Business Communication

**Peter Hartley and
Clive G. Bruckmann**

London *and* New York

First published 2002
by Routledge
11 New Fetter Lane, London EC4P 4EE

Simultaneously published in the USA and Canada
by Routledge
29 West 35th Street, New York NY 10001

Routledge is an imprint of the Taylor & Francis Group

© 2002 Peter Hartley and Clive G. Bruckmann

Typeset in Perpetua by Florence Production Ltd, Stoodleigh, Devon
Printed and bound in Great Britain by TJ International Ltd, Padstow, Cornwall

British Library Cataloguing in Publication Data
A catalogue record for this book is available from the British Library

Library of Congress Cataloging in Publication Data
Hartley, Peter.
   Business communication / Peter Hartley and Clive G. Bruckmann.
     p. cm.
   Includes bibliographical references and index.
    1. Business communication. I. Bruckmann, Clive G., 1946– II. Title
HF5718 .H2915 2002
658.4'5–dc21

                                              2001048113

ISBN 0–415–19549–7 (hbk)
ISBN 0–415–19550–0 (pbk)

Contents

List of figures   vii
List of tables   viii
List of boxes   ix
Preface   xi
Acknowledgements   xv

Introduction   **1**

Part one COMMUNICATION FUNDAMENTALS   **9**

1   Analysing communication   11
2   Communication codes and meaning   29
3   Intercultural communication   47

Part two COMMUNICATION AND ORGANIZATIONS IN CONTEXT   **67**

4   Organizational culture and communication   69
5   Information and communications technology (ICT) in organizations   90
6   Organizational structure and communication   112

Part three WRITTEN COMMUNICATION IN ORGANIZATIONS   **137**

7   Business writing: planning and organizing   139
8   Effective writing style   163
9   Effective design and visual aids   185
10 Effective business documents   209

Part four INTERPERSONAL COMMUNICATION IN ORGANIZATIONS   **239**

11 Effective interpersonal communication: defining interpersonal skills   241
12 Interpersonal skills in action: communicating face to face   264
13 Meetings and presentations   286
14 Building effective teams   311

CONTENTS

Part five COMMUNICATION AND CHANGE   **333**

15   Understanding organizational change   **335**
16   Making communication work: summary principles   **349**

Bibliography   354
Index   371

Figures

1.1	Action plan	16
1.2	Model of a communication process	18
1.3	Systems model of communication	20
4.1	Determinants of organizational culture	87
5.1	Winston's model showing restraints on the acceptance of new technology	93
6.1	Simple organization chart of a manufacturing company	113
6.2	Basic matrix structure of an organization	123
7.1	Sharples's model of writing as creative design	143
7.2	Structuring information: the planning triangle	145
7.3	Structuring information: pyramid structure	153
7.4	Spider diagram used to plan this chapter	153
9.1	Comparing sales and profits in Departments A and B	197
9.2	Example of line graph	202
9.3	Example of bar chart	203
9.4	Line graph with label to suggest the important conclusion	203
9.5	Line graph with suppressed zero	205
9.6	Line graph without suppressed zero	205
9.7	Sales data expressed as bar chart	206
9.8	Sales data in 3D cylinders	206
9.9	Fitting a line	207
10.1	The memo matrix	213
11.1	Hartley's model of interpersonal communication	243
11.2	Hargie's revised model of social skills	245
11.3	Styles of behaviour	252
11.4	Crossed transaction	256
13.1	Dimensions of meetings	289

Tables

1.1	The 'essential components' of communication?	19
2.1	Differences between spoken and written language	37
4.1	Components of organizational culture	71
4.2	Harrison's model of cultures and structures	77
5.1	Development of IT in business organizations	106
6.1	Organization subsystems and their communication	116
7.1	Suggested steps in business writing, as proposed by various authors	141
7.2	Main strategies used by writers	144
7.3	Paragraph structure	156
7.4	Elements of a persuasive letter	161
8.1	How a letter can be improved	169
8.2	Agreement on Plain English	174
8.3	Inappropriate corrections recommended by Word 97's grammar checker	178
9.1	Levels of heading in this book	193
9.2	Sales data	197
9.3	Matching story to visuals	198
9.4	Forms of visual aid	198
10.1	Basic report structure	223
10.2	Different report structures	227
11.1	Interpersonal communication as a staged process	261
12.1	The ladder of inference	269
12.2	The interview as planned communication	277
12.3	Stages in the selection interview	278
12.4	Appraisal as planned communication	281
13.1	Tropman's seven categories of agenda items	293
13.2	Group decision-making methods	297
13.3	Planning a presentation	303
13.4	Planning electronic presentations	308
14.1	Tuckman's four-stage model of group development	315
14.2	Wheelan's model of group development	317
14.3	Working through Wheelan's stages of group development	317
14.4	Comparing leadership and management	320
14.5	Team roles, as identified by Belbin	322

Boxes

1.1	Simple messages can fail	13
1.2	What do we do with this?	15
2.1	Language and social identity	32
2.2	A compilation of registers	33
2.3	Marilyn Monroe – the voice of safety?	35
2.4	The business card as communicator	38
2.5	Corporate-speak: new words or new actions?	44
3.1	The need for intercultural training	50
3.2	Different cultural approaches to rhetoric	54
3.3	Is the organization a system or a group?	57
3.4	The gender issue in English: an answer from another culture?	60
3.5	When talk is different	63
4.1	Organizational culture and creative design	72
4.2	A new company culture is announced	74
4.3	But how do the workers experience the culture?	75
4.4	The McDonaldization thesis	80
4.5	Expressions of the company culture	86
5.1	The technology has changed – what do we do now? And how do we continue to make money?	94
5.2	Commingling bits	95
5.3	Software with 'intelligence'?	97
5.4	IT can transform a business	98
5.5	Hypertext on the Web	103
5.6	Writing for the Web – the twenty-first-century version of desktop publishing?	104
5.7	The three waves of IT	105
5.8	The computer is in charge: nothing can go wrong, go wrong, go wrong ...	109
6.1	Communicating with stakeholders	115
6.2	The re-engineering process	121
6.3	Does the representative system communicate effectively?	125
6.4	The changing face of the office	130
6.5	Using new technology to support structural change	132
7.1	How should we plan Web sites?	142
7.2	Are you a bricklayer or an oil painter?	143
7.3	Who is your 'model communicator'?	146

7.4	Structuring documents	158
8.1	Contenders for the Golden Bull	165
8.2	The politics of language style	172
8.3	This organization has rules	173
8.4	Where Plain English disrupted the organizational structure	175
8.5	Simplified English	177
8.6	Microsoft may not know what you mean!	178
8.7	Why doesn't my word processor know I'm British?	181
9.1	The PC is not a typewriter	187
9.2	Typefaces in action	191
9.3	Example of a design grid	195
9.4	Using Ehrenberg's principles for presenting data in tables	201
9.5	Practical guidelines for producing graphics	204
10.1	Changing patterns of business correspondence	215
10.2	Bad letters can be expensive!	217
11.1	Can we teach the British to use more body contact?	248
11.2	Different types of assertive behaviour	254
11.3	Attending to culture	259
12.1	How important are the physical surroundings in the ways we communicate?	267
12.2	Communication can destroy a relationship in one easy sentence	270
12.3	Selection practices vary across cultures	273
12.4	Fair treatment or incompetent practice?	274
12.5	360-degree feedback	284
13.1	When Machiavelli comes to the meeting	298
13.2	Why don't the trainers agree?	301
13.3	Strategies for opening and closing a presentation	305
13.4	How to shoot your presentation in the foot in just the first few minutes	307
14.1	How not to move to teams	314
14.2	Groups can develop differently	317
14.3	Diverse views of leadership, from parable to starship	318
14.4	The leader as communicator	321
14.5	Belbin's recipe for success	323
14.6	Multiple views of reality	327
15.1	Environmental change and the Japanese convenience store	336
15.2	Who do you consult about change?	338
15.3	All change on British railway lines	341

Preface

People in organizations spend a lot of time communicating. For example, research studies regularly find that managers spend over 60 per cent of their time in meetings (Hargie *et al.* 1999, p. 1). In some cases they spend over 80 per cent of their day involved in communication (Hales, 1986). We also know that there are significant differences among organizations and cultures. In his study of European managers, Peter Collett (1998) found that Czech managers were most communicative (68 per cent of their time). British managers were average at 62 per cent but French and Bulgarian managers were much lower – 56 per cent and 52 per cent respectively.

But how *important* is communication to the organization's well-being? Is there enough evidence to support the claims that 'business communication is a critical success factor for any organization' (Misiura, 1996, p. 6) or that 'good management depends on effective communication' (Bovee and Thill, 1995, p. 15)?

The answer is clearly 'yes': 'research overwhelmingly suggests that improved internal communication brings large scale organizational benefits' (Tourish, 1997, p. 109). These benefits can include significant financial savings, both direct and indirect. For example, Scott *et al.* (1999) have shown that employees who feel satisfied with the communication they receive are less likely to leave their organization. Decreased staff turnover obviously reduces the expenditure on recruitment and selection. Other outcomes of effective communication are the less quantifiable benefits of a committed workforce. And we must also emphasize the ethical considerations. Don't all employees have a *right* to receive adequate communication?

Communication is time-consuming and important. But we believe it is often neglected in organizations – staff at all levels can ignore basic principles and create unnecessary misunderstanding and conflict. This does *not* mean that improved communication will always lead to less conflict or less work from the organization's point of view. David Bernstein tells how his company was employed to analyse and revise the communications of a public-sector organization. They revised the organization's newsletter into a newspaper format. After a couple of months, they had an 'annoyed client' – the organization was receiving more complaining letters from the public than before. The improved format meant that the information was easier to understand. This meant that the public were better informed of their rights – and they knew whom to contact about problems (Bernstein, 1984, p. 5). This story illustrates that communication can be improved if it is worked on. It also illustrates the ethical aspects: the organization had a moral obligation to communicate as effectively as possible. How would you have felt as a member of the public if it had gone back to the old format to disguise the information?

Communication is also complex. You need to understand the process to decide on the most appropriate strategy and behaviour. In a large organization, you will also find different responses to the same message. For example, DiSanza and Bullis (1999) investigated employees' responses to the company newsletter, which was designed to increase their sense of belonging and identification. They found that the newsletter 'worked' in the desired direction for employees who had positive experiences in the past and already felt positively towards the organization. But the newsletter actually made things *worse* for employees who already felt disenchanted – they interpreted the newsletter's stories in ways which reinforced their negative views.

This book aims to show both the complexity of communication and how it can be improved. But we do not offer simple recipes for success. Because of the complexities, you need to apply principles in ways which suit your specific context. We shall try to explain how this can be done.

THE AIMS OF THIS BOOK

After reading this book, you will be able to:

- outline basic principles underlying modern business communication, and apply these principles in varied contexts;
- critically analyse these basic principles, and their application;
- review the nature and role of communication in the changing context of modern business organizations.

It covers a wide range of business communication which has international relevance, and reflects the current and developing impact of information technology.

WHO SHOULD READ THIS BOOK?

This book is designed for undergraduate and postgraduate students who need a textbook on business communication. We use a direct style of language to make it relevant and attractive to people already working in business/commerce. So it can be used by:

- anyone studying business communication as part of a university or college degree course (both undergraduate and postgraduate) or as part of a post-school professional qualification;
- anyone working in a business or non-commercial organization who would like to review their ideas about and their own practice in communication;
- anyone who is studying communication as part of an advanced-level business course at school and has some experience of work.

CONTENT

This book offers the following features.

Practical examples *and* theoretical principles

The book explains both theoretical and practical aspects of communication, so it provides a framework you can use to assess your organization's and your own communication. It is as academically sound as we could make it, offering valid practical perspectives and techniques for business communication which arise from current theory and research.

Broad coverage

We offer a broad approach which covers all aspects of the communication process. For example, whereas some other business texts emphasize language much more than media, audience and structure, we cover each component. We also cover important aspects of interpersonal and group communication, including different types of group and their decision-making.

Not just one best way

We emphasize that communication depends upon the specific social and cultural context. As a result, we are critical of some other business texts which simply suggest that there is 'one best way' to approach a specific communication task. We always try to point out alternatives and highlight controversies.

Multicultural and structural factors

We emphasize the diverse multicultural composition of modern organizations, and identify practical implications for communication. We also summarize current and developing trends in organizational structures, and their impact on corporate and international communications.

Use of information technology

We incorporate up-to-date and progressive use of information technology whenever relevant. For example, use of Internet technology is emphasized.

Features

We have included the following features to make this book as useful as possible:

Boxes

Within each chapter, we include extra explanations, examples and illustrations in separate boxes to enhance the main arguments. We have tried to include a range of examples from different parts of the world and from different cultures and types of organizations.

Chapter summaries

Each chapter is summarized in a bullet list to highlight the main points.

Exercises

Every chapter includes practical exercises where you can apply the theories and techniques to your own situation.

Further reading

As well as the full list of references at the back of the book, each chapter suggests three or four specific texts so that you can further develop the ideas in that chapter.

Further materials

We are continually updating the materials and references on the topics in this book to support our own teaching and consultancy. Some of this additional material will be available through the World Wide Web. As Web addresses can change from time to time, please consult the Routledge Web site for details on this.

Acknowledgements

From Peter Hartley

Thanks to my family for support and encouragement.

Thanks to all the colleagues who worked with me on the courses where I developed my ideas on communication in organizations, especially (in approximate chronological order) Phil Radcliff, Ken Smith, Brian Gladstone, John Stannard and Clive Woodman.

This book is dedicated to the memory of David Jeffery.

From Clive Bruckmann

Thanks to my wife, Zoë, for her support and patience.

Thanks to my former colleagues at the University of the Witwatersrand who, over many years, helped to develop materials for Communication Studies courses.

I would also like to thank the following people who have helped me shape my ideas: Wim Mandersloot, John Kirkman and Adelé Thomas. I also wish to pay tribute to the late Len Lanham, who started me off on my academic career.

From both of us

Special thanks to Diana Railton, who brought us together and provided support and advice throughout this project.

We would also like to thank the reviewers who gave us such a detailed and valuable critique of our first draft, and all the staff at Routledge for their support and patience.

The following material has been reproduced with permission from the publishers: Figures 1.2, 11.1 and 11.4 from P. Hartley (1999) *Interpersonal Communication*, 2nd edition, London, Routledge; Figure 1.3 courtesy of Delta Consultancy, Pretoria; Table 2.1 from N. S. Baron (1999) *Alphabet to Email: How Written English Evolved and Where it's Heading*, London, Routledge; Figure 5.1 from B. Winston (1998) *Media Technology and Society: A History: From the Telegraph to the Internet*, London, Routledge; Figure 7.1 from M. Sharples (1999) *How We Write: Writing as Creative Design*, London, Routledge; Figures 11.1 and 11.3 from O. Hargie *et al.* (1994) *Social Skills in Interpersonal Communication*, 3rd edition, London, Routledge.

Every effort has been made to contact copyright holders for their permission to reprint material in this book. The publishers would be grateful to hear from any copyright holder who is not here acknowledged and will undertake to rectify any errors or omissions in future editions of this book.

Introduction

This book analyses how we communicate within business organizations and how this communication is changing. We focus on commercial organizations, but the main principles also apply to non-commercial and voluntary sectors, and to small, medium and large enterprises.

We focus on communication within the organization and do not say much about external communication (advertising, public relations, etc.). But all the principles we discuss do apply to both internal and external communication. For example, we emphasize the importance of understanding how different audiences may have very different perspectives on the same message; we emphasize the importance of clear language; and we emphasize the importance of careful planning and a clear strategy in formal communication.

Two examples from the UK illustrate the importance of these principles:

■ In a business speech, Gerald Ratner described some of his company's cheaper jewellery products as 'crap' and suggested that others would not last as long as a supermarket sandwich. He did not anticipate reports in the national press the following day. Although the immediate effect on sales was actually positive, the publicity had created an image which the company could not counteract when the economy dipped – people did not want to buy gifts from a store which now had a reputation for 'cheap rubbish'. Within months, sales had slumped and the company never recovered. The irony was that Ratner had used these remarks before in speeches, and had been quoted in the financial press. But this time the comments made the front pages in the popular papers. As he later reflected, 'Because of one ill-judged joke, 25,000 people lost their jobs' (quoted in Tibballs, 1999, p. 192).

■ The British railway company claimed that many trains were having trouble in winter because of the 'wrong kind of snow'. This was technically true – the weather conditions were very unusual. But the company should have realized that this explanation would not be taken seriously by a public who were already critical of the railways' poor punctuality and reliability. The phrase is still used and recognized in the UK as the classic example of a lame excuse.

These examples show the importance of communication and its long-lasting impact. They relate to external image and reputation. But the boundaries between internal and external communication are sometimes difficult to draw and they are obviously related: the most important external communicators in any company are the employees, as they determine the company image in their interactions with customers. We focus on these communicators as they work *within and across* their organization.

So we are not concentrating on what has become known as 'corporate communication', where the main responsibilities for managers include strategic planning, managing company identity, and public relations (Varey, 1997). This perspective tends to concentrate on communications management (Oliver, 1997). We shall obviously refer to these issues, but we are concentrating on communication as a process in which *all* employees of an organization participate.

In the rest of this introduction, we introduce some evidence which reflects the importance of communication, introduce some fundamental concepts, and explain how the book is organized.

COMMUNICATION WORKING WELL

In the Preface, we referred to research which shows the importance and benefits of 'improved internal communication'. If good communication is so important and can offer such tangible benefits, then why can we find so many examples where it does not seem to work effectively? Why do so many organizations seem to ignore the research into the practice of leading companies which have a reputation for effective communication? This research consistently highlights the following factors (based on research summarized by Tourish, 1997, and by Robbins, 1998, pp. 325ff.).

Management commitment

Senior management must be committed to the importance of communication and must act accordingly. Robbins regards this as *the* most significant factor: if the senior executive is able and willing to communicate his or her vision of the organization and regularly communicates face to face with employees, then this will set the expected standard for other managers. Of course, these other levels of management must also share that commitment. And managers must also act in ways which *confirm* their communication. This commitment by management must also extend to training. Communication training is given a high priority and is well supported.

Two-way communication

There must be an effective balance between downward and upward communication. Tourish highlights the importance of regular surveys of employee opinion, which must then lead to action plans and visible results.

Face-to-face communication

Wherever possible, communication is delivered face to face. This obviously allows for immediate feedback and discussion.

Messages are well structured to meet the audience needs

Management recognize what information their employees need to have and make sure that they receive it in the most appropriate form.

New technology is used to speed up communication

Many companies have made an enormous investment in new technology which enables them to spread messages very quickly across dispersed sites and offices.

Throughout this book we include exercises which invite you to apply our ideas to your own situation. An obvious exercise arising here is to consider how many of these apply to your organization, and to what extent. For example, what evidence do you have that your senior management are committed to fostering communication? If they are not, then what effect does this have on the rest of the organization?

Organizations may ignore communication because it is time-consuming and sometimes difficult, especially when the organization is going through a bad time. As we were editing this chapter, one of the major British retail chains was responding to a significant drop in profits by dramatic cost-cutting and management redundancies. Staff were quoted in the press as being 'furious' at the 'insensitive manner' in which this was done, and the process was described by one as 'barbaric'. Assuming that this press coverage was fair comment, what effect would this have on the long-term development of relationships and communication in that company? What if the press coverage was not representative of general staff feelings? Does the company have effective internal communication which could counteract the public criticism?

Although communication is important, we must always recognize that it is not a universal cure. We cannot turn a message about redundancy into good news by changing the words or tone. But organizations *should* respect their employees and treat them fairly and honestly. Communication can either support or destroy these obligations. We shall explore these issues on several occasions.

IMPROVING COMMUNICATION – USING RESEARCH

In this book, we try to show how communication can 'work' not just by analysing what happens when people communicate within organizations but also by suggesting techniques and strategies which can make communication more effective. This does make two important assumptions:

■ that we know enough about what happens in different types of organization;
■ that techniques and strategies which work in one situation can also be applied in others.

3

Both these assumptions can be questioned. We have tried wherever possible to back up our claims with research evidence but there is not enough research on everyday events in organizations. Some important processes do seem to be under-researched. For example, it has been suggested that 'the academic management literature does not adequately explore the shaping role of political behaviour in organizational change' (Buchanan and Badham, 1999, p. 2). This has important implications for communication: the success or failure of a proposal at a business meeting may depend more on political manoeuvring than on how clearly the proposal is expressed!

There are also problems with the balance of research in some areas. For example, Steve Duck (1998) suggests that researchers have been less willing to look at the negative side of (personal) relationships and that we need to know much more about the impact of events such as deception, hurtful messages, gossip, boring communication and so on. On a broader scale, we can find much more research on large organizations in western cultures than on, say, small businesses in Asian cultures. These imbalances make it difficult to generalize. The problem of generalization also applies to techniques and strategies.

Because of these limitations, you should approach all the recommendations in this book as *hypotheses* – as generalizations to be tested and not as absolute or binding truths. Even findings which are based on fairly substantial evidence are *never* 100 per cent reliable. For example, John Kirkman researched the reactions of scientists to papers which were rewritten using the plain language principles which we recommend in Part 3 of this book. Generally, the scientists clearly preferred the rewritten examples, feeling that they were 'more interesting' and also that the author had a 'better-organized mind'. But although this positive reaction was strong, it was not universal. Nearly 70 per cent agreed that the rewritten examples were better and 75 per cent agreed that the author was better organized (Turk and Kirkman, 1989, pp. 17ff.). In other words, a small but significant minority did *not* agree with the changes.

So deciding what is appropriate language is not just a simple technical problem – all sorts of social issues and pressures may be relevant. We know one consultant who produced a beautifully written plain language report for a major national organization. He was asked to revise it to make it look 'more complicated' and 'academic' so it would 'impress' the government department which had commissioned it. These issues of context and audience will recur regularly as we look at different types and levels of communication.

This means that you should consider your context and situation carefully before you apply techniques or concepts from this (or from any other) text on business communication. You should also try to check the most recent research; many of the topics we cover in this book are both controversial and subject to social change. For example, how do you respond to the research which suggests that women communicate differently from men? Do you:

- question whether there is sufficient research to arrive at such a firm generalization? (P. Hartley, 1999);
- consider the implications for the opportunities (or lack of opportunities) which women in organizations can access for promotion or leadership? (Tannen, 1994);

■ consider 'the value of women's communication patterns *sans* alteration or repair for progressive organizations'? (Bell and Smith, 1999, ch. 14).

It is to be hoped that new research will develop our responses to all three of these issues.

WHAT DOES COMMUNICATION INVOLVE?

As we shall see in Chapter 1, communication can be defined in rather different ways. For example, we can define it as 'shared meaning created among two or more people through verbal and nonverbal transaction' (Daniels and Spiker, 1994, p. 27). This emphasizes the sharing of ideas and/or information. Ideally, at the end of the process, all parties involved share the same ideas and information. What are the important factors which will either assist or detract from achieving this goal? We emphasize some important factors which are often neglected in practice, including for example the following.

Purpose and strategy

The 'art' of communication is finding the most effective means of sharing ideas and information. We need to study how people choose and develop the strategies and tactics of sharing ideas and information. Implicit in this is the idea of a communicative purpose or objective, such as informing or persuading. Many problems in communication arise from unclear or inappropriate purposes or strategies.

We also need to consider how these purposes are expressed. For example, business objectives may be set out in the organization's mission statement. But is a mission statement the best way of expressing objectives in a way that the employees will accept and understand? Some organizations explicitly reject mission statements. One British vice-chancellor has suggested that

> although universities should be run in a business-like way . . . there are some business techniques that we should tear up into shreds. Mission statements, for instance, are an abject waste of time. We were just as effective before we had one.
>
> (*Times Higher*, 24 July 1998)

Does your organization have one? What is it and what does it really mean? Does it make a difference? Who is it aimed at?

Social and cultural background

A range of important cultural and social differences affect the way we interpret what is meant. Some degree of common background is essential for exchanging messages. Sometimes, practical problems crop up because the communicators fail to establish early on what that common background might be.

Codes

A code is a coherent set of symbols plus the rules you need to structure a message. Our language is the most important code we use, but gestures, illustrations and mathematics are all codes that have important roles in communication.

Situation and relationships

Situation is the context in which a message is sent and received. It has both physical and relational aspects. For example, communication in a lecture room is influenced both by the layout of the room and by the relationship between the lecturer and the students.

We always interpret communication in terms of the type of relationship we have with the other person. In many business situations, the status relationship is particularly important. For example, consider the message 'Please bring me the Smith file.' What does this mean when said by manager to secretary, and what does it mean when said between two secretaries of equal status? In the first case, we hear an instruction or command presented in polite language. Between secretaries, we hear a request for help which can be turned down: 'Sorry, I'm busy, you'll have to find it.' This would be accepted as a reasonable response in the second case but what about the first case? Would the manager see this as a 'challenge to authority'? It would depend on the specific relationship and working arrangements. Thus the meaning of a message depends on the relationship between the people involved.

Reviewing these and other factors, this book aims to highlight the different reactions and potential ambiguities which can affect our communication.

HOW THIS BOOK IS ORGANIZED

The structure of this book reflects how we think business communication is best understood.

You need to understand what communication means and what it involves. This is what Part one is all about. As well as looking at how we can define communication (and the practical implications of how we define it), we investigate in more detail the factors which comprise communication. Finally, we investigate the problems of communicating across cultural boundaries.

Communication always takes place in a specific social context. Part two explores what this means in organizations by looking at their various structures and cultures and by exploring the impact and development of information technology (IT), now usually known as information and communication technology (ICT). This new label both reflects the convergence of computing and communications technologies and reflects the way that many organizations now see the use and development of computing.

The dominant form of communication in many organizations is by written means, and that is the focus of Part three. As well as looking at practice and research on the advantages of Plain English, we look at how effective design can influence how documents are understood. We also look at how documents can best be organized, and look at the range of documents which are used in most organizations.

Communicating face to face is as important as, if not more important than, written communication, and that is the focus of Part four. After defining the major interpersonal skills, we look at how these can be used in a range of contexts, including formal presentations. We then look at group dynamics and team development and how these principles can be applied to improve formal and informal meetings.

Part five has two functions: to raise issues of organizational change as they apply to all forms and types of communication, and to wind up the book by offering overall principles which we feel are the most critical aspects of communication for twenty-first-century organizations.

Part one

Communication fundamentals

Effective managers and professionals in all walks of life ... have to become skilled in the art of 'reading' the situations that they are attempting to organize or manage.

(Morgan, 1997, p. 3)

The same remark can also be applied to communication. But we suggest that *everyone* in the organization needs to develop the skills of understanding and interpreting the messages and meanings they encounter. This 'reading' is not necessarily a straightforward process. Morgan talks of the need to 'develop deep appreciations of the situations' (p. 3). We also suggest that you need to develop a 'deep appreciation' of the communication which characterizes your organization – and this involves *understanding* what communication means and how it works.

In this part of the book, we investigate what we mean by communication by looking at three different aspects:

■   Applying general models of communication to a specific situation. We suggest that you need a combination of approaches to 'capture the richness' of everyday communication. In other words, if you adopt an oversimplified model to analyse communication, you will ignore critical parts of the process.

■   Analysing the different codes we can use to communicate. In later parts of the book, we look at a wide range of communication events, ranging from writing reports to delivering presentations and on to working in groups, teams and committees. In all these different contexts, we have to manipulate a range of verbal and non-verbal codes. Failing to recognize the implications of speaking or writing in particular ways is one of the most common problems in communication. Understanding how codes work and what they mean can help to avoid these problems.

■ Analysing how we communicate across cultural boundaries. It can be very difficult to communicate with someone from a very different culture if we do not recognize or respect their assumptions and perspectives. Understanding the most important differences between cultural perspectives is the critical first step in improving communication, and this principle can be applied whenever we communicate with someone from a different social background. We highlight the need to clarify assumptions and avoid misleading stereotypes – further important principles which can be applied to every communication event.

This part of the book emphasizes the necessary link between theory and practice. The message (which we shall repeat regularly throughout the book) is that broad generalizations about communication may not apply in some specific situations. *Understanding* what is going on is important so you can *adjust* your behaviour to meet the specific circumstances.

Chapter 1

Analysing communication

INTRODUCTION

We are concerned that many popular guides to 'improving your communication' (*and* some management training courses) do not spend enough time working out what is *meant* by 'communication'. Our understanding of what communication 'is' influences how we act, and influences how we analyse situations. So it is important to work out what communication involves.

This chapter looks at how we define communication and how we can understand the way communication 'works'. We argue that you need to examine communication from two contrasting perspectives: analysing the process and interpreting the meanings. You need to use both these perspectives to decide what is happening. To demonstrate our approach, we analyse an example of a situation which virtually everyone has experienced: the first few hours of a new job. This analysis shows that even simple everyday interactions are worth analysing in some depth to unravel the complexities of communication.

 OBJECTIVES

This chapter will:
- show how our personal definitions of communication influence how we act;
- review popular models of communication and explain why we need a more complex approach;
- introduce our approach: the communication triangle;
- outline a practical example of communication in the workplace and show how we can use the communication triangle to analyse it.

COMMUNICATION AND ACTION

Deciding what we mean by communication is not just an academic exercise. As human beings, we *act* on the basis of our perceptions and beliefs. So if we have a particular view of human communication, then we will *act* on that view. If we have a faulty view, then our behaviour may cause problems. An example of how managers act upon their perceptions and cause problems will make this point clearer.

Consider Fred Davis, recently promoted telecommunications manager, who is responsible for implementing new telephone, voicemail and email systems in a large organization which has recently gone through a merger. This case is described by Finn (1999), and is based on experiences with organizations implementing new technology.

Fred is not having a good time: he has received several messages from senior management who are unhappy with the new voicemail system; he knows there were 700 complaints about the system in its first week; he knows that fewer than half the employees turned up for training sessions; and he knows that some units within the organization have purchased answering machines and cancelled their voicemail service. Fred is also worried because he knows that the organization will have to switch to a new email system in the very near future or the computer network will not be able to cope with the traffic. What makes it even more frustrating for Fred is that he cannot see where he has gone wrong. From the technical point of view, the changeover went very smoothly and the system can achieve everything which the organization wants – but only if people use it properly.

What is Fred's problem?

The main problem is his failure to manage. This is based upon his *perception* of his role and his belief about how he should act and communicate as a manager. He sees himself as an expert and as a 'doer'. He makes decisions based on his expert knowledge and then concentrates on making those decisions happen. During the planning and installation he arranged everything in precise detail. What he did *not* do was communicate in any meaningful way with the prospective users of the new system. He did not make sure that the users knew exactly what was happening, why it was happening, and how they could benefit from the new system. He had not built a consensus within the organization which supported his plans. Of course, such communication would have slowed him down and he would not have been able to implement the system in such a short time. But a system which is not used cannot be effective.

Unless Fred reconsiders his role very quickly, his career in this organization will come to an end. He needs to think what managing really means and what he can achieve by working *with* and *through* other influential members of the organization. Only by adopting a new managerial style will he be able to rescue the situation – 'he has not yet begun to shed his *doer* role to become an *enabler*' (Rogers *et al.*, 1999, p. 580). In the same way that we all have views about how to manage, which may be more or less effective, we also have views on how to communicate. In other words, we have an *implicit* view or theory of communication.

Different views of communication

If different views of communication have very real practical consequences, what are the main differences? Philip Clampitt (2001) suggests that managers typically use one of three different approaches to communication: the 'arrow', the 'circuit' and the 'dance'.

Arrow managers believe that communication operates one way, as in firing an arrow. If your aim is good, then you will hit the target. If you have a clear message, then you will communicate. On the positive side, arrow managers may well spend some time working out their ideas and making sure that their messages and instructions are as specific as possible. However, as we shall see throughout this book, it can be very dangerous to see listeners as simply passive processors of information. It is also very difficult to construct messages which are absolutely unambiguous. Arrow managers can also be insensitive to possible ambiguities in what they say and how they say it. For a couple of examples of misdirected messages, see Box 1.1.

BOX 1.1 SIMPLE MESSAGES CAN FAIL

During the Second World War, an acrimonious discussion broke out at a meeting of the combined chiefs of staff of Britain and the United States. The argument was over a proposal by the British to 'table a certain document'. It went on for some time until one person pointed out that *both sides* wished to *discuss* the document. The problem was the differing meaning of 'table'. The more common British meaning is to 'put forward for discussion' while in the United States it means 'to postpone the discussion indefinitely'.

The head office of an organization manufacturing pumps received a telegram: 'Send urgently Model XYZ pump rubber impeller.' As the pump model was available with both rubber-coated and steel impellers, they duly sent the rubber-coated impeller version. What the branch actually wanted was a rubber impeller *for* the pump. The branch had to remove the impeller for the customer and then return the pump to the factory. This meant considerable expense – all because someone wanted to reduce a message to the fewest number of words. Prepositions are important words – in this case the intended 'for' was interpreted by the receiver as 'with'.

In contrast, *circuit* managers concentrate on communication as a two-way process, emphasizing the importance of feedback. They usually emphasize the importance of good listening and trust in relationships. Clampitt argues that this approach also has some weaknesses. In particular, he feels that circuit managers can overemphasize agreement and fail to recognize real differences in views within the workplace. Circuit managers may assume that disagreement is simply a matter of poor communication and that more communication will almost automatically lead to agreement. It may be that more communication is necessary to work out how and why we have different opinions and values, and we shall see some examples of this in Chapter 3, 'Intercultural communication'.

Clampitt concludes that the metaphor of *dance* is the most appropriate way of describing communication. To support this metaphor, he discusses a number of similarities between communication and dance, including the following:

- Both are used for multiple purposes. You can dance to entertain others, to impress your partner, to express yourself, and so on. In the same way, you can communicate for different reasons: to inform, to persuade, to impress, etc.
- Both involve the co-ordination of meanings. The importance of co-ordination is an obvious feature of dance. You have to know what your partner thinks is the best way of doing the dance – you have to know what they are going to do next! When we communicate we also have to recognize how other people see the situation, recognize what they are doing and respond accordingly. We shall see how important this is in communication when we look at interpersonal skills.
- Both are governed by rules. There are sets of rules which apply to different types of dance: what sort of steps to use, how these steps are organized in sequence, what dress is appropriate. Again in this book we shall see how different rules apply to different communication situations – ranging from the rules and conventions of grammar through to social rules and expectations. Also, these rules can change over time and be negotiated by the participants.

This analysis has very important practical implications – these different views of communication influence how we behave. Confronted by a similar situation, these three different types of manager will respond very differently. And this is why it is important to think very clearly about how we define communication and what that definition involves. How we think about communication will influence what we do. Confronted by misunderstanding or conflict, the arrow manager will perhaps focus on developing a 'clearer message'. If that manager has a misleading picture of the employees' assumptions, then this effort may be completely wasted or even lead to further conflict.

EXERCISE

Think of a manager you know or have worked with. How would you describe their usual style of communication? Do they fit into one of Clampitt's categories? How well did this style work for them?

So you need to check how you think about situations (and be prepared to revise your thinking) before you decide how to act in them. The importance of our perceptions and beliefs is a theme which will be repeated many times in this book. Another business example of the importance of flexible thinking is the confusion that sometimes surrounds new ideas for products – see Box 1.2 for a few examples.

BOX 1.2 WHAT DO WE DO WITH THIS?

The following examples illustrate how organizations need to think flexibly and what can happen when they do not.

One large company lost a market opportunity worth millions when it decided not to purchase the right to the xerographic process (the technology used in photocopiers). It thought that a copying machine could *only* be used to replace carbon paper. It did not consider that copiers would be used by the *receivers* of the documents, who could then make multiple copies for distribution.

The television companies were very alarmed when VCRs first came on the market – they were simply worried about viewers taping television programmes. They did not anticipate that the main use of a home VCR would be renting movies.

The Post-It note originated because scientists at 3M had developed a glue which was not very sticky. Rather than throw all the hard work away, the originator took time to investigate possible uses for a 'temporary' glue. He developed some trial products and persuaded colleagues to try them. They clamoured for more and a new product line was launched.

ANALYSING COMMUNICATION

Our approach is based on what we call the communication triangle. We suggest that you need to think about communication by putting together two different perspectives:

- define the process: in other words, you need to examine major components of the communication process and the sequence of events which are taking place;
- interpret the meanings: in other words, you need to investigate the social and cultural context, and the historical background to see how the participants *interpret* what is going on.

Once you have compared these approaches, you can identify any differences in perceptions and develop an appropriate action plan – as in Figure 1.1.

In the rest of this chapter, we shall explain these different perspectives and show how you can put them together to arrive at a clearer picture of what communication involves. Before we introduce these perspectives, here is a practical case study you can analyse.

CASE STUDY: FIRST DAY ON THE JOB

You have accepted a new job as a technical writer for a large engineering company. Read through the following account of what happens on your first day. We shall give our analysis later. As you read through it, note your opinions on:

15

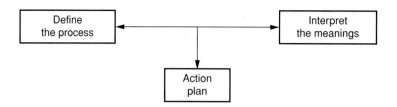

Figure 1.1 *Action plan*

- how you feel about the way you are treated;
- how the other members of the organization communicate to you;
- how you would analyse the communication 'habits' of this organization;
- how you could improve the communication to new members if you were the manager.

You arrive at the main entrance on the morning of your first day. You are obviously anxious to make a good impression. But you are also somewhat apprehensive, as you have been told by friends (after you accepted the job, unfortunately) that the company has a reputation for being rather formal and bureaucratic. When you report to the security desk, the receptionist checks your details very carefully and then gives you directions to the cubicle in the open-plan workspace which was used by your predecessor. You find the cubicle after spending some time hunting round the large open office. There is a desk, chair, a small filing cabinet and a desktop computer (not quite as powerful as you had hoped for). On the divider walls there are a few out-of-date notices. The desk contains a few sweets, two floppy disks and a memo pad. On the desk is a note asking you to telephone the department head, Jan Thompson, when you arrive. You remember that you met Thompson briefly at the employment interview.

How do you feel about the organization so far?

You follow the instructions on the note. In a few minutes, Thompson walks in carrying a stack of manuals, gives you a handshake and smiles. The following conversation takes place.

THOMPSON: Welcome to Ace Products. Hope you like your new office space. Here are half a dozen manuals – read them to get an idea of the work we do. Later this morning my secretary will bring over material on our new dump truck project which you will be working on. Tomorrow you will meet the engineer in charge of the project. Oh yes, please go down to the staff office sometime today; they want to complete your records. If you have any questions don't hesitate to ask, but I have to go to a meeting.

YOU: Thank you, I look forward to getting into the project. Also, I wonder if I could meet some of the salespeople who work with the kind of customers I will be writing for?

Thompson hesitates for a few moments, and looks away with a slight tilt of the head. You notice the change in eye contact and wonder what this means – could it be surprise? Does Thompson now think that you seem a little over-eager to make a good impression? Thompson says, 'In due time', and leaves the room. You are convinced by Thompson's tone of voice that you have spoken out of turn.

How do you feel about the organization now?

A little later you receive the following phone call from Thompson's secretary, whom you have not met:

SECRETARY: This is Bobby du Toit speaking, I have been asked to ring you. If you have any word-processing that needs special formatting, send it to me and I will get it done for you.

YOU: Thank you. And can I have the file on the dump truck project?

SECRETARY: I do not have the file; and by the way, I am not your secretary.

YOU: Yes, I know that, but Jan Thompson said you would bring the material.

SECRETARY: Jan may have said that but I have not received it. When I receive it, you can be assured that you will get it immediately.

Looking back on these two conversations, how do you feel now about the organization and your colleagues?

Before we try to analyse this case, we shall introduce one of the two perspectives we use to understand communication

THE PROCESS MODEL OF COMMUNICATION

The definition of communication in many management texts is based on a model first popularized in the 1950s, the so-called mathematical theory of communication. This was developed from work on telecommunications systems. It aimed to show how information is transmitted from source to destination and to analyse what can affect the quality of the information during this process. The model then became very influential with researchers in human communication (see Littlejohn, 1983, or Mattelart and Mattelart, 1998, for a more extended account).

Figure 1.2 shows a simple model of this communication process. Communication is essentially a one-way process with information passing from sender to receiver. This includes the following main concepts:

Codes

A code is a coherent set of symbols plus the rules needed to structure a message. For example, a language code consists essentially of a list of words, and a set of rules for preparing a text. These rules are the grammar or syntax of the language.

17

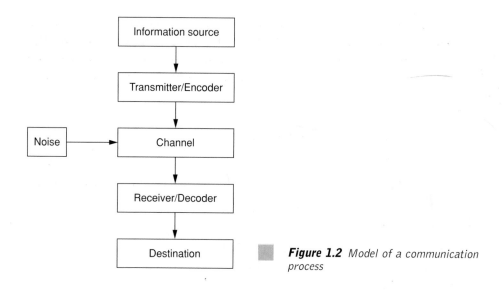

Figure 1.2 *Model of a communication process*

Encoding and decoding

Encoding is using a code to structure a message in an effort to achieve our communicative objective. Decoding is the reverse: we use our knowledge of the code to work out the meaning of a message we have received.

Medium/channel

The medium is the physical system which carries the message from sender to receiver, which can vary from the air carrying the voice between two speakers to something like an email where the author is separated from the reader by complicated electronic processes. Some texts use 'channel' for this concept and there is often confusion as to what constitutes a medium or a channel. In this book, we will not use the term 'channel'.

Noise

Noise is a random input which distorts a message or which interferes with its transmission or reception. Noise may be external or internal. Examples of external noise are traffic noise making conversation difficult or electrical interference on a telephone line. An example of internal noise is a temporary irritation which causes a communicator to lose concentration, such as feeling tired or having a headache.

Development of the process model

The most important early development added a feedback loop. Feedback refers to any signals which are received by the sender. In a face-to-face meeting such signals could include facial expression, gestures or other forms of body language.

Various authors have added slightly different emphases, but this basic model is still the only one offered in many textbooks (e.g. Taylor, 1999). Table 1.1 illustrates the common ground by comparing two definitions of the 'essential components of communication', one taken from a best-selling US text on organizational behaviour and one from a leading British text.

Table 1.1 *The 'essential components' of communication?*

Components according to Robbins (1998)	Components according to Hargie et al. (1999)
The communication source	Communicators (defined as the people involved)
Encoding	
Message	Messages
Channel	Channel
	Noise
Decoding	
The receiver	
Feedback	Feedback
	Context

EXERCISE

Taking these lists of factors, look back on the First Day in the Office case study. What factors do you think are the most important in this situation?

As communication is potentially always a two-way process, we will introduce a further, more elaborate version of this process model, the *systems model* (Figure 1.3). This demonstrates how the various concepts given above interact in the process of communication.

This model (analogous to Clampitt's circuit approach) suggests that communication comprises the following steps:

- Sender A wishes to achieve a certain communicative goal with respect to Receiver B.
- Taking into account B's background and their common background, A decides on a communication strategy and selects appropriate media.
- A encodes a suitable message and sends it to B using the chosen media.
- Using both knowledge of A's background and his or her own background, B decodes and interprets the message.
- A evaluates the feedback message to determine whether the message has been effective.

19

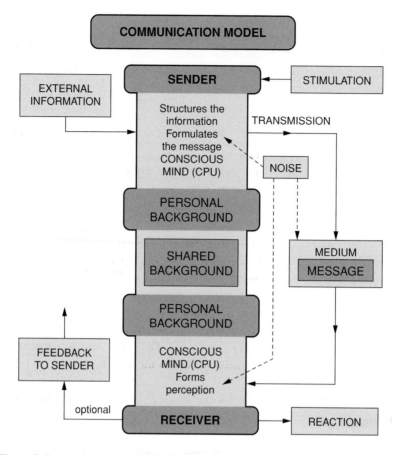

Figure 1.3 *Systems model of communication*

There may be a number of these cycles before A achieves the aim or decides to abandon the exchange. The important features of communication in this model are:

- The meaning of a message does not reside completely in the message, but is constituted by the receiver using their own background.
- Because of differences in background, this meaning can differ considerably from the intended meaning of the sender.
- Good feedback is essential in determining the effectiveness of a message.
- The greater the common background, the less information is needed to encode in the message.

Returning to the First Day at Work case study – a process analysis

We can use this process perspective to analyse the case study.

Your face-to-face meeting with Thompson

Sender: As both the initiator of the communication and the senior person, Thompson is the 'sender' and must take responsibility for the progress of the communication.

Receiver: As receiver you are at a disadvantage by being in a strange environment.

Background: Apart from a brief meeting at the employment interview, Thompson and you know little about each other. You have little knowledge of the firm and in particular of policies and procedures in the department. Thompson and you do share a profession, technical writing. One of your urgent needs is to get more background knowledge. Does Thompson help you do this?

Situation: As a new employee, you are in a strange situation which makes you apprehensive. This is not helped by the absence of any specific instructions about starting work. This is compounded by the fact that your office has been left untidy and unprepared.

Media: Thompson used two media for communication, first a note and then a face-to-face discussion. Is a note appropriate first contact for a new employee? Surely not, as it reinforces your view that the organization is impersonal. Face-to-face discussion is appropriate, but it is undermined by Thompson's need to rush to the meeting.

Message: Superficially, the messages exchanged are clear. However, at the level of attitude, there is the interpretation that Thompson sees you as 'over-eager'.

Noise: There is little by the way of physical noise to interfere with the message. You might consider your apprehension as internal or psychological noise.

Feedback: Has Thompson received adequate feedback from you? Can you be sure that you have interpreted Thompson's feedback correctly?

The phone conversation with Du Toit

Sender: In this case, Du Toit is sender.

Receiver: You are again the receiver.

Background: You have less in common with Du Toit than with Thompson. As secretary to Thompson, Du Toit is familiar with the work of the department. You immediately assumed that this covered Thompson's statement about the dump truck documents.

Situation: Though close by, Du Toit chose to telephone.

Medium: While the telephone can be an effective medium for passing on information, in this case a face-to-face meeting might have been worth the extra effort in terms of establishing a good working relationship.

Message: Du Toit's initial message was simple and caused no problem. But your message was based on an incorrect perception of common background. This was interpreted by Du Toit as an instruction, which was resented. But Du Toit also seemed to ignore your newness in the organization.

Noise: There was no significant external noise. Temporary irritation on the part of Du Toit and your apprehension constitute possible internal or psychological noise. But were these random events? We shall return to this issue when we look at the analysis of meaning.

Feedback: Feedback about the dump truck documents did not improve the communication.

Outcomes of the process

The objective of initial communication with any new staff member is to help you become a productive and contented worker in the shortest possible time. So the communication was unsuccessful.

There were several negative results:

- You received several messages which seem to confirm the view that the organization is impersonal and bureaucratic.
- Thompson seems to consider that you are 'pushy' and over-eager, but there has been no additional feedback to confirm or disconfirm this speculation.
- Du Toit seems to consider that you are 'pushy'.
- You feel Du Toit is officious and unfriendly.

The more fundamental problem is that most of these outcomes (if not all of them) are probably misconceptions which will take some time to dispel.

EXERCISE

Review the case study again and see if you can come up with any alternative interpretations of the outcomes listed above. What do your alternatives assume in terms of context or background?

Problems with the process approach?

The process approach has been fiercely criticized (e.g. Taylor, 1995). One criticism is that it does not take sufficient account of social or historical factors. It also seems to assume that the meaning of an event is 'given', as opposed to 'negotiated' between the participants (Craig, 1999). Other critics have suggested that it does not take account of business realities – it suggests one sender and one receiver, whereas most business communication involves 'multiple senders and multiple receivers' (Waller and Polonsky, 1998).

One response to these criticisms is to create a more complex model (as Waller and Polonsky do). Another response is to complement the process model with a more transactional account of communication (Mohan *et al.*, 1997). We take this latter approach as the process model does offer a useful starting point. It is not sufficient, though; we also need to emphasize the social and cultural background and look at how meaning is developed and negotiated through interaction – we need to interpret the meanings.

INTERPRETING THE MEANINGS

In order to fully understand how people communicate, we need to understand not just the immediate background but the much broader social context and history of their relationship. Not only do we have to examine how people *come to agree* on what is happening, but we also have to look at how they *feel* about events. The following two examples illustrate some of this complexity.

The case of the confused trainees

A colleague of ours was invited to run residential training events for managers in a large manufacturing organization. He came back from the first of these looking very dispirited, and complained that he could not understand the reactions from the group of managers, who were supposed to be very committed to personal development. There seemed to be at least three different reactions from different sub-groups:

- Some managers looked really interested and spent the weekend frantically scribbling notes.
- Some managers seemed over-anxious and did not seem to be concentrating on the events.
- Some managers seemed to see the event as a 'bit of a holiday'.

We suggested he questioned the managers more closely about *why* they had come. When he did this, he found that *none* of the managers had been explicitly told why they had been nominated for the training – their 'commitment' was a senior management *assumption*. As a result, they had tried to devise a meaning based upon their own experience, which then coloured their reactions to the event.

The first group of managers thought it must be some kind of test which might influence their next promotion or regrading – they were doing all they could to impress the trainer. They were convinced the trainer would be reporting back on their progress. The second group were worried that this training might indicate some problem with their performance and were mentally checking what they had done over the past six months to work out where or how they had failed; their minds were not on the training at all. The third group saw the event as a reward for good behaviour which need not be taken too seriously.

Our colleague was only able to communicate with these groups once these expectations and assumptions had been uncovered and discussed openly. In other words, the training could not begin until the participants had *negotiated* the meaning of the training event.

War in the training room

One of our colleagues was invited by the head of a training department to run a workshop on effective communication for his staff. The head was very insistent that the staff had requested this event and so our colleague was happy to oblige. When he arrived at the training room for the evening session, his first impression was a sense of unease and tension. Although he delivered a session which usually received very positive feedback, he was unable to achieve any real dialogue with the staff who attended.

After winding up, he managed to start a conversation with one of the participants and eventually discovered what was going on. The staff had definitely *not* requested the event! In fact, they were involved in a long-standing and bitter dispute with the head over staffing and workload. This training was seen as another opportunity by the head to assert his authority. He was seen by staff as dogmatic, authoritarian and insensitive. We later discovered that the head felt that the staff were lazy and incompetent. As the 'emissary' of the head, our colleague had inadvertently put himself in the firing line. The training session was a complete waste of time and only intensified the conflict. In this case it was not possible to negotiate an acceptable definition of the event, and our colleague retired hurt.

In both these cases, we are looking at communication which depended upon a complicated history of events. As a result of that history, people had developed shared meanings over time which meant that communication was based on *very different* assumptions and expectations. Potential consequences in both situations were further misunderstanding and possible conflict.

If we look at the way people develop shared meanings, then we can also look at the way people express those meanings. In the past decade, organizational researchers have become very interested in the way people in organizations tell stories, tell jokes and use metaphors to describe what is going on in their organization (Fineman and Gabriel, 1996). These stories and metaphors can provide very useful insights into the way people typically behave and communicate in that organization.

For an example of the power of these metaphors, and how they can influence communication, consider the case of the Disney Corporation. Disney is often used as an example by US textbooks of organizations which 'make communication a top priority' by sophisticated and systematic corporate message systems, and by encouraging employee feedback (Bovee and Thrill, 1995, p. 3). The powerful external image of an organization that provides quality family entertainment is certainly promoted vigorously within the company.

Smith and Eisenberg (1987) analysed the metaphors used by Disney employees and found two very strong metaphors in place: drama and family. Employees saw themselves as 'actors' using costumes to play out stories which would entertain the customers. They also used the concept of family not only to describe their relationship with customers, but also to characterize the relationship between management and employees. The strength of these feelings led to difficulties at Disneyland in the 1980s. Faced by increasing competition from newer parks and other economic pressures, management cut the various costs and benefits in a way which for some employees destroyed the metaphor. The depth and strength of feeling led to union action and conflict. Smith and Eisenberg argued that the way for management to rescue this situation was by reconsidering these metaphors.

In other words, the management communication about cuts and economies had undermined the widely-held values which were summarized in the family metaphor. If management had recognized and discussed these values more openly rather than focusing on the economics, they might have developed solutions which were not so threatening.

EXERCISE

Consider a group or organization with which you are familiar. What are the typical stories, jokes and metaphors used in that group? What do these stories imply about the values of that group? And how are these values expressed in communication in that group?

ANALYSING THE MEANINGS IN THE FIRST-DAY CASE STUDY

Go back to our case study and think about how you would have felt in that situation. After your first hour in the office, which of the following statements would summarize your reactions so far?

- 'I feel disappointed that I have not been able to make a better impression. I did not realize that Thompson would be taken aback by my request about meeting the staff. I also did not intend to upset the secretary. Tomorrow I shall have to be a bit more cautious about what I say I'm going to do.'
- 'I am angry that the organization seems to care so little about new staff. The people at the reception desk did not know who I was and spent ages checking my papers. Thompson gave me an impossible task – reading these manuals today – and then got upset because I showed some initiative. I was also annoyed because Thompson's secretary was so unpleasant and inefficient. If I do not receive better treatment in the next few days I shall be looking out for a new opportunity.'
- 'I am puzzled by the confusion and lack of organization which I experienced on my first day. There did not seem to be any systematic preparation for my arrival and I am not sure what impression I made on the other staff. Thompson seems pleasant but does not seem to have a clear view as to how I am intended to fit in. There seem to be issues about status and formality which I need to work out.'

Of course, there are other possible interpretations of the situation. But these three show how you can arrive at very different meanings by adopting a different perspective on the same series of events. These different perspectives reflect:

- different emphases on the different events;
- different interpretations of the motives behind the other people's behaviour;

25

- different personal priorities and agendas ('I want to be accepted' in A, compared with 'I deserve to be well-treated' in C).

Another implication of these three different accounts is their very different implications for future behaviour:

Perception – creates expectations – leads to specific behaviour and communication

A person with the first reaction will be trying harder the next day but will also be rather guarded about what they say and what they do. A person of the second type will be looking for further evidence of poor treatment and perhaps being a bit too impatient. The third type of person will be looking for more evidence to work out what is really going on in the department.

These differences also reflect broader expectations. Remember, you had heard that the organization was formal and bureaucratic. With a different expectation, the first day could have had more or less impact on you. And this is why we always need to consider communication from these two perspectives: defining the process and analysing the meaning. To add to the complexity, we have not fully discussed the meanings which Thompson or du Toit interpreted from the day's events. What implications could these have for future working relationships?

EXERCISE

When you imagined how you would feel about the first day at this office, what were your images of the people involved? We deliberately left their identities ambiguous. For example, did you *assume* that the manager was male and the secretary was female? Would your perceptions change if the genders were different? Would it make any difference if they came from different social or cultural backgrounds – would this change your expectations? We shall look at some of the complexities of communication caused by different social backgrounds in Parts two and four of this book.

As a final example of the complexity of communication, you will see that we have not fully explained one part of the case study: Thompson's reaction to your request to meet the sales staff. Was this simply surprise at an unexpected question? Or did it mean something more significant? Suppose that there has been some conflict in the recent past between the sales staff and Thompson's department. Have you unwittingly implied that you already know the politics of the organization? You can decide between these alternatives only by more detailed investigation of the context.

So we must beware of simple models of communication and try to take account of the full range of historical and cultural factors which influence how we think and behave. We must be critical of our own models and presuppositions.

MOVING TO ACTION PLANNING – WHAT COULD HAVE BEEN DONE DIFFERENTLY?

To illustrate some of the possibilities, consider the following suggestions on what could have been done differently, from a process perspective:

Sender: The sender has the initial choice on such matters as media and situation. In this case the person responsible (Thompson) should plan induction to achieve the desired objectives.

Background: Essentially, the purpose of induction is to try to bring the background of the new employee, as far as the work situation is concerned, to the level of other employees in the department. This can be done by personal discussion, arranging for a mentor, and supplying policy and procedure manuals. Departments should have clear procedures on induction of staff.

Situation: It would have been far better if first contact had been in Thompson's office to meet the secretary, a mentor and perhaps one or two colleagues.

Media: For rapid assimilation of background, face-to-face contact is most desirable. However, to avoid information overload, policy and procedure manuals give useful detail. But these should be backed up by having a senior colleague as a mentor.

Message: With new employees, messages can often be misunderstood because of lack of background. It is particularly important that instructions are clear and detailed.

Feedback: Being sensitive to feedback is particularly important with new employees. As we have seen, first impressions of an organization can have a long-term effect on attitudes.

But remember the meaning: A planned process like this would improve the organization's chances of building positive attitudes in new employees. But it could be carried out very mechanically and actually send the wrong message – for example, 'This is something we have to do but we do not really care about you.' So we must always watch out for the way that meanings are developed and negotiated, as we shall see in later chapters.

This case study highlighted the importance of communication within the induction process. We need more research on the ways new staff are integrated (or not) into the organization, especially on how the organization communicates the 'content' of socialization – the values, norms, beliefs, skills and knowledge which are expected of the organization's members.

SUMMARY

- Our understanding of communication influences the way we behave.
- Managers may define communication as a linear process which may or may not incorporate feedback.
- This definition is not sufficient and can be misleading in many situations.
- You can analyse human communication from at least two different perspectives: the process perspective and the interpretive perspective.
- The process perspective emphasizes the way messages are constructed and delivered, and the various factors which influence how those messages are received.
- The interpretive perspective emphasizes the meaning which we perceive in situations. This meaning is often the result of complicated historical and cultural processes.
- We need to consider both process and interpretive perspectives when we examine particular examples of business communication.

DISCUSSION QUESTIONS

- Is Clampitt right to say that managers adopt one of three different definitions of communication? Are there other definitions which managers use?
- Do we really know what managers believe about communication?
- If we need to investigate the historical and cultural factors in order to interpret meaning, which of these factors are the most important?
- How predictable are people's reactions to particular messages?
- Why do so many guides to business communication rely upon process models of human communication? Why do they seem to ignore historical and cultural factors?
- What are the strengths and weaknesses of our approach? Is it possible to integrate process and interpretive approaches?

FURTHER READING

Clampitt, P.G. (2001) *Communicating for Managerial Effectiveness*, 2nd edition. Thousand Oaks, CA: Sage. Chapter 1 gives a detailed explanation of the three views which managers seem to adopt. Chapters 2 and 3 explore the meaning of communication in greater depth and investigate the impact of organizational culture. At the Web site of Clampitt's consulting firm, you will find some useful materials based on the book, including self-tests on the main ideas in each chapter <www.imetacommm.com>.

Hargie, O.D.W., Dickson, D., and Tourish, D. (1999) *Communication in Management*. Aldershot: Gower. See chapter 1 for a recent restatement of the process approach and for discussion of the value of effective communication to the organization.

Mohan, T., McGregor, H., Saunders, S. and Archee, R. (1997) *Communicating: Theory and Practice*, 4th edition. Sydney: Harcourt Brace. See chapters 1 and 2 for an approach which complements a transmission model with a transactional model.

Chapter 2

Communication codes and meaning

INTRODUCTION

You cannot transmit your mental images, ideas and feelings directly to another person, unless you believe in telepathic communication. Such telepathy may be the staple diet of science fiction but business communication must rely on more tangible mechanisms. We have to translate or encode our thoughts in such a way that others can receive and interpret what we think.

This encoding is the focus of this chapter. We introduced the notion of codes in the previous chapter but we need to analyse the variety of codes we use in everyday communication. We focus on both verbal and non-verbal codes and consider how much scope there is for ambiguity and interpretation. If we can anticipate how other people will interpret what we say and do, then we can make our communication more effective.

Of course, we also need to bear in mind the implications of the previous chapter: that communication is not just the transmission and reception of information. No matter how carefully we feel we have 'encoded our message', we need to be aware of all the factors which can influence how other people will interpret our behaviour.

OBJECTIVES

This chapter will:
- introduce the range and variety of human communication codes;
- explain why we need to think of human language as a collection of multiple and overlapping codes;
- examine the nature and scope of non-verbal communication, and its relationship with language;
- identify practical implications for the appropriate use of language and non-verbal codes in business communication.

WHAT CODES DO WE USE TO COMMUNICATE?

There are several ways of categorizing the different codes we use to communicate with each other. For example, Ellis and Beattie (1986, p. 17) identify 'five primary systems of communication' which occur in face-to-face interactions:

- verbal: all the words, clauses and sentences which we use in speech and writing;
- prosodic, i.e. all the stress and pitch patterns such as pauses and intonation which we use in speech and which are 'linguistically determined' – we use them to punctuate the speech and make its meaning clear. Ellis and Beattie give the simple phrase, 'old men and women' as an example. If you leave a silent pause after 'men' when you say these words, then it changes the meaning;
- paralinguistic: all the pauses, 'ums', 'ahs' and other sounds which are not 'real' words and which do not have a clear linguistic function;
- kinesic: all the ways we move our bodies during communication, including our posture, gestures and so on;
- standing features: more static non-verbal features such as appearance, orientation (the angle at which you stand in relation to the other person) or distance.

There are two main issues with this and with other systems of classification:

- Does this mean that the different systems 'work' in different ways? Do we somehow interpret or process them differently?
- Do the different systems have different functions? For example, it is often suggested that non-verbal signals communicate our emotions better than words.

Both these issues have important practical implications. For example, what do you attend to when you are meeting someone for the first time? Do you concentrate on what they are saying or on some aspect of their non-verbal behaviour? How would you give them some clues that you liked them – what signals would you use?

As we shall see in the rest of this chapter, these issues are not easily resolved. We shall use the distinction between verbal and non-verbal codes but emphasize that the most important issue is how they work together to create a particular meaning.

EXERCISE

Compare two speakers or lecturers you have experienced – one whom you liked and one whom you disliked or who irritated you. How would you describe their verbal and non-verbal styles? Which features of their behaviour did you notice? What did you think these differences told you about their personalities?

UNDERSTANDING HUMAN LANGUAGE

Michael Clyne (1994) suggests that language has four main functions:

1 As our most important medium of human communication.
2 As a means of identification. We use language to express our membership of social groups, which may be national, ethnic, social, religious, etc.
3 As a means of intellectual development. The way that children learn and develop their language skills is very strongly related to the way they experience their surrounding environment. In adulthood, we use language to develop new ways of thinking and new concepts.
4 As an instrument of action. Much of what we say is directly linked to what we do. When we promise or apologize, we are not simply passing on information.

Although this book concentrates on function 1, we must recognize the practical implications of the other functions. People who concentrate on function 2 may have very strong views on what language use is appropriate in a given situation – see Box 2.1 for further discussion of this. Function 4 can cause difficulties if we do not recognize the action implications of what we say. This may be especially important in cross-cultural encounters, as we shall see in Chapter 3 when we discuss Business English as an international language.

Codes within language

Language is not just a carrier of information – it can convey various levels of meaning depending on the situation. In even a simple conversation, there may be several different codes which we can recognize:

A: I'm getting an error message – could be a driver problem.
B: OK, Bones, what are you going to do about it? They're all supposed to have the 3.5 upgrade.
A: Obviously you need to try it on the other two machines first.

In this brief conversation between two people trying to get a computer program to work properly for a demonstration, we can see various codes at work:

■ technical jargon as in 'driver problem';
■ the joke based on a *Star Trek* character;
■ the joking over who does what – 'you' do this.

All of these depend upon the relationship between A and B – recognizing that they both understand the jargon, recognizing the joke and the verbal sparring. B would have adopted a very different tone with a relative stranger or a new boss. This example illustrates Kurt Danziger's view that all communication simultaneously works on two levels:

- the presentation of information (he calls this *representation*);
- the presentation of a particular relationship which is implied in what is said and how it is expressed (he calls this *presentation*) (Danziger, 1976).

Danziger shows how certain individuals are very conscious of this distinction and manipulate what they say to entrap the other person in a particular relationship. His examples include sales representatives and interrogators! This is not the same as the distinction between verbal and non-verbal codes as we can express a relationship both verbally and non-verbally. One very important practical implication here is that we need to review both *what* we communicate and *how* we do it. We need to establish the appropriate relationship as well as convey the appropriate information.

BOX 2.1 LANGUAGE AND SOCIAL IDENTITY

You can see the importance of language as a symbol of broader social identities in the following examples:

- The campaign known as 'US English' has been active since the early 1980s in the USA, lobbying to ensure that English is the only language used for official functions (Crawford, 1992).
- The French Academy has attempted to protect the French language from 'foreign' words and expressions. It recently tried to stop female ministers in the French government from using the feminine definite article to describe themselves (*la ministre*) as this departed from the traditional masculine form for the word (*le ministre*).

These movements suggest that some varieties of language are inherently inferior. They try to define one version of the language which can be accepted as the ideal or standard. They face serious challenges on both these counts. All languages grow and develop. Any attempt to 'police' a language which does not recognize these processes is unlikely to succeed.

As another example of how strongly people feel about 'their language', consider the reactions to the *Encarta World English Dictionary*, published by Microsoft and Bloomsbury in 1999, and described in the introduction as 'a dictionary that accurately reflects the worldwide presence of the English language today' (p. xi). This claim was vigorously rejected by Christopher Howse (1999) who argued that 'many of the words are merely modish slang' and were 'included for no more reason than they are up-to-the-minute and American'. For example, are words such as *notwork* and *webisode* just temporary slang or lasting expressions? Neither appeared in the last *Oxford Dictionary of New Words* (Knowles, 1998) and both were highlighted as misspellings when this paragraph was written in Microsoft Word 97! Would you use them?

BOX 2.2 A COMPILATION OF REGISTERS

How would you describe the register of the following extracts? Which is the closest to your idea of 'good' business writing?

Did you like the previous version? Did you? Well? We would have liked it a lot more if it was, um, a bit better.

Gold discoveries were like No. 11 buses yesterday. None came for ages, then three arrived at once.

ABC Industries, the financial services conglomerate which is breaking itself up, is poised to go out with more of a whimper than a bang.

Fed up with the same old job? Then it's time for a change! Full training and uniform provided plus above average rates.

If you think we are just another high street retailer, allow us to open your eyes. This is a company that leads the field in many different sectors of retail, from small electrical goods to toys, from jewellery to furniture. Our computer technology is amongst the most sophisticated in the business, our stock control systems are the best around and we offer convenient shopping along with convenient service that keeps the customers coming back.

The first extract is from a computer games magazine; the rest are from a mass-circulation British newspaper – the first two from the editorial in the business section, and the last two from the job advertisements (for security guards and store managers respectively).

As far as written style is concerned, the grammar checker in our word processor (Word 97) does not like the structure of the first sentence in the last extract and also thinks that the second sentence is 'too wordy'. Do you agree?

Language variety

Here we need to discuss three main concepts: register, dialect and accent.

Register

The English language is not a single, coherent body. Different groups use different sub-sets of the language to suit their purposes. We can identify the characteristics of different sub-sets or registers. For example, one early study of scientific reports found common features which were very rare in everyday conversation, such as compound nouns, passives, conditionals, prepositional verbs and so on.

Without going too far into these linguistic technicalities, you can recognize main features of different registers, as in Box 2.2. The important implication is that certain registers are accepted as the norm in certain situations even if they are not very 'efficient', as we shall show in the discussion of Plain English in Chapter 8.

Dialect

A dialect is a language variety which is characteristic of a region or a socio-economic group. In England, for example, there are a wide variety of regional dialects such as Cockney or Liverpool ('Scouse').

Over the years in Britain there has been considerable pressure to achieve Standard English. Despite growing acceptance of regional dialects, most people still consider some dialects 'better' than others. This is also true in other parts of the world with other languages. We cannot look at the way language is used without investigating the *opinions* people have about language variety: 'Ordinary people (i.e. non-linguists), however, have been accustomed from time immemorial to make value judgements about language' (Milroy and Milroy, 1999, p. 10). We can illustrate the problems this may cause by looking at the impact of different accents.

Accent

Accent is often confused with dialect because a non-standard accent is often associated with a non-standard dialect. Accent refers to the distinctive pronunciation which characterizes a group or a geographical area. In a country such as Britain, accents tend to be regional, e.g. Scots, Welsh, Irish, Yorkshire, etc.

As with most aspects of language, people can feel very strongly about accents. For example, the British author Beryl Bainbridge caused some upset when she said in a speech that everyone should have elocution lessons to 'wipe out' regional accents. This remark, along with her claim that 'You don't take people seriously who speak badly', was widely reported in the media. Most commentators argued in favour of diversity: 'Accents are the thread that makes our nation such a rich and diverse cultural tapestry' (K. Knight, 1999). But that same newspaper article also took the opportunity to reinforce popular stereo-types of British regional accents: the 'unintelligent' Birmingham; the 'warm and honest' Lancashire; and the 'Cockney whine'.

Research confirms that certain accents are more highly regarded than others, and some organizations are deliberately selecting staff to deal with customers on the basis of these perceptions. This regard for certain accents may vary from country to country and group to group (see Box 2.3 for an example of the search for the appropriate accent to deal with customers). Of course, many people deliberately cultivate an accent as a means of rein-forcing group or cultural identity.

The great danger in our attitude to people with an accent that differs from our own is that we stereotype them with attributes that have little or nothing to do with ways of speaking, as in the British examples above. For example, we tend to consider people to be less well (or better) educated merely because they speak with a different accent. Of course, people may also discriminate against a particular accent in order to discriminate on racial or class grounds.

BOX 2.3 MARILYN MONROE – THE VOICE OF SAFETY?

According to a British newspaper report, London Undergound is considering replacing the voice on the existing recorded announcements for passengers – 'mind the gap', 'mind the doors', 'move right down inside the cars' and so on. The likely decision is based on its research which showed that 'a female voice was more acceptable than a man's for giving passengers information' and that a synthesized version of Marilyn Monroe's voice sounded 'genuinely helpful' and 'smiling' to most people (Hussey, 1999).

There is another, more serious aspect of this: how do we give warning messages to people in a tone which neither frightens them so much that they panic nor is so 'soft' that they ignore it?

The same article also commented upon rail chiefs' concerns that announcements on trains and stations were becoming 'too lighthearted'. New guidelines are planned, presumably to avoid situations like the rail driver who asked his passengers, 'Has anyone got a spanner we can borrow?' after a breakdown.

The problem for managers in this sort of situation is whether they could make customer relations worse by adopting standardized scripts for announcement. As we shall discuss later in this book, a standard script for an interaction can sound false and bureaucratic and increase customer irritation. On the other hand, there is obviously room for improvement in the information which passengers receive. One of our own favourites is the way a Scottish operator announced a breakdown: 'This train has been declared a failure.'

LANGUAGE FEATURES

Every language has certain structural features which has implications for how we communicate in (and how we learn) that language. For example, if I tell you 'it rained last night' then you have no way of knowing from my remark whether I know it rained because I was there, or because I heard the weather forecast or from some other source. If I were speaking to you in the Hopi language, then the source of my information would be clear from what I said. In other words, the language specifies the context as well as the event or information.

Among the most interesting features of the English language are the following:

Expanding and developing vocabulary

We can find many English words that appear in dictionaries but which are virtually extinct as far as everyday use is concerned. Does it matter if we no longer use terms such as 'velleity', 'aposiopesis', or 'mycoclonic jerk' (none of which is recognized by my Microsoft spell-checker)? (Bryson, 1990, p. 60). There is the regular debate in the British media over which new words should be recognized in the next edition of the Oxford English Dictionary. As with many aspects of language, the debate can be heated.

The important principle for our purposes is that new expressions are appearing all the time in various ways:

- We borrow words from other languages, such as 'shampoo' from India or 'ketchup' from China.
- We put new meanings into old words. An obvious example here is the word 'gay'.
- We add or subtract parts from old words, usually by abbreviating them. So 'examination' becomes 'exam', 'television' becomes 'TV' and so on. Sometimes we can take a long-standing word (such as 'political') and add to it to create a new expression. According to Bill Bryson, the word 'apolitical' appeared in 1952 (ibid., p. 76).
- We create new words, usually by making some analogy. So we now spoke of politicians talking in 'sound-bites' to mean short snatches of political rhetoric, a phrase that became popular during the 1988 American elections (Ayto, 1999).

Multiple meanings for words

An example of a word with multiple meanings is 'set'; this has 58 uses as a noun, 126 uses as a verb and 10 uses as an adjective. Many other words have multiple meanings and we have to work out how they are being used from the context.

Variety in pronunciation

The English language has more sounds than many others. This can be a particular problem for many language learners, especially when we find that many spellings and pronunciations do not match (for example, how would you pronounce 'chough'?) There are also changes in pronunciation which seem to reflect changing fashion and the obvious variations in dialect. These variations can be quite dramatic.

Flexible syntax

English does have rules of grammar but no formal ruling body to enforce them (see Box 2.2 for related issues). As we shall see in Chapter 8, some rules are more 'powerful' than others and they are subject to change over time.

The important practical implication of these features is that we cannot simply rely on a dictionary to help us choose the most effective language in a given situation. We need to assess the situation and context. For example, how can we recognize when a word or expression has become sufficiently accepted that it can be used, especially in more formal situations such as a written report or a public meeting? This depends on the audience. For example, are they familiar with expressions which arise from popular culture? Would you use any of the following phrases which appeared in a recent British daily paper: 'road rage', 'spin doctor', 'Spice boy', 'trend towards retro' and 'prosecution of spam king'? Or do you have an audience which is openly hostile to 'trendy catchphrases' or to 'Americanisms'?

Speaking versus writing

There is a long-standing academic debate about the differences between spoken and written language. Table 2.1 gives the most common distinctions. But how far are these affected by context?

OTHER BUSINESS CODES

There are other important codes to mention, especially in relation to written communication. Numerical and mathematical conventions and systems can be analysed as examples of communication codes. Graphic codes, such as illustrations and diagrams, are widely used to avoid problems associated with communicating to people of different languages. Pictorial road signs (often reasonably self-evident) circumvent the need for multilingual signs. Similarly, safety and freight-handling information is often encoded in graphic forms, but we cannot always assume that graphic symbols will be universally understood, and this can be very important, especially with health and safety information.

We shall examine issues of graphic codes in Chapter 9. For an example of how graphic and language codes interact, see Box 2.4, which looks at communication surrounding the business card.

NON-VERBAL CODES

When the media talk about non-verbal communication (NVC) or body language, they often focus on what is known as kinesics – the fourth communication system we introduced in

Table 2.1 Differences between spoken and written language

Writing is:	Speech is:
Objective	Interpersonal
A monologue	A dialogue
Durable	Ephemeral
Scannable	Only linearly accessible
Planned	Spontaneous
Highly structured	Loosely structured
Syntactically complex	Syntactically simple
Concerned with the past and future	Concerned with the present
Formal	Informal
Expository	Narrative
Argument oriented	Event oriented
Decontextualized	Contextualized
Abstract	Concrete

Source: Baron (1999)

BOX 2.4 THE BUSINESS CARD AS COMMUNICATOR

Business cards are a common device for exchanging contact details but do they communicate more than those details? Helen Pickles (1998) argues for their importance by quoting a leading designer ('The look, feel, layout can tell you a lot about how that company operates') and a consultant psychologist ('A business card is a snapshot of you and your company').

The different combinations of text, graphics and colour which you can put on a business card can certainly create an impression. But how do we decide what impression is created? Can we accept the conclusions which Pickles offers, such as 'a name and address, all in lower case, without job title suggests a democratic, teamwork atmosphere' in the company. Or are business cards decoded in a more complex way, depending on the context?

Chambers (1998) shows how professional designers use both graphics and specific typefaces to create certain images. For example, if you wanted to open a shop selling up-market decorative items for home and garden, which typeface would you select from the following? (see Chambers, 1998, pp. 10–11 for a real example of a design of this sort). Which of the following typefaces would be most likely to 'project elegance'?:

Smith & Jones (Garamond)

Smith & Jones (Arial Rounded MT Bold)

Smith & Jones (Rockwell Extra Bold)

Given developments in word processing, desktop publishing and laser printing, even the smallest organization can produce letterheads and business cards incorporating sophisticated typefaces like these. We return to this topic in Part three. For the moment, consider how your organization projects its image through devices like business cards and letterheads – what codes does it use? And how successfully are they used?

the list on p. 30. Signals which have been studied under this heading include facial expression, eye contact, gesture and body posture. Much of the time, such communication is unconscious. The face in particular signals a wide range of emotions, and there seems to be a range of 'basic emotions' which are very similar across many cultures: fear, anger, happiness, sadness, etc. (Ekman, 1992). We also seem to interpret facial expressions in terms of these clear categories rather than as a continuum. This can have unusual consequences: if you suffer a particular brain injury then you will find it difficult to recognize certain facial expressions but not others. You may recognize happiness and surprise but not fear or anger (Young, 1997).

There is an enormous amount of research on different non-verbal signals and we shall return to this in Part four of this book. This research has focused on how different signals are used and what they usually mean. For example, eye contact signals interest and helps to control social interaction. Body posture often signals the attitude towards the interaction, whether it be tense, relaxed, interested or bored. Gestures are often used to indicate submission. Sometimes gestures become ritualized as in an army salute. Body posture can also become ritualized, as in bowing, kneeling, etc.

The following are important aspects of non-verbal codes.

Non-verbal codes may contradict the verbal

Often body language contradicts a spoken message and we say that the sender does not 'mean what he says' and is insincere. This raises another fundamental question which we return to later – how far can you become adept at reading body language?

For example, in interviews can we use it to determine what the person being interviewed might rather keep hidden?

Non-verbal messages can be very important

Many of the books about NVC which are aimed at general readers make similar claims about its 'power'. For example, Judi James (1995, p. 9) suggests that certain research did 'discover exactly what it is that contributes to the total message', as follows:

- verbal – 7 per cent;
- tone of voice – 38 per cent;
- visual – 55 per cent.

In other words, the majority of the meaning does *not* come from the words, or as she says, 'Words take a definite back seat when compared to the impact of vocal tone and the non-verbal images' (ibid.). Burgoon *et al.* (1996, p. 136) suggest that 'this estimate has found its way into almost every popular article on nonverbal communication' despite the fact that 'unfortunately, it is erroneous'. They point out that it is based on early studies of NVC which investigated only very limited verbal cues.

Despite the fact that subsequent research has painted a much more complicated picture, this finding is still regularly repeated without any attempt to suggest any reservations. We shall return to this claim in Part four, where we advise you not to rely upon these statistics, which are actually difficult to interpret. Research has shown that non-verbal signals *can* be very important but they may not be so dominant in every situation. We must *always* consider the relationship between the words and the non-verbal cues.

Non-verbal communication cannot be avoided

You cannot avoid sending non-verbal signals. Even the purposeful avoidance of contact by one or both parties sends a signal that they do not wish to communicate. Eye contact, a smile or a proffered handshake all signal varying degrees of willingness to communicate.

Much non-verbal communication is culture-bound

Some non-verbal behaviour appears to be universal – we have already mentioned the 'basic, strong emotions' such as fear, surprise, sadness, and so on. However, the expression of less intense emotions and general social feelings is much more culture-bound. For example, in many situations in British and American culture, failure to 'look a person in the eye' is interpreted as shiftiness. But in many African and Hispanic cultures, averting the eyes is a mark of respect for a person of higher status. Similarly, the American 'OK' hand sign has an obscene or vulgar meaning in other countries as diverse as Brazil and Greece.

As a result, we now have books which offer dictionaries of non-verbal signs and guides to 'correct' non-verbal expression in a range of cultures (e.g. Axtell, 1998; Morris, 1994). Morrison *et al.* (1994) offer guidance on sixty countries, including cultural overviews and advice on behaviour styles, negotiating and protocol. They point out that 'eye contact among the French is frequent and intense' (p. 123) whereas the English 'maintain a wide physical space between conversation partners' (p. 113) and in Australia 'Men should not be too physically demonstrative with other men' (p.13). There are obvious problems with all these generalizations, including whether they apply equally across a culture and whether they are changing. There is also the problem of deciding which rules are really important. For example, we cannot agree with the observation that, in England, 'men's shirts should not have pockets' (p. 114) – which would mean that both of us have to buy a new wardrobe!

But how can we make sense of these differences? McDaniel (1997) argues that non-verbal behaviour reflects or represents dominant cultural themes. He uses the example of Japanese culture, where there are a number of clear themes, including social balance and harmony, strong group and collective loyalty, formality, humility and hierarchy. He then shows how Japanese non-verbal behaviour both illustrates and reinforces these cultural themes. For example, the Japanese tend to avoid direct eye contact 'unless a superior wants to admonish a subordinate' (p. 259). Thus, the typical behaviour reflects the norm of humility. This norm is broken only in order to reinforce another cultural theme, hierarchy.

As McDaniel acknowledges, this form of analysis is easier in cultures which have very strong themes such as Japan. It is much more difficult in more diverse cultures. And we have the problem of measuring cultural themes, which we shall revisit in Chapter 3.

The meaning of non-verbal behaviour depends on the context

Even within the same culture, we cannot expect a particular non-verbal signal to mean the same thing in different situations. For example, Mark Knapp and Judith Hall review research on the non-verbal signals associated with dominance (Knapp and Hall, 1997, pp. 453ff.).

A non-smiling face is seen as dominant, but does this mean that dominant people smile less? Some studies have found that dominant members of a group smile more! They suggest that people who are trying to *achieve* dominance may use a different set of non-verbal signals from those who have already achieved high status.

You can improve your interpretation of non-verbal communication

It is possible to improve your skill in interpreting body language. One key principle here is to look for 'leakage', where the person tries to control their expression in certain parts of their body but the true emotion leaks out elsewhere. I may feel very angry and put on a poker face but you may be able to spot my anger in my gestures, or the way my foot is furiously tapping, or some other leak which I cannot control.

NON-VERBAL SIGNALS IN EVERYDAY BUSINESS SITUATIONS

One point that we shall repeat in Part four is that you should interpret communication in a holistic way – you should interpret the total picture that is before you, looking at all the verbal and non-verbal codes together. However, there are situations where a particular non-verbal code can have particular significance.

The importance of paralinguistics

In the work situation, the paralinguistic message can be the most important. Thus when a subordinate says 'Everything is going well', the hesitancy in the voice may show that everything is *not* going well.

The reverse can also happen. You may have a perfectly sound proposal to put forward to management. But if your behaviour is badly affected by nervousness, then the proposal may come over as uncertain and hesitant. As a result, you may not be taken seriously. If you have an important verbal message to put across, you need to ensure that the paralinguistic message supports it rather than detracting from it.

Appearance

A person's appearance is often taken as an indicator – not only of that person's attitude, but also of the organization's attitude to the people he or she communicates with. Thus a waiter in nondescript, dirty clothes sends a negative message about himself and the organization. One study has even shown that overweight people have trouble getting job offers.

Clothing can have a significant effect on whether a person is employed, makes a sale or is believed by those with whom he or she communicates. Many organizations provide uniforms to ensure that employees project an appropriate image, as in the travel industry. Almost all airline employees who are in contact with customers have a uniform of some sort. This is intended to convey an image of discipline, reliability and orderliness to reassure passengers. Other organizations do not go to the extent of having uniforms, but have written or unwritten dress codes which define what is acceptable.

Dress also has a cultural dimension and can sometimes be a source of discord or discrimination. Certain groups signal their affiliation by clothes. Examples are the turbans of Sikhs and the yarmulkes of certain Jewish groups. In addition, certain minority groups have their own dress codes, which may clash with prescribed codes. As dress can be a source of miscommunication and friction in organizations, management should develop a sensible policy which should be reviewed regularly, as attitudes and fashions do change with time.

Eye contact

Barbara Shimko (1990) surveyed thirty-eight general managers of fast food restaurants about their employment practices and found that 9 per cent of applicants were rejected because of 'inappropriate eye contact'. She also noted the success of Project Transition in Philadelphia, which trained people on welfare to work in the fast food industry. One part of the training helped trainees to rehearse their interview behaviour. They were instructed to adopt the typical non-verbal behaviours of a 'middle-class, mainstream candidate'.

This study illustrates how people in organizations do have norms and expectations about non-verbal behaviour. People who want to gain entry to a particular organization may have to comply with these norms to get through the selection procedure. Posture may be very important here – it is usually seen as a strong indicator of a person's attitude to the situation and audience. In high-stake situations such as job interviews, the interviewee is unlikely to create a good impression with an 'over-relaxed' posture. In superior–subordinate interactions, the subordinate who wants to impress will probably try to take up a posture that is slightly more rigid than that of the power-holder. Of course, there are dangers here – an over-rigid posture can signal lack of confidence.

Personal space and distance

The effect of personal space and distance in communication is complex and depends on a number of factors, which include the social relationship, the situation, the status relationship and the culture. Edward Hall (1959) identified four distance zones for middle-class Americans:

- intimate – physical contact to 45 cm;
- casual–personal – 45 cm to 120 cm;
- social–consultative – 120 cm to 365 cm;
- public – over 365 cm.

In cultures which follow this pattern, business interactions tend to take place at the casual–personal or social–consultative levels. But expectations of the type of interaction influence the distance: if we expect an unfavourable message, we will distance ourselves from the sender. So, depending on the level of formality, we tend to alter the distance to where we feel comfortable.

One general rule is that the person with power or status controls the interaction distance, particularly in the intimate and casual personal interactions. In your organization, is it acceptable for a manager to pat a junior on the back as an accompaniment to encouragement or praise? And would the reverse be resented?

Comfortable interaction distances vary from culture to culture, and you need to understand this when working in intercultural situations. The 'comfortable' distance for Arabs and Latin Americans is much closer than it is for South Africans, British people or Americans.

EXERCISE

Look at the typical interactions in your organization. How do the participants use space to signal what they mean and the status differences? Do they 'obey' Hall's zones? If not, why not?

CAN WE DEVELOP PRACTICAL GUIDELINES ON COMMUNICATION CODES?

One of the themes running through this chapter is that we make judgements about people who are communicating to us based on various features of their behaviour: their accent, dialect, appearance, etc. Can we somehow 'control' these judgements, or at least eliminate possible negative judgements? Chris Cooke (1998) suggests that organizations can take some steps to eliminate what he calls 'unconscious stereotyping', where people make unconscious judgements based on certain language features in a message. For example, if you have a preset opinion that a northern accent is 'lazy', then you see anyone with that accent as lazy.

Cooke gives the example of the UK company that produced guidelines to help its managers adopt a communication style which 'would encourage positive attitudes among the workforce' (ibid., p. 184). It did this in three main stages:

- identifying linguistic features which could create the desired impression;
- identifying 'key audience groups' and deciding which linguistic features were important to each group;
- training managers to follow the guidelines and monitoring how they were being used.

This raises the general issue of how language codes can be used to control behaviour, an issue that will crop up several times in this book. Box 2.5 introduces the concept of corporate-speak.

To return to Cooke's example, general linguistic features were identified from previous surveys of employee communications and by a workshop with a group of staff looking at a specific publication. These features included formality (using formal language rather than more conversational or colloquial expressions); jargon; propaganda features (features which made it 'look like sales talk'); use of the first or third person; and headlines or leaders (using catchy slogans or more formal titles and subtitles).

Specific guidelines were then identified for specific groups of employees (e.g. middle managers, front-line staff, etc.) on the basis of further research. Cooke concludes by

BOX 2.5 CORPORATE-SPEAK: NEW WORDS OR NEW ACTIONS?

If company management start using new terms and expressions to describe aspects of the business, what impact does this have? Fiona Czerniawska suggests the company language ('corporate-speak') 'is a powerful way of instilling a common outlook and ideoology' (Czerniawska, 1997, p. 26). But she also argues that it is neither possible nor desirable for management to have absolute control through their use of language. She notes how many organizations followed Disney's lead in the United States and developed their own jargon.

She also suggests that the development of computer systems has been fundamentally affected by the way language has been used by computer experts to describe their activities – 'from a very early stage . . . computer-speak was loaded with words whose meaning was imprecise' (p. 70). As a result, computers have become 'mythologised', which makes it very difficult to have meaningful discussion about the 'realities' of computer implementation. She sees this as 'a significant obstacle' in contemporary organizations. The analysis of modern computer 'disasters' does confirm that many managements have a view of computing which is more rooted in fantasy than reality. And we shall see in Chapter 5 how important people's perceptions of computer technology are.

identifying four 'general features which will probably apply to most organisations' (ibid., p. 185). Two of these echo much of the advice on written communication we shall summarize in Part 3 of this book:

- that technical or business jargon can be very intimidating to a general audience and should be used carefully and always explained;
- that you should avoid language features which suggest 'propaganda' or 'sales talk', such as buzzwords, euphemisms and clichés.

The other two are more controversial. First, Cooke suggests that 'in general communication it is better to use the third person – e.g. "it is thought, they do this" rather than using the first person ("I think this"), as the first person can be seen as "patronising, or less dominant"' (ibid., p. 185). Of course, this is advice for management but we are not so sure that this emphasis on control will 'work'. The workforce may see such an obvious linguistic tactic as manipulative. It also assumes that the target groups are reasonably homogeneous in their response to language. We shall return to this issue in Chapter 7.

Second, he advises that 'important topics dealt with in briefings or publications lend themselves to more formal language to ensure they are taken seriously' (ibid., p. 185). Again, we wonder how the workforce responded to such formality.

With both of these recommendations, we wonder whether the background research has managed to uncover all the *meanings* which are presently circulating in this organization. In terms of our approach from Chapter 1, it seems to have investigated the process but perhaps not questioned the context and history. For example, if there is an issue about management being patronizing, then how was this impression created? If management did behave in a patronizing way in the past, then a more formal or official style of language may *emphasize* that impression. The workforce will respond to language in relation to the overall context. Language does not work in isolation.

Of course, *we* may be making assumptions about this organization which are not warranted. Unfortunately, Cooke's article is relatively brief so he does not discuss the detail of how the scheme developed and whether it was successful in the long term. Nor does he give any detail on the *level* of formality which is recommended. There is not an absolute distinction between formal and informal language – it is a continuum which has degrees of change.

We have given this article particular attention because it highlights important issues from this chapter, and relates back to the approaches we used in Chapter 1. It raises important issues: organizations can research and review their communication practices and change them if they wish. It also shows that communication codes are not just an abstract concept; they have everyday practical relevance for all of us.

EXERCISE

Using ideas from this chapter, review a particular example of a publication which circulates within your company. What codes does it use? What is its impact on different groups in the organization?

SUMMARY

- We use a variety of codes to communicate, including verbal and non-verbal codes.
- Social rules and expectations are associated with these codes, and they influence how the codes are interpreted (e.g. perceptions of accent).
- Our communication will reflect our attitudes and feelings and we need to make sure that we do not send out ambiguous or misleading signals.
- Although there have been exaggerated claims about the importance and meaning of non-verbal communication, we must make sure that our non-verbal signals create the appropriate relationship.
- *All* human codes are fuzzy and potentially ambiguous. As a result, we always need to consider their meaning in context.
- We must pay attention to the whole range of communication codes when we try to detect emotional states such as someone's consciousness of using deception.
- Using the concept of codes, organizations can research and review their communication practices and change them if they wish. An example of this work shows that communication codes are not just an abstract concept; they have everyday practical relevance for all of us.

DISCUSSION QUESTIONS

- What meaning is attached to regional accents and dialect in your area or region? What impact does this have on relationships at work?
- How far should regional differences in the use of language be incorporated into our business communication?
- How important are differences between speaking and writing?
- How do you interpret other people's attitudes and feelings in their communication?
- How far (and in what ways) are you affected by personal attributes of others when they communicate with you?
- How important is non-verbal communication in everyday business relationships?
- How can you tell when someone is not telling the truth?
- What would a survey in your organization reveal about the communication codes in use and their impact?

FURTHER READING

Bryson, B. (1990) *Mother Tongue: The English Language*. London: Penguin. One of the most entertaining introductions to the complexities of language, focusing on how English has become 'the undisputed global language'.

Cameron, D. (1995) *Verbal Hygiene*. London: Routledge. Essential reading for anyone who wants to explore the debates about what makes language 'good or bad' and the various attempts to control how people express themselves.

Hartley, P. (1999) *Interpersonal Communication*, 2nd edition. London: Routledge. See chapters 8 and 9 especially for further analysis of the relationship between language and non-verbal communication.

Knapp, M.L. and Hall, J.A. (1997) *Nonverbal Communication in Human Interaction*, 4th edition. Fort Worth, TX: Harcourt Brace. A comprehensive overview of research into non-verbal communication.

Montgomery, M. (1995) *An Introduction to Language and Society*, 2nd edn. London: Routledge. An excellent introduction to linguistic analysis.

Chapter 3

Intercultural communication

INTRODUCTION

This chapter examines communication between different cultures – intercultural communication, also known as cross-cultural communication. This is complex for a number of reasons. First, we know how difficult it is to communicate across social boundaries because of factors which we discuss in this chapter, such as social stereotypes. Second, the concept of culture is itself complex. It is a socially sensitive subject as people, usually subconsciously, tend to approach it from the viewpoint of their own culture.

We start by looking at the general problems of communicating across social boundaries and then define and discuss some of the key concepts associated with cultural analysis. We follow this by showing how cultural factors affect cross-cultural communication, and explain management's responsibility in bridging cultures and some strategies they can use to overcome cross-cultural problems.

OBJECTIVES

This chapter will:

- introduce problems and issues which arise when we communicate across social boundaries;
- define basic cross-cultural concepts and explain how cultural differences can be analysed and compared;
- show how differences in cultural background can affect communication in the workplace;
- show how we can develop strategies to overcome intercultural communication barriers;
- explain how management strategies can bridge cultural gaps through effective training, industrial relations and personnel practices, as well as in the general corporate culture;
- show how the difficulties of intercultural communication illustrate basic concepts which underpin all our communication.

The concept of culture can also be applied to organizations themselves and we will show in Chapter 4 how this type of analysis can be used to improve the ways in which organizations communicate.

COMMUNICATING ACROSS SOCIAL BOUNDARIES

Researchers who have adopted what is known as the social identity approach argue that most of the time people think, feel and act as members of some sort of group. In other words, we do not necessarily act towards another individual in terms of their unique personality characteristics; we consider (perhaps subconsciously) our own group memberships and theirs and then we decide to act towards them in a particular way. From this point of view, many face-to-face meetings between individuals are really experienced as examples of what psychologists have called intergroup communication (communication *between* groups) rather than just communication between individuals.

How far this happens depends on how *relevant* the social identities are to the people in the situation. For example, if you are meeting a manager and you happen to be an elected staff representative, then you will be very conscious of those group memberships, even if the meeting is not about specific staff business. There are a number of important practical issues which follow from this perspective:

■ Research on intergroup communication has shown that there may be predictable negative consequences unless the group members work very hard on their communication.
■ If we are using 'group labels' to categorize the other people we meet, then we will probably also attach social stereotypes which may be misleading

Research on intergroup communication

Much of this research has examined situations where two groups are in competition or in conflict. Typical processes include the following (for more detail, see Hartley, 1997, ch. 9).

■ Individual perceptions become biased and discriminatory. Group members tend to develop biased perceptions within each group. For example, they will exaggerate the value of their own efforts in comparison to those of the other group.
■ Group processes change to 'gear themselves up' for conflict. For example, there will be more emphasis on conformity to group norms, and a more authoritarian leadership style is likely to emerge.
■ Discriminatory and antagonistic behaviour will lead to escalation of conflict. The groups will actually discriminate against one another at every available opportunity.

The developing climate of hostility has obvious implications for communication. All communication from the 'other side' will be treated with suspicion, and scrutinized for evidence of their 'real intent'. Unfortunately, these processes can occur even when there is little direct advantage to either side from competing.

EXERCISE

Consider a situation you know about where two groups see themselves as being in competition with one another. How far have these groups become involved in an escalation of conflict as described above? How has this affected the communication between the members of the two groups?

Stereotyping

A stereotype is a generalization about a group of people based upon their group membership: 'To stereotype is to assign identical characteristics to any person in a group, regardless of the actual variation among members of that group' (Aronson, 1999, p. 307). Early research suggested that 'stereotypical beliefs are rigid, unresponsive to reality, and generally resistant to change'. However, more recent studies have shown how the specific context influences whether or how far people make stereotyped judgements (Oakes *et al.*, 1999, p. 64).

We know that many stereotypes have been very stable over time, but that may reflect a stable social context rather than the stereotypes being 'fixed' cognitive structures. For example, Oakes *et al.* researched Australian students' perceptions of their own national stereotype. This remained much the same between 1992 and 1996, including characteristics such as being happy-go-lucky, pleasure-loving, sportsmanlike and talkative. There was major change in 1997: some characteristics disappeared (including being sportsmanlike); the stereotype became less positive and more complex; and there was much less agreement. These changes appeared to be linked to broader changes in Australian society, which had 'become more divided' as a result of political changes, with 'a sense of deteriorating intergroup relations' (Oakes *et al.*, 1999, p. 73).

The link to communication

Jandt (1998) suggests four ways in which stereotypes can damage communication:

- They can make us assume that a widely held belief is true when it is not. This can be important when stereotypes are continually reinforced by the media.
- If we accept a stereotype, then we may believe that every individual in that group conforms to the stereotype.
- Stereotypes can lead to a self-fulfilling prophecy. If you are labelling someone according to the stereotype, then you will behave towards that person according to that label. They may well respond in ways which react to the labelling, rather than their genuine character (see chapter 7 of Hartley, 1999).
- We can interpret others' behaviour according to the stereotype, and ignore other possible interpretations of their behaviour.

When stereotypes are applied to cultures, they usually take the form of an overgeneralization about some characteristic of that group. For example, Italians are seen as emotional

49

while the British are seen as unemotional. While it is true that certain behaviours have a greater value, and thus frequency, in some cultures than others, it is wrong to overgeneralize. While the British may value an unemotional 'stiff upper lip' attitude, it is dangerous to characterize all or most British people as unemotional. This is particularly so when one cultural group does not value the characteristic attributed to another. See Box 3.1 for an example of how this type of problem emerged in one multinational company.

Stereotypes can be positive but still have some negative impact. For example, Jandt (1998) examined the stereotype of Asian American groups in the United States. He noted that 'Asian Americans of all groups are most often portrayed in the press as industrious and intelligent, enterprising and polite, with strong values, and successful in schools and business and in science and engineering' (p. 74). Evidence reported in other media also supported this stereotype, such as the fact that Asian American students usually scored higher than white students on maths exams. However, this positive stereotype had some

BOX 3.1 THE NEED FOR INTERCULTURAL TRAINING

Kim and Paulk (1994) analyse the difficulties experienced between Japanese and American co-workers in an American subsidiary of a large Japanese multinational organization. The main issues were summarized under three categories: language and communication; work style/orientation; and management style/orientation. Apart from problems caused by the Japanese managers' difficulties with the English language and the 'rapid' American speech, major language and communication difficulties included the following:

- The Americans complained that the Japanese 'lacked verbal clarity' whereas the Japanese complained that the Americans 'lacked intuitive understanding'.
- The Americans complained that the Japanese 'gave vague and unspecific instructions' whereas the Japanese complained that the Americans '*needed* exact and detailed instructions'.
- The Americans complained that the Japanese 'relied on written communication'.

All these difficulties represent different cultural perspectives and approaches to communication. Both groups commented on their efforts and strategies to understand the other's perspective, although Kim and Paulk comment that the problems 'have not been addressed seriously by the company leadership', despite the considerable evidence that 'intercultural strain can be reduced through effective language and cultural instructions' (ibid., p. 140).

This type of research raises many questions for multinational organizations, including the following:

- Are they aware of the effect of cultural differences?
- Do they understand the experience of the cultural minority person?
- Do they know enough about intercultural training?

negative impact. Asian American students complained that teachers were too ready to advise them to pursue careers in maths and sciences. Teachers stereotyped them in this scientific and convergent thinking mould and did not explore or suggest possible careers in the creative arts or in management.

EXERCISE

What are the common stereotypes of the different cultural groups in the workforce in your region? How do these stereotypes affect relations between members of different groups? How are these stereotypes reinforced by local/national media?

ANALYSING CULTURES: BASIC CONCEPTS

One of the problems we face in defining culture is that the various human sciences have differing views on culture. Also, in certain contexts it can be an emotionally charged word, particularly when certain cultures are considered superior to others. Even if we try to choose a 'neutral' descriptive definition, different authors will emphasize different aspects. Consider the following examples:

> Culture is defined as a historically transmittted system of symbols, meaning and norms.
>
> (Collier, 1997)

> Culture is the 'system of knowledge' that is shared by a large group of people.
>
> (Gudykunst, 1991, p. 44)

> An ensemble of social experiences, thought structures, expectations, and practices of action, which has the quality of a mental apparatus.
>
> (Clyne, 1994, p. 3)

This brings in the idea of a 'community', which can be a whole nation or a small group. There is also the idea of sub-groups within the larger community. These cultures-within-a-culture are often referred to as subcultures. Subcultures may have very different sources of identity. For example, in South Africa the two most important cultural determinants are language and ethnic identity. In other instances, religion, political affiliation and geographical location also play a part.

Whatever the textbook definition, the everyday reality is that organizations are becoming more multicultural in two senses: workforces are becoming more diverse, and organizations are more likely to communicate with customers and clients from different cultures. In addition, many companies operate internationally. They face the challenge of adapting to local cultures while still maintaining their international image.

Another intercultural complication is that even where we have common institutions or ideas, the perception of these by different communities may be different. For example, a country may have a common legal system but some communities may see this as a fair method of regulating affairs whereas others may see the system as discriminatory. A further complication is that the situation is not static. Factors such as urbanization are bringing about significant changes as people adapt to new ways of living.

Because culture is spread by communication, our communication is thus 'culture laden'. It is the cultural assumptions in our communication that raise difficulties when we communicate across cultures.

EXERCISE

Review your organization (or one you are familiar with) in terms of its cultural composition. How many different cultures are represented? How are these different cultural groups treated by the organization?

Cultural relativism (relativity)

The concept of cultural relativity derives mainly from the field of anthropology. In its extreme form it holds that cultures can be evaluated only in terms of their own values and institutions. From this perspective, we cannot even apply our own concepts of 'truth' and 'consistency' to other cultures. This suggests that the concepts used by people can be interpreted only in the context of their own way of life. But can we understand a culture only if we work from within that culture and accept its values, even if we see them as illogical and contradictory? This extreme view suggests that all cultural values are equally tenable. The weakness of this view is that we would then have to accept Nazism and apartheid as valid cultures and judge them by their own standards!

A less extreme view is that if we are to understand another culture we need to compare it, but not judge it, with reference to some other culture, usually our own. It is important that we should *not* take our own culture as the standard by which other cultures are judged. We need to encourage tolerance, and be sceptical of any claims for universal objective standards. Thus we can discuss whether the religious beliefs of culture A are more or less consistent than those of culture B. From a practical viewpoint, this less extreme form of cultural relativism has more to offer when considering intercultural communication.

Ethnocentrism

Ethnocentrism is the view that uncritically presupposes that one's own culture is the criterion against which all other cultures must be judged. It is almost always used in a negative sense to describe attitudes that refuse to recognize the validity of values that differ from their own. It is difficult to avoid some measure of ethnocentrism as many cultural values are considered to be universal values or truths.

ANALYSING AND COMPARING CULTURAL DIFFERENCES

One way of examining cultural difference is to look for the fundamental characteristics of different communities, in terms of their norms, beliefs and attitudes.

Norms

A norm is a rule, standard or pattern for action. Unfortunately, the term can be used in two different ways, with very different interpretations:

1   to describe what is normal or *usual* behaviour in some community or culture;
2   to set out an *ideal* or standard to which, it is thought, behaviour ought to conform, or which some legislating authority lays down.

One of the main problems in cross-cultural communication is that people take norms in the sense of 1 above as norms in the sense of 2. For example, the Ten Commandments are essentially norms of the Judaeo-Christian communities but are often spoken of as if they were universal norms (in sense 2). Cultural relativists argue that there are no universal norms but only cultural or community norms.

When we talk about ideals or standards, we can also think about these at different levels. For example, we can consider the traditional customs of a particular community (and how they come to be regarded as essential to its survival and welfare), or the moral attitudes of a community or social group, or the manners and customs of a community or social group. Examples of the first level are the Christian ideals of family and marriage, which have been incorporated into the laws of most Christian countries. An example of the second level would be the moral attitude of the Catholic Church towards abortion. The third level covers more transient standards – for example, teenage youths placing a high value on 'being a regular gang member'.

One practical difficulty here is deciding what force these different norms have. Are we talking about norms which people *should* obey, or rules which people *must* obey? And what happens if you disobey them? For example, in UK society, respect for the aged could be considered a norm; but contravention is not punishable by law and is merely considered bad manners. But what counts as 'good manners' is also subject to social change.

Attitudes and beliefs

Your attitudes predispose you to respond in some preferential manner. Beliefs within attitudes are usually considered to have three components:

■   a knowledge component, i.e. something that is true or false;
■   an emotive component, i.e. something which under suitable conditions will arouse feelings;
■   a behavioural component, i.e. something that predisposes you to act in a certain way.

53

Attitudes are likes and dislikes; they are cognitive states. They are expressed in statements such as 'I like John Smith' or 'I don't like modern art'. As attitudes are mental states, and not directly observable, we can determine someone's attitudes only from their own statements or from their behaviour.

As an example of how fundamental beliefs can have profound effects on cultural norms and behaviour, we can use Alan Goldman's analysis of the impact of *ninsengei* on communication in Japanese multinational organizations. Goldman defines *ninsengei* as a 'metaphor and symbol of a quality, style and construct for interaction permeating Japanese social and corporate cultures'. Based upon Confucian philosophy, it incorporates ideals of reciprocal caring and concern for in-group benefit which 'breeds conciliatory, win–win game plans for negotiating, delivering persuasive oral reports, or managing conflict' (Goldman, 1994, p. 49). It also incorporates respect for hierarchical status and a complex set of rules of etiquette which govern how relationships are expressed. Goldman shows how these fundamental values underpin behaviours which are very different from typical Western styles. For example, the American negotiator who bases his style on confrontation, assertiveness and direct communication is likely to find his Japanese counterpart using the completely opposite pattern of behaviour. The potential for misunderstanding and conflict is obvious. See Box 3.2 for more examples of important differences.

Dimensions of culture

One of the most widely quoted studies of cultural differences suggests that culture varies along four main dimensions (Hofstede, 1994). In his 1997 revision of this book, Hofstede

BOX 3.2 DIFFERENT CULTURAL APPROACHES TO RHETORIC

Anderson (1997) compares Arab and American conceptions of 'effective' persuasion and concludes that they differ in three important respects:

- they frame their arguments differently;
- they use different organizing principles;
- they use different types of justifications.

She analyses a specific 'debate' conducted through ads placed in the US press by the Mobil oil company and the Saudi foreign minister, and comments that 'While Mobil imposed a unitary perspective based on "objective facts", the Saudi ad concentrated on illustrating competing interpretations of reality' (p. 105). She describes the ads as 'mirror images' of each other in terms of their tactics and the mutual criticisms which followed. She concludes that cross-cultural understanding needs more than just understanding the words: 'It also requires an understanding of the different cultural rules for what constitutes "reasonable" political debate' (p. 106).

added a fifth (long-term versus short-term orientation), but here we concentrate on the original four:

- individualism–collectivism;
- power distance;
- uncertainty avoidance;
- masculinity–femininity.

Individualism–collectivism

An individualist culture values individual effort and ability. A collectivist culture values the group over the individual. There is likely to be a strong emphasis on maintaining and achieving good group relationships. If there is a conflict between your individual feelings and the group needs, then you will be expected to meet the group requirements.

The emphasis in an individualist culture is on the individual to achieve and do their best. If you come from a collectivist culture then you may find it difficult to come to terms with the level of individual competitiveness and aggressiveness of more individualistic cultures. The United States is usually quoted as the typical example of a highly individualist culture and contrasted with more collectivist cultures such as Japan.

High- and low-context communication

Some authors suggest that the individualism–collectivism dimension is the most important value dimension by which to compare cultures. It can certainly have very powerful implications for communication. For example, consider the theory that the predominant form of communication in an individualistic culture is low-context communication, where 'the mass of information is invested in the explicit quote' (Hall, 1976, p. 70). In other words, in a low-context message, you spell things out very clearly and directly – you say very directly and explicitly what you mean. It is no accident that the many advice books on effective communication from the United Kingdom and United States have very clear and direct titles, such as *Say What You Mean, Get What You Want* (Tingley, 1996) or *How to Get Your Message Across* (D. Lewis, 1996). In contrast, a high-context communication is one where most of the message is embedded in the situation and it is not made explicit in what is said. For example, Japanese business people find it very difficult to say 'no' directly because of their cultural norms. They will signal that they are unwilling to accept the offer or proposition in various subtle ways. The Western business people who are trying to 'close the deal' will become very frustrated if they are waiting for a clear verbal response, which could never come.

Power distance

The second dimension, power distance, is about how people use and respond to power differences. For example, if you are a manager, do you expect your staff simply to obey every instruction that you issue? How would you react if one of your staff challenged or disagreed with one of these instructions? Would you listen to what they have to say by treating them as an equal partner in a dialogue?

In a culture where there is high power distance, the more powerful people will be obeyed as a matter of course. They will not be argued with, especially in a public situation. Where there is low power distance, powerful people will be expected to defend their ideas. Ideas will be accepted if they are convincing, regardless of who produces them.

Uncertainty avoidance

Hofstede (1994, p. 113) defines uncertainty avoidance as 'the extent to which the members of a culture feel threatened by uncertain or unknown situations'. In a society with strong or high uncertainty avoidance, you are likely to find many rules and regulations which ensure that people 'know exactly what to do' in as many situations as possible. Where the rules do not seem to apply or where others make requests which are 'outside the rules', then members of such a culture can become very uncomfortable.

Masculinity–femininity

Men and women are expected to behave very differently in different cultures. However, this dimension is not just about sex roles. Cultures high on the masculinity index will typically value aggressive, ambitious and competitive behaviour. A low-masculinity culture will have friendly and compassionate behaviour where conflict is resolved by compromise and negotiation.

Classifying cultures by dimensions

Some examples of cultural differences using these dimensions are the following:

- English-speaking and northern European cultures tend to show low power distance and low uncertainty avoidance. Japanese culture has high power distance and high uncertainty avoidance
- German-speaking, Caribbean and Latin American cultures show high masculinity, with English-speaking cultures in the middle, and northern European cultures low on this dimension.

One important issue is the reliability of these classifications. They offer a snapshot of a culture at a particular time; the picture may change. For example, Jandt (1998) quotes recent research which suggests cultural change. A sample of Japanese students in 1995, using the original Hofstede questionnaires, scored much higher on individualism and lower on power distance than the original sample. This could be explained by a general change in Japanese culture *or* by the suggestion that Japanese college students are much more likely to value individualism and equality than Japanese society as a whole.

Work by Trompenaars (1994) also suggests that differences can be more complex. His research found that on some issues the Unites States and Germany differed strongly from Japan, while on others Germany and Japan differed from the United States. See Box 3.3 for an example of differences across managers.

BOX 3.3 IS THE ORGANIZATION A SYSTEM OR A GROUP?

Should the company be seen 'as a system designed to perform functions and tasks in an efficient way' or 'as a group of people working together'? What is your response? And what impact do different answers to this question have on behaviour?

Managers certainly differ in their response. The percentage supporting the company as a system ranged from 25 per cent in Malaya and 36 per cent in Japan to 74 per cent in what was then Czechoslovakia and 75 per cent in Hong Kong (Trompenaars, 1994).

DIFFERENCES IN CULTURAL BACKGROUND: EFFECTS ON COMMUNICATION IN THE WORKPLACE

Consider an organization with business practice based on the European–American pattern. It incorporates the norms and values of Western industrial civilization. If this organization is employing workers from different cultural backgrounds, what does the organization assume about their perceptions? Does it assume that once people move into the workplace they will readily understand, believe and accept the dominant norms and values?

This section focuses upon communication codes, but it is worth emphasizing that there are many aspects of culture which affect business and which may not be understood and accepted by the entire workforce. These include:

- history;
- experience with and attitudes towards institutions;
- traditions and customs;
- experience with and attitudes towards technology and the workplace;
- arts and religion;
- patterns of recreation and use of time.

Communication codes

In intercultural communication, the different codes used will be a major factor in the success or failure of that communication. Building on the concepts we introduced in Chapter 2, we need to look at the impact of language and other code systems on cross-cultural communication.

Language

We can highlight some of the main issues by looking at how the English language is used. 'For better or worse, English has become the most global of languages, the lingua franca of business, science, education, politics and pop music' (Bryson, 1990, p. 2). This growth is likely to continue, as it is reinforced by technological change such as the World Wide Web. English has been adopted by many non-English organizations as their international language. However, we must not forget the linguistic diversity in many cultures. For

57

example, South Africa is linguistically complex as it has eleven official languages and four major indigenous black languages. In addition, there are minor languages and dialects. There are also substantial minorities who use other African, European and Asiatic languages such as Portuguese and Hindi. The language situation is in a state of flux because of changes that have taken place since the 1994 constitution came into effect.

Because language is both the means of communication and the carrier of culture, there can be a fear that adopting English as a common language of communication will lead to the so-called 'hegemony of English'. This is not just a local attitude: it must be considered in the formulation of both national and business language policies. (For a recent evaluation of the South African situation, see Titlestad, 1998.)

There are general points which arise out of the general acceptance of English as a global language of communication:

- If English is the common language of communication, then it ceases to be the sole property of England and/or the United States. The 'Englishes' of the countries that have adopted English must be considered equally valid and acceptable dialects.
- Many people are happy to use English as a common language of communication but are not interested in it as a carrier of English culture.

THE ENGLISH LANGUAGE AS THE LANGUAGE OF BUSINESS

If English has become the leading international language for business, then which variety of English has become dominant? Are we actually talking about American English or are there a number of variants? We can point to countries where English has a very different status:

- as the dominant language for all purposes, as in United States, Australia, New Zealand, etc.;
- as one of many languages but with some official status, as in India, Singapore, Malaysia or Nigeria;
- as the typical language used for international communication, as in Japan, Korea or Taiwan.

We could draw finer distinctions to emphasize the complexity: Tom McArthur (1998) concludes that World English is used in '113 distinct territories' and he suggests eight categories of use. Global English or World English is a more or less standard English which is used for science, technology and business.

But there are significant differences in the way that English is used in these different contexts which have implications for communication. Bloch and Starks (1999) suggest the following differences and examples.

Differences in punctuation

Once you recognize these differences, then they are not a major barrier to understanding.

Code-switching

People can switch languages in systematic ways to reflect what they want to talk about. For example, in the Philippines, professional people often mix English and Tagalog in the same conversation.

Different norms for turn-taking

Turn-taking is the way conversation moves from one person to another. For example, I can pause as a way of inviting you to speak or I can ask you a question or use a gesture to offer you the turn. There are cultural differences in how this is done. For example, there are very different norms for interruptions. Japanese speakers use interruptions more to show agreement than disagreement, whereas British speakers will interrupt for both. If people bring their native norms to a cross-cultural conversation in English, there is the strong possibility of misunderstanding.

Different norms for format

There are also differences in written communication, such as the different format to Japanese business letters where date, sender and receiver are at the bottom of the page.

Grammatical differences

Grammatical differences may create both misunderstanding and possible tension if the speaker or writer does not use the expected word or phrase. For example, it is polite in Indian English to say 'we hope that you could join us' whereas a native speaker would say 'can'.

Style differences

The 'most problematic of the differences' (Bloch and Starks, 1989, p. 84) are those where the speaker or writer fails to recognize the contextual rules of the situation and uses an inappropriate tone or content. This often reflects different politeness strategies used in different cultures. For example, Asian job applicants often give an impression to native English selectors of being too 'casual' or 'detached' and therefore not very interested or committed, simply by the way they use English to express their norms of politeness.

We can see from this that second-language users often have special communicative problems. In a spoken language, much information can be conveyed by tone, which can often modify or even negate the meaning of the words. For example, it is possible to say 'You've had it' in such a way that it means 'You have not had it and are not likely to get it.' This meaning by intonation causes special problems for people who are not first-language users of a language. Business communication relies heavily on a common language between senders and receivers, so it is particularly important in structuring messages for the sender to be aware of the language experience and competence of the receiver(s).

BOX 3.4 THE GENDER ISSUE IN ENGLISH: AN ANSWER FROM ANOTHER CULTURE?

In times of particular sensitivity to sexist language, English suffers from a lack of a personal pronoun to cover both male and female. This leads to clumsy constructions such as 'he or she' and 's/he'. In several black South African languages there is no such problem as the pronoun *yena* covers both male and female cases. This does, however, lead to interference problems with their mother tongue, so native black speakers are likely to use English constructions like 'my sister has stayed at home, he is very sick'. Perhaps there is a case for importing *yena* into the English language.

Dialect and accent

The variations in dialect and accent we introduced in Chapter 2 are obviously important in cross-cultural meetings. For example, in South Africa, among first-language English speakers there is comparatively little variation. The two main groups that have affected the English of native English speakers were the 1820 settlers (Eastern Cape) and the Natal settlers. While there are dialect differences, the main differences are in accent. Thus the South African English as used by native English speakers may be considered as a single dialect which is not all that different from Standard (British) English. With non-native speakers a number of different dialects have been identified, including a number of varieties of Township English. As in Britain, most people still consider some dialects 'better' than others. Extreme dialects, particularly when they are coupled with very strong accents, are regarded as inferior for business purposes.

As far as accent is concerned, in South Africa the main distinction tends to be between English first-language speakers and English second-language speakers. Thus people are described as 'speaking with an Afrikaans [or Indian, etc.] accent'. Again the main cross-cultural problem is that certain accents are more highly regarded than others.

Language functions

We have already suggested that people use their first language for a wide variety of functions: to express emotions, to give instructions, to exchange small talk at a social occasion, etc. Each of these functions requires a different approach with different conventions.

The linguistic philosopher Ludwig Wittgenstein spoke of different 'language games'. That is, each function is a separate 'language game' with its own rules, strategies, conventions and ideas as to what is considered the correct thing to do. This can cause problems for people learning a second language. Unless they live fully in the society of the target language group, they may have difficulty in adapting to all the language functions. For example, a student whose second language is English may understand the university lectures easily but not be able to join in the small talk at the student canteen.

Written and spoken language differences

As well as differences in the spoken language and non-verbal codes, we can also expect differences in written documents which reflect cultural values. Clyne (1994, pp. 160ff.) reports a series of studies which highlight cultural differences. For example, he compared the essays of secondary school children in German and Australian schools and found very clear differences in teachers' expectations, which they used as a basis for awarding high or low marks. The English tutors placed much greater emphasis on strict relevance to the topic and a clear linear structure. The German writers were much more likely to digress from the main topic, and to give unequal emphasis to different parts of the discussion. In contrast, the native English writers were much more likely to define the key terms right at the beginning of the essay, to give equal attention to different topics in the essay, and to use more 'signposts' to indicate how the argument was progressing. He suggests that these differences in style reflect different cultural approaches to academic argument and debate.

Second-language users often use the written form as a model for the spoken form or vice versa. The two versions have different conventions and often differ in level of formality. Thus a lecturer will often use a personal, informal approach to liven up lectures. A student who takes down his or her words verbatim may be criticized for using the lecturer's style in a written assignment.

Phonological aspects

A major problem for second-language speakers of English is the phonetic differences between the first and second language. An instance of this is the difference in vowel structures. For example, South African English has about twenty-one vowel sounds while a typical South African black language has about five. Thus black South Africans speaking English have difficulties in both pronouncing and recognizing the different vowel sounds. An example would be interpreting 'bed' as 'bad' because of first-dialect interference.

Paralinguistics

Different cultures use different patterns of what linguisticians call 'back-channelling'. When you back-channel you show the speaker that you are listening and you encourage them to continue speaking. Examples of phrases used are 'oh', 'right', 'I know', 'really'. European and Latin American women tend to use 'mm': South-East Asian women tend to use 'oh' or 'ah'. It has been suggested that these are two very different ways of expressing politeness.

Other non-verbal codes

All the characteristics of non-verbal codes we introduced in Chapter 2 are obviously relevant to intercultural communication and many of our examples in that chapter were of cultural differences.

HOW INTERCULTURAL BARRIERS CAN BE OVERCOME

To provide a complete framework for analysing and understanding intercultural communication, Michael Clyne (1994) suggests that we need:

- general, global description of each culture in terms of its rules for communication. In detail, this would include the rules which govern how writing is organized in business, which communication media are used in which situations, and the rules for linguistic creativity – that is, how you express humour and irony in that culture;
- general description of the values which influence how people interact in that culture;
- full description of how that culture manages turn-taking in a conversation;
- full description of how the different cultures involved deal with the same action.

Although we now have a lot of useful research information on some of these issues, we are a long way from achieving this full analysis of intercultural communication. The most practical way forward is for organizations to take account of the existing research and adopt a systematic problem-solving approach. See Box 3.5 for further examples of issues which multinational organizations must confront. We suggest that solutions to the problems lie in five main areas:

- awareness of the problem;
- realistic evaluation of the problem;
- developing positive and constructive attitudes;
- developing a corporate culture;
- managing cultural diversity in an organization.

From an individual perspective, Stella Ting-Toomey (1999) advocates that we become 'mindful' communicators, paying particular attention to the meaning that people from different cultures will attach to behaviour in particular contexts.

Making people aware of the problem

We need to make people aware of the concept of cultural relativism and of the dangers of ethnocentricism. Once people realize that other cultures may have different value systems, there is a sound basis for communication. Discussion of these differences will also lead to a greater understanding of differing atttudes. Initially, it is usually better to discuss these matters in small groups rather than in large meetings.

Taking a realistic approach to the problem

Each organization will have its own set of problems, and attempts based on trying to accommodate all cultural differences are as likely to fail as those based on ethnocentricism. Attempts to accommodate all cultural aspects within an organization could be impractical.

BOX 3.5 WHEN TALK IS DIFFERENT

Carbaugh (1997) suggests that the cultural emphasis in Finland on the 'importance' of 'proper speech' in public is governed by implicit rules which are contrary to American patterns. As a result, Americans are seen as 'superficial'. For example, the American use of superlatives ('fabulous', 'magnificent', etc.) is 'troubling to some Finnish ears' (p. 223).

Friday (1997) contrasts the negotiating styles of American and German managers within the same multinational organization. Although both favoured direct confrontation and assertiveness, the Americans were reluctant to launch direct personal attacks on other individuals, a tactic which was an accepted practice for the German managers.

McDaniel and Samovar (1997) compare the different cultural backgrounds of Mexican, American and Japanese employees in industries along the US/Mexican border. Numerous cultural differences led to different behaviours: they observed divergent attitudes to status and formality, differences in non-verbal communication, and differences in negotiating styles. For example, the Mexicans and the Japanese adopted a similar indirect approach to negotiations, whereas the Mexicans and Americans used much 'closer' non-verbal communication than the Japanese.

In all these examples, the real problem is that the cultural differences may remain unrecognized and stereotypes therefore unresolved.

In addition, too great an emphasis on the need to recognize and accommodate cultural differences tends to emphasize human differences rather than the common needs and aspirations of people within the work situation. Management should aim for an even-handed and fair approach which leads to the developing of constructive attitudes and a shared corporate culture.

Once the various groups in an organization have identified the differences that cause difficulties in communication, they are in a position to identify the problems within the organization. Thus the organization would come to appreciate that they can provide a solution that will function in their own work environment. They can develop a corporate culture that all employees can accept and identify with.

Developing an appropriate corporate culture

We focus on organizational culture in Chapter 4, so here we shall make only a few brief comments.

Many well-meaning attempts to develop an 'inclusive' corporate culture have foundered because management has attempted to formulate a corporate culture without consultation with the constituent groups. With the best will in the world, management may not be able to avoid some ethnocentrism if they do not interact with staff from different cultures. It is often those things that are taken for granted in a culture that cause problems in cross-cultural communication.

MANAGEMENT RESPONSIBILITY FOR INTERCULTURAL COMMUNICATION

Improving intercultural communication is a management responsibility which extends over a range of activities listed below. These are just some of the areas in a business which may have cultural assumptions built into them, including:

- company policy and working conditions;
- training;
- industrial relations and the work of the personnel or human resources department;
- the house journal and other publications;
- customer relations.

The organization must set up effective consultation procedures. Albert Koopman suggests that managers should 'get out of our ivory towers, "value trade" with our workforce and change our perceptions' (Koopman *et al.*, 1987, p.9). Thus the comments below cannot be a quick-fix solution to intercultural communication, but do identify problem areas and provide an agenda for consultation. Each organization must identify its own problems and set its own agenda.

Company policy

As mentioned previously, management should enter the process of improving cross-cultural communications with as few preconceptions as possible. The company must be committed to improving intercultural relationships through genuine consultation and negotiation. The ultimate aim is to build a corporate culture to which all employees can subscribe.

Training

Training programmes often have a built-in cultural bias. Thus it is necessary to see that training programmes are based on the real entry standards of participants rather than on any preconceived ideas. For example, the following problems were noted with many training initiatives adopted by South African organizations:

- Training simply 'adapted' overseas programmes. These would tend to favour white South Africans, with their closer association with Western norms.
- Training made unjustified assumptions about the language competence of the people taking the course.
- Training made unjustified assumptions about the technological experience of the people taking the course.

Industrial and staff relations

Industrial relations policies can have very different fundamental principles. Western models are usually based on the work culture of European and US industry, reflecting the hierarchy of supervision with a gradation of status and privilege for each level. Some organizations have as many as thirteen levels in the hierarchy. By contrast, the Japanese industry goes more for a team approach, with fewer levels in the hierarchy. Thus in the field of industrial relations there is a need to adapt the systems to the corporate culture of the organization.

And a final word of caution

This chapter obviously offers only an introduction to this important topic, and cannot cover the full ramifications of the subject. Any organization wishing to set up programmes to improve cross-cultural communication should get specialist help to determine its needs and design an appropriate programme. This is not a field for the enthusiastic amateur. In this book, we can do no more than explain some of the concepts and outline some of the problem areas.

SUMMARY

- Organizations are becoming more multicultural and we must review the factors which create difficulties in intercultural communication.
- National cultures differ in terms of fundamental dimensions which have implications for communication.
- The communication codes discussed in Chapter 2 do have particular implications for intercultural communication.
- Problems in intercultural communication can be overcome if we know enough about the underlying factors.
- Improving intercultural communication is a management responsibility which needs careful and genuine attention.

DISCUSSION QUESTIONS

- What are the different cultures represented in the workplace in your region? What characterizes these different cultures?
- How do these cultural differences affect relationships in the workplace?
- How would you characterize your national culture in terms of dimensions?
- What implications does this characterization have for the way you communicate?
- What should management do to improve intercultural communication in the workplace?

FURTHER READING

Clyne, M. (1994) *Inter-cultural Communication at Work: Cultural Values in Discourse*. Cambridge: Cambridge University Press. A very interesting account of the impact of detailed language differences.

Gallois, C. and Callan, V. (1997) *Communication and Culture: A Guide for Practice*. Chichester: John Wiley. Offers an interesting range of approaches and strategies.

Gudykunst, W.B., Ting-Toomey, S. and Nishida, T. (1996) *Communication in Personal Relationships across Cultures*. Thousand Oaks, CA: Sage. A valuable summary of important research in this area.

Jandt, E. (1998) *Intercultural Communication: An Introduction,* 2nd edition. Thousand Oaks, CA: Sage. A comprehensive general introduction to intercultural communication.

Lewis, R.D. (1996) *When Cultures Collide: Managing Successfully across Cultures*. London: Nicholas Brealey. On the basis of his experience in cross-cultural and language training, Lewis offers a 'practical guide to working and communicating across cultures'.

Part two

Communication and organizations in context

One of the main principles we emphasize in this book is that communication is always influenced by the social context in which it occurs. For example, in Part one we saw how cultural differences influence how people respond to verbal and non-verbal signals. Here in Part two we examine the organizational context in which people work and highlight aspects which have major implications for communication.

In Chapter 4 we investigate the concept of organizational culture. In the same way that national cultures define how members of that culture are expected to behave, organizations develop norms and rules which their members are expected to follow. We learn a lot about an organization by analysing how people react to these (often unwritten) rules. And we also need to check whether the 'official view' of the organization is what the members believe and respond to.

In Chapter 5 we look at the increasing reliance on computer technology in modern organizations. We show how the computer has advanced from its early days as a 'number-crunching' device to its more recent role as the 'glue' which ties the organization together through advanced communications. Does this mean that we are creating new forms of organization where we need to learn new habits and techniques of communication, or is the technology simply speeding up old practices?

Finally, in Chapter 6 we look at what these changes mean for the way organizations are organized or structured. Is there or should there be a strict hierarchy? Are people to be organized in teams or departments? How do people communicate across these structural boundaries? We review different models of the organization and show how these have a fundamental impact on the nature and quality of communication. And we also show how the pressures to change and modernize organizational structures are placing increasing demands on our communication.

Chapter 4

Organizational culture and communication

INTRODUCTION

We discussed the concept of culture and its implications for communication in Chapter 3. But that was in terms of national culture and communicating across cultural boundaries. Can we also apply similar ideas if we treat an organization as a 'site' of culture? Although sociologists have used this sort of approach for many years, the notion of organizational culture did not become prominent in the management literature until the 1980s, possibly as a reaction to models of organizations which were seen as 'over-rational' or 'over-mechanical' (Albrow, 1997). Responding to this management literature, many large organizations have spent very large sums of money since the 1980s, both investigating and trying to improve their internal culture. Communication has been a central concern of all these initiatives.

This chapter compares definitions of organizational culture and shows how we can define culture by investigating everyday practices such as story-telling. The importance of this approach for communication is twofold. First, we can show that culture is expressed through communication, often in very subtle ways. So the investigation of how we communicate in organizations inevitably raises questions of culture and subcultural differences. Second, we can look at the content of communication to see how it reflects particular cultural values. This is particularly important when we look at how organizations change, which is investigated more thoroughly in Part five of this book.

OBJECTIVES

This chapter will:

- explain what we mean by organizational culture and why it is important;
- explain and compare major models of organizational culture;
- show how organizational culture is communicated and expressed.

WHAT IS ORGANIZATIONAL CULTURE?

Definitions of organizational culture usually echo definitions of national culture which we encountered in Chapter 3. They talk about typical or traditional ways of thinking, believing and acting. They talk about the way these ideas are shared by members of the group, and the way they must be learnt by new members of the groups. Two leading American exponents of the cultural approach describe how they 'are interested in the workways, folk tales, and ritual practices of an organization' (Pacanowsky and O'Donnell-Trujillo, 1990).

You can think how these ideas make sense if you consider how you feel when you join a new organization. You are very keen to find out 'the way they do things round here' and you probably behave rather cautiously to make sure that you do not offend anyone by breaking one of the 'unwritten rules'. So how can we define the components of an organizational culture in more detail?

Compare the two lists of components in Table 4.1 (adapted from different definitions in Senior, 1997). Although they have a lot in common, there are important differences between these two lists. List A seems to cover more of the ways that culture is communicated (myths, heroes, etc.) whereas List B seems to focus more on underlying principles (e.g. to what extent the organization uses teams). List B includes many of the formal rules of the organization, such as the reward criteria: the way in which salary increases and promotions are decided. It also focuses on notions of identity: 'members' identity' means the degree to which employees identify with the organization as opposed to identifying with their job or professional background. You can also use a list like this to develop a checklist to review and compare different organizational cultures (Senior, 1997, p. 103). List A focuses more upon informal characteristics such as jokes and stories, and also highlights the historical dimension.

Both these lists are long and detailed. Which aspects should we concentrate on? How do we decide what is most important? And what details should influence our interpretation? After all, we can observe lots of details even within one room in an organization:

> even the nature of an empty meeting room conveys something about the general organizational culture, since these rooms generally reflect and reproduce the structures of interaction expected in the organization. Straight lines of chairs and note pads, each guarded by a water glass as erect as a sentry, communicate a sense of conformity and order.
>
> (Morgan, 1997, p. 135)

EXERCISE

Analyse the characteristics of a meeting room in your organization or an organization you know well. How is the room organized and decorated? What does the layout suggest about the way business is done in the room? Compare your perceptions with those of a friend or colleague. How far do you agree on what the room 'means'?

Table 4.1 *Components of organizational culture*

List A	List B
Examples of common language: jokes, metaphors, stories, myths and legends	Members' identity
	Group and team emphasis
Behaviour patterns: rites, rituals, ceremonies and celebrations	People focus
	Unit or department co-ordination
Behaviour norms	Control
Heroes	Tolerance of risk
Symbols and symbolic action	Reward criteria
Beliefs and values and attitudes	Conflict and co-operation
Ethical codes	Company focus on goals
Basic assumptions	Relationships with external systems
History	

LEVELS OF ORGANIZATIONAL CULTURE

There have been several models which adopt the approach of examining levels of organizational culture. One of the best-known comes from Edgar Schein (1991). He suggests three levels. What he calls artefacts are the visible structures and processes in the organization. Here we can look at the language people use, the stories that circulate around the organization, the rituals and ceremonies, and the organization's environment (including the buildings and the way space is allocated).

The second level is what he calls the espoused values. These are the values which the organization *claims* to follow. We can find these expressed in the business plans, the annual report, the mission statement, and so on.

The third and deepest level is what he calls the basic underlying assumptions. These are the taken-for-granted beliefs which are the *real* source of values and actions within the organization and which may be accepted either subconsciously or unconsciously. Box 4.1 offers an example of how an organization can be designed on very explicit values.

The obvious implication of Schein's definition is that there may be very important differences between what an organization *says* it does and what it actually does. The organization that claims to value and support its employees in the mission statement may be extremely ruthless when it comes to hiring and firing people. The basic underlying assumption may be 'survival of the fittest' whereas the mission statement portrays a happy family. Employees will recognize these differences if they occur and will be very cautious when a new or changed management issue pledges about culture change. An example of the sort of commitments which can come from top management is given in Box 4.2.

BOX 4.1 ORGANIZATIONAL CULTURE AND CREATIVE DESIGN

An interesting example of how an organization can be developed from basic principles comes from Jerry Hirshberg in his book *The Creative Priority* (Hirshberg, 1998). The book explains the philosophy and development of Nissan Design International (NDI) from his perspective as the founder and president of the company. In his own words, it is 'a first-hand account of an ongoing enterprise, one that began by identifying idea making as the centermost concern of a business' (p. 237).

Nissan had decided to incorporate Western design skills into its car-building operation to make its cars more attractive to Western car-buyers. It wanted to establish an independent operation to concentrate on the design of new cars. Having chosen the United States as the home for this new operation, Nissan invited Hirshberg to set it up from scratch in 1980. He had already become disillusioned with the organizational culture in General Motors, which he describes as 'increasingly stifling' (p. 10). There were problems of increasing boundaries between different departments, which meant that creativity and collaboration were suffering. As a result, the company was no longer producing what he regarded as truly creative designs.

Determined to establish a new operation which would be organized 'around the priorities of the creative process' (p. 15), he reflected on the most important characteristics of this process. He concluded there were four themes, which underpin most creative activity:

- polarities, i.e. all those 'opposites' and ambiguities that encourage people to think creatively;
- unprecedented thinking, which must be encouraged at all times;
- the deliberate attempt to break down boundaries;
- an emphasis on synthesizing and integrating ideas.

As a result of putting ideas together from these four themes, eleven key strategies emerged which characterized NDI. For example, one practical strategy was to hire designers not as individuals but in pairs who, deliberately, were different from one another. Putting these two people to work together guaranteed that there would be some exchange of different ideas.

An example of a specific working practice that highlights the difference between the NDI culture and previous Detroit practice is the evaluation of a prototype. The traditional Detroit practice was to invite a very selective audience and expect comments only from the designers working on the particular model along with the major executives. Another 'rule' was that people could criticize only if they were able to offer an improved solution. In NDI the rules are very different. Invitations go to anyone in the company who feels interested enough to attend. Anyone can offer a comment and they do not have to offer a solution. Hirshberg quotes the example of the car design where the initial comments at the review were rather polite and indifferent until an executive secretary blurted out that the car looked 'fat, dumb and ugly' (p. 58). After the initial shock of this rather blunt reaction from someone who was normally extremely courteous and quiet, the designers realized she was right. The design was 'not working' and needed major revision. The design which later emerged from this process was an important commercial success and the designers paid special compliments to the importance of the executive secretary's intervention. Hirshberg claims that another by-product of this process is that everyone in the company feels much more involved in its creative aims.

EXERCISE

Apply Schein's definition to an organization you know well. What do you see at each level? Are there major differences between the espoused values and the 'real' values? If there are differences, what consequences are there for communication and interactions in the workplace?

There may also be significant differences between different groups in the way they perceive the same event. These differences can give us clues to how different groups view the organization in more general terms. Daniels and Spiker (1994, p. 10) contrast the administrators' view of the registration process at University X – an 'orderly, necessary set of procedures' – with that of the students. Students called the event 'the Gauntlet' and seemed to take delight in telling jokes and grim tales ('war stories') of how tedious and inefficient the process was: 'Sign up for at least twice as many classes as you really need. That way, you may actually get something.' Through these stories, new students were introduced to the shared perceptions students had about the administration.

If you accept Schein's proposal that the most fundamental level of organizational culture is the source of values and actions, then you can appreciate the importance of this concept. You can also see that different authors have placed different emphases on the notion of organizational culture. Some authors have treated culture as *one* variable which influences how organizations perform; other authors have treated culture 'as a metaphor for the concept of organization itself' (Senior, 1997, p. 105). Senior goes on to use the model from Johnson and Scholes to illustrate the second approach whereby culture covers virtually everything that happens within an organization. We shall discuss this in the next section.

It is worth emphasizing at this point that organizational culture is not simply an interesting backdrop to the organization. The culture can have very clear and important practical consequences. Philip Clampitt (2001) suggests that there are four consequences which are especially important:

- 'Culture affects the bottom line' (p. 51).
- Culture will influence how the organization both analyses and solves problems. He quotes the example of the company meeting where a manager admitted that she had

73

BOX 4.2 A NEW COMPANY CULTURE IS ANNOUNCED

An example of a commitment to corporate culture comes from a large British company, recently formed from a merger of two companies. The company newspaper reported the staff charter which all employees received and which outlined a number of commitments, including the following:

- promises to 'empower staff within boundaries';
- commitment to develop and support 'high-performing teams', which included a commitment to training and the commitment to foster a 'can-do attitude';
- commitment to an open, relaxed and performance-oriented management style;
- commitment to develop leadership and technical skills;
- commitment to 'valuing staff';
- the need to improve levels of trust;
- the need to improve the customer focus in the organization.

The newspaper also commented that staff would be able to assess whether these promises were kept.

Time will tell whether these commitments become embedded in the organization's practice or whether the practical difficulties of merging two organizations with very different histories and profiles will send it down a different path. The critical task facing the new executive group is to make sure that all management actions live up to these initial commitments. The staff charter has created a series of expectations throughout the organization; future management behaviour will certainly be measured and evaluated against these expectations.

not met her targets for the last period. The vice-president responded, 'I would have lied.' This remark from a senior executive was naturally taken very seriously. That one remark could well have created a culture of deception and smokescreens virtually overnight.

- Culture influences how the company responds to change. We shall revisit this point in Part five of this book.
- Culture has a profound impact on employee motivation. We shall see this illustrated later when we look at some employee tales. An important point here is that companies must 'live' their values and not simply 'publish the vision'. Box 4.3 gives further examples of how important this is.

MAJOR MODELS OF ORGANIZATIONAL CULTURE

As well as Schein's model, which we have already described, many models have emerged from research and business consultants (e.g. Trompenaars, 1994). This section outlines four further models to show how different authors have responded to the problem of defining organizational culture.

BOX 4.3 BUT HOW DO THE WORKERS EXPERIENCE THE CULTURE?

To examine how Japanese models of quality control were implemented in factories in Britain, Rick Delbridge spent four months working on the production line in two factories: one Japanese-run and one British operation which was trying to introduce Japanese methods (Delbridge, 1998). He found very dramatic differences in the British factory between the espoused values, such as worker participation, open communication and team involvement, and the actual practice. His examples include the 'counselling' sessions with workers who were having difficulties; these turned out to be one-way communication from the management to 'do better', with little if any genuine dialogue. He also noted the 'team meetings' where only the managers ever spoke.

EXERCISE

While reading through the different accounts which follow, decide which best characterizes an organization you know well. Or do you have difficulty classifying the organization as just one type? And which of these four models seems to fit your experience?

Harrison's four cultures

A model proposed by Roger Harrison in the 1970s, and later popularized in the work of Charles Handy, suggests that there are four main types of organizational culture – which will also tend to have different structures. We shall use the labels for the four cultures which he adopted in his later writings (where he talked of achievement and support cultures instead of task and person cultures).

Role culture

As you might expect from the name, an organization with the 'role' type of culture places a strong emphasis on defining roles for each worker and manager. The organization will usually have job descriptions which define each role; there will be written rules and procedures which cover the main activities of the organization; and there are also likely to be written principles which establish how much each person is paid. The organization will have the pyramid structure of a traditional hierarchy. There will probably be a lot of attention paid to making the roles and the procedures as clear and as precise as possible.

Senior management exercise control in a role culture by producing explicit plans and by monitoring the work which people do. For example, there is likely to be an annual business plan with set targets for each part of the organization. Examples of this monitoring will probably include staff working in quality control, staff who check inventories and stock control, audit and accounting procedures to check financial matters, and a personnel or human resources department with responsibility for checking staffing figures and costs. And there are also likely to be clear procedures which limit the responsibilities of the organization. Documents given to customers will probably contain very clear statements of this sort.

Achievement culture

Perhaps the most typical example of an organization with an achievement culture is the small family business, such as a local shop which is owned and run by a family group. In this culture, the individuals are all directly involved in the work and the focus is on getting the job done, with very little time spent writing down procedures or rules. Another example would be a small firm of management consultants.

In this culture, control is not achieved by regulation or specified procedures. The person who does the job is responsible for the quality of what they do. That person may well be working to standards which they have learnt through professional training.

Power culture

The key feature of the power culture is that all the important decisions emerge from and are taken by the few individuals who hold power at the centre. A small family business which is controlled by the family head is a typical example. Employees are expected to obey the directions and commands which come from the centre. In its most extreme form, an organization with this culture may be ruled by fear and intimidation.

In this culture, there may also be written plans made by senior managers which specify what needs to be done. Whereas in role cultures there are likely to be procedures to check that things are going according to plan, supervision is the key process in a power culture.

Support culture

An organization with a support culture is based upon mutual support and commitment. The members feel that they have a personal stake in the organization and are prepared to work hard to maintain it. An example would be a workers' co-operative or a commune where every individual has an equal share in the organization. A more commercial example would be a firm of solicitors where each solicitor has a defined share in the partnership.

Within this sort of organization, the members feel responsible to each other and accountable for their own contributions. As a result, members feel controlled by the consensus which they have helped to create in terms of what the organization needs to achieve.

This model suggests that each culture is tied to a particular organization structure, and we shall return to the implications of particular structures in the next chapter. Table 4.2 summarizes this relationship and also points out some general implications for communication.

We must also remember the influence of national culture. In countries that score high on Hofstede's collectivist scale, organizations often favour the support culture, as shown by Mike Boon's work on African organizations (Boon, 1996).

Table 4.2 *Harrison's model of cultures and structures*

Culture	Structure	Major implications for communication
Role	Bureaucratic hierarchy	This structure suggests that there are very definite 'rules', 'procedures' and 'channels' for communication, which we discuss more thoroughly in Chapter 6
Achievement	'Family' group	Provided the group is working to the same goals, then communication should be direct and effective
Power	Web with power source at the middle	The 'important' communication comes from the centre. Other messages may be discounted or ignored
Support	Equal partnership	The organization will survive as long as the members maintain their commitment to the ideals and values

Hall's compass model

Wendy Hall (1995) suggests three main ingredients to a company culture, which she calls the ABCs. A stands for the artefacts, the 'visible concrete elements of culture'. Examples of artefacts would be the language and the manners, the types of greeting, the clothing and so on. B refers to behaviours, the ways in which groups and individuals do what they do – 'this is how we do things around here'. This would include how decisions are made, how problems are solved, how conflict is handled and negotiated, and the way in which people communicate. These can obviously be observed, but they need to be interpreted carefully so that we can compare the different patterns of behaviour.

C refers to the core of morals, beliefs and values. This is what Hall calls the deepest level of culture and it determines what individuals and groups believe is good, fair, right or otherwise. For example, organizations may have very different views on the rights of shareholders, and those views will reflect fundamental values.

Hall went on to investigate differences between companies in terms of their styles of behaviour. She identified two critical dimensions of behaviour: assertiveness and responsiveness. She defines assertiveness as 'the degree to which a company's behaviours are seen by others as being forceful or directive' (p. 52). A highly assertive company is one which is quick to act, is seen as firm and decisive, and is likely to be seen as a leading force in its particular sector. Companies which are low on assertiveness will behave more slowly and more carefully. They will tend to wait before adopting a new technology or procedure. They will tend to be less aggressive in the way that they deal in the marketplace.

She defines responsiveness as 'the degree to which a company's behaviours are seen by others as being emotionally expressed' (p. 54). A highly responsive company will often be described as friendly or relaxed. A company with low responsiveness will behave in more serious and less open ways.

Working with these two dimensions, Hall concluded that there were four distinct company cultural styles:

- North style: low assertiveness and low responsiveness;
- South style: high assertiveness and high responsiveness;
- East style: low assertiveness and high responsiveness;
- West style: high assertiveness and low responsiveness.

A North-style company is likely to be very thorough and methodical in the way it acts. It will place a lot of emphasis on checking the facts and getting details right. It will tend to avoid risks and conflict, and try to make sure it gets things right the first time.

The South-style company will be entrepreneurial and unpredictable. It may make decisions spontaneously and will value independent and creative behaviour. It will take risks and pride itself on achieving new and different products.

The East-style company will emphasize the quality of personal relationships and teams. There will be an emphasis on consensus and agreement. Groups are very important and harmony is an important ideal.

The West-style company has a very direct and professional approach which tends to keep emotions hidden. There is a strong emphasis on control and clear quantitative targets.

The cultural web

Johnson and Scholes (1997) talk about the cultural web of the organization, which includes:

- rituals and routines;
- stories;
- symbols;
- control systems;
- power structures.
- organizational structure.

All these arise from the prevailing organizational paradigm: the beliefs and assumptions held by the people within the organization. For example, the concern for people within the central paradigm is reflected in several symbols: the leisure facilities for employees, the quality of the buildings and surroundings, and so on.

Corporate cultures

Another model of company cultures which made an immediate impact in the 1980s came from Deal and Kennedy (1982). After examining hundreds of companies, they suggested there were four main types of company culture, based on four key attributes:

- values, which are the shared beliefs and philosophies;
- heroes, the individuals who are seen to personify the organization's values;
- rites and rituals, the ways in which the members celebrate their beliefs;

■ a communication network, the informal communications channels (like stories and gossip) which spread the values.

The four main types of cultures which emerged were the following.

Tough-guy, macho culture

In a macho culture, we find individuals who work hard and fast, often take risks, and expect to receive quick feedback and awards. Such a culture favours the young and is very competitive. As a result, it may be difficult to get staff to co-operate.

Work hard/play hard culture

A work hard/play hard culture may thrive in a much less risky environment where staff are rewarded for hard work and there is an emphasis on 'team play' and conforming to recognized procedures.

Bet your company culture

In a 'bet your company' culture the risks are high but feedback may take quite a long time. Here we have large businesses that invest a lot of money in projects which take a long time to complete. Staff are valued for their commitment, technical competence and stamina/endurance.

Process culture

If an organization is exposed to low risk and receives slow feedback, it may embrace a process culture in which there is a strong emphasis on how things are done – getting the procedures right and attending to the detail.

CONTRASTING THE MODELS

We can make a number of interesting comparisons between these models and also highlight some of the differences.

One common theme is that certain cultures are more or less suited to a particular business environment. One major management text of the 1980s took this further to say that

EXERCISE

Before you read on, make your own list of the main differences which you see between these four models. And what differences in communication would you expect to see?

some cultures were *inherently* better than others (Peters and Waterman, 1982). Its authors claimed that effective organizations share the following values:

- a bias for action;
- closeness to the customer;
- autonomy and entrepreneurship;
- productivity through people;
- a hands-on, value-driven philosophy;
- 'sticking to the knitting' (concentrating on the business they know best);
- simple form, lean staff;
- simultaneous loose–tight properties (encouraging people to think creatively but within a framework of shared values).

Unfortunately for this analysis, some of the organizations they labelled as successful went on to struggle in the 1990s. This raises the question of how far an organization's culture is related to broader social and political issues. One controversial proposal is that many modern organizations are taking on the values of efficiency and predictability which were first promoted in the US fast food industry. Box 4.4 looks at this proposal in more detail.

BOX 4.4 THE MCDONALDIZATION THESIS

In a challenging book, subtitled *An Investigation into the Changing Character of Contemporary Social Life*, George Ritzer introduced the term McDonaldization. He uses this term to suggest 'the process by which the principles of the fast food restaurant are coming to dominate more and more sectors of American society as well as of the rest of the world' (Ritzer, 1996, p. 1).

He suggests that a wide range of organizations have adopted the four major principles which have been taken to their logical extreme in many fast food chains. The first principle is *efficiency*, whereby the organization develops systems which ensure that the service is provided as efficiently as possible. Second, there is an emphasis on *accountability*. This means that the quantitative aspects of both the product and the service are calculated in great detail. In the fast food restaurants, this means an emphasis on the exact measures of ingredients and helpings, and on speed of delivery to the customer. The third principle is *predictability*. The products you receive in the restaurant in New York will be exactly the same as the ones in London or Paris, and they will be exactly the same tomorrow as they were today. This predictability is also applied to the behaviour of the workers and the scripts of the service staff. The fourth principle is *control*, which also tends to emphasize the use of technology to control both the staff and the customer. Again one can look at the wide range of automatic processes which exist in the typical fast food restaurant.

Ritzer does not claim that these principles offer no advantages. For example, he points out that organizations have used these principles to deliver a wider range of goods and services to a wider range of people. He also notes the advantages of convenience and standardization. However, he is also concerned about the negative features of McDonaldization, which he contrasts with the early attempts to build 'rational, scientific organizations' and ideas of bureaucracy. As we shall see in Chapter 6, the bureaucratic structure can be very effective in a stable, predictable marketplace, but even the founding father of bureaucracy, Max Weber, later commented on what he called the 'iron cage of rationality'. In other words, the bureaucracy may not be a very interesting place to work. In the same way, Ritzer suggests that McDonaldization can have negative and dehumanizing consequences. He concludes that customers may not recognize some of the factors which make the organization inefficient from their point of view. For example, many of these systems make the customers do a lot of the work. They may also be rather expensive and may create a lot of waste in packaging, etc.

He is also very critical of the values which the system represents:

> rational Systems impose a double standard on employees. Those at the top of an organization impose rationalization on those who work at or near the bottom of the system – the assembly line worker, the counter person at McDonald's. The owners, the franchisees, top managers, want to control subordinates through the imposition of rational Systems. However, they want their own positions to be as free of the rational constraint – as non-rational – as possible. They need to be freed to be creative, but not their underlings.
>
> (Ritzer, 1996, pp. 123–124)

Needless to say, his work has received very powerful reactions, not least from the organizations that are the obvious targets of his criticism. We do not have the space in this book fully to debate the pros and cons. But we can highlight the important issue of possible conflict between value systems which are highlighted by Ritzer's analysis. The fast food industry also provides an interesting example of notions of corporate culture where the market leaders spend significant amounts in order to communicate their organizational values.

We can also question what happens to an organization when its economic environment changes. For example, Deal and Kennedy suggested that banks were typical examples of the process culture. However, if you look at the way modern banks operate in the UK, they have become more like sales-type organizations (Senior, 1997, p. 112). This is partly because of increased competition and partly because of the opportunities created by new technology. We now have supermarkets which are operating banking services; and the banks have responded by offering telephone or Internet banking. So should banks adopt the work hard/play hard model which Deal and Kennedy suggested for sales organizations?

In fact, Deal and Kennedy returned to their categories in the 1990s and concluded that they were still useful descriptions of important differences between companies. But they also concluded that 'within any single real-world company, a mix of all four types of cultures will be found' and that 'companies with very strong cultures . . . fit this mold hardly at all' (Deal and Kennedy, 1999, p. 14). They agree with other research that 'sustaining visions are . . . the driving force in strong-culture companies' (p. 27). In other words, if there is a long-term vision from the company leadership which is supported by action, then the company is likely to be successful. This conclusion is supported by other important studies of the relationship between company culture and performance (notably by Kotter and Heskett, 1992, and Collins and Porras, 1994).

Models of organizational culture differ in the importance they give to organizational structure. Obviously, Harrison's model is identified with particular organizational structures. Other models are less prescriptive about structure.

In the discussion so far, we have mostly implied that a single organization fits one culture. This is one problem with many cultural models: the assumption that the organization is a unified whole. There are a number of factors which argue against this assumption:

- Some cultures are stronger than others. In other words, the employees' acceptance of the general culture can vary.
- Different parts of the organization may reflect different cultures. For example, in a large organization, Deal and Kennedy (1999) expect clear differences between the production units (likely to be process culture) and the marketing unit (tough guy).
- Cultures can and do change, and we shall return to this issue in Part 5.

Another possible misconception is that culture develops only in large organizations. In fact, we can observe and analyse culture in organizations of all sizes, including the very small indeed. For example, Dean Scheibel (1990) compared the culture of two rock bands: one playing Top 40 hits and the other playing original material. He investigated the metaphors, stories and fantasy themes which were present in their everyday talk. Among the most powerful metaphors were those of 'family' and 'marriage', which were used to express how group members felt about each other's actions.

COMMUNICATION AND EXPRESSION OF ORGANIZATIONAL CULTURE

Corporate cultures can be expressed in various different ways. The official corporate culture is often symbolized in the organization's mission statement, which can sometimes be expressed as a set of values. What has been called 'the most famous set of corporate values in the United States' (Wind and Main, 1998) comes from Hewlett Packard. Wind and Main (ibid., p. 104) summarize the five fundamental values as follows:

- We have trust and respect for individuals.
- We focus on a high level of achievement and contribution.
- We conduct our business with uncompromising integrity.
- We achieve our common objectives through teamwork.
- We encourage flexibility and innovation.

Of course, it is very easy for senior management simply to publish and distribute slogans of this sort. As we have already suggested, employees will become very cynical very quickly if the organization does not live up to such claims, especially if they are well publicized. It has certainly been argued that one of the fundamental reasons behind Hewlett Packard's continuing success is that the management *do* genuinely believe in the company's corporate values, and that their daily business practice properly represents and symbolizes these values. So if an organization proclaims its cultural values, it must do its best to live up to them.

EXERCISE

Consider the way corporate values are expressed in an organization you know. How do the senior management represent and communicate these values?

So far in this chapter, the main examples we have used have looked at how management have tried to communicate corporate values to their employees. But, of course, this may not accurately reflect what happens in the workplace. As a result, researchers have paid increasing attention to the ways in which organizational culture can be revealed in more personal communication. For example, there is research on:

- stories people tell about the organization;
- stories which circulate about heroes in the organization;
- how people use slogans and catchphrases in the organization;
- graffiti in the organization;
- jokes which circulate about the organization;
- metaphors which people use to describe their experience of the organization.

Research on these areas can highlight the values which are accepted by the members of the organization and also the conflict which may exist between sub-groups (e.g. Gabriel, 1998). We can illustrate this type of research by giving some examples, showing different ways of reflecting on the organizational culture.

The founder as hero

The Hyundai Corporation was established in Korea by a young man from a poor peasant family who set up a car repair business after the Second World War. He is described, when at the height of his powers, as having been 'a fearsome figure'. One of the stories about him is the claim that there used to be a stretcher kept in the executive boardroom, ready for use whenever he would 'punch out underlings' who were unwilling to do what he wanted (Robbins, 1998, p. 604).

Stories from work placement

Stephen Fineman and Yiannis Gabriel criticize many traditional textbooks on organization life for offering a rather static and antiseptic view of organization reality. Their book offers forty-five stories from young people who were asked to recall an incident or conversation which symbolized what it was like to work for their placement (Fineman and Gabriel, 1996). Here we shall summarize two of the stories and illustrate their significance.

Geir tells about the fire exercise which was completely ignored by the management and supervisors: it was a nasty cold day outside and the managers specifically told staff to ignore the fire alarm. This lax attitude contrasted completely with the very strict enforcement of some rules. For example, it was completely out of order to introduce any 'degree of friendliness into letters I was about to send to clients . . . Not even a little "Merry Christmas" at the bottom of the letter was acceptable' (p. 43).

Arne's story is about the sacking of a senior accountant in the bank (pp. 105–107). The accountant made an abrupt departure early one morning: he was called to the manager's office, returned five minutes later and packed his briefcase, then left the office with a only a brief word to one of the four staff. About an hour later, all the office staff were seen by the head of the department, who told them that the accountant had resigned and there would be 'no talk of the incident'. Arne's account reveals that the department had a very 'strong culture'. The senior accountant had introduced some changes which seemed very trivial to Arne but which were taken by some members to be an attack on the established 'culture of trust'. Arne is sure that the sacking was the result of a deliberate strategy by these members. He concludes that the incident taught him that 'in a company, there is a hidden network of people who have immense power, mainly through gossip, malicious talk and knowing the right people'.

Both these stories paint a rather negative and depressing picture of organizational life, and this represents the overall tone of the book they come from. Fineman and Gabriel do comment on this, reminding us that these stories are not intended to be statistically representative and that they were collected at a time when many British organizations were suffering massive change and restructuring. This highlights the moral that organizations are well advised to pay particular attention to communication when economic conditions are poor or difficult. The organization needs everyone to be performing as well as they can in difficult times. Poor management communication may undermine staff commitment in ways which are suggested by these examples. The other point to make is that we only receive 'one side of the story' in these accounts. As we shall see in Part four, interpersonal relations often involve multiple different perceptions.

EXERCISE

Collect some stories and anecdotes from an organization which you know well. What is their overall tone – happy, light-hearted, cynical, pessimistic, or what? What do these stories reveal about people's feelings towards the organization and their acceptance (or not) of the main organizational values? And how do these feelings influence communication?

The power of metaphor

An example of the power of metaphor in a large commercial organization is the study of labour–management conflict at Disneyland (Smith and Eisenberg, 1987). From their analysis of interviews with employees, Smith and Eisenberg concluded that there were two fundamental (root) metaphors which represented the Disney approach: Disneyland was a 'drama' and a 'family'. Employees saw themselves as 'actors' putting on 'costumes' to act out a 'show' for the benefit of the 'audience' (which is how they described customers). The family metaphor was used to describe management or worker relationships and attitudes. When management responded to increasing competition by adopting hard economic measures, the workers felt that this was 'a breach of Disney's caring philosophy' (p. 374). Smith and Eisenberg go on to discuss how management could 'reconsider' these metaphors in order to convince employees that the new approach was required. And this raises the possibility of communicating new cultural values to support organizational change – a theme we return to in Part five.

Lists versus stories

Another continuing theme in the literature on organizational culture is the comparison between organizations. Browning (1992) suggests that two broad types of cultures can be identified by their preference for lists or stories. The 'lists' organization will tend to issue written lists to staff to tell them what to do and how to do it. This reflects the organization's values: the maintenance of standards, accountability, certainty, etc. On the other hand, the 'stories' organization will rely on face-to-face interaction and story-telling to communicate to staff. This is an organization which values humour, drama and performance.

Cultural differences

Much of the research to date on organizational stories has looked at Western organizations using English as the dominant language. In other cultures, members of the organization may have different ways of expressing themselves through stories. For example, whereas stories in British or US organizations often use images, jokes and metaphors drawn from popular television programmes, films and music, a study of story-telling in a Malaysian organization found that most stories used traditional legends and historical characters (Ahmad and Hartley, 1999). The one major exception was a story in several parts which used the *Power Rangers* characters to comment on current management preoccupations.

REVIEWING THE DETERMINANTS OF ORGANIZATIONAL CULTURE

As this chapter has suggested, there are a range of factors which influence the culture that an organization develops. Figure 4.1 summarizes these factors, and some brief comments follow concerning their implications for communication.

85

BOX 4.5 EXPRESSIONS OF THE COMPANY CULTURE

This box gives examples of company and employee behaviour which could be interpreted as significant symbols of the organizational culture. For each example, what do you think they express? What sort of impact could these behaviours make if they were introduced to a company or organization which you know well? And would you like to work for any of the organizations featured in these examples?

The reverse organization chart
One US telemarketing firm places great emphasis on customer service. Its official organization chart is 'upside down'. The customer is placed at the top of the chart and the board of directors is at the bottom (Clampitt, 2001, pp. 57–58).

The quality newsletter
A US company which produces high-quality paper products also produces an internal newsletter where the quality of the layout and the pictures is on a par with those in *National Geographic* magazine (Clampitt, 2001, p. 57).

Pie in the face
Several US and British sales companies have interesting ways of rewarding the sales representative who produces most custom in a given month. In one British firm, the 'winning' sales representative of each month is invited to a meeting where they can thrust a custard pie into the face of the sales manager.

Bring the clothes back when the child grows up
Hannah Anderson is a US company which sells children's clothing by mail. Its statement of corporate values includes a reference to 'social action', where it promises to research opportunities to 'contribute to the community'. One activity is a programme which the company called Hannahdowns. If customers return children's clothing once their child has outgrown it, they receive a 20 per cent credit. This returned clothing is then cleaned by the company and given to a community organization such as a women's shelter (Gordon, 1996, p. 472).

Follow the creator
In the manual which is given to recruits at the Hyundai Corporation in Korea is the following statement: 'the hard work of the creator [Chung] and the courage of the pioneer have helped us open the way for the expansion, sophistication and internationalization of the Industrial Society of our country' (Robbins, 1998, p. 604).

April Fool
The engineers at Sun Microsystems in California always play an April Fool's Day hoax which targets one member of the company's top management. One year they built a life-size replica of one of the managers' offices and placed it at the bottom of the shark tank in a San Francisco aquarium. The senior manager concerned was well known for his love of scuba diving. The hoax is videotaped and distributed to employees at all company locations (Robbins, 1996, p. 697).

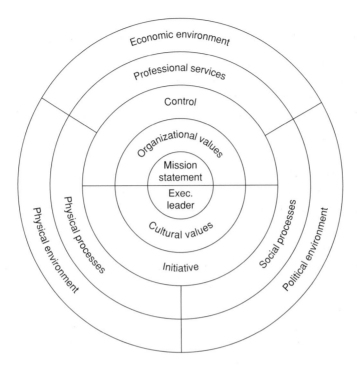

Figure 4.1 *Determinants of organizational culture*

Organizational mission – executive attitudes – organizational values – cultural values

In theory, the core of the organizational culture should be the organizational vision or mission. But this may not be the case if this mission is not 'echoed' by three other factors: executive attitudes, organizational values and cultural values. If the four factors are not aligned, then some level of conflict is inevitable.

Control – initiative

All organizations have to balance the competing tendencies to maintain control on the one hand, and encouraging initiative on the other. The larger the organization becomes, the more it becomes an issue. People in the organization need to 'know where they stand' on these issues and this is a very important issue to communicate.

Physical processes – social processes – professional services

A business may focus on physical processes, social processes or professional services – a chemical processing plant would be an example of physical process – but is likely to deal with all three to some degree. The mix of people involved will be an important factor. For example, many organizations employ professionals who have a professional code of practice. There may be conflict if the organization's demands clash with that professional code.

Political, economic, physical environments

Of the environmental factors, the political environment may be especially important for organizations whose parent culture happens to clash with the laws or customs of a particular country.

DISCUSSION QUESTIONS

■ Compare the lists of components in Table 4.1 (p. 71). Which list is the more useful in describing your organization's culture?

■ What organizations say they do and what they actually do can be very different. Have you experienced this? What consequences did this difference have?

■ Clampitt argues that culture has definite and tangible consequences. Do you have evidence or experience which supports this view?

■ Which models of organizational culture are most useful?

■ Does your organization show any signs of McDonaldization? If so, why is this happening, and what are the consequences?

SUMMARY

■ There are two key links between communication and culture. First, culture is expressed through communication, often in very subtle ways. Second, the content of communication reflects particular cultural values in an organization.

■ Definitions of organizational culture usually mirror the definitions of national culture which we encountered in Chapter 3.

■ There are different models of organizational culture; culture can be conceptualized in different ways and at different levels.

■ Whatever the precise definition, organizational culture can have very clear and important practical consequences. For example, it can influence how the company responds to change, and have a profound impact on employee motivation.

■ Organizational culture is communicated and expressed in terms of the 'official' corporate culture. This is often symbolized in the organization's mission or values statement. Employees will become very cynical very quickly if the organization does not live up to such claims, especially if they are well publicized.

■ Researchers have paid increasing attention to the ways in which organizational culture can be revealed in more personal communication, such as story-telling. This research suggests that these forms of communication can often highlight the discrepancies between the 'public face' of the organization and how its employees perceive its values.

■ Many factors influence or determine organizational culture, from the organizational mission to the political environment. The interaction between these factors is critical.

FURTHER READING

Ashkanasy, N.M., Wilderon, C.P.M. and Peterson, M.F. (eds) (2001) *Handbook of Organizational Culture and Climate*. Thousand Oaks, CA: Sage. A substantial overview of recent research and theory, including sections on measurement and organizational change.

Deal, T. and Kennedy, A. (1999) *The New Corporate Cultures: Revitalising the Workplace after Downsizing, Mergers and Reengineering*. London: Orion. As well as providing an interesting update of their important work from the 1980s, this challenges some 'myths' about culture and change which have important implications for communication (and for issues we shall raise in Chapter 15).

Fineman, S. and Gabriel, Y. (1996) *Experiencing Organizations*. London: Sage. Although this book does not focus on the question of organizational culture *per se*, the stories and commentary offer a fascinating introduction to the issues of how organizations are experienced by the members, and how the 'official' culture may not reflect how members experience their everyday working lives.

Goffee, R. and Jones, G. (2000) *The Character of a Corporation: How Your Company Culture Can Make or Break Your Business*. London: HarperCollins. This offers yet another model based on the authors' considerable experience in consultancy and research. A series of checklists are included so you can apply the model.

Hofstede, G. (1994) *Cultures and Organizations: Software of the Mind*. London: HarperCollins. A very important text based on research which examines culture at both national and organizational levels. The revised edition (1997) introduced a fifth cross-national dimension: long-term versus short-term orientation.

Pheysey, D.C. (1993) *Organizational Cultures: Types and Transformations*. London: Routledge. This text offers a useful overview of organizational behaviour, starting from a cultural perspective and covering the major concepts and research studies. There are nearly 100 pages of case studies and exercises which are drawn from both public and private organizations in Europe, Asia and Africa.

Senior, B. (1997) *Organizational Change*. London: Pitman. A very comprehensive and readable overview of this topic, with lots of material on organizational culture.

Williams, A., Dobson, P. and Walters, M. (1993) *Changing Culture: New Organizational Approaches*, 2nd edn. London: Institute of Personnel and Development. The first part of this book summarizes basic concepts of organizational culture and the second part looks at methods of change. The final part of the book has a very interesting set of case studies of real cultural change in UK-based organizations.

Chapter 5

Information and communications technology (ICT) in organizations

INTRODUCTION

In this chapter we shall briefly review how 'computers' have been transformed into 'information technology' (IT) and then into 'information and communications technology' (ICT).

We believe that this *is* a fundamental shift in terms of what the technology can do, although we must not ignore social and political influences on the way the technology is applied (MacKenzie and Wajcman, 1999). Organizations which fully embrace ICT do have significant opportunities which have not been available before. We outline some of these and suggest that they can have a profound impact on the way we communicate. But we also need to retain a healthy scepticism about some of the claims currently being made for the 'revolutionary' power of ICT.

OBJECTIVES

This chapter will:

- identify the fundamental features of computing technology and show how these have expanded into new roles and functions;
- review how 'computers' have been transformed into 'information technology' (IT) and then into 'information and communications technology' (ICT);
- show how modern organizations are using ICT to develop new ways of working;
- identify critical impacts of these changes on the way we work and communicate.

TECHNOLOGY AND THE DEVELOPMENT OF COMMUNICATION

Looking back on the history of communication, we suggest five major milestones:

- the invention of writing – this enabled people both to record events and to send messages;
- written media for the mass audience – the development of printing in the fifteenth century enabled mass production of books and other documents. This brought many

fundamental social changes, including the spread of literacy and education and the development of newspapers;

■ instantaneous person-to-person communication by electrical means – the development of the electrical telegraph enabled people to communicate instantly at a distance thanks to telegraph operators using the Morse code. This paved the way for the subsequent invention of the telephone;

■ instantaneous mass media – the development of the radio, and later television, meant that groups and individuals could broadcast to a mass audience simultaneously; and

■ communication with multiple *and* simultaneous senders and receivers, as enabled by computer developments. People now communicate with computers, computers communicate with people, and computers communicate with computers. And that is the theme of this chapter.

But how far advanced is the 'digital revolution'?

Many writers are enthusiastic:

■ 'We may safely conclude that *on average, about half of every business of the industrial world could be affected by the Information Marketplace*' (Dertouzos, 1997, p. 192, emphasis in the original).

■ 'We stand at the brink of another revolution; this one will involve unprecedently inexpensive communication. All the computers will join together to communicate with us and for us' (Gates with Myhrvold and Rinearson, 1996, p. 3).

■ 'As the business world globalizes and the Internet grows, we will start to see a seamless digital workplace' (Negroponte, 1995, p. 228).

According to these authors, we have developed very quickly into the 'information age' or 'information society'. However, there are important debates about what this means exactly (Webster, 1995), and we need to remember that the incorporation of digital technology within society depends upon social and political constraints (Winston, 1998).

In order to assess the likely future impact of ICT on business organizations, we shall briefly explore what factors can affect technological advance. We will then look at how computing technology has developed before analysing how its changing roles and functions influence business and commercial activities.

From science to application

New technology can be created when someone applies scientific ideas in a new way. Whether this technology develops into an established product depends upon a number of factors, including the following:

■ whether the technology is practical. For example, two different research teams developed the idea for the silicon chip some time before it could be practically produced. This was a bonus for the patent lawyers as they argued over who had the idea first (Reid, 1985);

■ whether the social, political and economic environment is ready to accept the new technology. The IBM Personal Computer (PC) became established in business and defeated competition from technically superior products because of a mix of social and economic factors (Hartley, 1990, pp. 6–7).

Brian Winston offers a more sophisticated analysis of these processes. At first sight, the early years of computing advance in the late 1940s and the 1950s look like a very impressive decade of technological advance. However, Winston suggests that the radical potential of these machines was significantly *suppressed*. For example:

■ Small machines could have been built much earlier, using the transistor (a few were, but they did not have any impact).
■ The early machines were very inaccessible and difficult to operate. Some of the 'old guard' obstructed the development of programming languages.
■ Business and commerce was largely indifferent to early machines. Only a few organizations saw the real potential.

Figure 5.1 represents these restraining forces in terms of Winston's model. Whether prototypes become fully fledged inventions depends upon what he calls a 'supervening social necessity'. This is the combination of social forces which determines whether the new technology is accepted. One combination of social forces which is particularly important acts as a 'brake' on the technological development. He calls this the 'law of the suppression of radical potential'. These constraints ensure that any new technology will take time to filter through to mass acceptance. The delay may be due to active resistance by established organizations within society.

Once the new technology is in full-scale production, it can of course fail (perhaps through redundancy) – do you remember the digital compact cassette, which was offered as *the* digital replacement for the audio cassette? A new technology can also generate spin-offs; for example, the CD was initially a product designed for computer memory – the audio CD was a very successful spin-off.

EXERCISE

Consider how computers are being used in an area of business you know well. Can you find any evidence that the development of computing in business and commerce is still being 'suppressed'? What is the mind-set in business today? Are we equally failing to exploit possibilities? You may like to repeat this exercise *after* reading this chapter. To give you some ideas, Box 5.1 gives examples of business organizations which have had to (or may need to) completely revise their strategies and methods because of IT developments.

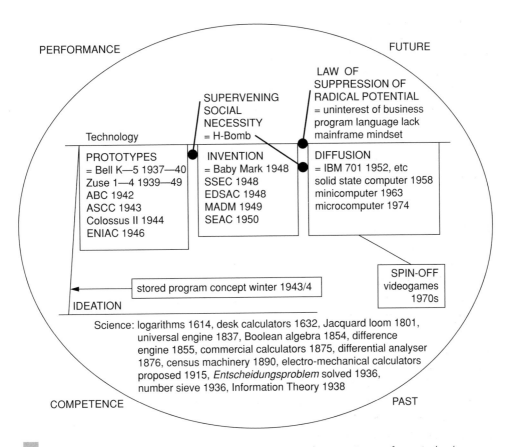

Figure 5.1 *Winston's model showing restraints on the acceptance of new technology*

FUNDAMENTAL FEATURES OF COMPUTING TECHNOLOGY

Dertouzos (1997, pp. 51ff.) proposes 'five pillars of the Information Age':

1   Numbers are used to represent all information.
2   These numbers are expressed with 1s and 0s.
3   Computers transform information by doing arithmetic on these numbers.
4   Communication systems move information around by moving these numbers.
5   Computers and communications systems combine to form computer networks – the basis of tomorrow's information infrastructures – which in turn are the basis of the Information Marketplace.

(Dertouzos, 1997, p. 317)

It is worth discussing some of these points in more detail. For example, Dertouzos's second point is that computers use binary code – this means you can represent numbers using the very simplest electrical circuit: the switch (see Hartley, 1990, or Gates with Myhrvold and

BOX 5.1 THE TECHNOLOGY HAS CHANGED – WHAT DO WE DO NOW? AND HOW DO WE CONTINUE TO MAKE MONEY?

In the past decade, paper encyclopedias have been completely overtaken by CD-ROM versions, stimulated by the heavily publicized appearance of Microsoft's *Encarta* at a price well below that of its paper competitors. This change had a major impact on the traditional market leader, *Encyclopaedia Britannica*, effectively forcing a restructuring of the company and its previous sales methods (and sales force). Having moved its product to CD-ROM, it took this process one stage further in 1999 and offered the complete encyclopedia online through the World Wide Web with *free* access.

As we were finalizing this chapter in late 2000, many newspapers and magazines were speculating on the long-term impact of MP3, which has become a standard for saving music files in computer format. Will all record companies be forced to distribute their product through the World Wide Web with customers downloading the music they wanted to be played on portable MP3 machines? Or will this downloading be restricted to certain music styles or audiences? And what will the changes do to the conventional distribution chain of record stores?

Microsoft is sometimes characterized as a company which 'changed overnight' when it seemed to decide 'in one step' to revamp *all* its main products to exploit the Internet. What actually happened is less dramatic (Gates with Hemingway, 1999, pp. 161ff.), but it is interesting to speculate what might have happened if it had not moved fast to exploit the growth of Internet use.

Rinearson, 1996, for more detailed discussion of how this works). An electronic circuit (a set of switches) can therefore store information and do calculations. And these circuits have seen major technological advances over the past forty years: they have become much more powerful, much cheaper and much smaller. We have moved from the valve or vacuum tube of the 1950s to successive generations of microchip.

What are the limits?

All information must be converted into binary numbers (digitization) before it can be used or manipulated by computer. Is there any information which we cannot convert? Computers started out as 'number-crunchers', manipulating numerical information to work out mathematical and scientific problems. They then became 'word-crunchers' – letters and punctuation can also be translated into numbers. Using mathematics, you can also express graphics in terms of numbers. And so computers became devices for visual presentation. Finally came the advances which enable us to digitize sound and video images – the age of multimedia.

As far as the computer is concerned, all it does is move numbers. In the words of one leading commentator on the digital age, this means that 'bits commingle' (Negroponte, 1995, p. 18). In other words, we can mix numbers, words, graphics, sound and video in *any* combination provided that:

- the source material can be digitized; and
- the hardware can cope with the amount of information involved. (For example, digitizing colour video generates a lot of information – you need machines with fast processors and a lot of memory to cope with it.)

See Box 5.2 for some examples of this commingling.

Computers can also handle instructions. They can follow an algorithm which leads to a decision. An algorithm is simply a chain of yes/no choices. Such choices mimic the way we often make everyday decisions. For example, you are about to leave the house when you realize you cannot find your door key. You will probably work through a series of binary decisions. Did you leave it upstairs or downstairs? If you left it upstairs, did you leave it in the bathroom or in the bedroom? And so on.

Another important implication is that we need clearly specified rules to form algorithms. This explains why computers have become quite expert at chess, a game with very clear and explicit rules, but are still struggling to recognize human speech, where there are enormous variations depending on context. Of course, technology is advancing very fast and there are several areas where computer programs can incorporate more flexible approaches (see Box 5.3).

BOX 5.2 COMMINGLING BITS

The obvious example of commingling bits is the multimedia CD-ROM, which can contain:

- text;
- data, in the form of numbers and calculations;
- graphics;
- still pictures;
- video clips;
- audio clips;
- Web links.

Another recent example of how this commingling can enhance services is the development of digital radio. As well as audio sounds, digital radio can broadcast a wide range of additional information. What you receive will depend upon your radio. The simplest (cheapest) set will receive the audio and perhaps one simple scrolling display to tell you what you are listening to. The more complex sets will offer more information and ultimately the opportunity to interact through an Internet link.

EXERCISE

Do you have any ideas for a new application of computing which would improve business communication and which would involve a novel 'commingling of bits'? Are there possible ways of 'expanding' the way we send messages through this technology?

Dertouzos also suggests that the key development in computing has been the way that computers and communication systems have combined, as we discuss later. We think that there are other important processes:

- IT developed new roles;
- IT has become 'embedded'.

Changing roles

Computers can automate processes. Examples of automation range from industrial robots which construct and paint new cars to computers which accept information from scanning devices at supermarket checkouts. The example of the checkout suggests a second main function for computers: they can *monitor and control* processes. As products are purchased and scanned, the computer reviews the stock levels for each item and generates orders when stock levels hit a predetermined level.

One interesting implication of computer control is the role of the human operator. For example, would you be happy to travel in an aircraft which was *completely* computer controlled from take-off right through to landing? Would you be prepared to fly in this aircraft if you knew there were no human pilots on board? Could the computer take account of all eventualities and deal with any emergency which arose? Or would you need a human operator on standby in case an unforeseen emergency arose?

When computers do take charge of a process, you have to consider what happens if something goes wrong. The near-disaster at Three Mile Island illustrates what happens if the human operators do not fully understand how the computer deals with emergencies. In this case, the computer took emergency action which the operators did not understand. They reversed the (correct) computer actions and very nearly caused a major accident.

Integrating

IT can also integrate processes in new ways. The ability to manipulate sound and video data through computers is demonstrated in recent movie blockbusters, such as the computer-generated ship in James Cameron's *Titanic* or the restoration of the original *Star Wars* movies. A commercial example of the way data can be integrated is the way that supermarkets can develop a profile of customers, as we see later. Another example of the way that IT can integrate functions is the way that it helped transform the British national newspaper industry in the 1980s – see Box 5.4.

BOX 5.3 SOFTWARE WITH 'INTELLIGENCE'?

There are also software programs which derive from attempts to develop computers with some degree of intelligence:

Expert systems

An expert system contains a set of rules which is modelled upon the behaviour of human experts in the particular situation. One example is the financial planning programs used by banks. The bank employee asks the customer a series of questions prompted by the computer. From this information, the program produces various options for the customer, together with their advantages and disadvantages. The bank employee does not have to be an expert to use the program. This has obvious advantages to the banks in terms of the expertise and qualifications needed by employees. It has the obvious disadvantage that the program is only as good as the experts who were used to develop it. Also, as the users of the system are probably not aware of the assumptions built into it, there can be problems if the customer's responses are ambiguous in any way.

Neural networks

A neural network tries to emulate the way the human brain operates in terms of its structure. Rather than processing a single instruction at a time, the neural network is an interconnected set of processors which act in parallel. For example, a whole range of data might be fed into the network to see which combination of data can predict share prices the following day. The system is trained on existing data until it can produce an answer which is as accurate as possible. It is then put into use to try to predict future events.

Fuzzy logic

Rather than working with the very definite 'on–off' rules of traditional computer programs, fuzzy logic aims to create rules which are more approximate and variable. The idea here is that this is more like the way we think as human beings, weighing up different probabilities in terms of likely events.

All these approaches are likely to become more important in commercial applications as computers become more powerful. For a more detailed description, see Laudon and Laudon (1994, ch. 17).

BOX 5.4 IT CAN TRANSFORM A BUSINESS

One dramatic example of this transformation was the British national newspaper industry in the late 1980s. At the start of 1986, all the British national newspapers were written and printed in a small area of London, around Fleet Street. By the end of 1989 they had *all* moved away, and all adopted computer technology as central to their newspaper production.

In the 1970s all the national newspapers used mechanical technology which had not changed fundamentally since the beginning of the century. First the journalist would type up his or her notes, then these notes would be typed up by a compositor on a Linotype machine to create lines of lead type. Then this type would be assembled into pages by another section of the workforce, and so on. This complex workforce generated a very complex pattern of industrial relations.

Of course, newspapers are a unique product in several ways. Their cover price does not include any profit margin – profit must be achieved through the sale of advertising. A newspaper can have healthy circulation figures and yet fail economically if it does not attract sufficient advertising. A daily newspaper also has a very limited shelf life: if it cannot be sold on the right day, it is no longer saleable. So any delay in getting the product to market is financially very damaging. This was one reason why the trade unions exerted considerable bargaining influence.

The critical change came in 1986 when Rupert Murdoch opened new plants at Wapping, with several key innovations:

■ new technology: the new plant used a US newspaper computer system;
■ new workforce: Murdoch recruited a completely new workforce to handle the printing side of the business, with a single union agreement;
■ new distribution: he moved off the railways and on to road distribution.

Perhaps ironically, his computer technology was not the most advanced available. However, once he had shown that national newspapers could be produced reliably using computers, other newspaper groups were quick to follow. This set the scene for much more advanced computer use in the late 1980s and through the 1990s.

This dramatic change was accompanied by industrial action, especially around Wapping. This was not too surprising given the scale of redundancies. For example, the last newspapers to leave Fleet Street were the *Daily Express* and the *Sunday Express* in November 1989. By December of that year, only 25 per cent of the workforce were still employed by these newspapers (Tunstall, 1996).

So this example illustrates many of the characteristics discussed earlier in this chapter:

■ Computer technology can simplify and integrate processes.
■ Combining computer and communications technology can enable remote locations to work together.

■ Introducing compriter technology can eliminate traditional processes and craft skills completely, and require a completely new set of skills.

This case study also highlights the importance of social and political factors. One of the key issues for the proprietors of national newspapers was the power of the unions. In provincial newspapers, this was much less of an issue and the new technology was adopted much more quickly and with relatively little conflict.

Informating

Another critical process is what Zuboff calls 'informating'. This is based on the notion that computers generate a lot of additional information as a by-product of their main function. In her own words,

> the . . . technology simultaneously generates information about the underlying productive and administrative processes through which an organisation accomplishes its work. It provides a deeper level of transparency to activities that had been either partially or completely opaque. In this way information technology supersedes the traditional logic of automation.
>
> (Zuboff, 1988, p. 10)

This principle of informating applies to *all* applications of computers. An example of how it can be used to control and monitor workers' performance would be the computerized telephone system used in a call centre. Management can discover at the press of a key exactly how many calls any operator has dealt with and how long they took. The quality of service provided in a phone call can be difficult to measure, so these crude statistics may be used (perhaps unfortunately for the customer) as measures of productivity.

Many retailers have invested in customer profiling. If you pay at the checkout using a credit card or one of the store's loyalty cards, then you are providing that store with a great deal of information about you. This information can then be related to the purchases you make on a regular basis to discover systematic patterns in your shopping. The possibility of targeting promotions and special offers at customers with known shopping habits then becomes a technical problem of data manipulation.

EXERCISE

What function or process in your workplace could benefit from automation through computer technology? What would the effects of such automation be? And what potential informating would result?

IT has become embedded

The best way to explain how technology becomes embedded in our everyday life is to use the example of the electric motor. If you had to count how many electric motors there are in your home, you would have to think about it. You would have to count the number of appliances which contain small motors, such as a hair drier or a food mixer. But around a hundred years ago, the electric motor was a large stand-alone appliance which needed significant skill and mechanical expertise to run and maintain. Around the turn of the twentieth century, the major US mail order retailer Sears and Roebuck was proud to announce its 'home motor' – reliable and affordable, and with a whole range of attachments. In other words, you purchased *one* motor and then connected up the appliances such as the cleaner or the mixer which needed the motor's power (Kline, 1996). That motor technology has now become embedded.

The microchip is already an embedded technology. There are microprocessors in many domestic appliances, such as the video cassette recorder, the microwave oven and the phone. Already these can carry out functions which were not feasible before digital technology. A simple example would be the 1471 feature on the UK phone system. Pressing these numbers gives you the number of the last person to call and has provided a major bonus in reducing nuisance or harassing phone calls.

Combining computer and communications technology means that devices can offer new functions. Linking sensors to computers which can communicate offers a range of new possibilities, including the car which diagnoses its own breakdown and calls a breakdown service without the driver's intervention.

EXERCISE

Review all the technology you can find in a typical modern office. How many embedded microchips are at work? Is there further scope for embedding?

MOVING FROM INFORMATION TECHNOLOGY TO INFORMATION AND COMMUNICATIONS TECHNOLOGY

The image of the 'information superhighway' which has excited some computer pundits – not to mention leading government figures – is usually based upon a combination of the Internet and the World Wide Web. These are not the same thing, although they are sometimes confused. The Internet can be simply defined as a 'network of networks'. It is the set of electronic connections which enables users to access and transfer information in various ways. *One* of these ways is the World Wide Web, which from now on we shall simply call the Web.

The Internet grew from a small network of US military and scientific sites in the early 1960s to the collection of networks which span the globe and which uses a common set of rules to transmit and receive files. For example, 'http' stands for Hypertext Transfer Protocol and is the set of rules which allows networks and individual computers to communicate with one another, and fetches files to and from servers.

A server is simply a computer which holds information that can be distributed over a network and then over the Internet. There are other protocols which enable you to do different things. For example, FTP (File Transfer Protocol) allows you to transfer a file from a remote computer on to your machine.

This technology allows us to communicate in ways which would have sounded like science fiction only a few decades ago. For example, if you have the right equipment and connections, you can from your *home* computer:

- access other computers worldwide within a matter of minutes (although this timescale is often rather optimistic at busy periods);
- download information from other computers across the world;
- send to and receive email from other users across the world;
- browse through information held in universities and libraries across the world;
- scan databases across the world;
- play computer games with other users across the world;
- publish your own database (which theoretically can be accessed by anyone across the world);
- retrieve and play back audio, video clips and multimedia documents.

All these facilities are also available to any business, *no matter how small*. And business users can now conduct business across the Internet – selling goods and services (often called e-commerce, which we return to later).

These facilities have been available through the Internet for a few years now. And these advances are built upon a number of quite old ideas (Winston, 1998, ch. 18). It is worth summarizing these ideas as they may suggest how this electronic communication will develop in future:

Computers can be operated at a distance. This was achieved to some degree back in 1940. This idea was later developed so that remote computers could enable many users to access them simultaneously.

Computers can be connected by networks which enable them to share resources. Early computers of the 1950s and 1960s – large machines which filled large rooms – usually controlled networks. Users sat in distant offices in front of a keyboard and a monitor and were connected to the main machine, which did all the processing work.

Messages can be sent flexibly across a network. The need for secure military communication prompted the development of the network which was the Internet's predecessor: the Arpanet. This used the idea that messages could be broken down into chunks (now known as packets) which could be sent separately through the network in the most efficient way possible. These packets would be reassembled into the complete message when they reached the destination machine. In this way, if one link on the network failed, the packets of information could be sent round the network in other directions and still reach their destination.

Information can be organized as a web of associations. Back in 1945, Vannevar Bush argued that it was possible to construct a machine which would enable the user to search through all available knowledge. Rather than use an index to move through the information, this would mimic the way the human mind works – by association. He talked about an 'intricate web of trails' through the information.

A related idea is hypertext, also first established in the 1940s. Ted Nelson developed the idea of a text which did not have the structure of the conventional book. You read a normal book from page 1 to page 2 to page 3, and so on. A hypertext document is a set of pages which enable you to jump from an idea on one page to a related idea or illustration somewhere else in the document. Perhaps the simplest example of this is the thriller or fantasy novel for children where you are the hero and have to make a choice on each page to decide what to do next. You are usually presented with three choices: if you decide to go into the cave you go to page 47; if you decide to climb the mountain you go to page 63; and so on. You are then presented with another page of the story – the monster chases you out of the cave – and another series of choices at the end – assuming you survive till the end of the page!

In the late 1980s, a computer program appeared on the Apple Macintosh which used this sort of structure: Hypercard. Using this package, you could present a series of pages on screen. Each page contained some 'buttons' and 'hot spots' which you could click in order to jump to another page which offered related information. This is the pattern of navigation which we now take for granted when we use multimedia CD-ROMs and search the Web.

The man who invented the Web, Tim Berners-Lee, wanted to use hypertext so that computer users could free-associate between ideas in the same way that the human mind does. Box 5.5 shows an example of hypertext navigation through a series of Web pages.

Berners-Lee also wanted to reproduce the informal collaboration which you would find in the coffee area of a research department: somewhere where people could get together and share ideas. In 1994 he set up the World Wide Web Consortium (W3C) to take on the job of managing the Web – not managing in the sense of controlling, but making sure that his original principles are maintained: common standards and openness.

Computers can exchange all types of information, provided they share standard rules (usually called protocols). The fact that there are standard rules has enabled the Web to become an international system. However, it is also one of the Web's biggest problems.

For example, the Web uses a standard publishing language – HTML (Hypertext Mark-up Language) – that allows you to specify which part of the text are headings, subheadings, bullet lists, and so on. But HTML is continually being developed to allow writers to produce more complex Web pages. For example, the first version of HTML did not allow you to put a table in a Web document; the latest version allows complex tables and also uses style sheets in similar ways to advanced word processors.

As well as an Internet connection, you need the software on your machine to interpret HTML files – browser software such as Netscape Navigator or Microsoft Explorer. This software is continually revised to keep up with HTML development. An older version of the browser may not be able to read certain Web pages which have been designed to exploit newer features.

BOX 5.5 HYPERTEXT ON THE WEB

Snapshots of linked Web pages from a programme called MediaWeb to show the principles of hypertext on the web.

Use of Hypermedia in CD-ROM Project

The screens featured on this page are taken from MediaWeb, a CD-ROM developed by the Centre for Multimedia in Education at Sheffield Hallam University to support students across the curriculum. More information is available on the web site at: http://www.shu.ac.uk/cme/mediaweb

EXERCISE

How is the Web used in your organization? Who produces the Web site and the pages? What are the plans for future development? How will these plans influence the way people communicate?

NEW WAYS OF WORKING AND COMMUNICATING USING INFORMATION AND COMMUNICATIONS TECHNOLOGY

Information technology (IT) became a common term because it emphasized the idea that computers could manipulate information in a very broad sense. This information could

BOX 5.6 WRITING FOR THE WEB – THE TWENTY-FIRST-CENTURY VERSION OF DESKTOP PUBLISHING?

In the early 1980s, word-processed documents were usually very simple and limited. They did not have features you could find in professionally printed texts. The arrival of desktop publishing (DTP) in 1985 combined new computer software with laser printing. The software imitated the way professional typesetters laid out a page and the laser printer could achieve high-quality printing. This meant that anyone could produce a document which looked as if it had been professionally typeset and printed with:

- a range of fonts with proportional spacing;
- graphics;
- multiple columns; and so on.

In the following decade, word processing software gradually incorporated the main features of DTP so that all these things can now be done with word processing software. DTP software has also became widely available and cheap. This software usually contains many templates, so it is easy to imitate an established design format. Good-quality printing can now be achieved with inkjet printers, so you can now achieve reasonably professional results on a very limited budget.

So DTP has moved from being a highly specialized professional activity to something which can be achieved in the office of a small organization. Of course, organizations still need professional graphics and printing expertise for very complex documents, especially involving colour printing.

We anticipate the same sort of change in Web production. You can produce a file in HTML in several different ways:

- type in a text file and add the HTML commands as you go along;
- use a word processor which allows you to save files in HTML (such as Word 2000);
- use software which is designed to produce Web sites and HTML files without your having to know HTML, such as Macromedia's Dreamweaver.

Professional Web designers often use 'raw' HTML. But the packages which mean you do not have to do this are becoming more and more sophisticated and easier to use. We think that in a few years' time, no one will need to learn HTML unless they are doing very highly specialized or imaginative graphics.

represent a variety of sources, from words to images. The move to *communications* technology (usually now referred to as ICT – information and communications technology) emphasizes that we are now using digital technology to communicate. There are a number of technical developments which have supported this move, as well as the applications we talked about in the previous section:

- *Developments in cable technology.* The use of fibre optic cable to wire up offices, and now cities, is a major advance. This type of cable can handle much more information much more quickly than previous types. This is particularly important when computers are exchanging video and audio data.
- *Developments in satellite technology.* Satellites in orbit round the earth can effectively cover the complete population.
- *Digital telecommunication systems.* Until recently, telephone systems used analogue signals. They are now being converted to digital coding, which means that the information coming down the phone line can be manipulated and integrated in the same way as the information stored on computer. So we can now deliver text, data, audio and video through the phone system.

If you look at the way computers can be applied in business, various authors have suggested stages in the evolution of computerization and information strategies, as in Box 5.7. For example, Thorp and DMR (1998) suggest that we have moved from 'automation', where ICT developments affected only small parts of the organization, to 'information' and on to 'transformation', which is characterized by many complex linkages right across the organization, and where everyone is affected to some degree.

BOX 5.7 THE THREE WAVES OF IT

Jeff Papows (1999) summarizes the development of IT in business organizations in three waves, summarized in Table 5.1. He also suggests that there are four technological developments which are 'integral components' of this third wave:

- the Internet;
- the Web;
- intranets (networks which use the software associated with the Web but are internal to the organization and usually protected from outside visitors);
- extranets (using similar technology to link businesses with their suppliers, customers, etc.).

We suggest that the development of secure intranets and growing interest in knowledge management may bring a fourth wave which is characterized by more creative communication within and across the organization.

Table 5.1 *Development of IT in business organizations*

From ...	the wave was ...	characterized by ...
Up to the late 1960s and early 1970s	'The back office (automated accountants)'	Large mainframe systems, using databases to automate functions such as payroll and accounts
The late 1970s and through the 1980s	'The front office (knowledge workers)'	The PC, enabling office workers to handle document production, spreadsheets, etc. for themselves
The arrival of the Internet and Web in 1994	'The virtual office (the global marketplace)'	The move to networking for organizations of all sizes

In a sense, this returns to an issue we raised at the beginning of this chapter. Just how dramatic and revolutionary are the possibilities offered by ICT? Box 5.7 offers another way of conceptualizing the growth of ICT by suggesting that we are in the 'third wave' of the 'IT revolution', where networking has become commonplace for all sizes of organization.

We cannot pretend to predict the future with any certainty. There are numerous examples of intelligent people giving spectacularly inaccurate assessments of the future:

- 'I think there is a world market for about five computers' (attributed to the chairman of IBM in 1943).
- 'There is no reason for anyone to have a computer in their home' (from the president of Digital Equipment Corporation in 1977).

And there are many more examples where these come from (see Milsted, 1999). Nonetheless, we suggest two major trends in the use of ICT which will have more impact over the next few decades:

- using ICT to support and enable new structures of work, such as the growth of networked and 'virtual' organizations, and the increased use of teleworking;
- increased use of electronic commerce (or e-commerce).

Both of these will influence the way we work and communicate. For example, the growth of teleworking and virtual organizations will place even greater emphasis on communication through electronic documents such as email and the use of the Web. The increased volume of information through these electronic means is already creating concerns about 'information overload'. Can we alleviate some of these problems with strategies to create better-organized documents?

One widely quoted collection of predictions of future social trends, that by Wieners and Pescovitz (1996), suggests that around 20 per cent of the US workforce will be telecommuting by the year 2003 but that the use of paper is so entrenched in our culture that the concept of the paperless office will *never* be fully realized. Their most optimistic projection is that offices might be around 80 per cent paper-free by the end of the first decade of the twenty-first century.

We shall discuss the potential for new structures of work in more detail in the next chapter. To conclude this chapter, we shall review recent developments in the use of e-commerce, and then suggest some final issues in the adoption of ICT.

Electronic commerce (e-commerce)

In one of the first books to explore the potential value of the Internet to business, Mary Cronin (1994, p. 284) suggested that 'The electronic highway is not merely open for business; it is relocating, restructuring, and literally redefining business in America.' E-commerce has certainly grown, but not yet to the extent implied, possibly because of financial caution: 'just as reliable transport and secure money are crucial to commerce in the physical world, so security and electronic payments systems will be at the heart of electronic commerce' (Cairncross, 1997, p. 144). These issues of security and payment do seem to have been resolved by software advances over the past few years. We feel that a major expansion is just around the corner.

There is certainly growing interest in purchasing across the Internet – notice the increasing coverage in newspapers, magazines and television. One important implication is that this technology is available to small businesses at a reasonable cost. Compare the costs of worldwide advertising through conventional means with the cost of setting up and running a small Web site.

Of course, you do need more than Web software to run a commercial site on the Internet. To set up your own infrastructure, *PC Magazine* suggests that you need the following (from *PC Magazine*'s Guide to E-business, distributed with its September issue, 1998):

- Web server (the computer which will host the Web site);
- Web server software to build and maintain the site;
- merchant server software, which enables customers to buy your products over the Internet;
- payment software, which enables customers to pay without any risk;
- peripheral software to deal with other information and functions such as shipping, taxes, etc;
- a security 'firewall' (software which protects your company network from any hackers or viruses);
- a high-speed telecommunication connection.

A small company does not have to invest in this infrastructure. By using a service provider to supply the network connections and security software, it can have a presence on the Internet at a relatively modest cost.

Another indicator of the growth of business across the Internet is the growth in advertising through the Web. We can also highlight the growth of the Internet itself: to reach

EXERCISE

Review the major business and computer magazines over the past few months. What statistics are they now quoting about the growth of Internet use and e-commerce?

an audience of 50 million, radio took thirty-eight years; television took thirteen years; cable television took ten years; and the Internet took only five years.

Some organizations are already using the Internet in quite radical ways to support all types of business activity. For example, many large companies are increasingly using the Web in their recruitment. Applicants may have to submit their CV electronically, which may then be checked (again electronically) to confirm basic information. Applicants may also have to complete a long and detailed Internet-based questionnaire which is designed to build up a profile. Candidates with unsuitable profiles may be eliminated at this stage.

COMMUNICATION PROBLEMS IN THE APPLICATION OF INFORMATION AND COMMUNICATIONS TECHNOLOGY

As we mentioned earlier, ICT is characterized by human-to-computer and computer-to-computer communication. The computer's ability to process information and to communicate is determined by software. This software depends on the skills of programmers as well as the amounts of money developers are prepared to spend. So it is easy to program a computer to play noughts and crosses because the rules are few and the strategies are very simple. But to program a computer to translate a text is a formidable exercise. As we have already seen, the rules of language are complex and changing, and the strategies of composition are ill-defined. So computer translation is not a problem that has been solved, although it is constantly improving.

Many human-to-computer interactions give rise to problems because of the limitations of the software being used, and because the system is *not* primarily designed from the user's perspective. An example is the telephone answering systems used by many businesses. These computerized systems are designed to:

- route incoming calls to the correct destination;
- give information that the caller may need;
- take messages for absent recipients.

Problems arise because information comes in a rigid sequence and you often have to listen to a mini-directory being read out before you reach the choice that you need. You may also have to listen to unwanted messages and music. The response of the system often gives the impression that it has been designed for the convenience of the organization and certainly not yours. The frustration of spending several minutes on the telephone without making contact with a human being has given rise to a new term: 'phone rage'. This is a direct

BOX 5.8 THE COMPUTER IS IN CHARGE: NOTHING CAN GO WRONG, GO WRONG, GO WRONG . . .

Stephen Flowers (1996) analyses 'failed' computer systems and highlights a number of common factors, many of which relate to communication. These factors include:

- 'Hostile culture' – in other words, a culture where staff feel unable to comment openly on errors and possible problems. In this context, staff may try to continue a project which is failing rather than admit the problems. This will usually make things worse in the long run.
- 'Poor reporting structure' – in other words, a situation where senior management do not have a clear idea of the progress of the computer project.
- 'Technology-focused developments' – in other words, a system design which has focused on technological possibilities and has ignored the important human factors which would make the system work.
- 'Poor consultation' with users and other stakeholders.

problem of having to communicate with a machine with a very limited and inflexible range of responses. Organizations should consider such applications very carefully as many of them clearly violate guidelines for good communication.

Of course, these systems may be replaced in the future by more sophisticated speech recognition technology which aims to allow computers to 'recognise, to understand, and to respond to normal human conversation' (Janal, 1999, p. 4). So voice recognition technology *should* allow you to ask for the information you need in your normal conversational voice rather than having to use restricted commands or responses or enter particular keystrokes on the telephone keypad.

Speech recognition software has improved dramatically over the past decade, although it has problems with less predictable speech. It is becoming more effective for personal dictation into a PC, although there are still important snags (Williams *et al.*, 2000).

There are other important issues for automated and electronic systems in organizations. First, there may be issues of accountability and responsibility. When most business was conducted by correspondence, there were often very strict rules about how this should be done. These rules covered how the correspondence was checked, who could sign particular letters, how letters were stored and filed, etc. Of course, you can do all these things with electronic mail, but many businesses do not seem to have the necessary systems in place. There are also issues of security. Box 5.8 gives a few more examples of how computer systems have failed by failing to take sufficient account of human processes.

CONCLUSION

We started this chapter with questions about the scale and impact of the information revolution. We end by suggesting that the technology *has* advanced to a point where 'revolution'

SUMMARY

- 'Computers' have been transformed first into 'information technology' (IT) and then into 'information and communications technology' (ICT). The fundamental features of computing technology – digital coding and programming (algorithms) – have expanded into new roles and functions.

- Among the most important new functions are monitoring, integrating information, embedding and informating – generating new information about the process itself. Organizations can exploit these functions to generate new commercial possibilities, as in the case of customer profiling.

- As well as taking on new functions, computers have expanded the range of information which can be digitally coded – we can now 'commingle' the bits which represent words, pictures and sound into coherent packages.

- Computers have also expanded into *communications* technology (ICT), thanks to advances in telecommunications. This *is* a fundamental shift in terms of what the technology can do, although we must be cautious about some of the claims currently being made for the 'revolutionary' power of ICT.

- Brian Winston's model shows that there were powerful restraining or limiting forces operating in the early days of computers. Such restraints are still relevant. These social, economic and political forces must be considered.

- Organizations which fully embrace CT do have significant opportunities which have not been available before. These opportunities are available to large and small companies, and can completely transform an industry.

- Modern organizations are using CT to develop new ways of working and new products which affect the way we communicate in organizations. How far these changes will become commonplace is still open to debate, but there are some trends which are very likely to have increased impact, such as recent increases in e-commerce.

- Finally, we must not forget that these new applications of ICT must aim to provide solutions which *resolve* problems of communication and control rather than simply creating new ones.

is at least possible. ICT offers the opportunity both to restructure the business internally and to develop new external relationships with customers and suppliers. It can support developments which could make business in the twenty-first century a very different proposition (Cairncross, 1997):

- Electronic communication means that distance is much less important and that companies are no longer tied to specific physical locations.
- Small companies will be able to offer services that previously only large companies could afford.
- Most people will have access to advanced networks.
- Companies can adopt looser and more flexible structures.

We must be cautious about extrapolating from a few well-known examples or case studies. For example, at the moment, online commerce is 'tiny'. The biggest online market is the United States. Yet till recently, online trading amounted to only around 10 per cent of revenue from television shopping, which in turn was only 10 per cent of catalogue shopping expenditure (Cairncross, 1997, p. 129). But such statistics change very quickly, and certainly have changed in the time since these words were put on paper.

A final important point is that new technologies often supplement previous processes rather than replace them. For example, the Virtual Society research programme reported in 2000 that:

- teleworkers often did more travelling than their non-connected counterparts;
- email and the Internet worked as an 'add-on' to phone and fax.

DISCUSSION QUESTIONS

- What are the most important features of modern ICT in terms of communication in organizations?
- How well is ICT used in your organization? Is the organization taking advantage of all the features now available through developments such as the Internet?
- How do new ICT developments work alongside existing technologies?
- What developments in computer power will have most impact on your organization over the next ten years?
- How important is e-commerce to organizations you know? How will its development change the way these organizations work?
- Many automatic systems operated by computers seem to frustrate customers. Is this problem inevitable? How can it be resolved?

FURTHER READING

Cairncross, F. (1997) *The Death of Distance: How the Communications Revolution Will Change our Lives*. London: Orion.

Dertouzos, M. (1997) *What Will Be: How the New World of Information will Change Our Lives*. London: Piatkus. This and the previous book are both interesting attempts to analyse the current and potential impact of ICT – one British and one American.

Gallia, P. (1998) *How the Internet Works*, 4th edn. Indianapolis, IN: Que. A very comprehensive introduction to and overview of Internet technologies with lots of illustrations to show how the processes work.

Gates, B., with Hemingway, C. (1999) *Business @ the Speed of Thought: Using a Digital Nervous System*. In this and the following book two leaders of the IT industry offer their views on the future of ICT in organizations and in society.

Papows, J. (1999) *Enterprise.com: Market Leadership in the Digital Age*. London: Nicholas Brealey.

Chapter 6

Organizational structure and communication

INTRODUCTION

This chapter looks at common organizational structures and reviews their implications for communication. Given the new opportunities offered by ICT (as we described in Chapter 5), and given the need to develop a positive and coherent organizational culture (as described in Chapter 4), we need to review the impact of organizational structures. Do particular organizational structures encourage or impede organizational communication?

One very important issue is whether more traditional hierarchical structures have had their day. We explore the work of organizational theorists who argue that we need to change the structure of our organizations in radical ways to meet current market challenges and ever-increasing competitive demands.

Whatever organizational forms finally emerge from these debates, they all depend on the quantity and quality of communication. And so we conclude that the role of communication has become even more critical to the success of modern business organizations.

OBJECTIVES

This chapter will:

- discuss how we can identify and describe different organizational structures;
- discuss how organizations can be described in terms of different models:
    1   the stakeholder groups
    2   the organization's subsystems
    3   the organization hierarchy;
- identify and discuss how communication is represented in these different models and look at issues which affect these formal structures, including the status and role of informal networks;
- review recent organizational theory and identify likely organizational changes and developments for the next decade;
- discuss how these changes will affect both organizational structure and communication.

HOW CAN WE DEFINE ORGANIZATIONAL STRUCTURE?

You will find many different ways of representing the structure of an organization in different textbooks. One of the most common is the organization chart, and a simple example is given in Figure 6.1. But what does this tell us? The vertical dimension shows the hierarchy and status relations; and the horizontal dimension shows the range of activities which the company is involved in. In this example of a manufacturing company, these activities include production, research and development, finance, marketing, and so on.

It is important to remember that this diagram is *one* way of *representing* an organization. As James Taylor (1995, p. 43) puts it, 'an orgchart is a theoretical construction, or conceptual model, meant to represent the structure of the organization in a way that captures the intuitive sense of what an organization is for the people who make it up'. Taylor goes on to argue that this is often 'taken for granted' and that the image of the organization as a well-ordered system with 'well-structured authority relations' (p. 45) can be very misleading. If management see the organization in this 'clear-cut' way, then they may implement policies which do not work because the organization does *not* actually work in such a systematic way. His main example is office automation systems which fail to recognize how the humans in the system actually need to work.

A similar point is made by Hosking and Morley when they argue that 'the entitative approach has dominated studies of organizations' (1991, p. 41). Organizations are seen as 'well-defined entities' with clear boundaries, identities, 'purposes which are relatively well defined' (p. 41) and formal structures. They argue that 'social organization is better understood in terms of relational processes' (p. 61). In other words, organizing is a process of ongoing negotiation between people and groups with communication as the 'oil' which lubricates this process.

Different ways of representing the structure of the organization are not just matters of technical detail. They can represent fundamentally different approaches and different theoretical assumptions. If you review some of the classic texts on organizations, you will find very different starting points. These range from the organization's contribution to the wider

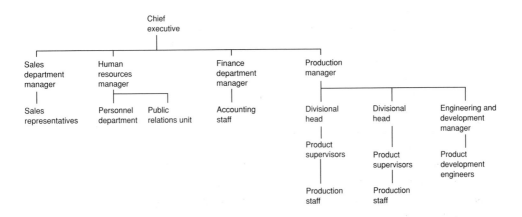

Figure 6.1 *Simple organization chart of a manufacturing company*

113

EXERCISE

Consider how you would try to describe the structure of an organization you know well. What would your description contain? What would it focus on? Would you end up drawing some form of organization chart? Or would you concentrate on the individuals or groups in the organization and the relations between them?

society, through approaches based upon how power and authority is organized, and on to approaches which reflect how the organization is structured to meet the demands of its environment. One very influential management text has argued that 'all theories of organization and management are based on implicit images or metaphors that lead us to see, understand, and manage organizations in distinctive yet partial ways' (Morgan, 1997, p. 4).

As our main purpose is to focus on communication, we will not provide detailed analysis of different theories and metaphors (for an alternative analysis, see Daniels and Spiker, 1994). What we will do is show how different structural perspectives have important implications for the role of communication, by offering three different ways of describing the organization's structure:

- as a set of stakeholder groups who are connected through communication;
- as a set of managed subsystems;
- as based on a command hierarchy which can be realized in different ways.

Defining the stakeholders

The leading British writer on organizations, Rosemary Stewart, defines stakeholders as 'people who have an interest in the organisation, which may cause them to seek to influence managers' actions' (1991, p. 80). She also comments that 'Managers have to take account of more – and more powerful – stakeholder groups than in the past.' Other commentators, such as the American writer Stanley Deetz, have argued that this model of business communication is much more relevant to modern organizations because they need to consider much more than simple economic motives. They must consider broader issues and implications, and so communication with both suppliers and the local community must forge long-term relationships for the common good (Deetz, 1995). This analysis has also generated new forms of communication, as described in Box 6.1.

EXERCISE

Take an organization which you know, either as a member or as a customer or user. How would you describe the different stakeholder groups which are involved with that organization? Would it be feasible to bring them together in the way described in Box 6.1? Does your analysis suggest any problems in communication?

BOX 6.1 COMMUNICATING WITH STAKEHOLDERS

Future search conferences are a method which some senior executives have used to try to improve connections and relationships between the different stakeholder groups, especially in periods of change or economic turmoil. These conferences are based on three essential features:

- They bring together the 'whole system' in one place to work through an agenda which focuses on the organization's task.
- They emphasize connections between the stakeholders.
- They encourage the stakeholders to 'take ownership' of the future development of the company and to commit themselves to future action.

With up to eighty participants, lasting up to three days, and involving external facilitators to manage the process, these are expensive and significant events for a company. They need to be carefully planned beforehand in order to create an agenda which all the participants will commit to.

Defining the organization's subsystems

The executive group in charge of an organization is responsible for maintaining a number of communication systems. These systems are interdependent, but they are described independently in Table 6.1, where we try to show the relationship of the executive group to these various communication systems.

EXERCISE

Take an organization which you know, either as a member or as a customer or user. How do the subsystems described above seem to work in that organization? Are all the communication channels used effectively? Does your analysis suggest any problems in communication?

Defining the hierarchy

We have already suggested that there are different forms of hierarchy in modern organizations. One fairly typical set of definitions comes from Andrews and Herschel (1996). They suggest six prominent forms of organization:

1   the traditional centralized structure;
2   the centralized structure with decentralized management;
3   the divisional form;

Table 6.1 Organization subsystems and their communication

System	Main purposes include:	Typical means of communication	Typical formal responsibilities
The shareholder system	▪ To communicate shareholders' directives, policies and decisions ▪ To communicate the executives' requests, reports and goals to the shareholders	▪ Articles of association ▪ Board meetings ▪ Board resolutions ▪ Annual general meetings ▪ Annual reports ▪ Minutes of meetings	The groups responsible are the board of directors and the executive group. The communication is controlled by the company secretary, who acts both as secretary to the board of directors and as a member of the executive group. Much of the communication by the secretary is prescribed by law or by the organization's articles of association
The regulatory system	▪ To comply with the state, provincial and local laws and regulations ▪ To provide information required by regulatory agencies	▪ Laws, government gazettes and regulatory documents ▪ Prescribed forms ▪ Prescribed reports	The prime responsibility here again lies with the organization's secretary, but legal responsibility is sometimes placed on other officials by their being designated as 'the responsible person' in terms of some legislation
The community system	▪ To convey the organization's objectives ▪ To improve the organization's image and co-operation with the community	▪ Mass media including TV, radio and the press ▪ Press releases ▪ Commercial and technical journals ▪ Special publicity material and events	The community system is usually seen as a function of the chief executive, who delegates much of this as a staff responsibility. Large organizations are tending to create special public relations or public affairs departments reporting to the chief executive. Some have seen it as part of the marketing function
The supplier system	▪ To ensure that the organization obtains regular supplies of goods and services at competitive prices	▪ Advertising in a variety of media ▪ Directories	The supplier system usually operates as two distinct subsystems: a purchasing system and a human resource system

Table 6.1 (cont)

System	Main purposes include:	Typical means of communication	Typical formal responsibilities
	■ To recruit, hold and develop the necessary human resources for the organization	■ Specialist recruiting organizations ■ Forms ■ Catalogues	Purchasing is a specialist function, which in large organizations is often carried out by a specialist department. It is also a critical factor of concern to line management. There is usually considerable interaction between the employment hierarchy and the supplier system. The interaction between the two systems is often a problem area
The customer system	■ To promote sales of the organization's goods and services ■ To receive and analyse information from the market ■ To provide customer support on request	■ Advertising ■ Mass media ■ Sales and information literature ■ Articles in the commercial and industrial publications ■ Live presentations ■ Audio-visual presentations ■ User manuals	This is usually the function of a specialist marketing division. The communicative requirements are part of the specialist study of marketing, and in this, there is often close interaction with the public affairs function
The administrative system	■ To maintain a sound administration ■ To ensure that the organization achieves its mission ■ To co-operate with the employee representative system to ensure employee harmony	■ Policy statements and directives ■ Job descriptions ■ Training courses and manuals ■ Operating manuals ■ House journals ■ Electronic communication media ■ Group communication system	The prime responsibility for communication in the employment hierarchy is with the chief executive and the executive group. However, everyone in the hierarchy has a responsibility, which should be defined in each person's job description. This should also define responsibilities for communication in any other system

Table 6.1 (cont)

System	Main purposes include:	Typical means of communication	Typical formal responsibilities
Employee representative systems	■ To set out and negotiate changes to wages and conditions of employment ■ To settle disputes ■ To negotiate with trade unions	■ Policy and procedure documents ■ Employment contracts and conditions ■ Contracts and agreements ■ Negotiating and discussion groups ■ Arbitrators, ombudsmen, etc. ■ Notices	From the organization's side, the chief executive has a major responsibility, some of which is delegated to personnel or human resource departments. From the side of employees, the responsibility may lie with trade union officials, elected representatives or appointed spokespersons.

Notes:

This definition of subsystems reflects the fact that an organization is deeply involved with its local community. The community provides suppliers of goods and services, employees and customers. As we noted above in the discussion of stakeholders, organizations are increasingly becoming involved with a community in a socio-political sense and have seen social responsibility as a necessary function of the organization.

These subsystems all exist to some extent but they can obviously be very different. For example, employee representative systems can range from virtually no system under an autocratic management to highly complex systems with written constitutions and an organizational infrastructure.

4   the decentralized structure;
5   the matrix structure;
6   what they call the 'type D' organization.

In the first two of these forms, we have strong control from the senior management group, who will usually be based in the same physical location. The traditional centralized organization emphasizes control and co-ordination through a very clear hierarchy. As you go down the hierarchy, you find people working on increasingly specialized tasks. There are standard ways of working, and these standard procedures may cause problems if staff are presented with new problems to deal with. In another type of centralized structure, the management is decentralized to some extent. In other words, the top management will control the main functions such as production or sales but the managers at lower levels will have some discretion when they make specific operational decisions.

In forms 3 and 4, we have structures where the senior management have devolved authority in rather different ways. Within a divisional structure, the organization has a central office which co-ordinates and controls but the main work of the organization is carried out in its divisions. These divisions may be based on different functions or products, or on different geographical regions. The divisions will have authority to make decisions within certain limits. It is even possible for there to be divisions within one organization which are in direct competition with one another.

In a decentralized organization, the sub-units are all owned by a holding company which may make little effort to co-ordinate provided that the economic performance of the different units meets targets.

In the matrix structure, we have a dual command structure so that employees report to senior staff in terms of their specialist role. This is very different from the traditional hierarchy where each employee tends to have a single line manager, and we discuss this in more detail later.

The final form – type D – is characterized by 'distributed work arrangements' where the work is distributed between the organization 'core' and peripheral units which might involve external subcontracting and various other mechanisms based on the use of information technology.

DEFINING STRUCTURES WITHIN STRUCTURES

Although broad characterizations of a hierarchy are useful, we can argue that few organizations (especially larger ones) conform entirely to a single basic structure. Thus we need to consider in more detail how some basic structures work: line, staff/functional, matrix and committee.

EXERCISE

For each of these four types of structure, find an example in an organization you know and assess how well communication operates within that structure.

Line structure

A line structure is based on the idea that at each level, people control and administer the work of a group in the level below them. Instructions and information pass from the top downwards, and information and requests are passed from the bottom upwards. Sideways communication takes place via a cross-over point.

Such a structure has potential advantages:

■ It clearly sets out the lines of administrative responsibility (you know what you have to do and who you report to).
■ All levels of the organization should be informed about matters which are relevant to their area.

But it also has potential disadvantages:

■ It leads to excessively long lines of communication (for example, when messages have to go across the organization).
■ People at higher levels can easily be overloaded with information.
■ It can lead to 'compartmentalization' of information.

Various techniques have been be used to overcome some of the problems of line communication, including:

■ *Contracting lines of communication.* A senior manager can address several levels at once, whether through meetings or by some form of general notice.
■ *Reducing the number of administrative levels.* If communication is passed through fewer people, misunderstanding is less likely.

One characteristic of many large organizations over the past twenty years has been regular restructuring which has reduced the layers of middle management (sometimes called de-layering or downsizing). This has often been done as part of a 're-engineering' exercise, using ideas described in Box 6.2.

Staff or functional structure

In terms of staff or functional structure, management includes both specialist and functional managers, each one instructing workers on an aspect of their work. A version of this model was advocated by one of the early management theorists, Frederick Taylor, who is usually associated with breaking down manual tasks into small functional tasks. He actually suggested that management should *also* operate in this way, but the managements of his day did not wish to lose their power base and simply applied his logic to the workers.

It would be virtually impossible for a business to operate as a purely functional organization, as there would be no one to co-ordinate the work, or take ultimate responsibility. (Taylor did advocate a central planning department to pull everything together.) However,

BOX 6.2 THE RE-ENGINEERING PROCESS

Business process re-engineering (BPR) was defined by its founders as 'the fundamental rethinking and radical design of business processes to achieve dramatic improvements in critical, contemporary measures of performance, such as cost, quality, service, and speed' (Hammer and Champy, 1993, p. 32). They suggested that radical rethinking of what the organization is about will lead to changes such as:

- changes in organizational structure such as a move to team-working;
- changes in job and role definitions with increased sharing of responsibility;
- changes to managers' roles – they become more like advisers or facilitators;
- drastic reduction in the number of levels of management – the hierarchy becomes flatter.

In other words, 're-engineering means that organisations start over, re-evaluating ways in which they create products or services that deliver value to their customers' (Andrews and Herschel, 1996, p. 351).

But does it work? In the mid-1990s, re-engineering came in for very serious criticism (Micklethwait and Wooldridge, 1996, ch. 1). It was suggested that:

- Many if not most re-engineering projects fail to deliver – that BPR has an 85 per cent failure rate (Birchall and Lyons, 1995, p. 237).
- Re-engineering fails to take account of the softer human factors which influence business performance.
- Simple reliance on cost-cutting and IT does not deliver the promised improvements and the organization should be 'investing in people first'.

Even articles which suggested that BPR had a more impressive record of success also suggested that it would not work without a strong emphasis on the skills of cultural change, including clear communications and the development of trust.

most organizations do make use of specialist functions, as there are potential advantages of functional structure:

- Workers are instructed by specialists with expert knowledge.
- Lines of communication are short.

But there are corresponding disadvantages:

- Workers have many supervisors and may receive conflicting instructions.
- Workers may have difficulty in assigning priorities.
- Workers may play one supervisor against another.

Some of these disadvantages can be overcome by a clear definition of responsibilities. But for most purposes, a purely functional organization is not practical.

Committee structure

The term 'committee' is used (and misused) for a variety of organizational structures. Strictly speaking, a committee is a group of people who are elected by the members of an organization to control its affairs. The committee members then elect certain office bearers, normally a chair, secretary and treasurer. The committee may also appoint an executive to carry out policy decisions and to attend to the day-to-day operation of the organization.

The chair, whose authority is conferred by the committee, is responsible for its smooth functioning. However, committee members may, under certain conditions, remove the chair from office.

Committees often appoint subcommittees to assist them with specific tasks. These subcommittees may be either standing or ad hoc (constituted for this purpose) committees. Standing committees are usually responsible for ongoing activities such as finance, publicity, etc., while ad hoc committees are constituted for a special task and are dissolved once the task is completed.

Clubs and professional organizations are often run by committees which operate on democratic principles. Decision-making is usually by majority vote, though they often try to achieve consensus. Some committees, particularly in business, are not truly democratic but have variations on the democratic principle. Traditional universities, for example, often operate on a system of interlocking committees, and membership of these committees is often determined by status or invitation. Increasing managerialism in higher education has weakened these structures.

There are few 'true' committees in business and industry in the sense we have defined above, but most business organizations appoint committees for co-ordination and special purposes. For example, the representative system usually operates with committee-type structures.

Potential advantages of this structure include the following:

- It permits a rapid exchange of information and ideas.
- It encourages co-operation.
- It generates new ideas and information.

There are also potential disadvantages:

- Decisions depend on the frequency of meetings.
- Effectiveness is highly dependent on the secretariat and chair.

We shall revisit these problems in Part three when we look at groups, teams and meetings.

Matrix structure

The matrix structure (Figuure 6.2) is a variation of the basic functional structure. In this structure, the following report to the overall manager:

- a number of executive project managers, each responsible for the execution of a specific project;
- a number of specialist managers, each responsible for a specialist activity.

The project manager has direct control over the specialist staff allocated to the project. Both the project manager and the specialists may call on the specialist manager for advice and support. The allocated staff are still responsible to their specialist manager for the quality of their work, whereas the project managers have full control over the work allocated to the teams.

This type of structure can work well in situations which require flexibility. Potential advantages include short lines of communication, ready access to specialist information, and

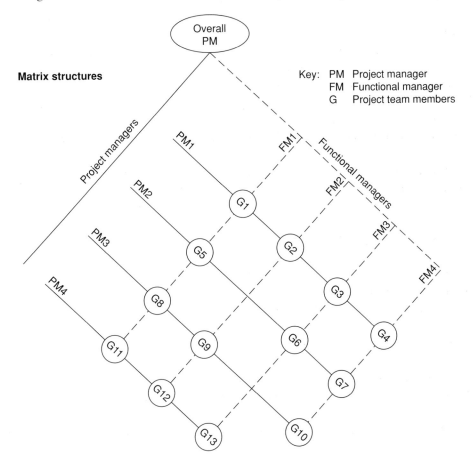

Figure 6.2 *Basic matrix structure of an organization*

effective interdisciplinary co-operation. Where the life of the project is limited, teams may be built, expanded, contracted and dismantled as the work requires. As a permanent arrangement, a matrix structure presents difficulties, as the specialist managers tend to lose control of their staff.

Matrix structures have been used successfully for finite projects in research, development, design and contracting.

COMPLEXITIES WITHIN STRUCTURES

Most organizations use some combination of these structures. Large organizations often use line and staff functions, alongside elements of the matrix system and the committee system. For example, a research and development department may be organized on a project system with the interdepartmental co-ordinating functions (such as safety, public relations, research planning, etc.) handled by a modified committee system. There are a further range of complexities which have implications for communication:

- *Distinctions between employment and representative roles.* The *people* may be the same but the two *systems* are different. They have different objectives and different structures, and the roles people play in them are different. For example, in the employment hierarchy, John Smith is a welder and takes instructions from his supervisor, Bill Jones. On the works council, John Smith is the elected representative of his shop and Bill Jones has been nominated by his departmental head as a member. On the works council, they both have the same status and an equal voice in decision-making, at least in theory. There will also be differences depending on the type of representative system: is it purely employee-established, or a joint management–employee structure, or a quasi-judicial structure? Communication between management and this structure is obviously very important, and we set out some issues to consider in Box 6.3.
- *The nature of advisory roles.* Some structures contain staff with purely advisory functions; others contain staff with both advisory and some delegated administrative responsibility. Examples would include staff with specialist expertise in human resources.
- *The role of informal communication.* As this raises important issues about how we define the 'real' organization structure, this will be discussed in more detail in the following main section.

The growing organization

Sometimes textbooks give the impression that these are issues only for large firms. However, structure is just as much an issue for a small and developing company, although there are obvious differences in scale. Structure may become especially important when the company tries to grow.

Consider the case of a small service organization set up by two partners. How many extra staff can they recruit before they need to establish a layer of management? What if they decide to open a second site? How will this be managed? This development might also create strains in the relationship between the two partners. At the start, they may be able to share the work out equally and not worry about specialization. But once they have a significant workforce, they will have a number of additional concerns. For example, how will they deal with the complexities of employment law and welfare rights? Will they employ some advisory staff or will they ask some outside firm to handle these aspects? All of these are critical issues of organization structure.

THE ROLE OF THE 'INFORMAL ORGANIZATION'?

Many authors make a distinction between the 'formal' organization and the 'informal' organization. The formal organization is the organization as expressed in the organization chart: the official job roles and the lines of responsibility and communication. The informal organization is that network of relationships which coexists, based on personal and political relationships: 'many members of an organization may draw power from their role in [these] social networks' (Morgan, 1997, p. 187).

Communication across this informal organization is often dismissed as of low quality, being a mixture of leaks, rumour and speculation. However, sometimes very accurate information (and sometimes very embarrassing to management) can reach employees through this network, which can be defined in various ways, including the grapevine, the 'old boy' network and company social gatherings. We can examine this 'informal organization' more closely by looking at this notion of the grapevine.

BOX 6.3 DOES THE REPRESENTATIVE SYSTEM COMMUNICATE EFFECTIVELY?

We could devote an entire text to the complexities of management/union communication. This is very important, as management and employees often have widely differing perceptions. Among the most important questions which we can ask of this form of communication are:

- Are procedures clear? Do participants know the constitution, decision-making powers, procedures and method of decision-making? Are relevant documents readily available to all? Are meetings conducted in a fair and open way?
- Are there effective records?
- Are the information and any decisions clearly communicated? The information handled by the representative system is obviously very important to employees; inaccurate leaks and rumours can have a very negative effect on employee morale.
- Is there adequate education and training? Workers and their representatives must be fully trained in the communication procedures used, to avoid any suspicion that they are being manipulated.

The grapevine

Gary Kreps (1990, p. 208) defines the grapevine as 'the communication that develops among organization members and is not necessarily prescribed by the formal structure and hierarchy of the organization but grows out of organization members' curiosity, interpersonal attraction, and social interaction'. His survey of research and writing about the grapevine suggests that it:

■   is that mixture of leaks, conjecture, educated guesses and gossip that circulates in an organization;
■   is often seen as 'evil' or 'malicious';
■   can be very fast and *accurate*;
■   'is a very powerful and potentially useful channel of communication' (Kreps, 1990, p. 209).

A British guide to internal communication methods lists the grapevine as a method 'which needs to be included in any communication strategy as part of the media mix' (Scholes, 1997, p. 139). And this notion of using or managing the grapevine is a fairly common theme in several management texts and articles.

But we think that this notion of the 'formal versus informal' organization can be misleading. It suggests two parallel systems of communication – one based on the rational pursuit of the organization's goals and the other based on emotions and relationships. In Part 1 of this book, we argued that *all* communication has both information and relationship aspects. If management feel that they can deliver their 'official' messages through the hierarchy and use 'ever-faster methods of communication' to 'circumvent the grapevine' (Scholes, 1997, p. 141), then they are adopting a flawed view of the communication process.

EXERCISE

Identify a rumour which recently circulated in an organization you know. How did that rumour develop? What was management's role in the communication process? Does a distinction between formal and informal processes help to explain this?

ARE BUREAUCRATIC STRUCTURES DISAPPEARING?

Although we have argued that most organizations have a mix of structures within them, the most common description of large modern organizations still conveys the characteristics which Weber defined as bureaucratic. For example, Laudon and Laudon suggest that 'all modern organisations are alike because they share . . . characteristics' (Laudon and Laudon, 1994, p. 89). These characteristics include hierarchy, clear division of labour, explicit rules and procedures, and impartial judgements. Employees are hired and promoted on the basis of their technical qualifications and professional expertise. The organization is devoted to maximizing its efficiency.

126

Of course, there are many examples of bureaucracies which have been badly managed. But there are more fundamental problems: Heckscher and Donnellon (1994) suggest that bureaucracy has fundamental and inherent limitations even when it is well-managed. They suggest that one of its basic principles – that people are responsible only for their own jobs – is a fundamental flaw in today's economic environment. This principle creates three major undesirable consequences:

Intelligence is wasted. Employees do not work to their full capacity.

The informal organization cannot be 'controlled'. He argues that bureaucratic rules can never be so clear and explicit and comprehensive that they cover everything that happens. In other words, the organization will grind to a halt if all the staff follow the rules to the letter. This is often the case when staff involved in an industrial dispute decide to work to rule. So he argues that 'a whole set of informal systems and relationships is essential if the bureaucracy is to work at all' (Heckscher and Donnellon, 1994, p. 21).

The organization cannot change effectively. It is difficult to imagine how a strict bureaucracy can evolve smoothly over time rather than in fits and starts. Things start to go wrong, the organization restructures, and a new routine sets in until things start to go wrong again.

And this takes us to the search for new organizational forms.

NEW FORMS OF BUSINESS ORGANIZATIONS

Paul Thompson and Chris Warhurst (1998, p. 1) suggest that there is 'a considerable amount of common ground among popular business and academic commentators about what the trends in work and workplace are'. This common ground is based upon the notion that we have moved into an information age, where the dominant form of employment and production is no longer manufacturing. This move from manufacturing into service industries not only creates new types of worker, the so-called knowledge worker, but it also demands new organizational structures and new patterns of communication.

Moving away from the pyramid

One common prediction is that organizations will adopt flatter structures with fewer layers of management. But simply removing layers of management cannot be an end in itself, although this did seem true of many downsizing operations in the 1980s. Many writers suggest that this de-layering will work well only if staff further down the pyramid are allowed to increase their capabilities and competence. This may well have particular implications for those middle managers who remain: they will have to 'manage the heartland of the organisation' (Cannon, 1996, p. 245) by improving the way they manage both the people and the information systems.

Another, related recommendation is that these new organizations must become less rigid and mechanistic. They must become more 'organic'; the clear distinctions between roles which characterize formal organizational charts will become blurred as people co-operate to achieve the necessary tasks.

Another suggestion is that organizations will restructure so that there is only a small core of people who are directly employed by the organization.

Does this mean a paradigm shift?

One interpretation is that organizations are moving towards a completely new way of working. Rather than being a continuous development from previous practice, this means radical and revolutionary change. Consider the following quotations from Don Tapscott (1996, p. 12): 'the new enterprise is a network of distributed teams that act as clients and servers for each other' and 'companies need fundamentally new strategies for the new economy. Networking is enabling new structures and new strategies.' These remarks give the flavour of some of the new ideas and prospects which underpin the development of the so-called 'virtual organization'. This form of organization 'has no identifiable physical form . . . its boundaries are defined and limited only by the availability of IT' (Harris, 1998, p. 75). Martyn Harris discusses several models of virtual organization and suggests that they are all based on three fundamental ideas:

- The changes needed for organizations to thrive and prosper mark a radical change from past practice. In other words, we are experiencing a paradigm shift.
- Technology, ICT, will play a central role in this change. These visions invariably rely upon IT to provide flexible communication links and to store and distribute information (as we discussed in Chapter 5).
- The 'ethical/moral fabric of the organization' must be overhauled. In other words, behaviour based on hierarchy and control must be replaced by new patterns of relationships. One key concept is that we must move towards 'high-trust' relationships.

We can certainly find examples of organizations which are difficult to classify in conventional terms. For example, consider the international property consultancy that was formed by merging two real estate associations from opposite sides of the globe. The management brought together thirty-four separate firms under a common logo and computer network. This enabled the firms to exchange local knowledge and collaborate. But is this *one* organization?

Henning (1998) describes an engineering company that has only thirty-five employees, with no staff in finance, personnel, manufacturing or public relations. All these functions are subcontracted to outside organizations. The employees concentrate on what they do best: developing solutions to engineering problems and forging marketing relationships. Everything else is done from outside.

Henning also talks about two 'major forms of liability which a virtual organisation must face' (1998, p. 145). The first is that the teleworkers may lose touch with the organization, leading to low morale and dwindling motivation. The second liability is conflicting interests. If the organization is made up of a series of alliances, then these may need almost permanent consultation and negotiation to maintain.

Although the virtual organization is not yet a dominant form, we can see that many organizations are moving in that direction – by increasing reliance on networking, and by the growth in teleworking.

The networked organization

The networked organization can be visualized as a cluster or federation of business units which is co-ordinated by the central core of the organization – potentially very different from the classic hierarchical organization structure.

The central core provides the broad overall vision and strategy, provides coherent administration, and ensures that the sub-units work together to support the common purpose. The network will constantly change to serve the needs of customers and to adapt to changes in the business environment. Electronic communication is absolutely central to this model, allowing speedy communication not only between the core and sub-units but also between the units. As a result, the network organization can be described in terms of two distinct components:

- the technological infrastructure; and
- the social structure: the people on the network and how they use it to interact with one another.

The Future Work Forum at Henley quotes numerous examples of organizations that have taken advantage of ICT to restructure their organization in less radical ways, often by relocating part of their work (Birchall and Lyons, 1995). A few of these examples are:

- The English company producing materials for conferences and sales presentations. After a day spent working with the client to produce an appropriate design for the presentation, draft sketches are agreed and then sent to New York where the professional layout is completed. The client receives the completed product back in England the following morning. As far as they're concerned, the work has been finished overnight. Because of the time difference, time has been shrunk to improve customer service.
- The supermarkets who wish to improve service from their suppliers. The development of electronic data interchange (EDI) means that data on stock levels can be communicated instantly from supermarket to supplier. This data is automatically updated whenever the stock is purchased. Linking computer information in this way means automatic reordering of stock.
- The multinational engineering company which works on over 150 sites in over thirty countries. This company developed its own telecommunications network which supported voicemail, email and videoconferencing. This system was linked to a database which enabled each site to draw upon the library of computer-aided design

tools. Work is distributed to wherever there is spare capacity; virtual teams are created for projects made up of staff located throughout the world; and small local offices have an international facility to draw upon.

Another implication of these changes is that many organizations are revising their concept of 'the office', and we give some examples of this in Box 6.4.

Teleworking

Many newspapers and magazines of the late 1990s painted dramatic visions of remote or distance working: the notion of teleworking. These popular accounts often painted either a very positive or a very negative image. Positive accounts tended to emphasize the 'liberating' aspects of being able to work in your own environment and being able to control pace and timing. Negative accounts tended to emphasize problems of isolation.

Government reports echo these comments. For example, the Department of Trade and Industry's Information Society Initiative in the United Kingdom published its international benchmarking study in 1997. This suggested that businesses could gain from teleworking by 'more flexible working practices, significant cost savings, increasing productivity and the ability to target services more closely to customer needs' (p. 57). Worldwide, the United States had the highest proportion of businesses which used teleworking. In Europe, the United Kingdom took the lead. The use of remote access was closely correlated with use

BOX 6.4 THE CHANGING FACE OF THE OFFICE

The new headquarters of British Airways, opened at the end of 1997, was seen as 'a catalyst for change and a way of transforming the way people work together' (Steenstra, 1999, p. 307). The design uses a metaphor of villages, streets and neighbourhoods. Each of the six four-storey buildings has its own courtyard, which acts as a focal point for that building. The central eating, shopping and meeting places were designed to 'give the largest number of possible random connections between the people of any building in Europe' (p. 307).

Management have claimed performance improvements of up to 20 per cent based on saving space over traditional offices, and increased efficiency. In this new environment, there are no individual desks. Staff have individual lockers that contain files which they can move to the nearest desk, where they can also plug their laptop into the network. Staff can easily work from home by setting up email links and videoconferencing as necessary. They can meet in one of the coffee shops or in more formal bookable space.

There are many similar experiments in office layout. One common thread is that the office worker has three basic items of equipment: the laptop computer, the mobile phone, and a locker or mobile trolley for storage. Some of the proposals appear more gimmicky, such as the meeting room where there are no seats and which you cannot book for longer than five minutes.

of the Internet. The one exception was Japan, where only 8 per cent of employees worked from home at least one day a month using remote access, compared to 14 per cent in Germany, 24 per cent in the United Kingdom, and 34 per cent in the United States. The report suggested that 'this could reflect more rigid business structures and working practices, characteristic of Japan's highly collectivist work culture' (p. 59). Once again we see the importance of culture, both at national and organizational level.

Debates about the value of teleworking have also been different in different cultures. Early European debates tended to view telework as simply unskilled, low-paid office work which was done at home. The assumption was that the work was organized by a distant but central office. In the United States, the debate mainly focused upon the costs and benefits of eliminating commuting (Qvortrup, 1998, pp. 22, 23). More recently, there has been more systematic debate on the international level which has recognized that there are very different forms of teleworking. This makes measurement and comparison quite difficult. For example, Qvortrup outlines five common ways of organizing teleworking:

- Electronic home offices, where the worker operates from home most of or all the time.
- Shared facility centres. Here there is a building, equipped with IT facilities, used by various workers from different companies or the self-employed. These centres can be in a rural location or in a residential area.
- Satellite work centres. These are similar to shared facility centres except that they are owned by one company.
- Private enterprise centres. These are privately owned centres which are usually located in rural regions. They offer facilities for local workers who provide IT-based services to distant customers.
- Flexible work facilities. This category covers workers who operate at a distance from the main organization's facilities: they tend to be mobile, using portable equipment and communications.

Teleworking is more complex than might first appear. Jackson and Van Der Wielen (1998, p. 340) conclude that we need 'social innovation – new attitudes and forms of behaviour – as well as technical innovation – if new forms of working are to succeed'.

EXERCISE

What does teleworking mean in the business sector you work in (or intend to work in)? What are its applications and social implications?

BOX 6.5 USING NEW TECHNOLOGY TO SUPPORT STRUCTURAL CHANGE

Several commentators suggested at the end of 1999 that e-procurement would be the 'next big thing' in e-business, where firms use Internet technology to handle the way they procure supplies. There are basically three ways of doing this:

- The company can host the supplier's catalogue on its own Internet or intranet system with regular updates from the supplier.
- The company can put hot links on its intranet to supplier sites.
- The company can set up what is basically an auction site which allows suppliers to bid for specific contracts.

In the first two of these models, staff in the company log on and purchase supplies within predetermined limits and following standard procedures. This new way of relating to suppliers aims to cut costs and to provide the company with much better information about what it is spending.

For another example, financial commentators suggest that there have been three major revolutions in British banking. The first occurred over a long time when privately owned local banks gradually merged to become the national banks. The second revolution was stimulated by the availability of new technology in the 1970s and brought us the 'hole in the wall' machines (ATMs), which most people now rely on as a way of withdrawing cash. This second revolution allowed the banks to close many of their smaller branches and become more profitable. The proposed third revolution integrates the established ATM technology with Internet access. At the end of 1999 the Co-operative Bank announced plans to install machines in Co-op stores all over Britain, linking them through satellite technology.

This raises the interesting question of what will happen to the remaining branch offices of banks. Will people still want to talk in person to financial advisers and develop some form of relationship? We must not forget the importance that people attach to relationships even within relatively automated practices. For example, Castells (1996, p. 396) notes that one of the first telephone banking services in the UK located in West Yorkshire because of research which suggested that this accent was the most 'easily understood and acceptable' throughout the UK.

BUT HOW FAST ARE ORGANIZATIONS REALLY CHANGING?

Although the advocates of new organizational forms may offer persuasive examples, we cannot assume that all organizations are so progressive. Nor can we ignore the political implications of new forms of working. A more pessimistic picture is painted in papers from the annual International Labour Process conference (Thompson and Warhurst, 1998). These suggest that claims of 'revolutionary' and wholesale change may be exaggerated when we consider evidence such as the following:

- that much 'knowledge work' is in fact extremely routine and repetitive;
- that organizations may wish to ensure consistency and 'quality' by using strong control principles akin to the ideas of 'McDonaldization' discussed by Ritzer (see Box 4.4 on pp. 80–81);
- that some modern human relations practices which claim to 'empower' workers are devices 'to achieve nothing less than the total colonization of the . . . workforce' (Thompson and Warhurst, 1998, p. 7);
- that 'most companies in the US remain traditionally managed, wedded to a low-trust, low-skill, authoritarian route to competitiveness' (ibid., p. 9);
- that relatively few workers are currently able to take advantage of the flexibilities which are offered by ICT.

However, they also point to situations where there has been significant positive change.

Harris (1998) suggests a further complication: larger organizations may contain a number of different structures within them – some based on older forms and some based on new principles and/or new technologies. He quotes examples as diverse as the Japanese Ministry of International Trade and Industry and the BBC to illustrate the point that 'markets, hierarchies and networks may co-exist as complementary alternatives *within the same institutional setting*' (p. 85, emphasis in the original). He goes on to complain that theorists often ignore this diversity, especially those who advocate the virtual organization.

WHAT THESE CHANGES MEAN FOR COMMUNICATION

If organization structures do change (if only partly) in the ways advocated in the previous sections, then business communication must also change. For example, Tom Cannon characterizes new forms of organization in terms of communication: 'communication follows natural flows and people work together on a "need to" not a "must do" basis' (1996, p. 249).

This sort of change will certainly have impact on the style of management. For example, if we assume a broadly networked organization with lots of external links and subcontracting, then the managers in the 'core' of the organization will have to adopt a much more co-operative and less directive style. There will also be increased needs for horizontal co-operation and the need to manage the growing importance of teamwork.

SUMMARY

- Organizational structures can be defined in terms of different models, such as the 'stakeholder' groups and the organization hierarchy, which highlight different aspects of communication.

- The hierarchy can also be subdivided in different ways, and this is complicated by notions of advisory and representative systems.

- Communication is a critical aspect of all these systems, and affects all these formal structures. We also have to consider the role of 'informal' networks.

- Most organizational descriptions focus upon certain core structures: line, committee and matrix. This raises the question of how far modern organizations have moved from classic bureaucratic forms with some of their inherent limitations.

- A number of organizational theorists now argue that we need to change our organizations to meet ever-increasing competitive demands and realize the potential of new technology.

- It may be that claims of revolutionary and wholesale change may be exaggerated when we consider what happens in many large organizations. Even so, the role of communication remains critical to the success of modern business organizations.

DISCUSSION QUESTIONS

- What structures exist in organizations with which you are familiar?
- How do differences in structure affect communication?
- What is your experience of organizational restructuring? How successful are such change programmes?
- How would you define the 'informal organization'? What is the real impact of the grapevine?
- What is your organization's view of teleworking? How will this change over the next decade?
- How has teleworking developed since the statistics in this book were compiled?
- How far have the organizations you know moved towards 'virtual' or 'network' models? What factors have influenced or impeded any changes?

FURTHER READING

Buchanan, D. and Huczynski, A. (eds) (1997) *Organizational Behaviour: Integrated Readings.* Hemel Hempstead: Prentice Hall.

Deetz, S. (1995) *Transforming Communication, Transforming Business: Building Responsive and Responsible Workplaces.* Cresskill, NJ: Hampton Press. Deetz's ideas are also very important for organizational change.

Kolb, D.A., Osland, J.S. and Rubin, I.M. (eds) (1995) *The Organizational Behaviour Reader*, 6th edition. Englewood Cliffs, NJ: Prentice Hall. This and the book by Buchanan and Huczynski are two collections of readings on organizational behaviour, one British and one American. Both offer important studies which relate to this chapter and the previous chapters in Part two.

Ostroff, F. (1999) *The Horizontal Organization: What the Organization of the Future Actually Looks Like and How It Delivers Value to Customers*. Oxford: Oxford University Press. An organizational model which focuses on teams, decreases hierarchy and places emphasis on ICT. Ostroff explains the model and describes how organizations have used it.

Stacey, R.D. (2000) *Strategic Management and Organizational Dynamics: The challenge of complexity*, 3rd edition. Harlow: Prentice Hall. Chapters 3 and 4 explain strategic choice theory and show how organizational structures follow from this, thereby raising the question of how far rational managerial approaches take account of communication processes.

Part three

Written communication in organizations

New technologies such as the Internet and email have given organizations new methods of written communication. But one fundamental question remains the same, whatever the method: is the written communication achieving what it should do? Written communication should achieve some business objective – it should help to get some necessary job done. For example, it could:

- tell someone what to do or how to do something – through instruction sheets or manuals;
- give someone accurate information – as in a product information sheet;
- market a product or an event – through an advertisement or a press release;
- persuade someone to set up or continue with a project – a project proposal or report.

So we can use one overriding criterion to judge the quality of business documents, whether paper or electronic – *are they effective?* For example: is the instruction understood and carried out correctly? Is the user well informed about the product? And so on.

We argue that written communication will be effective only if writers plan and organize their documents (Chapter 7). A good plan enables writers to choose the appropriate language (Chapter 8), use effective layout and visual aids (Chapter 9), and use a document format which makes sense to their readers (Chapter 10). This may mean that they have to depart from some established conventions and adopt a flexible approach. But one advantage of modern word processing is that it gives us all the potential to be 'document designers' rather than just writers. Every good design comes from sensible objectives and planning, and this is where we start.

Chapter 7

Business writing

Planning and organizing

INTRODUCTION

Many books on business writing start by offering advice on the most appropriate business style. For example, the book which describes itself as 'the most widely used writing course in the English-speaking world' starts by emphasizing that good business writers should write so that readers receive a clear and accurate impression of the writer's message. It then moves on immediately to five principles of clear writing, where principle 1 is 'to prefer clear, familiar words' (Joseph, 1998, p. 12). We comment on principles like this in the next chapter, but we think that all writers need to start by taking a step back to reflect on their approach to writing and the way they organize information. Our starting point is represented in the following quotation from well-known British researchers and consultants in communication: 'the real effort in writing is in the thinking required for planning and preparing, in the judgement required for organising and laying out, and in the continual need for sensitivity in the encoding of ideas in words and phrases' (Turk and Kirkman, 1989, p. 126). Turk and Kirkman here identify *three* critical steps which we reflect in this book: planning; organizing the material; and choosing the best way to express yourself. They also put the initial emphasis on planning and preparing. So how do you plan and prepare to write? Is there a best way of going about this process? For example, in this chapter we emphasize the importance of clear objectives. A document can be beautifully written, but if it does not have clear objectives and does not satisfy the needs or expectations of its readers, then it is *not* an effective business document.

The chapter starts by examining different approaches to writing. We highlight the way that a document's structure affects our perception and demonstrate that the way it is organized influences how readers respond to it. Accordingly, it is important for the document's writer to have clear objectives and we suggest ways in which these might be prepared and phrased. Finally, we discuss different methods and techniques for planning the structure of documents, and give examples to show how particular structures can support particular objectives.

OBJECTIVES

This chapter will:

- review different approaches to writing and suggest that you need to decide which approach suits you best;
- explain why organizing and structuring information is so important;
- discuss how to establish clear objectives;
- explain different methods and principles for structuring information, including the use of outliners and other relevant software, and show how these can be used to plan documents;
- show how we can also use these principles to organize information at different levels, including how to construct paragraphs and link them into a well-organized text;
- show how the structure of a document can and should support its objectives.

IS THERE A BEST WAY TO APPROACH BUSINESS WRITING?

One well-known handbook for technical writers offers a very clear answer:

> The best way to ensure that a writing task will be successful . . . is to divide the writing process into the following five steps:
>
> - Preparation
> - Research
> - Organization
> - Writing the draft
> - Revision
>
> At first, these five steps must be consciously – even self-consciously – followed . . . With practice, the steps in each of these processes become nearly automatic.
>
> (Brusaw *et al.*, 1997, p. xiii)

Under 'preparation', they suggest three main steps. First, you need to establish the purpose of the document. In other words, you need to decide what your readers should know or do after reading the document. We return to this later. Second, you need to 'assess your reader' to decide what they already know and what level of terminology or jargon will be acceptable. Finally, you need to establish the 'scope of the writing project'. In other words, how much detail do you need to research or include to make sure that your document achieves its purpose?

What these authors call organization is the best sequence in which to present your ideas. We deal with this later when we talk about structuring information. They talk about using the most appropriate 'method of development', which we shall also discuss later in this chapter.

Many texts on business communication recommend this approach – that writing is best achieved through a definite sequence of steps. Different writers use different labels for the steps, but the ideas are very similar, as Table 7.1 shows. This table is based on texts that focus on word-processed or printed documents. As many organizations now publish many documents via the World Wide Web, we can also ask whether this staged approach can be applied to Web sites. Box 7.1 discusses this.

EXERCISE

Consider the last piece of business or extended writing which you did. Did you follow these steps? If not, why not? Would the writing have been more successful if you had adopted a more organized approach?

Should we always follow the suggested steps?

If the *advice* from business communicators is clear, is this advice supported by research evidence? Can we ensure success by following these steps?

As with most aspects of human communication, reality is more complex than some of the advice. In one of the most accessible and interesting reviews of what we know about the writing process, Mike Sharples concludes there are three 'core activities' in writing – planning, composing and revising – but the 'flow of activity, however, is not just in one direction' (Sharples, 1999, p. 72). His model is reproduced in Figure 7.1. It shows a flow of material in a clockwise direction – from notes and plans to draft to final copy – *and* a flow of ideas in the opposite direction. For example, reading a draft may generate an idea which alters the plan.

Sharples also reviews specific studies on the impact of the initial planning phase, as well as looking at some of the methods we cover in this chapter. He concludes that 'time spent on planning is time well spent' (p. 88) but that there are different ways to plan. Writers need to find the combination of methods that suit their situation rather than relying on a single 'model approach'.

Table 7.1 Suggested steps in business writing, as proposed by various authors

Heller and Hindle (1998)	Stanton (1996)	Barker (1999)
Decide what you want to say	Write down your purpose	Create a message
Research the information	Assemble the information	
	Group the information	
	Put the information into logical sequence	Organize the information
Write your draft	Produce a skeleton outline	
	Write the first draft	Write a first draft
Edit and revise	Edit and write the final draft	Edit and revise

BOX 7.1 HOW SHOULD WE PLAN WEB SITES?

Many recent guides to Web site creation and design also advocate a staged approach. A typical example comes from Jennifer Fleming, who suggests a development cycle with the following phases:

1   *Information gathering*. This means collecting all the information you need to plan and implement the site, including the aims and target audience.
2   *Strategy*. You work out the scope of the project and decide what would best meet the user needs.
3   *Prototyping*. You create a rough plan for the site and decide how users will move about it.
4   *Implementation*. You then build the site.
5   *Launch*. This is the period just before and after the site goes live, where you need to check and test it very thoroughly.
6   *Maintenance and growth*. You need to keep the site up to date over time.

These stages are broadly similar to recommendations for written documents: planning, followed by drafting, followed by revising and editing. The last two stages are more specific to Web sites. However, Fleming is very quick to point out that although this process can be described as 'tidy and controlled ... and strictly linear' as above, it is usually very different in practice, where mistakes and delays can disrupt progress (1998, pp. 75–104). As we see with written documents, the design process is more flexible and dynamic than linear models suggest.

We can extract practical conclusions from this brief review:

■   It is important to develop plans and objectives,
■   but this does not mean that you have to write in a rigid sequence of steps,
■   and you should review your initial plans and objectives as your writing develops,
■   so you need to find an approach to planning and organizing your writing which suits you.

Another research finding is that writers can have very different ways of approaching all three main components of the writing process, and we summarize some of the important differences in Box 7.2.

Planning is more than the text

Another important point which is not always emphasized is that planning should not just be about the words or the text – it should consider the whole of what we call 'document

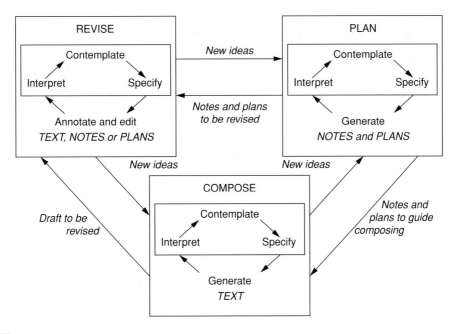

Figure 7.1 *Sharples's model of writing as creative design*

BOX 7.2 ARE YOU A BRICKLAYER OR AN OIL PAINTER?

Several research studies have tried to investigate the main strategies used by writers. Sharples (1999, pp. 114ff.) identifies two major studies which came up with very similar results. Table 7.2 highlights major differences between strategies.

Some writers seem to use one strategy almost exclusively; others adopt different strategies for different tasks. We can find examples of successful professional authors who use each of these strategies. The key to successful writing is being aware of what you need to produce rather than following a specific process. As Sharples concludes, 'Being a writer is, above all, having control over how you write and trust in your ability to make progress' (1999, p. 128).

design'. This is summarized in Figure 7.2 – the planning triangle. This diagram suggests that there are *three* interlinked aspects which will create the finished document:

■ Style of writing, i.e. choice of words, jargon, the way you address the reader and so on. We shall cover this in Chapter 8.
■ Layout and design, i.e. the design of the page, and the use of any visual aids such as illustrations or diagrams and so on. We shall cover this in Chapter 9.
■ The way the information is structured, which is the focus of the rest of this chapter.

Table 7.2 *Main strategies used by writers*

'Watercolourist'	'Architect'	'Bricklayer'	'Sketcher'	'Oil painter'
Tend to write 'in one pass' from mental plan	Make detailed plan	Build the text up, sentence by sentence	Produce rough plan	Start by drafting rather than planning, working from broad headings
Tend to review and revise on screen rather than print out drafts	Do a draft, then print out. Revise paper version and then return to computer	Revise on screen as they go	Make frequent revisions and review/revise both on screen and from paper draft	Review drafts on paper

One advantage of a clear plan is that the completed document should be easier to understand from the reader's point of view.

WHY IS STRUCTURING INFORMATION SO IMPORTANT IN BUSINESS COMMUNICATION?

We know from decades of research into human perception, cognition and memory that our brain continuously anticipates, organizes and reorganizes the information it receives. A lot of the time we are not conscious of the amount or extent of this processing. As a result, we can be misled by the way information is presented. Scott Plous demonstrates this very convincingly in his summary of research on human decision-making and problem-solving. For example, he quotes research which asked students to comment on film clips of road accidents. Students who were asked how fast the cars were going when they 'smashed' estimated an average speed which was 30 per cent higher than students who were asked about the speed when the cars 'hit'. Students who were asked about 'smashed' cars were also likely to 'remember' a week later that the accident involved broken glass – something which was *not* on the film clips. In other words, these students had not just remembered – they had *reconstructed* an image of the accident based on the notion of a 'smash' and subconsciously exaggerated elements of what they had actually seen. Other research has shown the power of suggestions in particular formats of questions – for example, it makes a difference to people's estimates if you ask 'how *long* was the movie' rather than 'how *short* was the movie' (Plous, 1993, pp. 32ff. and 66ff.).

So our retention and understanding of messages depends on how they are presented. We cannot easily absorb or remember information which is not clearly structured. For a simple example, read the following list of animals once and try to remember and repeat them before you read on:

- chacma
- cheetah
- gorilla
- impala
- leopard

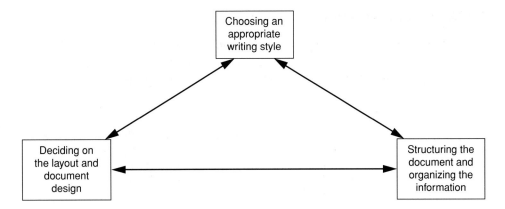

Figure 7.2 *Structuring information: the planning triangle. Whenever we write a business document, we need to plan three factors which influence each other:*

- *how we are going to structure the document and organize the information;*
- *how we are going to design the document and lay out the sections and pages;*
- *what style of writing we should use to express our ideas to the intended audience.*

- vervet
- wildebeest
- wolf
- zebra

Most people find this list difficult to remember. It is organized – it is arranged in alphabetical order – but this does not help you to structure the list in any meaningful way. It does not give you much help remembering the information, especially as some of the animals are not very widely known. A meaningful structure would make recall much easier. Consider the following reorganization:

Herbivores	Carnivores	Primates
impala	cheetah	chacma
wildebeest	leopard	gorilla
zebra	wolf	vervet

Recall of this classification is easier for two reasons:

- A long list has been subdivided into three short lists.
- There is some logic in the subdivision.

However, we must use sensible structures. If we examine these three sub-lists closely, the logic is not consistent. 'Herbivores' and 'carnivores' refer to eating habits while 'primates' refers to a zoological order. If we added 'bear' to the list it would not fit into any of the classifications as it is neither a herbivore, a carnivore nor a primate. To get a logically consistent classification we would have either one based on eating habits (herbivores, carnivores and omnivores) or one based on zoology (primate and non-primate).

145

This illustrates the point that, while classification helps us to order our information, we need to use a system of classification which is consistent – it should use one criterion at a time. It is, of course, possible to have sub-classification. We can classify the animals into primates and non-primates and then again subdivide each group into herbivores, carnivores and omnivores.

If you were trying to help people remember a list of this sort, then you would also need to choose criteria to suit the subject matter and the needs of the audience. For example, an animal nutritionist would be more interested in a dietary classification than a zoological one.

The practical point here is that if we can present information which is clearly organized *and* organized in a way which makes sense to the audience, then that audience will find the information easier to understand and remember.

DEFINING OBJECTIVES

Many discussions of objectives imply that you must have them 'perfectly' worked out before you do anything else – see Box 7.3 for a controversial example. We see objectives as more flexible, in line with the more fluid description of the writing process we gave earlier. There are two aspects of objectives we want to highlight in this chapter:

■ Phrasing your objectives in a particular way can help you decide what information to provide.
■ Clear objectives help you to improve the document by revising or redesigning it.

After we have discussed these we will look at one common business objective – to persuade – and show some of the complexities of translating this into writing.

BOX 7.3 WHO IS YOUR 'MODEL COMMUNICATOR'?

One interesting category of management texts uses historical and sometimes fictional figures to act as role models for management behaviour. So we have had texts on leadership based on Moses, Genghis Khan and even *Star Trek*. Another recent example suggests that Jesus Christ provides a model of effective marketing and communications (Finan, 1998). The argument here is that communication was one of the major tools used by Jesus, and that his life illustrates the power of some basic principles:

■ clear and simple objectives;
■ careful planning for long-term success. One of Finan's main points is that all Jesus' reported actions contributed to his overall strategy;
■ using each and every opportunity to explain his message;
■ assembling a committed team to 'spread the word' and support him.

Phrasing objectives

Ros Jay gives an example of how useful it is to refine your objectives and make them more specific. Suppose you had to write a proposal which would convince a customer to 'buy one of our swimming pools' (Jay, 1995, pp. 14ff.). This could cover a range of different models. Suppose we believe that the 'deluxe' model would suit the customer's needs best. But what needs, are they? Jay suggests 'quality' and 'ease of maintenance' as needs, but of course we could be more specific. We could develop an objective which helps to structure the communication: for example, to demonstrate that the de luxe model would satisfy customer X by being well built and reliable, easy to maintain, safe for all the family members to use, and economical to run. We can use a simple layout to show how this objective is structured:

To demonstrate that the deluxe model would satisfy customer X by being:
1   well-built and reliable;
2   easy to maintain;
3   safe for all the family members to use; and
4   economical to run.

This layout demonstrates that this objective is structured in two parts:

■   the overall purpose; and
■   a list of the main criteria or arguments which support this purpose.

    You can structure the main objective for an investigation or report in the same way. For example:
    To show that replacing our current management information system with the Genesis system will:

1   improve our management decisions;
2   give operating staff more satisfying jobs; and
3   save on running costs.

Once again, this is an objective which then supplies the main structure of the argument. You would expect this report to have three main sections: one about management decisions, one about staff jobs and one about running costs.

Clear objectives can lead to new (and better) documents

David Sless (1999) shows how a large company used several rounds of customer testing to refine the format of what had been a complex multi-page document – a traditional letter plus several forms. The single page which resulted satisfied all the necessary objectives:

■   telling the customer that their insurance policy would be cancelled if payment was not received by a certain date;
■   reminding the customer of the details of the policy in question; and
■   providing a payment slip which customers could use by mail or at a post office.

The previous design put these objectives on separate pages. This created practical problems – if customers inadvertently separated the letter and the forms, they had no idea which policy was being chased up. Using a single sheet eliminated this problem. The layout of the new form also clearly highlighted the three sections by the use of shading behind the text:

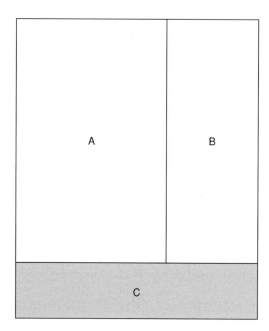

Section A was the 'letter' explaining the timetable for cancellation, section B summarized the policy and section C was the payment slip.

WHEN THE OBJECTIVE IS TO PERSUADE

The study of persuasion goes back about two thousand five hundred years to the time when the Greek Sophists taught people to argue their cases in courts and in a public forum. Aristotle (though not a Sophist) realized that there was more to persuasion than logical argument: 'We ought in fairness to fight our case with no help beyond the basic facts . . . other things affect the result considerably owing to the defects of our hearers.' He recognized that there were three basic elements:

- *ethos* – establishment of sender credibility, or believability;
- *logos* – appeal to reason; and
- *pathos* – appeal to emotions.

These three basic elements still underpin many modern theories of persuasion.

Sender credibility

Aristotle correctly reasoned that if people could impress an audience with their credibility, then what they said was likely to be accepted. In the business context, sender credibility operates at a number of levels. For example, a group within an organization can achieve credibility by reaching its targets, and individuals within the organization by living up to their promises. ('If Juliet Smith says it will be ready tomorrow, you can rely on that.') We are also inclined to believe in communication from presentable and helpful staff. Outward appearances can give an impression of credibility.

Rational argument

We cannot just rely on the strict rules of logic which the ancient Greeks used. In most business situations, you do not progress from irrefutable facts to logical conclusions; rather, you have a mass of evidence, often contradictory, which has to be weighed before a decision is taken. You have to show that the weight of the evidence favours certain conclusions, and that these conclusions suggest certain actions.

So, persuasive argument in business writing usually consists of the following:

- a clear presentation of facts and inferences;
- an objective analysis of this information;
- reasoned conclusions from the analysis;
- a proposed course of action based on these conclusions.

Appeal to the emotions

While business communication is not generally emotive, it is important to realize that the audience will often react emotionally to a message. It is important to know those areas where an audience is influenced by strong emotion, particularly where political, religious and moral beliefs and values are concerned.

Audience analysis

As persuasive correspondence aims at changing the audience's world-view in some way, it is important to have some idea of the audience's *present world-view* and the factors that are likely to *motivate* the audience to adopt the desired view.

Format of correspondence

In persuasive correspondence it is most important that the correspondence should encourage the audience to read it as there is usually no compulsion to do so. The minimum requirement for a persuasive letter is that it is clear and well set out.

Deciding on the content of persuasive writing

You can use all three of Aristotle's principles. For example, when applying by correspondence for financial support, sender credibility (*ethos*) can be established by a number of factors, such as:

- the high status of the writer or the organization;
- the obvious legality of the document, for example by the use of proper organizational stationery and inclusion of the fund-raising number;
- stating (briefly) some achievements of the organization.

We must also use logical argument and provide some evidence that the appeal is necessary. Such evidence can come from:

- facts and figures;
- expert opinion.

The emotive appeal must be carefully handled. It has been shown that overly emotional appeals do not necessarily result in the desired action, although they may often elicit an emotional response. For example, people usually want to forget unpleasant emotions as soon as possible. Charities have found that focusing on a bad situation during appeals is less successful than placing some emphasis on the potentially happy outcome of a successful appeal.

METHODS AND PRINCIPLES FOR STRUCTURING INFORMATION

There are several different ways of looking at structure.

Chunking, ordering and signposting

Much of the communication skills training that we have been involved in over the past twenty-plus years has used these three basic principles (Hartley, 1984):

- Chunking is the way that information can be broken down into sections or 'chunks' which make the information easier to digest. An example would be the way we sorted the list of animals on p. 144–145 into three chunks to make it easier to remember.
- Ordering is the way we put those chunks into an order which will make them more or less useful or meaningful.
- Signposting is the way we can offer clues or signals to explain or demonstrate the way the information is structured.

We can illustrate these principles with an everyday example. The news bulletin on US or UK television is usually clearly organized along the following lines:

- The bulletin is presented in a series of specific events with some use of overall categories – for example, the sports stories are clustered together towards the end (chunking).
- The introduction at the beginning lists the main stories or 'headlines' (signposting). This summary is repeated at the end and sometimes also about halfway through.
- The most 'important' stories come first (ordering). There is often a short, amusing story at the end to provide light relief.

EXERCISE

Review a document or publication using these three principles. Were the principles used effectively to make the document easy to follow? Would you have preferred a different way of chunking or ordering?

All the methods we go on to describe use some combination of these three basic principles. They often use some visual analogy as a basic idea, and so we start with the 'magic' of pyramids.

The pyramid principle

The pyramid principle is explained in detail in the book of the same name by Barbara Minto, which was first published in the United States in 1987 and has since inspired many business writers and trainers, including Alan Barker (1999). It is based on the idea that the human mind will look for patterns in the information presented, as we have suggested above, and that the pyramid is a common and convenient pattern. So she suggests that 'every written document should be deliberately structured to form a pyramid of ideas' (Minto, 1991, p. 1).

She explains how to construct pyramids which can then be translated into documents, emphasizing that any level in the pyramid must summarize the ideas grouped below it *and* that you must logically order and cluster ideas into sensible groups (what we would call chunking). She recommends a top-down approach, although she also shows how you can build a pyramid from bottom up, where you have a collection of information but do not have a clear idea of how to put it together.

With a clear objective, you can use the top-down approach. You start by defining the top level of the pyramid. To do this you need to decide what question you are dealing with and what your recommended answer is. This answer then fills the box at the top of the pyramid. For example, suppose that you have been asked to produce a written report which evaluates a proposal to replace an existing information system with a new one. If you decide that the new information system is a good idea, then this proposition becomes the top box in the pyramid. You then have to ask yourself how to convince your reader to go along with the proposition. For example, you may want to argue that a new system will actually provide more comprehensive information than the present one. It may be cheaper to run. It may be easier to use and allow staff to spend more time on other, more important jobs.

You can see from Figure 7.3 that you can use these ideas to build the second layer of the pyramid.

By generating a logical question which follows from these three propositions, you can produce of the third layer of the pyramid. The key question here is 'how'. How will the new system deliver more comprehensive information? How will it be cheaper to run? How will it allow staff to spend more time doing more important jobs? To construct the complete pyramid, you simply repeat this question-and-answer sequence to generate as many levels as appropriate.

EXERCISE

Find two reports which have recently been produced in your organization – one which received a favourable response or led to definite action, and one which didn't. Try to summarize the structure of these reports in pyramids as above. Is the 'better' report easier to translate into a pyramid? Minto argues that the more closely a report follows the pyramid principle, the more effective it is likely to be.

Minto also provides a very interesting model to form the introduction to any document. This is based on her suggestion that we need to spell out the history of events which have led up to the document. This can be represented by what she calls a 'classic pattern of story-telling – situation, complication, question, answer' (1991, p. 18). This sequence is explained in a bit more detail below.

Spider diagrams and mind maps

The pyramid principle advocates that we should visualize the structure of our argument as a pyramid. But what other visual analogies can we use?

The spider diagram

Another way of developing a structure of ideas is to create a spider diagram. You write your central idea or topic in the middle of the page and then build a 'spider's web' of associated ideas which link from it. This then gives you a structure which you can amend and revise until it covers what you want. Figure 7.4 shows a spider diagram which was produced to try to plan an early version of this chapter. We have used this very simple method of summarizing ideas in various ways – to take notes of lectures, to plan lectures, to give as handouts, to plan reports and papers, and so on. The spider diagram has a number of potential advantages over linear notes or a full transcription:

- It is quick and easy to do.
- It gives a visual map of the topic which can make it easy to remember.
- It can summarize complicated ideas.

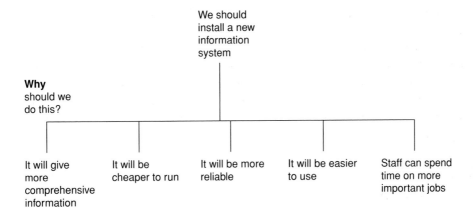

Figure 7.3 *Structuring information: pyramid structure. The diagram shows a pyramid with the main proposition and one layer which answers the fundamental question 'Why?' To expand the pyramid to the next layer, you will have to expand what you mean for each of the five statements (answering the question 'How?'). For example, how can you show that a new system will be more reliable or cheaper? You may have data on the rental or maintenance costs which proves your point. What information will a new system supply which will be 'more comprehensive'? And so on for each structure.*

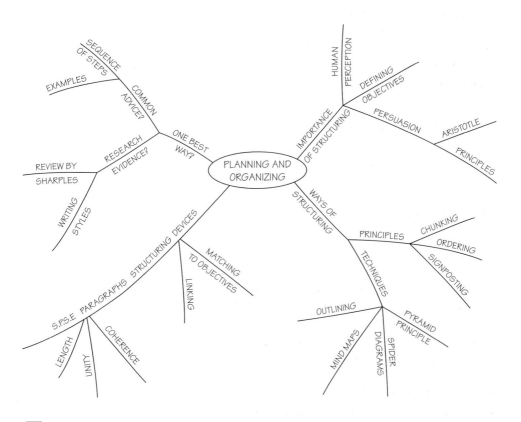

Figure 7.4 *Spider diagram used to plan this chapter*

Mind Maps

A more sophisticated development of this idea comes from Tony Buzan, one of the leading advocates of the Mind Map®, which he describes as 'a powerful graphic technique which provides a universal key to unlocking the potential of the brain' (Buzan with Buzan, 1995, p. 59). He argues that these maps work best when you incorporate a variety of techniques, such as:

- emphasis, by including images, colours and spacing on the page, and by variations in the size of lines, text and images;
- association, by making links across the diagram and by developing your own codes to represent ideas.

As a result, many of the examples in his main book are much more visually complex and colourful than the spider diagram we gave earlier. Several of these come from business or commercial applications such as the maps by Boeing engineers and Digital executives (p. 171) and the map used by Vanda North to decide whether to move her business headquarters (p. 126).

Building electronic maps

There are now various software packages which allow you to build different types of spider diagrams and mind maps, including packages from Buzan himself.

EXERCISE

Construct a spider diagram on a topic of your choice and then consult the book by Buzan to see if his additional techniques would make it more useful.

Outlining

We have tried to show that even the simplest written communication needs some form of planned structure. This can vary from a three- or four-point outline for a response to an enquiry letter, to an outline with headings and subheadings for an investigative report, and we shall show examples of this in later chapters. Modern word processing software includes an outliner so you can type in your text either in normal page fashion or directly into the outliner. Provided you have used the hierarchy of headings which your word processor allows, then you can also review your text in outline at any time. You can also move the text around in outline view, which can be easier than using 'cut and paste' in normal view.

So you can produce an outline straight into the word processor to see if your plan looks sensible and then expand it. For example, one junior administrator was asked to produce a short report on replacing the carpeting in the main office. He started with the following outline:

- carpet qualities available and suitability for various types of work areas;
- cost of the various grades;
- colours available (need pamphlet showing colours);
- fitting services offered by local firms;
- guarantees.

For longer documents, such as reports on investigations, you can use the outliner function to produce a plan of action as a guide before you start your investigation. Once the investigation is complete, this can be expanded in the outline for the report. For example, if you were asked to investigate the copier needs of your organization for the next five years, your plan could look something like this:

- present copying facilities;
- estimate of future requirements;
- technology – current and developing;
- operating costs;
- back-up service and spares.

Once the information has been collected and examined, you could develop this plan into a more comprehensive outline. For example, under operating costs you would want to investigate the comparative costs of purchase or lease and the different forms of lease available.

In the next few years we are likely to see major advances in the way computer software supports our writing through functions such as outliners and other advances (see Sharples, 1999, ch. 12).

EXERCISE

If you have not experimented with the outliner function in your word processing software, use it to review a report you have already done and then try to prepare something by drafting it in the outliner first and then revising it in normal page layout view. Does this help you organize your thoughts?

STRUCTURING DEVICES IN WRITTEN DOCUMENTS

There are a range of devices we can use in documents to make the structure clear to readers. To illustrate how this can be done, we shall concentrate on features of the paragraph: structure, length, unity, coherence, and linking devices. In later chapters, we show how features like typefaces and page design can supply similar cues, including the use of headings and subheadings linked to layout on the page.

Structure of paragraphs

Consider the following paragraph:

> Any substantial written business text contains a number of different pieces of information as part of a presentation to achieve some communication objective. Any substantial text without subdivision presents problems for readers – they can have no clear idea of the units of information that go to make up the total information presented. Subdividing into paragraphs is the most basic method of presenting units of information. A paragraph is a collection of sentences dealing with a single topic or theme.

If you examine this paragraph, you will see that it deals progressively with a single line of thought: the different pieces of information in a written text. It then considers the problem this presents to the reader and how this can be solved. So the paragraph has the structure shown in Table 7.3.

This sequence is a common structure in paragraphs in business writing as it presents a logical progression:

Situation

⇓

Problem

⇓

Solution

⇓

Evaluation

Table 7.3 Paragraph structure

Sentence	What each sentence does
Any substantial written business text contains a number of different pieces of information that are part of a presentation to achieve some communication objective	Introduces the situation/topic
Any substantial text without subdivision presents problems for readers – they can have no clear idea of the units of information that go to make up the total information presented	States the problem
Subdividing into paragraphs is the most basic method of presenting units of information	Gives the solution
A paragraph is a collection of sentences dealing with a single topic or theme	Gives an evaluation or judgement

The same sort of structure is also used as a model for structuring documents – see Box 7.4 for some examples. Often, only two or three of the components are present, but they follow the same sequence:

- situation – problem – evaluation
- situation – evaluation.

For example, the following paragraph follows the 'situation – evaluation' pattern:

> Any substantial written business text contains a number of different pieces of information that are part of a presentation to achieve some communication objective. These pieces are usually related in a structured way.

Another common structure is to follow the time sequence:

> We were travelling by car to Springfield. Near Halfway House the left-front tyre burst and the car skidded off the road into a barrier. We were extremely lucky to escape without injury.

This paragraph also follows the 'situation – problem – evaluation' sequence.

You can also use physical or spatial arrangements as the basis for paragraph structure. For example, you can describe a house in terms of its downstairs features, followed by its upstairs features.

The most important point to emphasize is that paragraphs should have a clear and consistent structure.

Length of paragraphs

As you have just seen, a paragraph can consist of a single sentence. Short one-sentence paragraphs are often used to emphasize a point.

There is no upper limit to the number of words in a paragraph. Good business writing tends to have shorter paragraphs than does literary writing. For long documents such as reports, a maximum of 100 words per paragraph is a rough guideline. For shorter documents such as letters and memos, about 60 words is suitable, but you must not destroy the unity of a paragraph in an effort to reduce its length.

To maintain the reader's interest, you should use paragraphs of varying lengths.

Unity

Unity here means that the paragraph deals with a single topic and contains no irrelevant material. Any sentence that does not refer to the topic should be excluded and moved to a new paragraph. This enables the reader to follow your train of thought one step at a time. However, a paragraph may have linking sentences which connect it with preceding or following paragraphs, and we shall look at those later.

Coherence

It is not sufficient that all sentences in a paragraph refer to the topic; they should also develop the theme in a logical way. Each sentence should follow on naturally from the previous one. Consider this variation of the first illustrative paragraph of this section, where we have transposed the last two sentences.

> (1) Any substantial written business text contains a number of different pieces of information that are part of a presentation to achieve some communicative objective. (2) Any substantial text without subdivision presents problems for readers – they can have no clear idea of the units of information that go to make up the total information presented. (3) A paragraph is a collection of sentences dealing with a single topic or theme. (4) Subdividing into paragraphs is the most basic method of presenting units of information.

This destroys the coherence of the paragraph: the new sentence (3) comments on the concept of a paragraph *before* this concept has been fully developed (sentence 4 in the original paragraph).

Linking devices

We can use linking to help the reader follow our train of thought. Linking can apply to the sentences within a paragraph and to the paragraphs within a text. Various ways of linking are:

- linking punctuation;
- linking words;
- linking phrases;
- linking sentences.

Linking can slow down the reader, so avoid excessive use. It can also be irritating, particularly where the linkage is obvious.

BOX 7.4 STRUCTURING DOCUMENTS

Suzanne Sparks (1999, p. 48) advises that you should 'structure your writing to reach your reader' and offers five possible structures for letters and memos which are similar to the paragraph structures we talked of above. For example, she suggests that a persuasive communication should be based on the following five paragraphs:

1 You try to establish some common ground.
2 You explain the problem which will be resolved if the reader agrees to your request.
3 You explain the solution and show how it has significant advantages for the reader which outweigh any disadvantages.
4 You list all the benefits for the reader.
5 You clearly specify what you want the reader to do.

Linking punctuation

The semicolon is commonly used to show that two statements which could have been written as separate sentences are closely related, for example:

> The company has applied for an overdraft to finance increased stock levels; this will be essential for the continued expansion of the business.

The clause after the semicolon could have been written as a separate sentence, but the use of the semicolon emphasizes the close relation of the two ideas.

Linking words and phrases

Linking words are those such as 'thus', 'therefore', 'also', 'but', 'first' . . . 'second'. For example:

> The programme has been designed to meet the needs of large businesses. *However*, it can be adapted for small businesses.

Repeating key words can also provide linking, as in:

> The programme has been designed to meet the needs of large businesses. *The programme* can also be adapted for small businesses.

Similarly, phrases such as 'next in importance is . . . , 'we conclude therefore . . . , 'to sum up' . . . can all help the transition between sentences and paragraphs.

Linking sentences

Where one topic has been dealt with in detail and a completely new topic is to be explored, it is sometimes necessary to signal this with a transitional sentence at the end of a paragraph. For example, if we have been considering the causes of inflation and wish to move to the cure for inflation, a transitional sentence can make this clear:

> Having examined the causes of inflation we will now examine the possible cures.

MATCHING STRUCTURE TO OBJECTIVES

To conclude this chapter, the most important point is that the structure of your written communication should support your objectives (this also applies to face-to-face communication, as we shall see in Part four of this book). We can illustrate this by looking at possible structures for a persuasive letter. The following are some of the elements that may be included. Not all of these elements are required in every case and they do not necessarily follow the sequence given:

- attention-getting introduction;
- statement of situation;

- statement of needs of or advantages to receiver;
- statement of needs of sender;
- visualization of outcome;
- reconciliation of sender's and receiver's needs;
- call for action.

For example, consider the appeal letter shown as table 7.4. It is based on a real letter from an animal charity which has been slightly modified to illustrate the above points.

EXERCISE

Compare the structure of this letter with other examples you can find. What structure is most likely to have the desired impact?

SUMMARY

- Many texts divide the writing process into a series of steps and suggest you follow them in that order, moving from preparation and research, to organizing the material, and on to writing and revising.
- Research suggests that life is more complex. Writers need to find the combination of methods that suit their situation. It is important to develop plans and objectives, but this does not mean that you have to write in a rigid sequence of steps.
- Research shows that if we can present information which is clearly organized *and* organized in a way which makes sense to the audience, then that audience will find the information easier to understand and remember.
- Clear objectives are an important part of planning. Phrasing your objectives in a particular way can help you decide what information you then need to provide.
- There are various ways of structuring information which you can use as the basis for a written document. They are all based on three basic principles: chunking, ordering and signposting.
- There are many useful techniques for structuring material. Often they use some visual analogy as a basic idea. It is worth considering the pyramid principle, the use of Mind Maps and the use of outliners.
- There are also devices we can use in documents to make the structure clear to readers. To illustrate this, we concentrated on features of the paragraph: argument structure, length, unity, coherence, and linking devices.
- The structure of your written communication should support your objectives, and we illustrated this by looking at possible structures for a persuasive letter.

Table 7.4 *Elements of a persuasive letter*

What each paragraph does	Text of the letter
Attention-getting introduction	When a dog lies crippled and crying on the roadside, the call automatically goes out for the ANIMALCARE ambulance.
Needs of receiver	When a stray is found – a family pet, abandoned by its owners and left to fend for itself – everyone reacts in the same way: 'Get ANIMALCARE on to it.' Even a child knows that if his beloved pet is sick or in pain, there'll always be someone at ANIMALCARE to help.
Statement of situation	But how many people know what goes on behind the scenes – or even realize where the money comes from for the care and attention of the animals who cannot speak for themselves?
Background to sender's needs. Statement of situation	Last year, because of lack of funds, it was touch-and-go as to whether we would be forced to close our doors, but miraculously, through the help of many generous friends in the community, we've managed to stay open.
Background to sender's needs. Statement of situation	We receive no state aid, and because 90% of our work is done free of charge, our funds are stretched to the limit. We battle to cope with escalating costs and the frightening increase in the number of animals needing attention.
Sender's need	But the crisis is by no means over.
Sender's need	Frankly, the situation is desperate. Which is why I am writing to you – as someone living in an area covered by the ANIMALCARE service – for your support.
Visualization of outcome. Receiver's need	Your gift, whatever the size, will not only help to eliminate suffering among animals, but will assist your local ANIMALCARE to protect you and your family from health hazards such as rabies.
Reconciling sender's and receiver's need	You can assist in the elimination of animal suffering by supporting our work. A donation of 50 ecus will support a dog for two months.
Call to action	For your convenience we are enclosing a donation form and an addressed envelope.
	Please help us, as we rely entirely on kind people such as you.
	Yours sincerely
	J Jones
	Organizing Secretary
Attention-getting	PS. This region's only Bird Hospital is run by ANIMALCARE. Wouldn't it be a tragedy if it had to be abandoned due to lack of funds?

DISCUSSION QUESTIONS

- How would you describe your current style of writing and what would you like to change/improve?
- How can we decide which structure is 'best' for a given document?
- If different readers prefer different ways of structuring, how can you meet all their needs?
- Techniques such as Mind Maps ask you to visualize the structure of your document. Does this visual approach suit everyone?
- What linking devices work best in business documents?
- Assuming that we have structured documents to reflect our objectives, what other factors can influence the way they are interpreted by readers?

FURTHER READING

Minto, B. (1991) *The Pyramid Principle: Logic in Writing and Thinking*. London: Pitman. This gives the complete description of the pyramid principle and its practical application. Includes lots of relevant business examples.

Plous, S. (1993) *The Psychology of Judgment and Decision Making*. New York: McGraw-Hill. Probably the best (and certainly one of the most entertaining and thought-provoking) introduction to the complex ways we process information.

Schriver, K.A. (1997) *Dynamics in Document Design: Creating Text for Readers*. New York: John Wiley. Perhaps the best general introduction to the general area of document design. The whole book is relevant to our concerns. In relation to this chapter, chapters 3 and 4 show the dangers of ignoring the needs of readers.

Sharples, M. (1999) *How We Write: Writing as Creative Design*. London: Routledge. An excellent summary of what we know about the writing process (and what we don't) which raises many interesting practical questions. Part 2 of the book is particularly relevant to this chapter.

Chapter 8

Effective writing style

INTRODUCTION

As we said in the previous chapter, business writing should achieve some business objective – it should help to get some necessary job done. For example, you might be writing to give someone accurate information (as in a product information sheet) or to persuade someone to set up a project (as in a project proposal).

How effectively you achieve your objective will depend in part on your writing style. So we need strategies which will increase the likely effectiveness of business language. These strategies are what this chapter is all about – how to write in an effective style for business communication.

We start by identifying some common criticisms of official and business language and then work through the main criteria we use to identify effective style – appropriate content and appropriate tone. Many business communicators advocate Plain English as the appropriate style to meet these criteria and we review both the main supporting claims and the criticisms of this approach.

Finally, we look at some detailed strategies for improving writing and assess the value of methods which are supposed to measure the readability of a document. But we cannot offer a 'magic solution' to language problems. Throughout this chapter we shall point out the difficulties and pitfalls of relying on simple or absolute rules of 'effective' language. As we illustrated in Part one, communication is both complex and dependent on context.

OBJECTIVES

This chapter will:

- identify common criticisms of business writing;
- explain the main criteria we use to identify an effective business writing style;
- outline the main characteristics, potential advantages and possible limitations of the Plain English approach;
- summarize important strategies of 'plain language' and suggest how to improve your style by using appropriate words and effective sentences; and
- evaluate methods to measure the readability of a document.

WHAT CAN GO WRONG WITH BUSINESS WRITING?

There are two main aspects of business communication: how the business communicates to its customers and to the general public, and how the business communicates within its own walls. Both aspects of business writing have come in for their fair share of criticism. Looking at external communication, Wind and Main (1998) conclude that 'business does a very poor job of explaining itself, and too often puts its foot in its mouth'. They continue to criticize the style of business representatives: 'on TV, CEOs [Chief Executive Officers] show up as tongue-tied grouches, and corporate speak squeezes the life out of language'.

As an example of the 'lifeless' and jargon-infested language which they see as typical of corporate-speak, they highlight the following announcement from an otherwise innovative American company: 'Human resources goes beyond the traditional personnel function by partnering with internal customers to discover meaningful solutions to people related issues and needs' (Wind and Main, 1998, p. 3). What does this mean to someone who does not have a very sophisticated understanding of theoretical debates in personnel practice? Probably not a lot! Unfortunately, this use of language may rebound on the organization. Rather than impressing an external audience, it may create an image of pompous or overblown communication which creates mistrust.

Criticisms of the written materials which circulate *within* organizations can be equally scathing. Again this is nothing new. At the height of the Battle of Britain in the Second World War, the British Prime Minister, Winston Churchill, still found time to write a memo to his staff recommending 'reports which set out the main points in a series of short, crisp paragraphs'. He complained that the majority of official papers were 'far too long', wasted time and energy by not highlighting the main points, and contained too many 'woolly phrases'. Box 8.1 gives some examples of business writing which have achieved notoriety thanks to publicity from the Plain English Campaign in the United Kingdom.

If business writing is so often ambiguous, over-complex and unattractive, what can we do about it? Perhaps we should accept William Horton's suggestion that we need a new type of business document – 'one that answers questions in a hurry' (1997, p. 3). One common response has been to adopt Plain English. Before we investigate this in detail, we need to examine the general criteria which are often applied to business writing to achieve an appropriate style.

WHAT IS 'GOOD STYLE' IN BUSINESS WRITING?

'Style in writing is concerned with choice' (Kirkman, 1992, p. 6). Even if you work in an organization which has very strict rules about how letters and reports are presented, you will still have to make choices about which words and phrases to use, how to organize your paragraphs, and so on. You will have to make stylistic choices to create a document which has the appropriate content and tone – and we shall investigate these two aspects in search of the 'best' business style.

BOX 8.1 CONTENDERS FOR THE GOLDEN BULL

The British Plain English Campaign is renowned for its annual 'Golden Bull' awards which are given to organizations that manage to produce really horrendous examples of incomprehensible writing. Despite the impact of the campaign and other moves to improve business communication, they still have little difficulty finding 'worthy entries'.

Back in 1984, Martin Cutts and Chrissie Maher from the campaign compiled a hilarious collection of 'gobbledygook' (updated in the Plain English Campaign's 1994 collection, *Utter Drivel*). This collection demonstrates how government departments and commercial organizations frequently resort to 'bizarre use of language'. Examples include:

- the council that decided to replace the term 'bottlenecks' with 'localised capacity deficiencies' in one of its planning documents;
- the bank that included a 585-word sentence in an overdraft document;
- the company that threatened its workforce that 'If you neglect to obey this order in the time referred to herein, you will be liable to process of execution for the purpose of propelling you to obey the same';
- the council that added the following helpful erratum to its district plan: 'For the justification statement read the implementation note and vice versa.'

In 1998, Cutts (who is no longer associated with the Plain English Campaign) was involved with the European Union's translation service to improve the style of documents emerging from Brussels. Examples of odd language from Brussels were reported at the time in the British press, including:

- 'involuntary conversion' to describe a plane crash;
- 'grain-consuming animal unit' to describe a cow;
- 'improving the interoperability of inter-modal transport systems' to describe the streamlining of bus and train timetables.

Content criteria

What criteria can we use to evaluate the content of a business text? The most common are listed below, although many texts on business communication focus on the first three:

- accuracy;
- brevity;
- clarity;
- emphasis.

Accuracy

In business writing, accuracy is the most important criterion. Inaccurate and incorrect information can often be more harmful than no information at all. Would you wish to travel on an aircraft that had been serviced according to an inaccurate manual?

But this raises a problem: *how* accurate must your writing be? A high degree of accuracy often requires considerable detail and qualification of the information. The result could be long and turgid texts which nobody can bring themselves to read.

Consider for example the following simple memo:

TO: General Manager
FROM: Personnel Manager

Support for Staff Canteen
Pursuant to your memo requesting information on staff attitudes to a staff canteen, I wish to report as follows.

In the week beginning 25 January 2001, Messrs Smith, Jones and Kbumalo of this department carried out a survey of staff opinion using a simple questionnaire, which had been prepared by Jo Singh of the Human Resources Department as part of a project for his management development qualification. They were able to give the questionnaire to 470 staff which is 69.24% of the workforce who take lunch and eat in the vicinity of the factory.

In the following week, the questionnaire was analysed using the scanner and soft-ware in Human Resources. The results indicated that 89.47% of those questioned were in favour of a staff canteen.

A full copy of their report is attached for your perusal.

Although this memo is only 136 words long, it manages to demonstrate many examples of poor style. For example,

- The reader does not need this level of accuracy. The writer should have rounded off the figure to 89 per cent or even 90 per cent.
- Opinion surveys depend on responses which can change from day to day, and it is not justified to report the result to two places of decimals. Again, rounding off the figures would be much more sensible.

This is a very simple (and perhaps trivial) example, but we have seen this problem in many more serious and important management reports.

Brevity

The example given above also fails on the criterion of brevity. Over-long documents are usually caused by unnecessary material and/or long-winded writing. In any communication situation, the writer usually has more information than is necessary and must therefore determine:

- what the audience already knows;
- what the audience needs to know;
- what the audience wants to know.

Once you have a clear idea of this, you can trim the message without leaving out important information. If we consider the memo above, we can ask the following questions:

- Is the exact date of the survey needed or wanted?
- Are the names of the investigators relevant?
- What level of accuracy is needed?

If we remember that the detailed information is all included in the report (which the manager could read to check it), the text of the memo can be reduced to the following:

Re: your request for information on attitudes to a canteen.

We have surveyed staff attitudes by questionnaire. We surveyed 70% of the staff and 90% of them were in favour. Our report is attached.

This reduces the passage from 136 words to 34 words, i.e. by 75 per cent.

Of course, you can take brevity too far! The above message can be reduced to only seven words: '90% of staff favour a staff canteen'. But this message would place a greater burden on the reader, who would have to recall the background to the request. There is also the problem of accuracy: *90 per cent of 70 per cent* were actually in favour. This brings us to the next criterion: clarity.

Clarity

Lack of clarity is often due to poor style, rather than difficult subject matter, and may be caused by:

- stilted phrases and clichés;
- too much detail and repetition;
- lack of logical structure;
- excessive use of abstract and generic terms.

Consider for example the following letter:

Dear Sir

PACKING AND REMOVAL OF OFFICE FURNITURE AND EQUIPMENT

We are in receipt of your esteemed favour of the 30th ult. and subsequent communication with regard to the estimate you require for the packing and removal of your office furniture, equipment and records from your premises at 123 Main St to your new premises at 456 Rivonia Rd on the 20th inst.

We wish to confirm the arrangement whereby our representative, Mr S Strydom, will call on you at 09:00 hrs on 6th inst. at the above-mentioned address, to make an inspection of the above-mentioned items with a view to estimating the number of packing cases and vehicles we will need to effect the packing and subsequent removal of same.

We trust that the suggested time will suit your convenience. We will then submit our quotation for your consideration and hope that we may be entrusted to under-take the aforementioned work. Our quotation will remain valid for seven days. The time you suggest for removal, 08:00 on 20th inst., will be entirely convenient provided we receive your timeous response.

We beg to remain
Yours faithfully

W Smith
Removals Manager

This letter is unclear for a number of reasons:

- use of outdated abbreviations and clichés, such as ult. and inst., and 'your esteemed favour';
- unnecessary detail. Does the customer need to know that the cartage contractor has to estimate the number of 'packing cases and vehicles' needed?
- fuzzy facts. What precisely is meant by 'subsequent communication' and 'timeous response'?
- pompous words, e.g. 'timeous', 'in receipt of'.

EXERCISE

Before reading on, produce a simplified and improved version of this letter.

Emphasis

Important information should be emphasized. But how do we decide what is important? It is:

- information that is important to the audience; and
- information that will support your arguments as writer.

Less important information should be left out or placed later in the text.

Using these criteria, the previous letter can be further improved (Table 8.1).

Apart from ranking items in order of importance, emphasis can be achieved by other methods, such as the following:

- *Format and typography*. The layout and typography of a document can be used to highlight important points. We shall say more on this in Chapter 9. Techniques include use of white space, use of lists and bullet points, and use of headings.
- *Grammatical structure*. We can emphasize a word by making it the subject of a sentence. For example, rather than 'The temperature was measured by an optical pyrometer', you can say 'An optical pyrometer measured the temperature.' This puts the emphasis on the means of measurement.

Of course, emphasis should not be carried to the point where information is distorted or where important facts are concealed.

Balancing the content criteria

A good text depends on achieving a successful *balance* of the four criteria in order to meet the reader's needs. In the simple examples we have used above, the criteria are relatively easy to apply. But even in simple examples we can dig deeper and discover possible

Table 8.1 How a letter can be improved

Improved letter	Comment
REMOVAL OF OFFICE CONTENTS	
Thank you for your letter of 30 June about moving the contents of your offices. We wish to confirm the following points from our telephone conversation.	Gives an immediate audience orientation.
We are able to move the contents of your offices at 08:00 on 20 July as required. We have provisionally included your move in our work schedule.	Immediately confirms that the work can be done.
Mr S Strydom will visit you at 09:00 on 6 July to prepare a quotation and he will submit this to you within 24 hours.	There is no unnecessary information here.
We will hold your move on our removal schedule until 12 July to give you time to decide on our quotation. If there is anything you wish to know about these arrangements, please contact me at 706 2345(ext. 6781).	Gives a definite date. Also clarifies how the customer can respond.
Yours sincerely	
W Smith Removals Manager	

ambiguities. For example, the memo about canteen facilities discovered that most of the staff 'were in favour', but what exactly does that mean? What sort of facility did they want? And how often would they use it? This general approval might mask very strong differences in terms of what particular groups of staff want from a canteen. Of course, this detail may be in the attached report, but the memo should highlight the key findings. At the moment, this memo does not give a very clear pointer to any management action. So the criteria must always be applied in relation to what the written communication needs to achieve.

EXERCISE

Revise a business letter you have received using these criteria. How easy is it to apply the criteria?

TONE CRITERIA

Even if the content of a message is good, business writing can still fail to achieve its objectives if its tone offends the reader. We have already argued that communication always conveys two simultaneous messages: information and relationship. We can examine the style of business writing to see if it establishes or reinforces an appropriate relationship. This is especially important because everything you write can be taken to be written on behalf of your organization (or, in an internal communication, your part of the organization). Any attitudes you express are assumed to be those of the organization. You must therefore be aware of the image your organization wishes to project and write accordingly.

For a simple illustration, compare the following sentences from letters to customers and decide which organization is projecting the most 'professional' and positive image:

- 'If this does not sort out your gripes, give me a ring.'
- 'If this does not solve your problems, communicate with the undersigned at your earliest convenience.'
- 'If this does not solve the problem, please telephone me at . . . '

Of course, the different relations that exist in business mean you must be sensitive to the requirements of these situations. Therefore, you do not use the same tone when writing to a customer who has not paid his account for six months as you would to a potential customer. There are, however, certain tonal requirements that almost invariably apply to written communication. The fact that written communication constitutes a permanent record means that writers should:

- avoid undue familiarity;
- adopt a professional tone;
- use a tone appropriate to the status of the receiver;
- be sensitive to the existence of different business practices;
- be sensitive to cultural differences.

The last two points are particularly important in international business, where there is always the danger of unintentionally giving offence.

If we are searching for a business style which satisfies these criteria of content and tone, can Plain English provide the answer?

THE RISE OF PLAIN ENGLISH

Criticisms of official and business writing are nothing new. Equally long-standing are the pleas for plain and understandable writing; Martin Cutts (1995) produces examples of these pleas going back to the sixteenth century. We shall outline the rise of Plain English in the United Kingdom as a typical case study, with brief comments on the impact of these principles in other countries.

One of the major issues which prompted the rise of Plain English was the poor quality of official forms and government publications. Earlier in the twentieth century, there were several attempts to simplify the language of government, including the very influential book by Sir Ernest Gowers, *Plain Words* (later revised and extended into *The Complete Plain Words*; Gowers, 1987). Another influential article, still quoted in modern guides, came from George Orwell in 1946 ('Politics and the English language'). See Box 8.2 for discussion of some of the broader implications of his approach. His six elementary rules are worth repeating as a useful summary of early Plain English thinking (and are still recommended in leading guides to written style such as *The Economist Style Guide*, 1996):

1   Never use a METAPHOR, simile or other figure of speech which you are used to seeing in print.
2   Never use a long word where a SHORT WORD will do.
3   If it is possible to cut out a word, always cut it out.
4   Never use the passive where you can use the ACTIVE.
5   Never use a FOREIGN PHRASE, a scientific word or a JARGON word, if you can think of an everyday English equivalent.
6   Break any of these rules sooner than say anything outright barbarous.

These rules are echoed in many modern guides to effective business language. For example, in a book published by the British Industrial Society, Alan Barker (1999, p. 1) offers three 'golden rules of effective writing':

■   Use words your reader will recognize easily.
■   Construct straightforward sentences.
■   Make your point, then support it.

A recent American book (Joseph, 1998, p. 12) offers five main principles:

■   Prefer clear, familiar words.
■   Keep most sentences short and simple.
■   Prefer active voice verbs; avoid passives.

- Use conversational style as a guide.
- Revise, revise, and revise again.

There is a lot of common ground between these sets of principles, and we shall explore the most important recommendations in more detail later in this chapter.

The growing impact of Plain English

Early attempts to promote Plain English in official documents had little impact. In the United Kingdom, the situation in the mid-1970s was summed up as follows: 'Official forms in Britain were a national joke, had been for years. The public expected them to be impersonal, incomprehensible, pompous, long winded, and full of pitfalls' (Cutts and Maher, 1986, p. 9). Cutts and Maher, who had worked to pressurize government departments and offer alternative forms and advice to the general public, decided to promote a national initiative. In 1979 the Plain English Campaign was founded and received considerable publicity in the national press after mounting a public shredding of government forms next to the Houses of Parliament. Consumer groups in the United States were also making progress, and President Carter ruled that regulations should be written in Plain English, although his executive order was later repealed.

In the 1980s, several governments formally responded to this increasing pressure. A British government White Paper in 1982 ordered *all* government departments to review *all* their official forms, to eliminate any unnecessary ones, and to make sure that all forms were clear and easy to understand. Similar initiatives were successful in other countries. For example, the Australian government adopted a similar policy in 1984.

One feature of the pressure groups has been their continuing efforts to publicize examples of poor official writing. Perhaps prompted by the prospect of such public ridicule, many UK

BOX 8.2 THE POLITICS OF LANGUAGE STYLE

George Orwell was not simply interested in improving the quality of official documents. One of his main concerns was the way that totalitarian states used 'corrupt' forms of language in order to disguise the true intentions behind political dogma. A key weapon used by the state in his classic novel *Nineteen Eighty-four*, is the language – Newspeak. This language systematically destroys the link between words and meanings and is used to make the dogma of the ruling party both meaningless and indisputable at the same time. Orwell's arguments for clear and transparent language were all arguments to prevent specific linguistic features being used to confuse and dominate.

Another important aspect of Orwell's thinking is also very relevant to modern thinking on Plain English: the notion that plain language will be 'automatically transparent'. This assumes that there is a fixed code whereby a word corresponds to a fixed meaning. This is not our view. As we showed in Part one of this book, language is a fuzzy code where flexibility is the norm. Although Plain English may assist understanding, it can *never* guarantee it.

commercial organizations adopted Plain English policies in the 1980s. This continuing pressure has made an impact; for example, the Plain English Campaign now claims that 'today it is difficult to find a truly atrocious central government form' and many commercial companies have adopted their techniques and training materials (Plain English Campaign, 1993).

Developments in Plain English

One major difference between modern Plain English recommendations and those of previous writers such as Gowers is the attention paid to the organization, design and layout of documents; good writing is not just about 'getting the words right'. We also follow this philosophy, which is why we shall look at organization and layout in the next chapter.

EXERCISE

Investigate the impact of the Plain English movement in one organization or commercial area: do the organization(s) have any explicit language policies? Do they train staff in particular styles of English? How far do the reports and official documents use plain language? Does the organization house style include any odd or arbitrary rules? Box 8.3 lists some unusual rules which organizations have insisted upon.

BOX 8.3 THIS ORGANIZATION HAS RULES

Some organizations publish very definite rules to control their staff's writing. Some of these rules owe more to the personal preference of the management in charge than to any 'rules' of grammar or communication. For example (both examples from Lauchman, 1998, p. 8):

- One major telecommunications company tells its employees, 'NEVER USE SPLIT INFINITIVES!'
- One large company claims that 'personnel' is singular and so recommends sentences such as 'All personnel is required to report to work by 8.30 am.'

Current agreement on plain language

If you read a selection of texts on business communication, then you may be struck by the consensus that emerges over language style. Table 8.2 illustrates this agreement – and also suggests some differences in emphasis – by listing eight major characteristics of plain language style and showing how they are summarized in three important texts:

- one of the best British summaries of the Plain English approach, by Martin Cutts;
- 'the most widely used writing course in the English-speaking world' (Joseph, 1998);
- a recent US text published by the American Management Association (Lauchman, 1998).

Table 8.2 *Agreement on Plain English*

Language characteristic	Cutts (1995)*	Joseph (1998)	Lauchman (1998)
Short sentences	Average 15–20 words	Average 15–20 words (pp. 19ff.)	'Let emphasis dictate length . . . Length dilutes. Brevity emphasizes.' (pp. 59–60)
Familiar words	'Use words your readers are likely to understand.'	'Prefer clear, familiar words.' (p. 12)	'Give yourself permission to use ordinary words.' (p. 84)
No unnecessary words	'Use only as many words as you need.'	'the need for clear, simple language.' (p. 14)	'Avoid redundancy.' (p. 42)
Prefer the active to the passive voice	'Prefer the active voice unless there's a good reason for using the passive.'	'Prefer active voice verbs; avoid passives.' (p. 36)	'Use it [the passive voice] when emphasis and context demand its use. It is senseless to make every sentence active; when you do that, you alter emphasis.' (p. 38)
Style	'Put your points positively if you can.' 'Use the clearest, crispest, liveliest verb to express your thoughts.'	'Use conversational style as a guide.' (p. 39)	'Write with verbs, not with nouns.' (p. 31)
'Good' punctuation	'Put accurate punctuation at the heart of your writing.'	'Punctuation marks are like traffic signals. They guide readers; they tell readers when to go and when to stop, and when to turn, and in what direction.' (p. 209)	'Punctuation has a single purpose: To clarify the writer's intended meaning.' (p. 105)

* All quotations taken from his summary of guidelines on p. 9.

But is Plain English always the answer?

As well as the arguments in favour (e.g. Kimble, 1994/5), Plain English also has its critics. Robyn Penman argues that we need to consider the context when we write and we cannot rely on a universal principle of plain or simple English. There is some evidence that Plain English revisions do not always work: Penman quotes research including an Australian study which compared versions of a tax form and found that the revised version was 'virtually as demanding for the taxpayer as the old form' (1993, p. 128).

We agree with Penman's main point – that we need to design appropriate documents – but we still think that *all* business writers should consider the recommendations coming from Plain English sources. Unless you have clear contrary evidence, they are the 'safest bet', especially if you have a general or mixed audience. For the rest of this book, we shall talk of 'plain language' to refer to this approach – using the simplest and clearest expression which is appropriate for the audience.

One further word of caution: changing language styles in an organization does not just change the language. Language use reflects important aspects of organization culture, as we saw in Part one of this book. There may also be specific implication for organization relationships, as the study in Box 8.4 illustrates.

APPLYING PLAIN LANGUAGE STRATEGIES

In this final section, we summarize plain language strategies which you can consider in your own writing.

BOX 8.4 WHERE PLAIN ENGLISH DISRUPTED THE ORGANIZATIONAL STRUCTURE

Jim Suchan studied how report assessors (RAs) in a government agency made decisions based on information in written reports from subordinates (with whom they had no direct contact). The RAs felt the reports were badly organized and difficult to read, but they had various strategies to 'make sense of all the garbled stuff in these reports' (Suchan, 1998, p. 312). Despite these criticisms, they did not suggest that their subordinates should change their writing style – it was accepted as part of the job. The RAs had 'become very skilful in manoeuvring through the reports to find the information they needed to make a decision. They were proud of that skill: it differentiated them from others.'

A few reports were rewritten using techniques such as the inclusion of headings and subheadings, bulleted lists, active verbs, shorter paragraphs, etc. However, these revised reports did not lead to better decisions. They were disliked, and described as 'abnormal discourse'. The new report style was seen as a fundamental change in the relationship between them and their subordinates – deskilling the RAs and 'usurping their authority'. Rumours circulating in the organization about possible cutbacks and restructuring were an obvious factor in these perceptions.

This study shows that we cannot simply impose a new language style on an organization without considering the broader impact and implications. As Suchan concludes, 'a document's perceived value and most importantly the organisational outcome from its use are contingent on factors outside of the document's design, organisation, and style' (1998, p. 321).

Hit the right point on the 'word scales'

You need to use appropriate words in a specific situation. Some organizations have tried to control word choices by introducing simplified English. Unfortunately, this can bring other problems (see Box 8.5). Assuming you have free choice, consider where your words fit on the following four scales:

- *Abstract – concrete.* An abstract word is the name of something we experience as an idea or a disposition such as freedom, justice or boredom. A concrete word names something we can experience directly with our senses such as a book, a dog or a trumpet. The main problem with abstract terminology is its vagueness. It often requires a concrete example to *clarify* it. Although a statement like 'Inflation is affecting our administration costs' may be true, it is vague. The statement could include a concrete example, like 'Inflation is affecting our administration costs – the costs of printing and stationery have risen by around 7 per cent per year for the last three years.'
- *Generic – specific.* 'Vehicle' is a generic term, as it covers a variety of things. There is a range from generic to specific, as in: vehicle – motor vehicle – motor car – Toyota car – 1998 Toyota Corolla – 1998 green, 1.6 litre Toyota Corolla – and so on. Business writing tends to be too generic.
- *Formal – colloquial.* On informal occasions, such as casual conversation in the workplace or on social occasions, we tend to use more colloquial words. 'The company is in financial difficulties' is more formal, while 'The company is going down the drain' is more colloquial. Excessively formal language can sound pompous; it also tends to distance the writer from his or her audience. It is very important to pitch your writing at the point on this scale which is appropriate; colloquial words are often frowned on in business writing as they suggest a less than serious attitude towards the subject matter.
- *Emotive – referential.* Emotive words may be considered as words that convey both facts and attitudes or dispositions. Referential terms convey facts rather than attitudes. Therefore 'The shop floor was covered with sawdust' is essentially factual, whereas 'The shop floor was filthy' conveys the writer's attitude. Often words which were not originally considered to be emotive acquire an emotive connotation because of circumstances. This may be especially important in intercultural communication. For example, black South Africans have been successively referred to as natives, non-Europeans and Bantu. Each of these words has acquired a negative connotation, and the current referential term is 'blacks'. In the United States, however, the preferred term is 'Afro-Americans' instead of 'black Americans'.

Avoid jargon and technical slang

Jargon is technical language which is usually unintelligible to a wide audience. A term such as 'discounted cash flow' would be unacceptable jargon to a general audience, if no explanation was given. Technical slang means slang terms that are used in technical conversation: expressions such as 'the bottom line'.

176

BOX 8.5 SIMPLIFIED ENGLISH

Basic English was developed by C.K. Ogden to help non-native speakers to communicate in English but it never really caught on. After the Second World War, the Caterpillar Corporation used Ogden's principles to develop a simplified English which could be used in its maintenance manuals worldwide and taught to non-English-speaking technicians. Other international manufacturers produced similar versions. The basic approach is to:

- use a very restricted vocabulary;
- use a simplified grammar.

The biggest users today are the aircraft industries, where clear instructions can mean the difference between life and death.

Avoid clichés

Clichés are expressions which were once fresh and insightful, but have become stale through constant use. Some current phrases which have probably now gone 'past their sell-by date' include 'address the critical issues', 'action the problems', 'on a learning curve'.

Avoid piled-up nouns

Nouns are often 'piled up' so that it is difficult to disentangle the meaning, as in: 'staff induction emergency training procedures'. Apart from the difficulty of disentangling the meaning there is always the danger of ambiguity. In this example it is not clear whether we are dealing with emergency-training procedures (how to train people to deal with an emergency) or emergency training-procedures (how to organize the training if there is some sort of crisis).

Simplify the sentence structure

While there is no set formula for writing sentences in business English, simple straightforward structures make for easy reading. The most common structure is to start the sentence with the subject as in 'The company increased its profits by 25 per cent compared with the last financial year.'

A common alternative structure is an adverbial opening such as 'In the last financial year, the company increased its profits by 25 per cent.' Adverbial beginnings are particularly useful when you wish to link the sentence to something that has gone before, as in: 'However, unfavourable trading conditions may not continue after the first quarter.'

It requires considerable skill to structure long sentences. Modern word-processing software has built-in spelling and grammar checks which will identify 'poor' or over-long sentences. But these checks can give some strange results, as we illustrate in Box 8.6.

177

BOX 8.6 MICROSOFT MAY NOT KNOW WHAT YOU MEAN!

Table 8.3 gives six examples of corrections to sentences and phrases which are recommended by the grammar checker in Word 97 (set for British English) and which range from the unnecessary to the completely nonsensical.

This shows that you should approach these automatic devices with some caution. Often their recommendations are based on rather strict interpretation of grammatical rules, or on misinterpreting the context, or on slavish obedience to supposed 'good practice' (like avoiding the passive at all costs). There are also problems with different cultural norms – see Box 8.7.

Table 8.3 *Inappropriate corrections recommended by Word 97's grammar checker*

Original phrase or sentence	What Word 97 recommends	Comment
What's it like to live around here?	What's it *liked* to live around here?	The changed version no longer makes sense as a question.
The idea for the silicon chip was developed by two different research teams.	Two different research teams developed the idea for the silicon chip.	This changes the emphasis; it does not improve the clarity.
You are described by a colleague as the single most important figure in popular music.	A colleague as the single most important figure in popular music describes you.	The recommendation is gibberish!
[As part of feedback on a student essay] I would highlight the following as especially good.	I would highlight the following as especially *well*.	Our students would think we had started to suffer from stress if we accepted Word's recommendation.
Whether what you have learned matches the type of opportunity you are applying for.	Whether what you have *taught* matches the type of opportunity you are applying for.	This change completely alters the meaning of the original phrase – which was advice to interviewees about what they should emphasize in interview answers.
First the journalist would type up his or her notes; then these notes would be typed up by a compositor on a Linotype machine to create the lines of lead type.	First the journalist would type up his or her notes; then a compositor on a Linotype machine to create the lines of lead type would type these notes up.	To avoid the passive, Word produces a very tortuous sentence.

Use the appropriate balance of active and passive sentences

There is a common misconception that the passive form is the 'preferred' business style for official documents. However, active sentences are usually preferred in Plain English. In practice you need a judicious *mix* of active and passive.

The criterion for choice between active and passive should be emphasis. Consider the following sentences:

1   *The company* gave each employee a bonus.
2   *Each employee* was given a bonus by the company.

In 1 the emphasis is on 'the company'; in 2 the emphasis is on 'each employee'. Both sentences are perfectly clear. Your choice depends on whether you wish to emphasize 'the company' or 'each employee'.

Use clear and simple punctuation

Punctuation is important: it can change the meaning or emphasis within a sentence: 'Punctuation marks are an integral part of the code on which written communication is based' (Kirkman, 1992, p. 81).

Consider the difference between these two simple examples:

1   Insert the ID card into the slot, with the label on the top right.
2   Insert the ID card into the slot with the label on the top right.

In 1 the punctuation tells you that the label is part of the ID card; in 2 the punctuation tells you that the label relates to the slot. In more complicated instructions, possible ambiguities of this sort could be very dangerous. You could punctuate the following to give very different meanings:

Send replacement mother board if the system fails again we will need to shut it down.

But how do we decide which punctuation to use and when to use it? Here the situation becomes more complicated. Different punctuation marks have different rules attached to them. For example 'There are simple, definite rules about the use of the full stop at the end of sentences. There are no equally simple rules for all the various uses of the comma' (Collinson *et al.*., 1992, p. 19). So how do we decide how to use the comma? Although guidebooks on English grammar offer extensive guidelines, they may not offer absolute rules:

Commas are in a no man's land of punctuation, where few routes are charted and mostly we have to find our own away. It was easier before World War Two, when commas could be used all over the place. But the style now is to use them as sparingly as possible, so there is more reason to hesitate before slipping one in.

(Howard, 1993, p. 87)

179

This highlights the importance of changes in taste and style. For example, the use of the comma in addresses and dates in business letters is now often ignored. Instead of '24, Acacia Drive, 24 March, 2001', we would write '24 Acacia Drive, 24 March 2001'.

There are several useful guides to modern punctuation (Kirkman, 1991; Trask, 1997). We would emphasize the following points:

- Make sure that you are familiar with the conventional uses of the main punctuation marks.
- Make sure that you are using these main punctuation marks consistently.
- Punctuation marks are very important signals to the reader about when to pause and which parts of the sentence go together.

One strategy is to use only a limited set of punctuation marks. We do not agree with some advice which suggests that you only really need to use the full stop and the comma. But we could write virtually every type of business document using only the punctuation marks discussed in one of the well-known British advice books, *The Economist Style Guide*. The 1996 edition offers advice on apostrophes, brackets, colons, commas, dashes, full stops, quotation marks, question marks and semi-colons (pp. 58–60) and a useful discussion of different uses in American and British English (pp. 85 and 86).

As additional help, most modern word processing packages offer some help. This chapter was prepared with Word 97, which:

- automatically puts a capital letter after every full stop – at the beginning of every sentence;
- highlights incorrect or unknown spellings;
- suggests when our sentences 'fail' its in-built grammar checker.

However, do not be tempted to rely too heavily on these automatic systems – they offer only very crude guidance which can be misleading (see Boxes 8.6 and 8.7). For example, I tested Word 97 by entering part of the quotation from Howard above. It was happy to accept the following with no punctuation: 'It was easier before World War Two when commas could be used all over the place but the style now is to use them as sparingly as possible so there is more reason to hesitate before slipping one in.'

READABILITY

There are several readability formulae which claim to predict how easy or difficult it is to read a particular text (see Hartley, 1994, p. 49–55). These usually combine some measure of sentence length with some measure of average word length. Rather than the more common Fog index, we shall use the Flesch formula as an example, as this is supplied as an automatic feature in word processors such as Word 97/2000.

BOX 8.7 WHY DOESN'T MY WORD PROCESSOR KNOW I'M BRITISH?

Another problem with computerized grammar checkers is that they may be insensitive to cultural variations. Word 97 continually criticizes us as we do not follow one of the rules laid down by one of the main *American* authorities on written style, *The Chicago Manual of Style*. According to this manual, you should use the word 'that' to introduce a restrictive clause and the word 'which' to introduce a non-restrictive clause. For example, the *Manual* approves of the following sentences:

1   The book that Nigel gave me was no good.
2   The book, which Nigel gave me, was no good.

In example 1, the clause is restrictive because I'm talking only about the specific book which Nigel gave me and not any of the other books which I own. In example 2, the clause is non-restrictive, as the fact that Nigel gave me the book is simply added as extra information – the clause is not used to identify which book we are talking about.

Native English-speakers often do not make this distinction, although it does crop up in some well-known guides to good English which are used in Britain. This is an interesting example of a stylistic rule which makes little or no difference to communication. This reinforces the point made by Deborah Cameron that 'statements about "good writing" are not self-evident truths about language but value judgements upon it'. Her book on popular attitudes towards language should be required reading for anyone who advises others how to write good English (Cameron, 1995).

The Flesch formula

You need to work out what Flesch called reading ease (RE).

$$RE = 206.835 - 0.846W - 1.015S$$

where
W = the average number of syllables per 100 words;
S = the average number of words per sentence.

The higher the RE score, the better. We used the Flesch scale on Box 8.2 (p. 172). This gave an RE of 49 with 20 per cent passive sentences, and a grade level of 10.9 (which roughly equates to the years of education you need to understand the text). This suggests that Box 8.2 is 'fairly difficult' – it would be understood by someone who is working at college level (but then that is a main target readership for this book).

EXERCISE

How would you adjust the text in Box 8.2 to increase readability? Which of your changes would make most impact?

Readability formulae can give a useful check – they can be used to revise texts to make them easier to understand. However, the results must be interpreted with caution as they ignore some critical points (Hartley, 1994):

- Some short sentences can be difficult to understand.
- Short technical abbreviations may be very difficult to understand.
- Some long words are very familiar (e.g. 'communication').
- The formulae ignore any graphics or visual aids which can help readers to understand.
- The formulae ignore the impact of any layout, such as headings and subheadings.
- The formulae ignore the readers' past experience and knowledge.
- The formulae ignore the readers' motivation.

James Hartley (1999) has also shown that you can increase the readability of text according to the scales, yet make it *more* difficult to understand. Our favourite example of a short text which would pass a readability test but which is difficult to understand is the following notice, stuck by the elevator doors in a large multi-storey American office block:

> Please
> Walk up one floor
> Walk down two floors
> To improve elevator service

If you take the notice at face value and walk up one floor, you discover the same notice by the elevator doors on the next floor (in fact, on every floor). The writer managed to construct a very tortuous way of advising users not to take the elevator for very short journeys! For more examples of this type of problem, see Chapanis (1988). Another of our favourites in the same vein is the following notice on a fence in the middle of a large national park in the UK:

> The land within is outside open land.

SUMMARY

- Business writing often fails to communicate because of poor expression.
- We need to evaluate our writing using both content and tone criteria, bearing in mind the demands of the situation.
- The Plain English movement has made a significant impact on official writing but we need to consider research studies which suggest that this approach is not as straightforward as might at first appear.
- 'Plain language' should be considered as a company strategy, remembering that this argues for an *appropriate* style of language and *not* the same simple style for every document. Also, it is not just about using the right words; we also need to examine organization and layout and consider the needs of users/audiences.
- We can use 'plain language' ideas to evaluate and improve our words and sentences.
- We should follow standard conventions on punctuation while remembering that the rules are both flexible and changing.
- Readability texts offer some useful information but should be interpreted cautiously.

DISCUSSION QUESTIONS

- If Plain English has been shown to be effective, why doesn't every organization use it?
- Can we always apply the five content criteria consistently? In other words, do they always point in the same direction?
- If we all interpret the world rather differently, how far can we agree on the tone of a written document?
- Are words as easy to categorize on the four scales as we imply?
- How can we define what counts as jargon?
- What rules of punctuation *must* we obey?
- Modern word processing software offers automatic grammar and readability checks. Do these help writers or add to their confusion?

FURTHER READING

Cameron, D. (1995) *Verbal Hygiene*. London: Routledge. This is an important book which should be read by everyone who is interested in how we make value judgements about the English language. It examines various attempts to prescribe 'correct language', ranging from debates over grammar to the linguistic practices in assertiveness training, which we discuss in Part four.

Cutts, M. (1995) *The Plain English Guide*. Oxford: Oxford University Press. This is probably the best British book to date which explains both the purposes and the techniques of Plain English.

Plain English Campaign (1993) *The Plain English Story*, 3rd revised edition. Stockport: Plain English Campaign. A very interesting account of the campaign's history and principles, with many useful examples.

Schriver, K.A. (1997) *Dynamics in Document Design: Creating Text for Readers*. New York: John Wiley. Perhaps the best general introduction to the general area of document design. Chapter 6 discusses how readers interpret words and pictures.

Turk, C. and Kirkman, J. (1989) *Effective Writing: Improving Scientific, Technical and Business Communication*, 2nd edition. London: E&F Spon. This book contains lots of useful examples and illustrations from scientific and engineering contexts as well as explaining many of the techniques introduced in this chapter.

Chapter 9

Effective design and visual aids

INTRODUCTION

It is worth emphasizing how quickly the process of producing business documents has changed. Back in the 1980s, many if not most business documents in large organizations were produced on electric or electronic typewriters. These offered very limited scope for page design and virtually no flexibility to use visual aids. The growth of the PC means that these limitations have gone for ever – and the decreasing cost of PCs and peripherals means this is true for even the smallest organizations.

Modern word processing software has copied many of the techniques and facilities which were first introduced when desktop publishing arrived on personal computers in 1985. As a result, we can use many of the fonts which used to be the exclusive property of professional typesetters; we can use clip art and graphics; and we can add a relatively inexpensive laser or inkjet printer to achieve near-professional print quality. Other software has also

OBJECTIVES

This chapter will:

- explain why effective design and layout is such an important part of effective business writing;
- review the main design features which we need to consider when we produce business documents;
- explain what business writers need to know about typography;
- show how page layout can be used to show the reader how the document is structured;
- analyse when and where you need to incorporate a visual aid into a business document;
- review main types of visual aids used in documents and highlight their principal advantages and disadvantages;
- show some of the dangers of using inappropriate visual aids and how you can avoid misrepresentation.

added many useful features. For example, all the graphs mentioned in this chapter can be produced from a spreadsheet table with a few mouse clicks.

Because of these changes, *all* business writers now need to understand basic principles of document design and need to know how to construct simple and effective visual aids – and these are the main themes of this chapter.

WHY IS EFFECTIVE DESIGN AND LAYOUT NOW SUCH AN IMPORTANT ASPECT OF EFFECTIVE WRITING?

Most general introductory texts on business communication discuss visual aids in some detail (e.g. Stanton, 1996). However this topic is sometimes ignored in more advanced texts (e.g. Baguley, 1994). This suggests that document design is seen as less advanced or less important – that it is a skill secondary to the effective use of language. Graphic designers offer the opposite view:

> Anyone looking at the printed message will be influenced, within a split second of making eye contact, by everything on the page: the arrangement of various elements as well as the individual look of each one. In other words, an overall impression is created in our mind before we even start reading the first word.
>
> (Spiekermann and Ginger, 1993, p. 37)

Psychological research supports the designers' view that the 'look' of a document influences how it is read (Hartley, 1994). But despite the importance of good design, many organizations have been content to treat the PC as 'just a typewriter' – a view which can be easily challenged (Williams, 1992). One example of this misguided approach is the way that many administrators are taught word processing in a way which simply reflects old typing conventions. But many old typing habits simply do not make sense when you are word processing. More seriously, the real advantages of word processing – using styles and templates – are treated as advanced features and ignored by many users. See Box 9.1 for a brief discussion of these problems.

MAIN DESIGN FEATURES OF BUSINESS DOCUMENTS

We think of newspapers and magazines as being professionally designed. Can we apply similar criteria to business documents? Every business document has a characteristic layout; this can range from the simple layout of an inter-office memo to that of a glossy multi-colour annual report from a large company. Only the latter may have received much attention from professional designers but all documents have been put together with some attention to their design. And design is important no matter how humble the document. A well-designed document has two main advantages over a poorly designed one:

- It makes a good impression on the reader by suggesting a professional and competent approach. So it can enhance the credibility of the person who prepared the document. In this way, it improves the chances of its message being accepted.
- The content or information is easier to understand.

BOX 9.1 THE PC IS NOT A TYPEWRITER

Some interesting habits which were part of traditional typing practice still survive in many organizations using modern word processing (Williams, 1992). For example, leaving two spaces after a full stop (period) makes sense on an old typewriter where all the characters take up the same amount of space (monospaced). The two spaces help to separate the sentences. But on a computer we now use typefaces where each character is proportionally spaced – for example, the letter 'i' takes up less space than the letter 'm'. So you do not need more than one space to separate sentences. There are other habits which seem to be a legacy of typing such as the use of underlining; professional printing avoids underlining and uses italics or bold for emphasis.

The most effective way to word-process is to take full advantage of its automatic features such as styles and templates. Yet these features are often discussed later in the manuals as if they were more advanced rather than part of the fundamental logic of the system. We have visited several large organizations where the administrative staff were unaware of styles and were formatting each new heading or subheading on its own – a complete waste of time, especially if someone later needs to change the overall format of the document. Changing the style characteristics of 'Heading1' takes a few seconds – every Heading 1 in the document will then change automatically. Changing every heading individually in a long document can take some time.

Conversely, poorly presented material can put the reader off and create a poor image. A simple example would be coursework assignments which students have to complete at college or university. A well-prepared word-processed assignment is likely to gain more marks than its handwritten equivalent not because the tutor is consciously awarding marks for presentation but because the word-processed assignment is easier and quicker to read and looks as if it has been carefully prepared. Conversely, the poorly word-processed assignment – no page numbers, no subheadings, poor-quality print, etc. – can lose marks because it gives the impression of having been 'knocked together' at the last minute. Memos and reports in business can create similar impressions on the reader, depending on the way these look.

There is now no excuse for poorly formatted documents. We can use modern word processing software to produce most of the characteristics of professional typesetting. As a result, readers have come to expect documents which satisfy the criteria used by graphic designers (Lichty, 1989):

- proportion – where all the elements of the page are clearly in proportion to each other;
- balance – where there is a clear sense of balance to the design of each page;
- contrast – where contrasting parts of the design are used to focus the reader's interest on the page;
- rhythm – where the reader's attention is drawn smoothly down the page without distraction;
- unity – where the various components of the page fit together to give a coherent impression.

EXERCISE

Analyse a report or other long document which circulates in your organization in terms of the design criteria listed above. Does the document look as though it has been designed with the reader in mind?

What business writers need to know about typography

With modern word processors, writers have a wide variety of typefaces at their disposal. Some writers have abused this facility and produced documents containing many different typefaces. The result is usually messy. For most purposes, two typefaces are sufficient. The choice of a typeface is largely subjective, but you need to consider the conventional image and likely impact of the chosen typefaces. We shall discuss some of the main types below. Also, see Box 9.2 for some further possible choices.

There are a few technical aspects of typefaces and page layout which are worth knowing so you can make sensible choices. You also have to understand some technical terms with rather odd names; much of the terminology has been carried forward from the days when printing was a mechanical process using letters made from 'hot metal'. We outline these terms below before returning to the issue of which type is 'best' for particular business documents.

Type families

Any single typeface can appear in different styles, which make up its 'family'. For example, Arial can appear as: Arial; **Arial Black;** Arial Narrow. A specific size and style of typeface is usually called a font, as in **'this font is 10 point Times New Roman Bold'**.

One important type style is italic. This is not a separate typeface but a right-sloping version of the basic font. It has several main uses:

- to *emphasize* a particular word or phrase;
- to show the name of a book, newspaper, magazine or film;
- to indicate a technical term or foreign word;
- to indicate a quotation.

Type size

Type size is usually measured in 'points', one point being approximately 1/72nd of an inch. However, this does *not* mean that different typefaces which are the same point size will look the same. The points measurement is taken from the top of a capital letter to the bottom of a lower case-letter which extends below the baseline. But when we look at a typeface we are more inclined to notice its 'x-height' – the distance from the baseline to the top of a lower case-letter such as x. The example below shows the difference between two fonts which have the same point size but different x-heights.

This is Times Roman in 12 point.
This is Arial in 12 point.

Despite these differences, we can make reasonable generalizations. Eleven point or 12 point is common for body text, with larger sizes usually used for headings. Eight point or 10 point is often used for less important information as well as the 'small print' which you are always advised to read before signing a document. Consider your audience before you finally decide on the type size. For an older audience it is worth avoiding small print completely.

Space between lines

The space between lines is called leading (pronounced 'ledding') after the old printing practice of putting extra slices of lead between lines of metal type to increase the spacing. It is measured in points, so that 10 on 12 point Times Roman means a 10 point font with 2 extra points of leading. A rough rule of thumb is to use leading which is about 20 per cent of the font size, and this is what word processing software tends to do as the default on body text.

> You can see the difference on this paragraph where we have put the leading back to zero. On the next paragraph, we have increased it to double the normal setting. Increasing the leading does not necessarily make the text easier to read beyond a certain point.

> You can see the difference on this paragraph where we have put the leading to double the normal setting. Increasing the leading does not necessarily make the text easier to read beyond a certain point.

Alignment

Most word processing systems allow you to align your printing on the left-hand side and/or the right-hand side of the paper. Traditionally, professionally typeset material has been aligned on both sides. On early word processors this usually left unsightly gaps between some words, as the control of the space between letters (letter spacing) was not very sophisticated (from a distance, you can see 'rivers' of white space winding down the page). Although this control of spacing has improved, we recommend that documents leave a ragged right margin, as there is some evidence that this improves readability (Hartley, 1994).

Categories of typefaces

There are literally thousands of different typefaces, so we need some system of classification. There are official systems such as the Vox system, which is recognized both as a British Standard and by the Association Typographique Internationale (McLean, 1980, pp. 58ff.).

This puts typefaces into eleven groups, categorized by their historical development and function. For practical everyday purposes, a simpler classification will do, and we use five main categories (after Spiekermann and Ginger, 1993, p. 50):

- Serif, where the endings of the letter shapes are decorated in a way which harks back to the way that letters were carved out of stone in Roman times (Sutton and Bartram, 1968). Famous examples of serif type are Times Roman, which was designed as a readable and economical typeface for the *Times* newspaper in London, and its computer equivalent Times New Roman, supplied with Microsoft Windows.
- Sans serif, where the letters are without (sans) serifs. Examples include Helvetica and Arial.
- Script, where the typeface imitates the letterforms of handwriting.
- Display, where the typeface has been designed for use in displays such as advertising or posters.
- Symbols, where the alphabet is replaced by symbols. For example, the phrase 'I like zebras' would print in the typeface Wingdings as '☜ ●✠&🖐ⅢⅢ 🌢Ⅲ♌☐♋✦'. As an example of the practical application of fonts like Wingdings, we have often used the 'r' symbol when we have created a letter or form which needed a tick box. You can resize the symbols in exactly the same way you can resize conventional letters: compare 12 point – ☐ – with the same symbol in 16 point – ☐.

And which typeface is best?

It is almost impossible to say what the 'best' typeface is, although there is a conventional view that you use serif typefaces for body text and sans serif for headings. Many graphic designers have very definite views. For example, McLean states that one of the 'rules' of legibility for continuous reading is that 'Sans-serif type is intrinsically less legible than seriffed type' (1980, p. 44). The superiority of serif type for body text is often presented as 'fact' in this way, and yet researchers are not so sure: 'the available research really gives no clear guidance on this issue' (Hartley, 1994, p. 29).

Many organizations have now adopted sans serif typefaces as standard and do not seem to have suffered as a result. This suggests that people do get used to a particular typeface over time and that any intrinsic advantages or disadvantages may be less important than designers have argued. We suggest that the choice of typeface should depend on a number of factors:

- the purpose of the document;
- what the readers are used to and what they might expect;
- how the document might be used. For example, some fonts do not stand up to repeated copying or faxing as some of the letter shapes are too thin.

EXERCISE

What are the standard typefaces used in the documents in an organization you are familiar with? How were they chosen? Are there any particular advantages or disadvantages to these typefaces? For example, how clearly do they photocopy?

BOX 9.2 TYPEFACES IN ACTION

Below we give some examples of typefaces which are readily available on your PC or Apple Mac. Which would you use in a business report?

This short paragraph is written in 12 point Times New Roman, a typeface which is often used in business as it is so widely available. It is the default font in Microsoft Word. As a serif font which was designed for body text in columns (originally for newspapers), you can argue that it is 'readable' as body text. But does it give an 'old-fashioned' impression?

This short paragraph is written in 12 point Arial, a typeface with short ascenders and descenders which means lines can be placed close together and which was originally designed for email. It is increasingly used in business as it is so widely available. It is a sans serif font and so you can argue whether it is 'readable' as body text. But it will photocopy well and looks 'modern'.

This short paragraph is written in 12 point Garamond, a typeface which is often used in books. It is also a serif font and so you can argue that it is 'readable' as body text. It appears 'thinner' and 'fainter' than Times New Roman so may well not photocopy as clearly. But what impression does it convey? There are also several different versions of Garamond with different x-heights for the same point size.

This short paragraph is written in 12 point Verdana, a typeface which is often recommended for body text on Web sites. It is also a sans serif font and so you can argue whether it is 'readable' as body text. It 'works' on screen where the resolution is poor, but what impression does it convey on paper?

Page layout and document structure

Chapter 7 emphasized the important of clear structure. As we know that appropriate spacing can increase the clarity of text (Hartley, 1994), we should make sure that the document design and page layout emphasize the structure of the document. This can be done in a number of ways.

Clear numbering

The decimal numbering system is popular because it provides an easily identifiable hierarchy of headings:

1	Main heading
1.1	Subheading
1.1.1	Sub-subheading

There is obviously no limit to the degree of subdivision, but beware of using more than three levels for most business documents. Excessive numbering and subdivision can create a fragmented and difficult-to-read document.

It is also possible to use space on the page to further emphasize the hierarchy of headings, as below. We have mixed opinions on this as it can use up a lot of space.

1 Main heading in 14 point Arial bold

The text under the main heading is in 12 point Times New Roman and will be set out like this on the page so that it lines up ...

1.1 Subheading in 12 point Arial italic bold

The text under the sub-heading is in 12 point Times New Roman and will be set out like this on the page so that it lines up ...

1.1.1 Sub-subheading in 12 point Times New Roman bold

The text under the sub-subheading is in 12 point Times New Roman and will be set out like this on the page so that it lines up ...

Table 9.1 shows how the three levels of heading have been formatted in this book. It illustrates how:

- different typefaces can distinguish main headings from body text;
- spacing can be used to emphasize the hierarchy of headings and subheadings.

Although these applications of spacing and numbering may seem fairly obvious, they are often ignored or not understood. For example, most undergraduate students nowadays are fairly experienced in word processing. But, when asked to use space and typographic cues

Table 9.1 *Levels of heading in this book*

	Typeface	*Size*	*Characters*	*Spacing*
Heading 1	Bell Gothic	11 pt	Bold caps	Before 24 pt After 12 pt
Heading 2	Bell Gothic	9 pt	Bold	Before 24 pt After 12 pt
Heading 3	Bell Gothic	11 pt	Italic	Before 24 pt After 12 pt
Body text	Perpetua	11 pt	Normal	Standard line spacing

EXERCISE

Refer to the article on text layout by J. Hartley (1999) and reorganize the short text given at the top of p. 347 before you read the rest of the article. How many layout cues did you use? Was your use of these cues consistent?

to improve the readability of a short text, psychology undergraduates were often inconsistent or failed to use the variety of cues (J. Hartley, 1999).

Using lists

Lists are a simple way of presenting information to make it more readable. For example, sometimes a sentence becomes long because a number of items are governed by the main verb, e.g.

> When leaving at the end of the day make sure that: all the windows are closed; the back and side doors are locked; the burglar alarms are set; and all the lights are switched off, except the one at the front door.

This sentence can be made more readable just by listing the items:

> When leaving at the end of the day make sure that:
> - all windows are closed;
> - the back and side doors are locked;
> - the burglar alarms are set;
> - all lights are switched off, except the one at the front door.

You can also change the style:

> When you leave at the end of the day, make sure that you:
> - close all the windows;

193

- lock the back and side doors;
- set the burglar alarms;
- switch off all the lights, except the one at the front door.

Page grids

A good page layout can also contribute to ease of reading: 'All documents stand to benefit from the use of a grid . . . [which] . . . guarantees consistency throughout the document, identifies margins, and determines the orderly placement of columns and illustrations on the page' (Lichty, 1989, p. 99). In other words, you need to have a plan for your page design which shows where you are going to set your margins, how wide your columns will be, page numbering, use of white space on the page, and so on. For example, Box 9.3 shows the grid we used for the page design in this book.

Of course, your word processor will provide default settings for all these features.

For correspondence, a common practice is to use 25 mm for the side margins and 35-40 mm for top and bottom margins. You need to decide whether these settings create the effect you want.

EXERCISE

Compare a range of documents from companies in terms of their page layout and design. Are there any grids which seem to be particularly effective or appropriate? Could you use these formats in everyday documents?

Use of colour and texture

Colour and texture can be used to enhance the appearance of a document, but of course they make it more expensive. If you produce diagrams or charts in colour, then you also have to consider whether anyone will want to photocopy the pages. At the moment, colour photocopiers are too expensive for many organizations.

There are also a number of practical considerations which need to be reviewed before deciding on the format for a document which will be widely distributed, including:

- *Type of binding*. This can range from simple stapling to expensive book-type bindings, which often include covers.
- *Folding and packaging*. Frequently, documents require folding before they are packaged, so it is often advisable to design the document round the folds. For example, an A4 sheet, when folded into three, fits into a standard 220 mm × 110 mm envelope. By designing the document to fit into three or six panels, you can produce an attractive document with increased text.

BOX 9.3 EXAMPLE OF A DESIGN GRID

The diagram below shows the grid which was used to prepare this book:

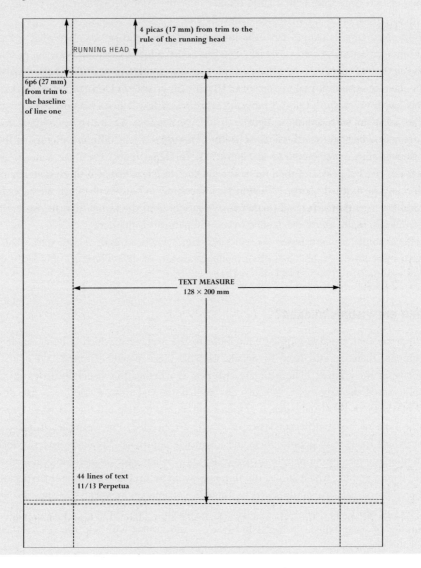

4 picas (17 mm) from trim to the rule of the running head

RUNNING HEAD

6p6 (27 mm) from trim to the baseline of line one

TEXT MEASURE
128 × 200 mm

44 lines of text
11/13 Perpetua

INCORPORATING A VISUAL AID INTO A BUSINESS DOCUMENT

One of the most respected academic writers on the presentation of statistical evidence and information design, Edward R. Tufte, argues that good graphics should '*reveal* data' (1983, p. 13). We extend this idea to all the visual aids which you might use in a business document. They should not simply display data, but should *reveal* its importance and meaning. They should present an argument which supports the argument being expressed in the text. Unfortunately, many visual aids in business documents fail to do this, either because they

195

have been put in simply to make the document look 'attractive' or because the writer has not really worked out what the data means.

For example, consider Table 9.2, a simple set of business data which gives the sales and profits of two departments in a large retailer over the same period of time. Before reading on, make a few notes on what this data tells you.

Both departments overall have the same overall sales and profits, but what is the relationship between these two variables? You can notice a lot of variation between periods and between the two departments. For example, we can see that in period 9, both departments made the same profit but sales were over 10 per cent greater in Department A. Both departments had low sales in period 8 but sales were much lower in Department A.

But what do we want these figures to tell us? Suppose we construct a graph for each department which shows sales against profits. This gives a very different picture of the relationship in each department, as in Figure 9.1. In Department A we see a steady growth until sales reach a peak and then there is a decline. In Department B there is steady growth with one very unusual quarter. Obviously, interesting and different things are happening in these departments which need further investigation. And the initial format of presenting a table did not really allow the reader to see the pattern in the data.

This example was not based on real sales data – we used part of data sets which Tufte uses to show how a graphic can often highlight aspects of data which are not easily spotted in the raw figures (Tufte, 1983, pp. 13–14).

When are visuals needed?

If we argue that visual aids must contribute to the argument which is being made in the document, then we still have to decide *when* they are worth inserting. Of course, this depends on the context. The ultimate criterion is whether the visual aid helps the reader to understand the argument. We use one tool borrowed from Eric Meyer. He discusses how newspapers use visuals such as graphics and photos to help tell their stories. Depending on the type of story, different types of visuals are needed. For example, if it is a 'who' story which focuses on people, then you might use photos or 'breakout boxes' which give potted biographies of the people involved. If it is a 'when' story which looks at events over time, then a graphic which shows the timeline could be useful. The different types of story and possible visuals are summarized in Table 9.3 (based on Meyer, 1997, pp. 36–38).

You can apply the same logic to business documents. For example, a report might cover a number of these types – what? why? how? – and visuals will help the reader to understand the material.

Another important point from Meyer is that graphics should be *organized* to make a point. He argues that all graphics should employ the 'inverted pyramid' form, which is the classical form of newspaper narrative; you express the most important point first, then the second most important, and so on. Translating this idea to graphics, he recommends a three-step strategy for design:

- Start with the main point and make sure this is 'loud and clear'.
- Go to the secondary point.
- Offer supporting details.

196

Table 9.2 Sales data

Period	Department A		Department B	
	Sales	Profits	Sales	Profits
1	914	100	746	100
2	814	80	677	80
3	874	130	1,274	130
4	877	90	711	90
5	926	110	781	110
6	810	140	884	140
7	613	60	608	60
8	310	40	539	40
9	913	120	815	120
10	726	70	642	70
11	474	50	573	50
Totals	8,251	990	8,250	990

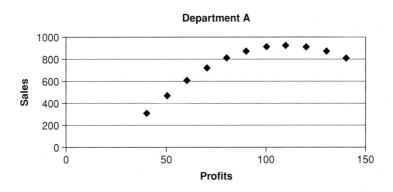

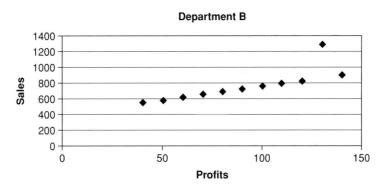

Figure 9.1 Comparing sales and profits in Departments A and B

197

Table 9.3 *Matching story to visuals*

Story type	Focus	Useful visuals
Who?	People	Illustrations of the people involved
What?	Particular agreement or plan	Graphic of the main points of the plan
When?	Chain of events, or schedule	Some sort of timeline
Where?	Place	Map or diagram of the location
Why?	Pros and cons of a particular position or argument	Table or chart which summarizes and contrasts the pros and cons
How?	How things work or happen	Graphics, photos or diagrams which show the process

If details do not support the main point, they should be omitted (Meyer, 1997, ch. 3). We shall return to this point later when we look at some visual aids in action.

THE MAIN VISUAL AIDS AND HOW THEY WORK

You can use a wide range of visual aids in business documents and you need to be aware of their main advantages and disadvantages. There are three main types, which we have summarized in Table 9.4.

Even this division is not entirely watertight, as a map is both pictorial and schematic.

Table 9.4 *Forms of visual aid*

Type	Includes:	Main advantages	Main disadvantages
Visual representations of numerical data	Tables, charts and graphs	■ Can summarize a lot of data very effectively ■ Can show trends	■ Audience must have sufficient technical knowledge to interpret them
Schematic presentations	Diagrams, signs, flow charts, organization charts, algorithms	■ Can convey information more efficiently than text	■ May rely on implicit knowledge which audience may not share
Pictorial presentations	Drawings, photographs, artistic illustrations, maps	■ Realistic representations	■ Can be expensive to produce

Visual representations of numerical data

If you have to present numerical data, then you have to decide whether to represent it in tables, charts and/or graphs. As we shall see, all the methods have potential disadvantages.

Tables

Readers find difficulty in absorbing numerical information when it is embedded in a sentence. It is often better to use a small table. Consider the following:

> Comparing the 1989 and 1990 results it can be seen that while sales of electrical appliances increased by 20 per cent from 2.5 million to 3 million, furniture sales only increased by 10 per cent from 3 million to 3.3 million.

This can be rewritten as a simple table:

> The figures show that electrical appliances increased their sales much better than furniture:

	1989 Sales (in millions)	1990 Sales	Percentage increase
Electrical goods	2.5	3	20
Furniture	3	3.3	10

The formatting feature in word-processing software means that you do not have to leave this as a simple set of boxes. Using Word 97, you can present it as follows:

	1989 Sales (in millions)	1990 Sales	Percentage increase
Electrical goods	2.5	3	20
Furniture	3	3.3	10

As with all such automatic features, you should ensure that the formatting does not interfere with or detract from the main point you are trying to put across. You also need to consider how readers might use the document. Some of the formats offered for tables in packages such as Microsoft Word do not photocopy very clearly.

Tables like the one above are intended to be read as part of the text. They usually obey the following conventions:

- They present a limited amount of numerical information.
- They are not identified by a table number and often do not have a title.
- They are not listed in the table of contents.
- They form part of the text and must not be moved for typographical convenience.

Formal tables

It is better to use formal tables for more extensive datasets, as these can substantially stand alone. This is necessary because it is not always possible to insert tables exactly where they are first mentioned.

An effective formal table has the following characteristics:

- It appears in the text in a convenient position after its first mention in the text.
- It has an identifying number.
- It has a clear and informative title.
- The data is arranged in some rational order.
- Columns should have clear descriptive headings.
- Where appropriate, the units of measurement should be stated.
- Important data should be emphasized by its position in the table.

Unfortunately, many complex formal tables you will find in business documents are not well organized. Some of the most powerful criticisms of the way tables are used come from Ehrenberg (1977), who offers the following four principles for presenting data in tables:

- Round off numbers so that readers can make comparisons quickly and easily.
- Include averages for each set of data so that readers can quickly work out the spread of values.
- Organize your table so that the reader compares the columns. Figures in columns are easier to compare than figures in rows.
- Order rows in columns by size with larger numbers placed at the top. Again this helps the reader compare the data.

See Box 9.4 for a worked example to illustrate these principles.

Charts and graphs

Modern spreadsheet software will allow you to convert a spreadsheet table into a chart or graph. But we can choose from an enormous variety of graphs, as the following list shows:

- line graphs;
- scatter diagrams;
- bar charts;
- pie charts (area graphs);
- histograms;
- frequency polygons;
- cumulative frequency curves.

Which type is the best to use in a given circumstance? We do not have space in this book to offer a comprehensive comparison of them all, but we can bring out the main issues by

BOX 9.4 USING EHRENBERG'S PRINCIPLES FOR PRESENTING DATA IN TABLES

Consider the following table, which compares the composition of the workforce in the ABC Corporation over the past few decades. All figures are in thousands employed:

	1970	1980	1990	2000
Total	201.66	342.54	410.44	567.21
Males	150.64	278.50	323.22	441.16
Females	51.02	64.04	87.22	126.05

After revising the table using Ehrenberg's principles, it is much easier to see possible patterns in the data.

	Males	Females	Total
2000	441	126	567
1990	323	87	410
1980	278	64	342
1970	151	51	202
Average	298	82	380

Of course, we always need to question the purpose of a table like this. If the real purpose is to investigate whether there is any gender bias in ABC's employment practices, then this should be the focus of the table:

	Total	Females	Females as percentage of workforce
2000	567	126	22
1990	410	87	21
1980	342	64	19
1970	202	51	25
Average	380	82	22

contrasting some of the main types (for further discussion and examples, see Mort, 1992, ch. 10). For example, suppose that you need to present sales data which shows that a particular initiative has reversed a decline. Would you use the line graph in Figure 9.2 or the bar chart in Figure 9.3? We would suggest that the line graph is a more immediate visual demonstration of the trend, especially if you label the main point, as in Figure 9.4.

EVALUATING THE EFFECTIVENESS AND APPROPRIATENESS OF VISUAL AIDS

Graphic messages can be evaluated in terms of certain criteria, just as messages in written communication are evaluated: for content and tone. It is also worth emphasizing the importance of a clear purpose and making sure that the audience will be able to interpret the visual aid in the way you intend.

Checking the audience

You need to consider your audience's background whenever you choose a visual aid. For example, one important study found that information presented in a table was preferred by readers with a strong technical background whereas less technical readers found a flow chart better for the same information (Wright and Reid, 1974). Unfortunately, we do not think that graphic literacy is as widely taught in our education systems as it should be, so, for most audiences, the simpler and more pictorial the device the better. Of course, many professions such as engineering, economics and architecture do have their own graphic languages and conventions, which can be used where appropriate.

In general, you have more information available than can be used in the visual aid, so the selection and processing of information is essential. Where the information is numerical, you need to use a form which matches the purpose and the needs of the audience. You can then decide the content of the message using the content criteria we have already discussed in this book:

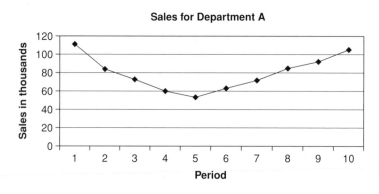

Figure 9.2 *Example of line graph*

- accuracy;
- brevity;
- clarity;
- emphasis.

Choosing the graphic

Once the audience analysis has been done, you should have a reasonably clear idea of the most suitable visual aid. You should then experiment with the following factors:

- type (e.g. horizontal or vertical bar charts);
- scale (this can affect the emphasis);
- complexity (there is a trade-off between detail, and accuracy and clarity);
- use of colour (certain colours are conventionally associated with certain attitudes and emotions but beware of any cultural differences that may affect your audience).

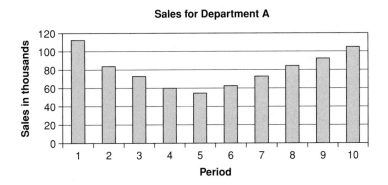

Figure 9.3 *Example of bar chart*

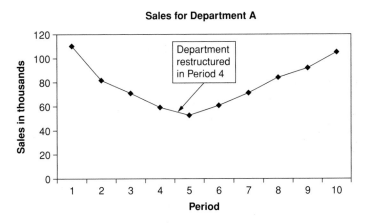

Figure 9.4 *Line graph with label to suggest the important conclusion*

203

You should also check whether the size of the graphic may be reduced to fit column or page sizes. If so, make sure your graphic can be reduced without loss of clarity.

Tone

Graphic devices do not offer the same opportunity for tonal variation as written material. However, you need to consider the appropiateness of graphic material and the extent to which attitudes can be expressed in graphics.

Graphics which treat any part of the audience without respect for their essential human dignity are unacceptable. This is particularly the case where humour is used to make a point.

BOX 9.5 PRACTICAL GUIDELINES FOR PRODUCING GRAPHICS

If you intend to produce your own graphics, the following are some practical guidelines.

- Keep the graph simple. Bear in mind the purpose and the audience; provide no more detail than your purpose requires and your audience needs.
- Place captions either above or below the graph, but be consistent throughout the document or presentation.
- Without being long-winded, ensure that your caption accurately reflects the contents of the graphic. Phrases like 'Graph of . . . ' or 'Diagram of . . . ' are unnecessary as this should be apparent. An explanatory note below the title can help the reader.
- See that your graph has some logic behind its presentation, e.g. largest to smallest, most important to least important, by provinces, or by time sequence. Use the ordering of information to emphasize the point you wish to make.
- Make the illustration attractive. It should provide a welcome break from the written word and not be a distraction or puzzle.
- Use specific devices to help your reader and to emphasize important points. Examples of such devices include: colour, arrows, heavy lines, distinctive plotting points, annotation and keys.
- Avoid bias in presenting information. This will be discussed in more detail later.
- Make sure that axes are clearly labelled and that units are unambiguous and consistent.
- Wherever possible, use horizontal labelling in preference to vertical labelling.
- Where possible, label line graphs directly rather than using a key, but do use a key if the graph becomes cluttered.
- Do not place a graphic before its first reference in the text, but place it as soon as practicable thereafter.
- Do not repeat information from graphs in the text but rather use the text for comment, explanation or interpretation.
- For scales, use multiples or submultiples of 2, 5 or 10.

A more subtle form of incorrect attitude to audience is stereotyping, for example where supervisors are always portrayed as white and workers as black.

AVOIDING BIAS AND MISREPRESENTATION IN VISUAL AIDS

Graphic devices can be used to deceive. Sometimes the line between honest emphasis and deceit is not always clear. In the final analysis, the author's or the professional illustrator's professional integrity is the best guide. The following are some of the methods that can, intentionally or unintentionally, deceive an audience.

Suppressing the zero

The zero on a graph is sometimes suppressed to save space or to emphasize a small but significant change. Note that in Figure 9.5 there is no indication on the graph that the zero has been suppressed. The graph suggests that sales are rising much more steeply than if the full range was included, as in Figure 9.6.

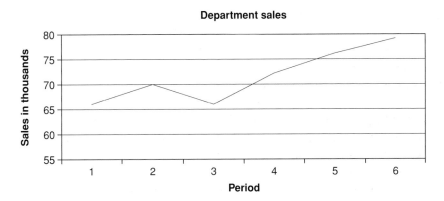

Figure 9.5 *Line graph with suppressed zero. The effect is to exaggerate the change*

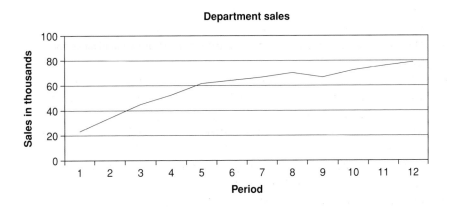

Figure 9.6 *Line graph without suppressed zero*

Mixing the scales

Often two- or three-dimensional presentations are used in pictographs, but the scale used is linear. Spreadsheets like Microsoft Excel offer you a range of 3D presentations but this can lead to distortion. The data in Figure 9.7 is turned into three-dimensional cylinders in Figure 9.8 to suggest that the difference between sales is much bigger than it actually is. Tufte suggests that you can quantify the distortion by working out what he calls the 'lie factor', which is:

$$\frac{\text{Size of effect shown in graphic}}{\text{Size of effect in data}}$$

This formula is take from Tufte (1983, ch. 2), which also contains many other examples of distorted graphics.

Unjustified line-fitting

Where the data shows a considerable scatter there is a temptation to fit a line or curve which supports the particular hypothesis favoured by the author. Even where sophisticated curve-

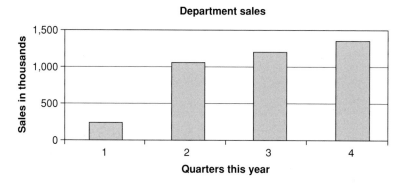

Figure 9.7 *Sales data expressed as bar chart*

Figure 9.8 *Sales data in 3D cylinders. The effect is to exaggerate the differences*

fitting methods are used, the result will not necessarily represent the best interpretation of the data. Ideally, any relationship derived from the data should be used as the basis for planning and testing further observations. This is, however, not always possible. Figure 9.9 shows that attempts can be made to fit both a straight line (AB) and a curve (CD) to the data.

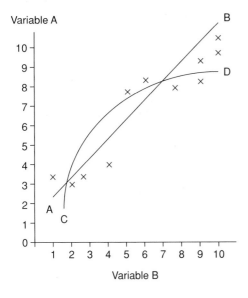

Figure 9.9 *Fitting a line*

SUMMARY

- Psychological research supports designers' views that the 'look' of a document influences how it is read. But despite the importance of good design, many organizations have been content to treat the PC as 'just a typewriter'.
- A well-designed document has two main advantages: it makes a good impression on the reader by suggesting a professional and competent approach, and it makes the content or information easier to understand.
- Writers should consider basic technical aspects of typefaces and page layout so they can make sensible design choices, such as using page layout to emphasize the structure of the document.
- Good visual aids should *reveal* data. It is important to highlight the main points you wish to make in whatever form of visual aid you decide to use.
- There are three main types of visual aids you can use in documents: visual representations of numerical data, including tables, charts and graphs; schematic presentations such as diagrams, flow charts, etc.; and pictorial presentations such as photographs. Although computer technology has made these easier to produce, there are still cost and production issues. These need to be weighed against the advantages.
- Graphic devices can be used to deceive. You must recognize the potential for misrepresentation and avoid it in your own documents.

DISCUSSION QUESTIONS

- How does your organization decide on the 'look' of its documents? Does it follow (or even consider) sound design principles?
- Review a sample of the documents your organization produces. What impressions do they make? Does the design make the content or information easy to understand?
- What technical aspects of typefaces and page layout do you really need to worry about? Cannot we just rely on the templates provided in word processors?
- Which of the main types of visual aids are the 'best' to use in business documents?
- Will advances in computer technology mean further dramatic changes in the layout of business documents (e.g. digital cameras, scanners, etc.)? What changes are most likely? Will these changes help us communicate?
- We have argued that you need to emphasize main points in visual aids but also avoid misrepresentation. Is there a conflict here?

FURTHER READING

Harris, L.H. (1996) *Information Graphics: A Comprehensive Illustrated Reference*. Atlanta, GA: Management Graphics.

Hartley, J. (1994) *Designing Instructional Text*, 3rd edition. London: Kogan Page. Although this focuses on instructional text, it offers a very comprehensive survey of research, and practical advice on document layout and design.

Meyer, E.K. (1997) *Designing Infographics*. Indianapolis, IN: Hayden. This and the book by Harris are both useful sources on the best ways to present information through graphics.

Spiekermann, E. and Ginger, E.M. (1993) *Stop Stealing Sheep and Find Out how Type Works*. Mountain View, CA: Adobe Press. Reviews the main characteristics, the design features and 'usability' of typefaces from a designer's perspective.

Tufte, E.R. (1983) *The Visual Display of Quantitative Information*, Cheshire, CT: Graphics Press.

Tufte, E.R. (1990) *Envisioning Information*, Cheshire, CT: Graphics Press. Both books by Tufte have become recognized as classic contributions to the debate on the impact of visual presentation.

Williams, R. (1992) *The PC Is Not a Typewriter*. Berkeley, CA: Peachpit Press. Although this is now dated as regards some of the technical references, it makes the important argument that we should approach the PC as word processor and 'page designer'.

Chapter 10

Effective business documents

INTRODUCTION

This chapter applies principles from the previous three chapters to common business documents, ranging from the informal to the official and from the individual to the corporate: memos and notes; letters; reports; email and fax; Web sites and Web pages; and finally, CVs and applications.

Principles of structure, style and design are summarized at the beginning of the chapter. If you want to read only about particular documents rather than the whole chapter, we recommend that you read this summary first.

We also highlight general issues, such as the impact of change. For example, email has been described as a 'new form' of communication as it seems to mix characteristics of both spoken and written language. But is this true and, if so, what are the consequences?

OBJECTIVES

This chapter will:

- summarize main principles which we need to consider when preparing any type of business document;
- review typical characteristics of the main forms of business documents, using these principles;
- raise important issues about the changing nature of business documents, including the importance of new forms of communication.

SUMMARY OF GENERAL PRINCIPLES

There are general principles to consider when preparing *all* business documents. We summarize these using main points from Chapters 7–9.

Planning and structure

- It is important to develop plans and objectives. This does not mean that you have to write in a rigid sequence of steps.
- Clear objectives are important in planning. Phrasing your objectives in a particular way can help you decide what information you need to provide.
- You must consider the particular needs of your audience when you decide your objectives.
- If we can present information which is clearly organized *and* organized in a way which makes sense to the audience, then that audience will find the information easier to understand and remember.
- There are various ways of structuring information in written documents. They use three basic principles: chunking, ordering and signposting.
- The structure of your document should support your objectives.

Style

- Business writing often fails to communicate because of poor expression. We need to evaluate writing using both content and tone criteria.
- 'Plain language' should be considered as a company strategy, remembering that this argues for an *appropriate* style of language and *not* the same simple style for every document. We can use plain language ideas to evaluate and improve our words and sentences.
- We should follow standard conventions on punctuation while remembering that the rules are both flexible and changing

Layout and visual aids

- The 'look' of a document influences how it is read.
- A well-designed document has two main advantages: it makes a good impression on the reader by suggesting a professional and competent approach, and it makes the content or information easier to understand.
- Writers should understand basic aspects of typefaces and page layout, and use them to make sensible design choices.
- Good visual aids should *reveal* data. It is important to highlight the main points you wish to make.
- Different types of visual aid have important advantages and disadvantages.
- Graphic devices can be used to deceive. You should avoid misrepresentation in your documents.

There are other general issues:

You are the organization!

Whenever you write to another person, you are representing your organization or your part of it. If you create a poor impression, then the organization suffers.

Format, image and house style

Business stationery projects your image. Large organizations usually employ professional designers to design their corporate stationery. Although the current trend is towards simple stationery, you may have to work within a certain format dictated by the house style.

Legal and statutory requirements

There are certain legal requirements, which obviously vary from country to country. For example, in South Africa, letters *must* carry the company's registration number and the names of its directors. The following list covers most requirements:

- name of organization;
- postal address;
- registration number;
- telephone, fax number, email and/or Web address;
- organization's logo;
- date;
- reference numbers.

How this information appears depends on the image that the organization is trying to project.

Document designs reflect organizational structures and culture

Susan Katz suggests that 'every organization, and every department within an organization has its own conception of what makes "good writing"' (1998, p. 109). She found that some managers very carefully coached new staff in their writing, explaining the importance and purpose of documents, providing models of good practice, and commenting on drafts and outlines.

As we saw in Jim Suchan's study of report formats (Box 8.4, p. 175), changing the design of documents may also change relationships between staff and their perceptions of their roles. So we cannot assume that making documents easier to read and understand will automatically make the organization more effective.

MEMOS AND NOTES

In every business, you need to take messages. If they are badly recorded, then this leads to irritation or frustration and, sometimes, commercial loss. For example, cryptic messages on small scraps of paper can easily be overlooked, mislaid or misunderstood. The advent of the Post-It note may have helped here, as they are very visible and flexible. But they can still be easily overlooked. So organizations need suitable stationery and should ensure that staff are competent in message-taking.

Structure and layout

A well-designed form – A5 is a common and appropriate size – prompts the message-taker to record all the necessary information. The important step is deciding the printed subheadings so that the right information is recorded, for example:

- Date;
- Time;
- Message for;
- Message from (Name, Organization, Tel. No., Email);
- Message title (subject or topic);
- Message;
- Action required;
- Taken by (useful on a telephone message form).

Even if your organization does not use printed forms, this structure is useful as it makes sure you include important details.

Chunking the message

If the message is more than a simple few lines, then you also need to consider how best to chunk it (as discussed in Chapter 7). For example, Thomas Clark (1998) asks his students to draft business memos using these headings:

- Objectives;
- Background;
- Findings;
- Issues;
- Action steps.

He then suggests that they use a matrix, as in Figure 10.1, so that they can check the relationships between the components. For example, do the findings relate clearly to the objectives? Do the action steps follow from the findings? The advantage of this system is that you can easily check whether your memo is logically coherent.

Style

You obviously do not need some of the formalities of business letters, such as the salutation or complimentary close, but how informal can you be? There is no single answer here – the formality expected in memos differs between organizations. For example, consider the differences in tone in the following two examples. The first is a request for information; the second is a response:

Objectives	Findings	Actions
1.	1.	1.
	2.	2.
2.	1.	
	2.	
Background		Issues

Figure 10.1 *The memo matrix*

Example A

MEMORANDUM
To Dave Smith
From Ian Williams
Date 11 June

STAFF TURNOVER
I am sorry to give you an extra task at this busy time. Before my meeting with the Head of Human Resources on 20 June, I need the staff turnover figures for the last three financial years. Please let me have these by the 15th.

Example B

MEMORANDUM
To: General Manager
From: Manager of Human Resources
Date: 13 June

Subject: STAFF TURNOVER FIGURES 1987-89

Financial year	Number of staff leaving	Staff leaving as % of total
97/98	182	22
98/99	212	25
99/00	240	27

There are differences in these memos which might indicate differences in the organizational culture and communication up and down the hierarchy:

- the use of names (and first names) in A as opposed to titles in B;
- the show of politeness in A ('I am sorry . . . ' and 'Please'), whereas these are completely absent in B;
- the lack of explanation in A of why the figures are needed.

We cannot decide what these differences mean without knowing more about the context. For example, did the writer in B leave out any comments so that the memo could be easily photocopied for the meeting? Or was he/she simply too busy to give anything other than a straight answer? Or was he/she annoyed by the request and determined to supply the minimum answer? The figures are not very detailed – would not the reader want some further breakdown by staff category?

EXERCISE

Find some memos which have circulated in your organization. How would you describe their tone? Compare them with your analysis of the two memos above: under what circumstances would a certain tone be inappropriate or damaging?

Importance?

The memo also provides an example of how technology is changing the way we communicate. In textbooks produced in the 1990s, the memo was described as 'a' or 'the' main method of written communication (for example, in Baguley, 1994, and Stanton, 1996). Nowadays, in many organizations, memos have been virtually replaced by emails. Both the examples above could easily be sent by email, and this is part of the changing form of business correspondence which we highlight in Box 10.1.

LETTERS

The writing of business letters has a long history. Their main advantage is that they provide a permanent record of what is said. On the other hand, letters are expensive, they have to be composed with care, and feedback may be slow or non-existent. For these reasons, it is important to question whether a letter is appropriate in any given business situation. Also, careless letters can have very expensive consequences, as in Box 10.2.

Standard and circular letters – defining effective style

Our example is a letter sent to staff about increased contributions to the staff medical aid fund (we have not reproduced the specific design of letterhead, etc.). How would you evaluate its tone and content?

BOX 10.1 CHANGING PATTERNS OF BUSINESS CORRESPONDENCE

According to Hargie *et al.* (1999, p. 181), 'the Internet has transformed business communication'. They point to the 'phenomenal' expansion in the number of email addresses and Web connections. They also highlight a study of email traffic in one large company where '60 per cent of the messages ... received by this means would not have been received by other channels' (p. 181). Email has become an indispensable communication tool in modern organizations.

Another recent survey found that 53 per cent of UK business people felt that the use of email had increased their level of communication, and 28 per cent suggested that staff felt more involved in the company after the introduction of email (survey reported in *Mind Your Own Business*, March 2000, p. 19).

There are cultural differences in the patterns of business communication. A survey by the Pitney Bowes company in 1999 suggested that whereas US and Canadian staff preferred asynchronous or time-delayed communication, European staff preferred real-time and more formal methods. There was very heavy use of voicemail in the USA (90 per cent of staff), less in the UK (58 per cent) and much less in Germany (32 per cent) (survey reported in *Mind Your Own Business*, July/August 1999, p. 30).

Another rather frightening statistic from this last survey – that the average British worker receives 171 messages per day – suggests that information overload is a real problem. Researchers such as Charles Oppenheim suggest that this overload 'seems to screw people up. The sheer pressure is immense' (quoted in *PC Pro*, March 1999, p. 56). Once again there are cultural differences, with overload being much more serious in countries where there is most use of the Internet. This reinforces the need for systematic staff training in these new technologies – training that discusses more than which buttons to press.

Increased contributions to the Staff Medical Aid Fund

Dear Member

As you may be aware from reports in the press, general medical costs have risen substantially in the past year – the statutory scale of benefits (i.e. tariff rates) have increased by about 15%. In addition, the VAT rate has been increased, which will add about a further 6% to costs.

In spite of a substantially increased company contribution, we must increase members' contributions by about 20%. The precise increase is given in the attached contribution tables which come into operation on 1 May 2001.

Yours faithfully

A Naim
Chair
Management Committee

215

Is this letter effective? Does it include all the appropriate information? What tone will it convey to staff? Which of the following responses is more likely:

1   'I understand what has happened and it looks as if management have done their best to protect our interests.'
2   'I don't understand all the detail and it does look as though management have passed on all the increase to us.'

We can identify parts of the letter which are likely to evoke response 1:

■   The writer has tried to explain the context.
■   The writer has said what has been done to improve the situation ('substantially increased company contribution').

But we can also identify parts which support response 2:

■   Will everyone know what is meant by 'the statutory scale of benefits (i.e. tariff rates)'? Doesn't this need further explanation?
■   Are the statistics a complete picture of the 'substantial rises'? (And why use this emotive phrase?)
■   Are the total increases 15% + 6% = 21%? If so, what is the 'substantially increased company contribution' if the members' contributions are going up by 'about 20%'? Why is the company contribution not specified?
■   Has there been any consultation on this? Have any alternatives been explored such as altering the benefits? It looks like a management *fait accompli* as the new tables 'come into operation on 1 May 2001' (which happened to be the following week).

This interpretation may seem cynical and pessimistic – but that depends on the relationship which management have established with staff. If management have not established trust and confidence, then each and every message will be interpreted from a negative and suspicious perspective, as in 2 above.

There is another important implication of circular letters: you cannot guarantee that everyone will see them at exactly the same time. As a result, some staff may 'hear the news' by being told about it before reading it, and this may give them another interpretation. Advance warning and preparation by managers may also be important here.

For example, consider the following message in a circular letter from the relatively new general manager of a large multi-site organization:

> From September to December this year, we shall be holding consultations with all staff on the Greenfield site to consider proposals to amalgamate the departments on that site.

Many staff on the Greenfield site received this news by word of mouth. But the meaning of the grapevine message was more definite than the written message: 'The new general manager has decided to amalgamate the departments on that site.'

This interpretation was strongly justified by its advocates. They pointed to several clues to management's 'real intentions':

- the way that the circular had been issued, out of the blue and just before the annual holiday period;
- the fact that the current department managers were completely unprepared for it;
- the 'fact' that the new general manager obviously wanted to establish her authority.

The important principle here is that circular letters must take account of the context and anticipate different interpretations. In the last example, some of the problems could have been avoided by briefing department managers and by issuing the circular after the holiday period.

Style in individual letters

We can write individual letters of various types, including making/answering enquiries; appointing an employee; submitting or accepting a quotation; and so on. We highlight main principles and issues with one example where the tone is particularly important: responding to a complaint.

An example letter: responding to a complaint

Responding to letters of complaint requires tact to avoid giving further offence. People who take the trouble to write letters of complaint feel, rightly or wrongly, that they have good reason to complain. Even if you feel the complaint is unjustified, it deserves a reasonable response.

BOX 10.2 BAD LETTERS CAN BE EXPENSIVE!

Mr A is annoyed; he has decided to move his personal finances from a particular bank. His annoyance will influence any future professional dealings with it. This stems from one letter.

He wrote to the bank to cancel a credit card. A few days later he received a credit card statement which ignored his letter and which included an annual charge for the following year. When he wrote to the bank to point out the mistake, he received a standard circular letter confirming that the account was closed and thanking him for his custom in the past. The letter made no reference to his letter or to the problem of the next year's charges. To Mr A, this letter symbolized poor and impersonal service, not to mention his frustration at having to write again to sort it out. That one letter cost the bank several decades of business.

Our Imaginary Company Ltd
Millionaire's Row
Anywhere
333 XXX

Our ref:
Your ref:

12 June 2001

Mr J Jones
Box 24
Sandtown
2146

Dear Mr Jones

Carpet cleaning service – your letter of 4 June 2001

We are very sorry that you were inconvenienced by the late arrival of our cleaning team on 30 May which meant that the job could not be done on that day. Our team were unexpectedly delayed at an emergency job and were unable to contact you.

I have instructed Mr Phillips, our Service Manager, to send a cleaning team at a time convenient for you, and to reduce your bill by 10%. Please phone him at 8131345 to arrange a time.

We do aim to provide a quality service at all times, and we hope that this will resolve the problem.

Yours faithfully

Jan Smith
Service Manager

Notice what this letter does:

- apologizes;
- makes a fair offer of restitution;
- explains what happened;
- treats the incident as unusual;
- tries to restore the company image.

And it does not:

- overdo the apologies;
- express disbelief in the complaint;
- give over-long explanations of what went wrong (which might suggest a badly run organization).

Chunking letters

In the example above, we tried to follow chunking principles from previous chapters. Each paragraph had a specific theme (the situation – what we are going to do – repeat apology and contact details). We can think of business letters in terms of the basic begin–middle–end structure, as recommended by many trainers and teachers (e.g. Ramey, 1999):

Begin	Explain why you are writing
Middle	Explain the detailed information
End	Explain what action you are going to take

Deciding on the tone

As well as making sure that the content was accurate, we also tried to ensure that the tone was positive and neutral. This also applies if you have to write a letter of complaint to another person/organization. One issue with any letter of complaint is the possible assumption that the other person is directly to blame. As accusations usually put the other person on the defensive, they are not a good strategy to resolve the problem, especially in the first letter. It is much safer to assume that your audience is someone who wishes to provide a good service, but that something has simply gone wrong.

And a final word on style in letters

A study published in 1987 compared a selection of business letters written in English, French and Japanese. The authors found lots of examples of what they called 'ritualized and formulaic writing' (Jenkins and Hinds, 1987, p. 328). We criticized this sort of language in Chapter 7. But how much has changed in the past two decades? More recent studies have suggested a change towards the principles adopted in this book (for example, see Akar and Louhiala-Salminen, 1999). But it is difficult to assess how widespread this change has been. The fact that organizations such as the Plain English Campaign in the UK are still very active does suggest that we still have a lot to learn.

Layout conventions in letters

Our example above used the block format of presentation which is now adopted by many organizations:

- Everything starts at the left-hand margin except possibly the company letterhead/logo at the top of the page.
- The right margin is either justified or ragged (we recommend the latter for word-processed documents).
- Punctuation is kept to a minimum with only the necessary full stops (periods) and commas (we did not abbreviate the date to avoid any confusion because of differences in usage between Britain and the USA – 2/6/00 can be read as either 2 June 2000 or 6 February 2000).

219

> **EXERCISE**
>
> Collect a sample of business letters from different organizations and compare the format with our example and with each other. Do particular formats have advantages or disadvantages? You might like to compare our approach with one of the texts or software packages which offer model letters (e.g. Taylor, 1998).

One further issue is the practicality of using printed stationery with word processing. We found one organization whose stationery had been designed without considering the default spacing used by the organization's standard word processor software. As a result, staff found it impossible to line up certain parts of the letter, such as the individual reference number with the pre-printed 'Our reference:'.

REPORTS

A report is an official or formal statement, often made after an investigation and usually made to the immediate line manager, or to a working group or committee. The audience(s) may be either internal or external to the organization, or, on rare occasions, both. The audience may not share the writer's expertise.

Analysing the audience

The structure and content of any report must meet the needs of up to four distinct categories of audience:

Primary audience

As a report aims to achieve action, these are people who have the authority to act on the recommendations. A report may thus be aimed primarily at a single person, such as a general manager, or at a group, such as a committee or even the board of directors. Key parts of the report, such as the synopsis, discussion, conclusions and recommendations, should be targeted specifically at this primary audience.

Secondary audience

Few decision-makers act entirely on their own; they seek advice from departments and specialists. This group of advisers are the secondary audience, and they often have limited or special interests.

Tertiary audience

If the recommendations of a report are approved, then it may be distributed to further readers who have to implement the recommendations. They will need detail which was not necessary for decision-making, so place this in the appendices.

And other readers

There may well be other readers who need to be considered. For example, there may be those who, for policy reasons, 'need to know' (often senior staff in other parts of the organization). Or there may be people at a later date who may find the report useful for similar investigations.

By assessing what these audiences may want to do with your report, you can decide what information and what level of detail you need to include. For example, we recently trained housing officers. Their managers understood their reports on house inspections but they were often too short and technical for another audience – when the report was given as evidence in a court case against offending tenants, perhaps as much as several years after the inspection. Although this did not happen very often, it was very important that they could defend the report in court if necessary. They had to develop reports which legal representatives could easily understand.

Types of report

Reports can cover a variety of communications, ranging from a brief, oral report of an incident to the large, complex reports of government commissions on some aspect of public life. There are different ways of categorizing these different reports. For example, Simon Mort (1992) describes fourteen different types. We discuss three main categories which cover most of this variation:

- form reports;
- short reports (sometimes called letter or memo reports);
- long, formal reports and proposals.

FORM REPORTS, FORMS AND QUESTIONNAIRES

Form reports, forms and questionnaires all share important features:

- They are designed to compile specific information from a variety of respondents.
- They collect information which can then be collated, analysed and interpreted.

Form reports are regular and standardized. They typically include documents such as production reports, sales reports, accident reports and progress reports. There are definite advantages in having standardized forms for these:

- The same information is in the same place each time.
- Users can check that all the required information is submitted.

Forms and form reports can be set up in the organization's computer system – by extracting information from a database or having on-screen entry forms. Information can be entered directly and the computer will collate and process it before presenting it in the desired format. The computer can also be programmed to act in certain circumstances – for example, by automatically printing orders for material required. As an example of automation, many office photocopiers now order their own replacement toner automatically through a Web connection.

Designing forms and questionnaires requires high levels of skill. It is all too easy to create ambiguous or misleading questions and collect data which is effectively useless.

SHORT REPORTS

Certain internal reports, usually of less than five pages, do not require all the formalities of long reports. They often have simple subsections, such as:

- introduction;
- investigation;
- conclusion.

Descriptive reports of this sort are usually intended to supply information, rather than recommend specific action. In terms of effective style and structure, we echo what we said about memos, emails and letters, emphasizing the importance of informative headings and subheadings to guide the reader through the text. You can also use techniques such as Clark's memo matrix, as discussed earlier.

LONG, FORMAL REPORTS AND PROPOSALS

Long reports deal with a complex investigation or issue, and are often addressed to a number of different audiences. To cater for different audiences and to provide a logical structure, reports are subdivided into sections with distinct functions. A complete investigation (from problem definition through to recommendations) requires a logical sequence of actions, which are reflected in this sectional structure.

Proposals might be for a new company or departmental initiative. These have a format similar to that of reports, but use some sections differently.

Objectives

Writing a report is easier if you have a clear objective. You can use the approach suggested in Chapter 7 to summarize your objective. A. Barker (1999, p. 99) offers another useful suggestion: summarizing your objective in what he calls a 'function statement' as follows:

- the first part ('the aim of this report is to . . . ') expresses the report's immediate aim . . .
- the second part ('so that . . . ') looks to the *future*. What benefit, payoff or actions do you see as a result of producing the report?

Having a clear view of the objective is especially important with complicated reports which involve a lot of preparation. It is also useful to have a clear function statement like this as you can then check it with whoever commissioned the report.

Structure and report sections

Basic report structure is an expansion of the begin–middle–end structure we have come across before, as shown in Table 10.1.

We shall discuss the report sections individually before looking at variations in order and purpose.

Title page

The title page serves as a protective cover, and can also be designed to impress clients. The minimum information expected is title, author and originating organization. You can also add:

■ name of staff or organization the report is submitted to;
■ date and place of publication (this should always appear somewhere if not on the title page);
■ identifying or reference number;
■ author's status.

The title obviously appears on the title page, and may be repeated on the synopsis page and the contents page.

The title should describe the contents without being over-long, avoiding words that carry little or no new information. For example, a title like 'A report on an investigation into

Table 10.1 Basic report structure

	Report structure	Report sections
Begin	Introduction	■ Title page
		■ Synopsis or summary
		■ Contents list
		■ Introduction
Middle	Main body	■ Methods of investigation
		■ Results
		■ Discussion of results
End	Conclusions and recommendations	■ Conclusions
		■ Recommendations
		■ Appendices

factors influencing the choice of office copiers' is verbose, since it is obvious that it is a report and reports are usually about investigations. It can be shortened to: 'Factors influencing the choice of office copiers'. But does this tell you enough about the content of the report? What is the focus of the report? Would readers get a clearer idea from a title such as – 'How this department should choose new photocopiers'?

Some writers recommend even more explicit titles. Joseph (1998, p. 121) recommends that 'The title should be a highly condensed version of the *whole* report'. This means it should contain the conclusion. In our copier example, the title could be 'Why the Sales Department needs to lease three new Acme photocopiers'. You also need to consider the tone which your audience might expect. Would this very direct style be 'acceptable' in your organization? Would a more neutral style be preferred: 'Leasing new copiers for the Sales Division'?

EXERCISE

Look at a selection of title pages of long reports in your organization. Do the titles really tell you what the report is about? What style and layout do they adopt?

Summary

The summary (also called an 'abstract' or 'synopsis') should be a concise overview of the report (unless you are told otherwise, we suggest fewer than 100 words). It should enable readers to understand the main aim and the main results, the conclusions and any recommendations.

EXERCISE

Look at a selection of summaries of long reports in your organization. Do they really provide a comprehensive summary – main results, conclusions and any recommendations? What style do they adopt?

List of contents

The contents page lists the divisions and main subdivisions of the report, with page numbers. As reports are usually read selectively, readers can find those sections they are interested in. You may also want to include lists of tables and figures.

Introduction

The aim of the introduction is to explain any necessary *background* so readers can understand the rest of the report. You need to tell the reader:

- what the report is about;
- why the work was done;
- the scope of the report;
- what methods were used.

A common fault in descriptive reports is to give or anticipate results in this section. In a persuasive report, where there is usually a problem to be solved, this problem should be clearly stated, together with its constraints.

Where *written terms of reference* were given, these should be quoted verbatim. (Terms of reference state when the report was commissioned, and by whom, as well as the full instructions that were given.) If they are extensive, they are usually given in full under a separate heading before or after the introduction.

Methods of investigation

One requirement of a good investigation is that others should be able to repeat it. Therefore, the methods used in the investigation should be described. If these methods are detailed and not necessary to understand the report, they are often given in an appendix.

Results/discussion of results

In the traditional scientific report, these are two separate sections, and you can see this structure in many scientific journals. It may not be the best way to present a business report if you follow pyramid or chunking principles from Chapter 7 where you discuss both the results and the implications of a particular topic under the same subheading.

Whatever structure you choose, you need to make sure that results are presented clearly. To avoid cluttering the main body of a report with detailed information, you can place details in an appendix and report only the key information in the main body.

Simple descriptive reports usually do not need detailed discussion of results. However, this discussion is one of the most important parts in persuasive reports – here the results of the investigation are evaluated and alternative solutions to the problems considered, together with the conclusions. You need to bring together the following information from other parts of the report:

- problem statement (from introduction);
- results of investigation (from results);
- constraints (from introduction, or developed in investigation);
- criteria for evaluation (from introduction, or developed in discussion).

Conclusion(s)

Descriptive reports rarely need detailed conclusions. You might need only a brief, simple statement after the results, such as 'The water, sand and air samples submitted by XYZ Holiday Resort on 15 June met all the requirements of the new "Clean Beach" standards.'

In long and complex reports it helps the reader to have a clear summary of the conclusions in a separate section. You can also list your conclusions in order of importance.

Recommendation(s)

Any recommendations must follow logically from discussions and conclusions. As the objective of a persuasive report is to instigate action, the recommendation section should be a set of clear directives, without any additional discussion and conclusions.

Each recommendation should propose a single action. If two separate actions are proposed, the decision-maker may reject the entire recommendation because he or she disagrees with one of them.

Appendices

Appendices contain information that you do not need in order to understand the main report, but that interested readers might want to check, including:

- detailed literature surveys;
- theoretical background;
- detailed data-gathering methods;
- detailed results;
- methods of interpreting results.

Variations in structure

Not all reports will contain all these sections – how they are subdivided depends on the contents and the audience requirements. Table 10.2 gives a few variations to meet specific needs. The important principle is to choose a structure which supports your objectives and which readers will follow easily. For example, many writers advocate the SPQR approach which we used in Chapter 7 (e.g. Barker, 1999, pp. 100ff.):

S = the situation (this company is the leading producer of grommits)
P = the problem or problems which have arisen (sales of grommits are falling)
Q = the question which arises in the reader's mind (how can we restore the profit in grommit sales?)
R = response (solutions and recommendations, which may of course challenge the assumptions behind the original question. For example, it may be impossible to revive grommit sales as this technology is in long-term decline – what should the organization do about this?)

Whatever the final structure in terms of headings and subheadings, it is essential that this reflects *the structure of your argument*. Having a visual summary of your argument can be very useful, perhaps using pyramid or spider diagram techniques as in Chapter 7, or perhaps just summarizing the building blocks of your argument as in the example on page 228.

Table 10.2 Different report structures

Report which summarizes the results of an investigation to arrive at a conclusion: 'the new manufacturing process does/does not meet Health and Safety standards'	Report which investigates three possible solutions to a specified problem and recommends the best course of action	Proposal which recommends that the department or organization adopts new working practices (e.g. adopts new computer system)
■ Title page	■ Title page	■ Title page
■ Title	■ Title	■ Title
■ Summary	■ Summary	■ Summary
■ Contents list	■ Contents list	■ Contents list
■ Introduction	■ Introduction (which specifies the problem)	■ Introduction
■ Investigation, which comprises	■ Solution 1	■ Analysis of present working practices
– method of information-gathering	– advantages	– problem 1
– results	– disadvantages	– problem 2
– discussion	■ Solution 2	– and so on
■ Conclusion	– advantages	■ How a new system would deal with these problems
■ Appendices (e.g. detailed test results)	– disadvantages	– advantages
	■ Solution 3	– disadvantages
	– advantages	■ Conclusion and recommendation
	– disadvantages	■ Appendices
	■ Conclusion	
	■ Recommendations	
	■ Appendices	

General statement – A
Supporting statements Bl, B2, B3, and so on.

A – We should include a small bar refrigerator in our product range.
    B1   We have received requests from our agents for such an item.
    B2   Two of our competitors are successfully marketing such models.
    B3   We have a suitable design for such an item.
    B4   Market research indicates 20 per cent growth in this market.
    B5   We have spare manufacturing capacity.

Report style

All the general issues of language style we discussed in Chapter 8 are relevant, but there are two issues which are worth emphasizing:

Style and organizational structure

A particular language style can reflect deep-rooted organizational attitudes which may be difficult to change.

Style and accuracy

Some of the traditional conventions of formal reports, like avoiding the first person and using the passive voice, were justified by the claim that this writing style was more 'accurate' or 'objective'. Some organizations still insist on some of these conventions. But you cannot automatically assume that your writing will be accurate by adopting these strategies. In fact, they can lead to tortuous expressions which can be vague or misleading.

The best practical solution is to make your reports compatible with the organizational house style, and avoid any constructions which can confuse. For example, Kirkman (1992) warns of regular problems in more technical reports, including:

- Excessive abstraction. General and abstract terms are used instead of more specific and concrete terms which would clarify the meaning. This often leads to:
- Excessive nominalization. A noun is used instead of the verb which it comes from. For example, we write 'the function of *allocation* and *distribution* of revenue will be performed by the Business Development Department' instead of 'the Business Development Department will *allocate* and *distribute* the revenue'. One way of checking for this is to review any sentence where you have used expressions such as 'take place', 'carry out', 'perform', etc., as these often occur in sentences which can be simplified.

EXERCISE

Review a sample of reports from your organization in terms of the style of writing and also in terms of how they reflect your organizational culture and structure.

EMAIL

Email dates from around 1970 when Ray Tomlinson wrote a couple of programs which allowed people in a computer lab to send messages between machines. His programs were incorporated into the early development of the Internet and by the mid-1970s people could send email across Internet connections, and give immediate responses using the reply button. Email then provided an important stimulus to Internet development; within a few years it was 'the driving force behind the network's expansion' (Naughton, 1999, p. 210).

This brief history is important because it explains the way email developed – as a simple message system which did not incorporate the formatting offered by word processing. It has developed over time so that modern email software can offer quite sophisticated ways of storing messages. But the basic rationale has not changed.

Denise Murray (1995, ch. 5) suggests that this pattern of development has created some problems. Because of the system's perceived simplicity, she suggests that most current users have received very little formal training or education in its best use. And this has had three important consequences:

- Senders often use the attachment facility to distribute long reports or other documents rather than summarize their content. Users can become overloaded with too much detailed information.
- As email was designed to exchange information, it is limited in what it can convey. Users have developed their own codes to supply additional meaning.
- Because it is so easy and quick, it is easy to send angry or rude messages before you have had a chance to think about it. We discuss this notion – that email inspires emotional outbursts, often called flaming – later in this chapter.

Structure and layout

At first glance, emails look like electronic memos – with a space for the sender, the receiver and the title. The date and time of sending is automatically supplied. There are none of the politeness features that we expect in letters (yours sincerely etc.).

The layout is very restricted on most email systems:

- They use a single font.
- You can highlight phrases only by using bold or a different colour.
- You can use space to suggest subheadings or emphasis.
- You can use techniques such as 'emoticons'. For example, the smiley face is a common signal of happiness, created by the following keyboard characters :-)

Email systems may become more design-conscious over the next decade, but that might not actually help communication.

Users are increasingly swamped by emails (refer back to Box 10.1), so it is very important that the title reflects the nature and urgency of the content (Whelan, 2000). As some email systems have a word limit to the length of title they show in the list of messages, a clear, short title can be very important. Apart from this specific issue, we suggest that emails are structured in terms of the principles outlined in Chapter 7. Given that readers have to scroll long messages, it is a good rule of thumb to organize the message in terms of descending importance – most important paragraph first.

Style

Mulholland suggests that 'minimalism or brevity in language use . . . is becoming the preferred style for email messages' (Mulholland, 1999, p. 74). Is this just a further development of the concise style we see in written memos? Some writers believe that it is a more fundamental shift. This has even caused concern that computer-mediated communication (C-m-C) may have long-term negative effects on our use of language. At the very least, there does seem to be a shift to more conversational forms of writing.

Is email talk or text?

Email and other forms of C-m-C do blur the distinction between talk and text. In other words, people adopt a style of communicating which is more conversational and does not have the more complicated features of written language. For example, Denise Murray (1995, pp. 79ff.) suggests the following characteristics of email style:

- use of abbreviations;
- use of simple words;
- use of simple syntax;
- disregard for 'surface errors'. In other words, people will ignore any spelling errors or typos or minor errors in syntax;
- use of symbols to represent non-linguistic information. For example, you might use emoticons, or write 'I *did* say', using asterisks to emphasize the word 'did'.

The obvious problem with these features is the assumption that the reader will recognize the code. For example, a reader may react to typos as evidence of a careless rather than hurried message. One of our colleagues once got himself into trouble by putting a sentence into capitals in an email. He meant to suggest irony/sarcasm; his reader interpreted this as 'bullying'. Luckily, their relationship was such that they could discuss and resolve this.

Is flaming inevitable?

Hargie *et al.* (1999, p. 182) report one survey where over half of email users claimed to have 'received abusive e-mails . . . which irreparably damaged working relationships'. Over half of these came from their managers, and were much more likely to be written by men than women (five times more likely, according to this study). But how do we explain this? A number of factors could help to create this situation:

■ Does C-m-C inevitably create a lack of social restraint because of the absence of face-to-face cues and because of its immediacy (unlike memos or letters, you can reply instantly)?
■ Was the culture of this organization characterized by conflict and aggression anyway? Did email just provide a new arena for the conflict?
■ Does the male–female difference reflect different management styles or power relationships?

Issues of flaming and email abuse have been debated by social scientists and in the mass media. Some have suggested that concern has been exaggerated and reflects people's lack of skill in using the medium – 'there are plenty of cases where people have dashed off e-mail messages without thinking properly about who's going to read them or what they're going to think when they do' (Jackson, 1997, p. 101). From a theoretical point of view, recent studies have found little evidence to suggest that the technology itself is to blame. Flaming may occur with particular users in particular contexts. It is also worth remembering that concerns about antisocial behaviour also characterized the early days of the telephone (Baron, 1999).

What is your individual style?

Individuals do develop their own style of writing emails. This covers such things as how politeness is expressed, the typical use of short sentences and abbreviations, and the absence of what linguists call metalanguage, where you use language to comment on itself as in the phrase 'can I ask when the minutes will be distributed?'

Your style should be appropriate to your audience. Reviewing our own use of email, we noticed how our style varies from very conversational with close colleagues to a more impersonal style in messages which may reach a large group. You also need to consider your organizational culture.

How is email used in your organization?

How email is used depends upon your organization's culture and working practices. For example, a study of email use in an Australian university, at a time when the organization was experiencing significant changes, found a wide range of attitudes to C-m-C, both negative and positive (Mulholland, 1999). The introduction of email to support committee work had important consequences. For example, draft papers were circulated more quickly and this also allowed committee members to propose amendments, although some committee members lacked the skills to do so effectively – another example of the importance of training in this new technology. One potential long-term outcome *could* be to make the committee process more open and democratic.

There are other important issues to consider:

- Emails may be kept on record. In the past few years, several court cases have argued over responsibility for the content of particular emails. For example, one large oil company was taken to court by a group of women workers who complained about a 'joke' email which they found sexually offensive. The company lost the case as the court concluded that its email policy was inadequate. As a result, many large organizations have developed 'a documented backup and storage policy that determines what email is stored and for how long' (Winder, 1999).
- Emails may be monitored. Partly for these legal reasons and partly because of concerns about staff 'wasting time' on personal concerns, many companies routinely monitor staff email, and this surveillance is becoming more common and more sophisticated (Barkham, 1999).

EXERCISE

Review the use of email in your organization in terms of how people use it and its effect on other channels of communication.

FAX

In the 1990s, fax was described as the 'preferred form for electronic transmission among businesses' (Murray, 1995, p. 94), and the 'most widely distributed modern messaging system' (Chesher and Kaura, 1998). It is still very important and useful despite the dramatic growth of email and Internet traffic. For example, recent statistics show that the market for fax machines is *growing* in the UK, with manufacturers commenting that staff often prefer hard copy to electronic documents (*PS Workplace*, July/August 2000).

Apart from being fast and simple to use, the most obvious advantage of fax is that you can send any hard copy to anyone who has a fax machine (or fax facility on their PC) anywhere in the world. Faxes are increasingly accepted as commercially valid documents for transactions such as orders. And you do not have to worry about the compatibility of file formats, which you need to check when sending computer files as attachments.

Developments in colour faxes and multi-purpose machines, which include copy and print functions, should maintain fax's popularity. One important disadvantage is that the quality of printed output on many fax machines is not very good, so you may lose detail on diagrams, etc.

Messages specially written for fax seem to share many of the characteristics we discussed for email, although 'flaming' does not seem to be an issue. They are short (often less than one page, not counting the cover sheet with the contact information); they mainly supply or request information; and they are written in a more conversational style than traditional business letters (Akar and Louhiala-Salminen, 1999).

WRITING FOR THE WEB

We now take for granted that our printed documents will use professional typefaces and incorporate graphics and flexible page design, thanks to the development of word processing. A similar process is affecting writing for the Web as the software is becoming easier to use. Producing a very simple Web page can be just a matter of saving a word-processed file as an HTML document, and Web authoring software has become more automated and flexible. Deciding whether a document should be a word-processed file or part of a Web site is a regular decision for many employees in different sizes of company.

Most organizations now have a Web site which they use for marketing, public relations and, sometimes, sales. This same technology of browsers and hypertext links can also be used to create an internal Web site – an intranet. Jacob Nielsen, one of the most influential contemporary writers on Web design, suggests that companies should have different user interface designs for these two Web sites so that employees can immediately recognize when they are looking at internal as opposed to publicly accessible information (Nielsen, 2000, p. 264).

Effective design

There are common design principles, whether you are writing for an internal or an external audience. These are compatible with ideas we have introduced in the last few chapters about printed information. For example, Robert Tannenbaum includes the following in his list of general principles for screen design (1998, p. 453):

- Develop clean, attractive, informative titles.
- Keep screens simple, conveying one major idea per screen.
- Choose type fonts and sizes that are clear and easy to read, yet direct emphases appropriately.
- Keep screen design uncluttered, using adequate margins and sufficient white space.

There are of course some important differences between print and screen information:

- Your screen design may be interpreted differently by different makes and different generations of browser. As a result, many Web designers recommend that you create Web sites which display in the same way on different machines (e.g. Siegel, 1996). This is one major advantage of designing for an intranet, as you should know exactly what equipment your pages will be displayed upon.
- Web pages have to be assembled on the screen; they do not appear instantaneously. You need to ensure that the download time is minimal and that the page components appear in an order which makes most sense to the viewer.

Nielsen suggests that the most important factors which determine the usability of public Web sites are what he calls 'learnability' – how quickly and easily you can work out how to find your way round the site – and 'subjective satisfaction'. He suggests that external users have to be 'kept happy' because they are using the site at their own discretion. In contrast, employees using an intranet will do so because they *have to* gain important information and are also likely to be very regular users. Accordingly, he suggests that 'efficiency, memorability, and error reduction' are the most important attributes for an intranet. The important thing is to ensure that users can navigate the site efficiently without wasting time.

EXERCISE

Review your own organization's policy and practice regarding Web pages. Is there a clear distinction between Internet and intranet information? How is this managed and controlled?

Structure

Perhaps the most important feature of Web documents is that they use hyperlinks. The structure of the Web site has to be very carefully designed so that users do not 'get lost' and they know where to find the information they are looking for.

Developing Web technologies

One important development is the increasing ability of the Web to carry audio and video information, which means that multimedia can be delivered over the Internet. Other important developments include:

- Integration of Web and database technology. Web pages can be constructed to respond to enquiries by lifting information out of a database. When the information in the database is updated, the Web page is automatically updated.
- 'Push' technology. Surfing the Web is often described as 'pull' technology – you pull information from the Web site. Push technology is where the Web software 'pushes' information at you on the basis of previous experience of your preferences and needs. A simple example is how Internet retailer Amazon suggests new books from an analysis of your previous purchases. This technology is likely to become more important on intranets as organizations develop more sophisticated information systems.

CVs AND APPLICATIONS

'An effective CV gets you shortlisted for a job that you are suited for, and provides a structure for the interview that follows' (Vandevelde, 1999, p. 24). The CV (curriculum vitae or résumé) is a powerful document. It is not just a summary of your achievements; it is a document which must *persuade* the reader that you are the person that the organization is looking for, and it can signpost areas which *you* want to discuss in the interview. In order to do this, it must be carefully prepared so that:

- you highlight your strengths;
- you demonstrate particular skills and qualities for which the organization is looking;

- it is easy to read quickly (various surveys suggest that recruiters look at a CV for less than a minute before their initial decision).

This last point argues for layout techniques such as the use of bulleted lists. It also suggests that you should use clear headings such as 'qualifications', 'career history', 'personal qualities'.

We suggest that you prepare a new CV for each job you apply for, as the mix of skills required is unlikely to be exactly the same. In practice, you can have a 'standard' CV on file and adapt it for each new opportunity.

Chunking the CV

This approach means that you do not necessarily follow the traditional order of information. For example, we have seen many CVs from undergraduates which start as follows:

- Name
- Address
- School qualifications
- College or university qualification
- And so on.

This chronological approach presents information in an order which is probably the least relevant to the selector. We ask students to consider an approach like the following:

- Name
- Address
- Personal qualities (a paragraph summarizing main strengths and highlighting main ambitions)
- Work experience (highlighting relevant experience, including any placement or project work)
- University qualification (giving a brief description of the course as well as the final grade – it is easy to assume that recruiters will understand the implications of university titles)
- And so on.

Similar principles apply if you are a manager looking for further promotion – you need to adapt the CV to suit the audience.

The letter of application

Job applications often demand two documents, the CV and a letter of application. The letter of application is also a persuasive document. Again you need to think carefully about the structure of the letter. As a basic structure, we suggest the following chunks:

- heading (application for post of . . .);
- first paragraph explains which post you are applying for and how you know about it;
- second paragraph explaining your interest in this post;

- third paragraph explaining how you have all the necessary skills and qualities;
- fourth paragraph confirming your availability for interview and re-emphasizing your enthusiasm.

This structure can obviously be adapted to suit the job opportunity and your level of experience:

- *Do* expand on your CV by giving relevant information.
- *Do* show an interest in the type of work indicated.
- *Do* relate your qualifications to the work offered.

You might be surprised how often these basic points are ignored, even in applications for senior posts.

Electronic assessment

Some organizations now ask for CVs in electronic form so they can use software which assesses CVs against specific criteria. This software may just look for keywords or may have more sophisticated search procedures.

These developments emphasize the need to be explicit in your CV. For example, if you have teamworking skills and experience, then this must be mentioned explicitly some-where on the CV so that this message comes across clearly to both human and machine recruiters.

SUMMARY

- General principles apply to *all* business documents: deciding on appropriate objectives, meeting audience needs, organizing the message, writing in an appropriate style, and using layout and design to support your message.
- Effective business correspondence meets both content and tone criteria.
- Written messages can be interpreted in different ways depending on the context in which they are received.
- The design of documents reflects aspects of organizational structure and culture, so there may be resistance to change.
- Each type of business document can be analysed in terms of structure, style and layout, and it is important to understand both the conventions which readers will expect and the potential problems caused by limitations of the system (for example, the limited formatting in email messages).
- You need to adapt the structure and style of your documents to the specific situation, as for example with the different ways of structuring long reports. Relying on a standardized approach will not usually be successful.

And finally

Of course, there is a lot more we could say about the organization and content of effective applications. But we need to end this chapter by emphasizing a point which applies to *all* the documents we have covered. You need to prepare every business document by considering how its intended audience will use it. In the case of CVs and applications, we have seen far too many which have been prepared using a standardized structure and format. As a result, they have not targeted the particular job opportunity and have been beaten by those which were better prepared.

DISCUSSION QUESTIONS

- What are the most important requirements in business stationery?
- What is the best format for different types of business letter? How far can the quality of correspondence affect the efficiency of the business?
- What should managers do to ensure the effectiveness of circular letters?
- How can you establish sender credibility?
- Are persuasive letters to the public really effective? Aren't members of the public so fed up with junk mail that they will ignore even the most persuasive written circular?
- Given the growth and advances in electronic communication, can we satisfy most of the demand for reports through electronic means?
- We have made a distinction between descriptive and persuasive reports. How useful is this distinction?
- Some texts on report writing suggest formal conventions which are at odds with Plain English recommendations. How can we reconcile the differences?

FURTHER READING

Bargiela-Chiappini, F. and Nickerson, C. (eds) (1999) *Writing Business: Genres, Media and Discourses*. Harlow: Pearson. This collection of studies examines how written discourse works in business contexts, with an emphasis on linguistic analysis.

Bell, A.H. and Smith, D.M. (1999) *Management Communication*. New York: John Wiley. Provides comprehensive coverage of writing and speaking skills with lots of American examples and illustrations, and a supporting Web site.

Jay, R. (1995) *How to Write Proposals and Reports That Get Results*. London: Pitman. Good example of a 'how to do it' text using many Plain English ideas and approaches.

Lynch, P.J. and Horton, S. (1999) *Web Style Guide: Basic Design Principles for Creating Web Sites*. New Haven, CT: Yale University Press.

Sklar, J. (2000) *Principles of Web Design*. Cambridge, MA: Thomson Learning. This and the above are both very useful introductions to Web design.

Mort, S. (1992) *Professional Report Writing*. Aldershot: Gower. A very thorough analysis of the conventions and practices of professional report writing from a British perspective, with many industrial and commercial examples.

Part four

Interpersonal communication in organizations

The rules for work are changing. We're being judged by a new yardstick: not just by how smart we are, or by our training and expertise, but also by how well we handle ourselves and each other.

(Goleman, 1998)

The notion that we need more than just intelligence to be successful at work and in life is not especially new. For example, we can probably all think of someone who is very good at intellectual or academic tasks but who is not very effective at getting more practical jobs done. This may be because they do not feel motivated to do a good job, or because they find it difficult to co-operate with other people. The importance of these more personal abilities has been emphasized by organizational theorists in recent years, especially given the increasing pace of social change.

In this part of the book, we focus on the social skills which are essential in modern organizations in various contexts: communicating face to face in both informal and formal settings; preparing and delivering presentations; and working in groups, teams and committees. As well as highlighting the behaviours which usually contribute to effective social skills, we shall stress the importance of understanding and planning in social interaction. We need to be both socially aware and flexible. Some of the broad generalizations about effective behaviour which you will find in textbooks (including this one) may not apply in some specific situations. You need to *understand* what is going on so you can adjust your behaviour to meet the specific circumstances.

Chapter 11

Effective interpersonal communication

Defining interpersonal skills

INTRODUCTION

The importance of face-to-face communication in organizations has been recognized by both business managers and organizational theorists for many years. For example, we know from research that managers spend enormous amounts of time in conversation, meetings and discussion. How effective is this major investment in time and energy? What can managers (and, of course, other staff) do to 'improve' their interpersonal communication, and what do we mean by 'improvement'?

Various methods have been proposed over the years to develop interpersonal skills. For example, in the 1990s many organizations were persuaded of the importance of personal understanding and interpersonal abilities by the best-selling books on 'emotional intelligence'. This concept emphasized self-awareness and the importance of handling relationships: 'a new competitive reality is putting emotional intelligence at a premium in the workplace and in the marketplace' (Goleman, 1996, p. 149). Goleman and others argued that organizations which failed to recognize or value these skills in their employees would simply not generate the trust, co-operation and creativity which are needed for long-term success.

This chapter reviews research and theory which suggests that effective face-to-face communication depends on interpersonal skills which *include* personal awareness and understanding. We shall examine what effective interpersonal communication involves, highlight the main characteristics of essential skills, and show how these skills can be used together in everyday situations. We shall also warn against the 'over-mechanical' use of certain techniques.

OBJECTIVES

This chapter will:

- explain what effective interpersonal communication involves;
- identify and explain the most important interpersonal skills;
- comment upon popular models of interpersonal skills and communication;
- identify important implications of this analysis for your behaviour towards others at work.

WHAT DOES EFFECTIVE INTERPERSONAL COMMUNICATION INVOLVE?

One answer to the question posed by the heading to this section is that we need 'good' interpersonal skills so we can respond or react to the other person or persons in ways which appear 'natural' and which are 'effective'. This suggests that we have accurately assessed what the other person is trying to communicate, and that accurate assessment depends upon how we perceive that other person. But what if our perception is misleading? Suppose that you worked behind the counter in an English bank and offered a male customer either cash or a cheque for a certain amount. Suppose the customer responded 'give me the money' with no change in intonation over these four words. Would you interpret this behaviour as 'rude'? Many native English-speakers would – to them it sounds too abrupt or even aggressive. The most common 'polite' English expression would be to say this phrase with a slight rise in intonation on the last word (assuming that the person does not have a strong regional accent for which different rules might apply).

If you interpreted the flat intonation as rude, does this mean that you would deal with this customer in a correspondingly abrupt way? Or perhaps you would not give him quite the same positive greeting you would give to other customers? But suppose your customer came from a Middle Eastern country. He has in fact used the pattern of intonation which is seen as polite in his native culture. Would you be sufficiently aware of this cultural difference to avoid an inappropriate reaction?

The definition also suggests that we know what the conversation is trying to achieve – unless you know what the goals are, how can you judge what is effective? And most texts on business communication stress the importance of clear goals. For example, Stanton (1996, p. 1) suggests four general objectives which can apply to any spoken communication: to be received; to be understood; to be accepted; and to get action.

This line of argument suggests that successful social interaction involves a lot more than just some 'correct' behaviours. The process of interpersonal communication is complex – unless you understand some basic features of this process, you can easily behave in ways which the other person will not accept or appreciate. For example, consider the model of interpersonal communication in Figure 11.1 (from P. Hartley, 1999). This suggests that there are a number of fundamental processes:

- Social perception – how person A interprets the behaviour and characteristics of person B. An example of this is the bank customer example we discussed above.
- Social identity – how person A sees him- or herself in terms of their role and status. We communicate in ways which support this sense of social identity.
- Coding – how A and B choose to express themselves. Do we use slang or jargon or technical words? What non-verbal signals do we use?
- The dual nature of 'the message', which always includes both information and relationship aspects.
- The influence of the social context.

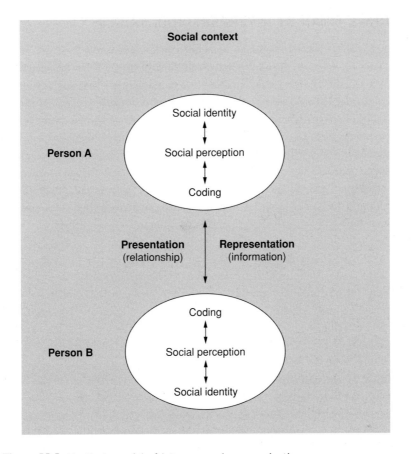

Figure 11.1 *Hartley's model of interpersonal communication*

We mentioned most of these processes in Part one of this book where we stressed the potential ambiguity which is inevitable in our everyday communication and which effective communicators anticipate and avoid. The more you investigate these processes, the more you realize that effective interpersonal communication demands both social understanding – recognizing the processes – and social skills – being able to use the behaviours and techniques. We shall look at fundamental behaviours and techniques before we return to this question of how they all 'fit together'.

EXERCISE

Analyse an interpersonal situation where there has been some conflict or ambiguity using Hartley's model. Does the model identify the important processes? Does it miss or neglect anything important?

WHAT DO WE MEAN BY INTERPERSONAL SKILLS?

Suppose you have been asked to nominate someone you know to lead a discussion group. Who would you choose? What do they do to make you think of them? What makes them good at getting people to talk? Do they make you feel that they really are listening and interested in what you are saying? How do they do this? How do they encourage you to contribute? What are the specific behaviours which make them successful? How and when do they smile, nod, invite you to speak, gesture, etc.? If you do this analysis in detail, then you will be doing a social skills analysis – you will define some of the social skills possessed by that individual.

This detailed approach to our social behaviour was pioneered in Britain by Michael Argyle in the 1970s. He developed the analogy between a motor or physical skill (like playing tennis or riding a bike) and a social skill like having a conversation with someone. He suggested that they had the following features in common (Argyle, 1994):

- *Goals*. You need to decide what you want to achieve. If you talk to someone, are you trying to persuade them, sell them something, make friends or what? Of course, my goals may differ from yours and this could lead to problems or conflict.
- *Perception*. You need to perceive what is going on around you and you need to do this accurately to achieve your goals. In a game, are you looking out for the opportunity to hit a winning shot? Will you recognize the opportunity when it comes? If you talk to someone, what do you think they are interested in?
- *Translation*. In order to perform effectively you have to 'translate' your idea of what you want to do into the correct action. If your customer is obviously not persuaded by your presentation, do you have another strategy? Can you think of another approach?
- *Responses*. Even if you have the correct idea of what you need to do, can you physically do it?
- *Feedback*. If you talk to someone, can you work out how interested they are? Can you recognize when they are getting bored or irritated? Can you accurately interpret the feedback you receive? For example, suppose you express your point of view and they lean back and cross their arms. What does this signal mean? Does it mean agreement or disagreement? If you think it means disagreement, then do you try to restate what you think more clearly or in a different way? This example illustrates that there are several problems in reacting to feedback. First of all, did you notice the signals? You might have been concentrating so hard on expressing yourself clearly that you did not notice the other person's NVC. Secondly, did you interpret the signals correctly? And finally, were you able to respond effectively?

There are other important analogies between physical and interpersonal skills:

- We have to learn how to perform effectively, and we can always learn something new or some improvement.
- We can benefit from good coaching and tuition.
- As we learn a motor skill, our actions become more fluent and better timed. We become less aware of what we are doing; the action becomes subconscious. The same

process can apply to interpersonal skills. For example, if you have to learn interviewing skills, your first interviews are likely to be hesitant and nervous until you gain some confidence. After some successful experience, you will no longer have to concentrate so hard as the behaviour will have become more 'automatic'.

■ We can let our skills 'lapse' by failing to practise. This is the downside of the previous point. As with a motor skill such as driving a car, we can become lazy and careless – and we can fall into 'bad habits'.

One recent development of this approach comes from Owen Hargie (1997). While endorsing Argyle's main ideas, he developed a more elaborate model – see Figure 11.2. This incorporates the following important ideas:

■ The social context is an important influence on our behaviour. The skills that are effective in one context may not work in another.
■ We gain feedback from our own actions as well as the other person's reactions. We are continually aware of our own behaviour and feelings, and this awareness can help us decide what to do next.
■ We are influenced by our emotions as well as by our thoughts, and so the term 'mediating factors' is used instead of 'translation'.

Note that these authors do *not* think that social skills are just the same as motor skills. We have already highlighted some important differences – the fact that other people may have different goals, the importance of feelings – and there is another, more complex problem, that of meta-perception.

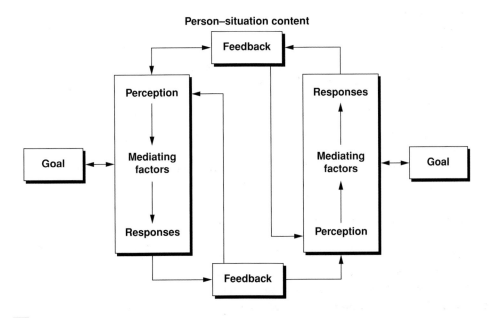

Figure 11.2 *Hargie's revised model of social skills*

Meta-perception

As well as directly perceiving our own behaviour and the behaviour of others, we can also reflect on how those other people are perceiving us. This has been called 'meta-perception' and has been shown to be an important factor in determining how people react to one another. For example, if we are having a conversation and I get the impression that you think I am being too 'chatty', then I might become more reserved to counteract this impression. If my initial impression is wrong, then I will probably confuse you or even offend you with my sudden and unexplained change in behaviour.

EXERCISE

Think of someone whom you would regard as socially skilled at work. What do they do which you see as skilful? Make some notes on this and compare it with the techniques described in the next section.

WHAT ARE THE MOST IMPORTANT INTERPERSONAL SKILLS?

One of the most comprehensive texts on interpersonal skills includes the following topics (Hargie, 1997):

- non-verbal communication (NVC);
- reinforcement;
- questioning;
- reflecting;
- opening and closing;
- explanation;
- listening;
- self-disclosure;
- influencing;
- assertiveness;
- group interaction and leadership;
- humour and laughter.

We shall summarize the essential features of some of these to illustrate the importance of this analysis and approach.

Non-verbal communication

We have already suggested some of the important features of NVC in Part one of this book, notably the following:

- There are a wide range of NVC signals, including facial expression, gaze, gestures, posture, bodily contact, spatial behaviour, clothes and appearance, non-verbal vocalizations (paralanguage) and smell.

- We usually react to the combination of these signals. For example, we may decide that someone is lying to us because they fidget, avoid eye contact, hesitate when they talk, etc.
- These signals are ambiguous. For example, the indicators of someone lying are very close to the signals of nerves and anxiety. This problem of ambiguity is very important if you are considering adopting particular NVC strategies.
- There are significant cultural differences in the meaning of non-verbal signals.
- When verbal and non-verbal signals seem to contradict each other, we are usually more inclined to believe the non-verbal 'message'.

Bearing these points in mind, we can suggest some recommendations for the skilled use of NVC in business situations.

Use a combination of signals to show what you mean

For example, some texts suggest that managers should be very careful to choose the right seating position when they want to have a discussion with one of their staff. The usual recommendation is to avoid the direct frontal position as this implies confrontation, and to talk 'at an angle' – across the corner of the desk rather than directly facing the other person across the desk. This will help to establish an atmosphere, but other cues are also important. To achieve co-operation you also need to use appropriate eye contact and gestures. Just sitting at the 'correct' angle will not help the manager who continues to belittle his staff verbally and non-verbally in other ways, perhaps by constantly interrupting them! These other signals will create the lasting impression in the staff.

Make sure that your verbal and non-verbal messages are 'in harmony'

A person who tells you they are listening to you while looking at their watch will not be believed!

Make sure your NVC is appropriate to the culture and the context

A British manager who uses his or her 'native' pattern of eye gaze when dealing with Arab colleagues may well be seen as 'shifty-eyed' and perhaps untrustworthy because Britons do not engage in what Arabs would regard as sufficient eye contact.

Avoid NVC which has a popular interpretation that you do not want

Many popular books on NVC claim that particular signals definitely pass on a specific message. Even if this is not always true, what if the other person believes that it is? For example, one recent British guide for students preparing for selection interviews suggests that a posture of 'folded arms with the fists clenched' shows 'definite hostility' (McBride, 1993, p. 132). Another text suggests that crossed arms and a sideways glance will be perceived as 'suspicious', and that crossed arms indicate 'defensiveness'. On the assumption that many interviewers probably do believe this is what these gestures mean, the applicant should not use any of them.

Develop your awareness of your own NVC and its likely impact

Perhaps the most important way of developing your NVC skills is through awareness of your own behaviour. Does your NVC always reflect what you want it to mean? You can develop this awareness only by reflecting on your own behaviour and by getting feedback from others who are prepared to give you an honest response. If you decide to change your behaviour then you also need to monitor the effect of change. You need to behave in a way which comes across as 'natural' for you rather than relying on 'textbook techniques' (see Box 11.1).

Reinforcement

When you use reinforcing behaviours, you use behaviours which encourage the other person to carry on or repeat whatever they happen to be doing. Various experiments have shown how people respond to quite small expressions of praise, encouragement and support,

BOX 11.1 CAN WE TEACH THE BRITISH TO USE MORE BODY CONTACT?

Many research studies have shown that British culture uses much less body contact in daily social interaction than other cultures, say compared with Mediterranean conventions. Is this a problem? The Australian writer and trainer Alan Pease believes that touch is 'a powerful way to gain someone's co-operation' (as quoted in the British press in 1995). He suggests a three-point plan for the British to use:

- Nod more frequently as you talk.
- Make sure that your eye level is below the level of the other person, as looking down can be interpreted as being aggressive.
- Brush the elbow of the other person for not more than three seconds. The idea here is that the elbow is a 'neutral area' and so the other person will react positively and not see this gesture as intrusive.

Will this strategy work? It partly depends on whether the person can do this NVC in a way which appears natural and spontaneous. Even if they can, we still doubt that this strategy will guarantee co-operation from the other person. These signals would have to be reinforced by what the person was saying and their other NVC. Our advice is to concentrate on the total impression that you are making. You cannot just rely on one or two non-verbal signals to provide the dominant message.

including head nods, grunts and saying 'uh-huh'. For a quick demonstration of the power of these simple cues, ask a friend to listen to you talking for a couple of minutes without showing any signs of support or agreement. First of all, they may find it very difficult if not impossible to do. Secondly, you will find it very disconcerting to speak to what is effectively a 'blank wall'. And this bring us on to the importance of listening, which we talk about later.

Questioning

If you have attended a series of job interviews you will know that some professional interviewers are much better than others at extracting information from you. This will be due in part to their question technique – whether they are asking the right sort of question at the right time. For example, texts on interviewing technique usually distinguish between open and closed questions.

An open question allows the person to answer in whatever way they like. An example is 'What do you think of the government's economic policy?' A closed question asks for specific information or a yes/no response, An example would be 'Do you agree with the government's economic policy?' Open questions encourage people to talk and expand; closed questions encourage short answers. Inexperienced interviewers often ask too many closed questions and do not get the detailed answers which they really want. We say more on this in the next chapter.

Reflecting

Reflecting is a skill often used by counsellors and other people who have to conduct very personal interviews and who want the other person to talk in some detail about their own feelings and attitudes. Even the most open-ended questions can sometimes suggest the way in which the other person should construct their answer. Reflections are more neutral; they feed back to the speaker some aspect of what they have just said. This invites them to elaborate or extend what they have been saying.

You can reflect in different ways and achieve different results. This will depend on whether you are interested in the factual statements that the other person has made or in their feelings about what they are saying. Textbooks often distinguish at least three different forms of reflection:

- identifying a key word or phrase which will encourage the speaker to say more;
- summarizing what you have heard in your own words;
- identifying the feelings which seem to lie behind what the speaker is saying.

This last form of reflection is perhaps the most difficult and needs the most skill – you have to sense the underlying emotion accurately and read between the lines.

However, these different strategies focus on rather different aspects of the other person's communication. The first two relate to concentrating on what has been said; the third concentrates on how it was said, trying to interpret the non-verbal accompaniment.

249

Opening and closing

The ways in which we establish the beginnings and endings of a particular interaction require consideration. For example, sales staff often receive very detailed training on how to start the interaction with the customer. Often this involves making conversation to establish the sales representative as more friendly and helpful than 'just a salesperson'. Consider all the different possible ways of starting a conversation with someone; some ways would be much more appropriate than others in particular circumstances.

The choice of opening can be very important in more formal situations such as an interview, where the opening can establish either a positive or negative atmosphere, and we shall give some examples in chapter 12.

Listening

It is worth emphasizing the importance of listening as it is often taken for granted. Perhaps because we do it so much, it can be dismissed as a 'natural' behaviour which we have all learnt. But educators concerned with the development of interpersonal skills usually give it central importance: 'Listening is a core competence. People who cannot listen cannot relate.' . . . 'Poor listening undermines the ability to communicate with others' (Hayes, 1991, p. 8).

Developing your skills as a listener involves two major steps:

- recognizing (and eliminating) any barriers which prevent you listening with full attention;
- adopting and practising behaviours which help you listen (and which convince the other person that you are giving them your full attention).

Examples of important common barriers include being distracted by personal stereotypes or other perceptual biases, such as listening selectively for what you expect to hear.

Detailed analysis of the skills which are used by people who are recognized as 'good listeners' shows that they use a variety of techniques. For example, Bolton (1986) talks about three clusters of skills:

- *Attending skills*, where you show the other person that you are attending to them. NVC can be especially important here.
- *Following skills*, where the listener uses techniques which encourage the speaker to give a full account of what they want to say. Reinforcing behaviour can be very important here, or what Bolton calls 'minimal prompts' like 'mmm', 'uh-uh', 'yes', 'and', etc.
- *Reflecting skills*, which we talk about in more detail below.

So the typical recommendations to support active or positive listening include the following (P. Hartley, 1999):

- Being receptive to the other person – showing that you are prepared to listen and accept what they are saying. (Of course, this does not mean that you automatically agree with it.) Non-verbal signals are obviously important here and you need to avoid any signs of tension or impatience.

- Maintaining attention – using eye contact, head nods and appropriate facial expression.
- Removing distractions.
- Delaying evaluation of what you have heard until you fully understand it.

One research study which shows how important active listening can be in practical situations comes from Marquis and Cannell (1971). They compared the results of interviews about family illness when the interviewers used one of three techniques: active listening; sensitizing the interviewee by reading out symptoms at the start; and simply going through the questionnaire. Interviewees gave nearly 30 per cent more examples when the interviewer used active listening techniques.

Self-disclosure

When you communicate with other people you can tell them various things about yourself (or you can decide not to). Sidney Jourard coined the term 'self-disclosure': the process of sharing information about ourselves with other people. When you self-disclose, you provide some information to the other person about yourself: how you are feeling, what your background is, what your attitudes and values are, and so on. Jourard was interested in how people came to reveal aspects of themselves to others and what this meant for the way in which they developed relationships with others.

Self-disclosure and relationships

You need to self-disclose to develop a relationship with another person. And this raises several practical issues:

- What do you tell them? What sort of information do you pass on? When is it 'safe' to reveal your personal feelings?
- How quickly do you reveal yourself? There are important social and cultural differences here. For example, in the United States, you are often expected to say a lot about yourself very early in a relationship. In Britain, a more leisurely pace is the norm.

In business, we have to develop good relationships with other people in the organization, and so self-disclosure is an important issue. How far can we (or should we) keep these relationships on a strictly formal basis and not self-disclose? If you develop a very close and open relationship with a group of staff and are then promoted to be their supervisor, can you maintain the relationship at the same level?

Assertiveness

Over the past two decades, assertiveness training has become one of the most popular ways of developing social skills. As well as training courses and workshops, many popular books on business communication use assertiveness principles even if they do not use the term. And some of these endorse it very strongly, even claiming it can 'change your life' (See P. Hartley, 1999, ch. 12).

What do we mean by assertive communication?

The following quotations summarize essential points:

- 'Assertive behaviour . . . gives you the right to say what you think and feel calmly and clearly, without giving offence and denying the rights of others to have different views or expectations' (Willcocks and Morris, 1996, p. 2).
- 'The aim of assertive behaviour is to satisfy the needs and wants of both parties involved in the situation' (Back and Back, 1999, p. 2).

What are the different styles of behaviour?

Books on assertive behaviour usually define three styles of behaviour: assertion, aggression and submission (or non-assertion). These are often expressed as a continuum with assertion in the middle.

Aggression ——————————- Assertion ——————————- Submission

But a better way of comparing styles of behaviour is to look at the two underlying dimensions:

- from indirect expression through to direct expression;
- from coercive behaviour through to non-coercive behaviour.

This gives Figure 11.3 below.

The fourth style is where you express aggression in an indirect way without direct confrontation. Most texts concentrate on the three main styles, and so will we in this chapter (descriptions taken from Hartley, 1999).

	Coercive behaviour	
Indirect aggressive		**Aggressive**
Indirect expression		Direct expression
Submissive	Non-coercive behaviour	**Assertive**

Figure 11.3 Styles of behaviour

Aggressive behaviour

Aggressive behaviour includes some form of threat which undermines the rights of the other person. It is about winning, regardless of the other person's feelings. The verbal and non-verbal accompaniments to aggressive behaviour include loud and abusive talk, interruptions, and glaring or staring eye contact.

Submissive behaviour

Submissive behaviour gives in to the demands of others by avoiding conflict and accepting being put upon. Verbal and non-verbal accompaniments include apologetic and hesitant speech, soft speech, nervous gestures and a reluctance to express opinions. Submissive individuals will be seen as weak and easily manipulated. They will certainly not inspire confidence in others.

The verbal and non-verbal behaviours associated with these styles have been demonstrated quite clearly in research studies as well as from observation of everyday life.

Assertive behaviour

The characteristics of assertive behaviour are open and clear expression, firm and fluent conversation, and quick, spontaneous answers. The non-verbal components include medium levels of eye contact; appropriate facial expressions; smooth gestures; relaxed but upright body posture; and appropriate paralinguistics.

Using assertive behaviour

There are various ways of categorizing assertive behaviour. For example, Ken and Kate Back (1999) define six main types of assertive behaviour, which can be divided into two levels as summarized in Box 11.2. Other texts concentrate on what they regard as the main assertive techniques. To illustrate the approach, we can quote a typical example from Linehan and Egan (1983). They offer the 'broken record' technique as a way of resisting influence. This technique simply involves repeating your initial request or response, without being sidetracked, until the other person accepts it. For example, suppose your boss asks you to work late one evening and you are already committed to an important social event. What do you say? If you say, 'I'm sorry, but I can't stay tonight', how do you respond if the boss says, 'But it's really urgent and important.' Applying the broken record technique, you should say, 'I'm sorry about that but I really cannot work late tonight' and continue to do this until your point is accepted. (See Linehan and Egan, 1983, pp. 80ff. for more discussion of this example.)

BOX 11.2 DIFFERENT TYPES OF ASSERTIVE BEHAVIOUR

Ken and Kate Back (1999, ch. 7) define six main types of assertive behaviour which can be divided into two levels, listed below. The practical implication of their work is that you should normally start by using a low-level assertion. If this is not successful, then you try a high-level assertion. The three types at the lower level are:

- basic assertion (a straightforward statement of what you need, want, believe or feel);
- responsive assertion (where you check what the other person needs or is feeling, by asking them in a straightforward way);
- empathetic assertion (where you make a point of recognizing the other person's point of view or feelings, before you state what you want).

The three high-level types are:

- discrepancy assertion (where you point out the discrepancy between what you have agreed previously on what seems to be happening or is about to happen);
- negative feelings assertion (where you point out the effect that the other person's behaviour is having upon you);
- consequence (the strongest form of assertion – where you tell the other person what will happen to them if they do not change their behaviour).

Back and Back suggests that you should 'use the minimum degree of assertion for achieving your aim' (p. 91, their emphasis). If you do not, then you may be seen as aggressive, and you will have fewer options if the other person does not wish to co-operate.

Does assertiveness always work?

Most texts on assertiveness emphasize the possible benefits of this style of behaviour. But there are also potential problems:

- Assertive behaviour may be 'misread'. It may be seen as aggressive, especially when the person is behaving differently from the way they have acted in the past.
- People have different definitions of assertiveness. For example, untrained women stress the importance of consideration for others, whereas untrained men seem to see assertiveness in terms of power and influence.
- There are issues of gender roles. Male assertion and female assertion can have different consequences, and so reliance on the same techniques may actually work out differently.
- There are situational factors to consider. Certain types of assertiveness may well work better in some situations than others.
- There are cultural differences to consider. Behaviour which is culturally acceptable in the United States and Western Europe may not be accepted in cultures that place very different values upon humility and submission.

POPULAR THEORIES TO IMPROVE YOUR COMMUNICATION

Books on business communication often summarize specific theories of interpersonal communication which are often used on training courses but which you will not find in mainstream social science texts. In other words, they have achieved wide popular acceptance but have often been dismissed or neglected by professional and academic social scientists. To illustrate why this may have happened, we shall briefly introduce a few key concepts from two of these systems – Transactional Analysis (TA) and Neurolinguistic Programming (NLP) – and highlight some important issues.

EXERCISE

Review two or three popular 'self-help' books on how to improve your interpersonal communication. What processes and skills do they emphasize? What research or theories do they seem to be based upon?

What is Transactional Analysis and how does it work?

Suppose you need to talk to Paula Jones, who works in a different department which has just moved into a new office block. You find the right floor of the new block – it has been organized on an open-plan basis but there are no notices to tell you which section people are in, as everyone is unpacking. You notice someone you recognize setting up a computer on a desk. You go across to ask them, 'Where can I find Paula Jones?' How would you feel if you received one of the following responses? For each alternative, imagine how the other person is feeling and thinking, and how you would react:

1   'Paula is in the far right corner over there.'
2   'I have to tell you that I'm not a secretary.'
3   'This computer never works properly for me.'

TA exponents would analyse this interaction using the concept of ego states, which the founder of TA, Eric Berne, defined as 'A consistent pattern of feeling and experience directly related to a corresponding consistent pattern of behaviour'. He decided that there were three distinct categories of ego state, which he called Parent, Adult and Child. In the Parent ego state, you adopt feelings and behaviours which you learnt from the parent figures who cared for you when you were a child. In the Adult ego state, you feel and behave in a logical and rational way in order to cope with whatever is happening in the world around you. In the Child ego state, you feel and behave in ways which are emotional and playful, and which can be described as 'relics' of your own childhood self.

Transactions

Berne called a transaction the 'basic unit' of social interaction. The simplest transaction is a single communication from me and the response from you, as in:

'Hello' – 'Hello'
'Good morning' – 'Morning'

To go back to our example above, response 1 looks like an Adult–Adult transaction. My adult addresses your adult and receives an adult response. This is also what Berne called a complementary transaction – you receive a response from the ego state which you addressed. You can have complementary transactions involving the other ego states, P–P, P–C, C–C and so on.

But what of response 2: 'I have to tell you that I'm not a secretary.' This looks more like Figure 11.4 An A–A stimulus has met a P–C response! And this is an example of a crossed transaction where we will have to adjust our ego states if we do not want this conversation to develop into a row. Perhaps the row has already started!

In the third alternative I gave at the start of this section, you seem to have met someone who needs some help and is using a C–P message to invite you to help them: 'This computer never works properly for me.'

The final main type of transaction is what Berne called the ulterior transaction, which you need to analyse at two levels:

■ the social level – what seems to be happening on the surface, usually Adult to Adult;
■ the psychological level – the covert or hidden message which reflects how the people really feel.

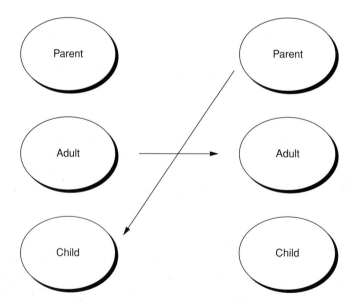

Figure 11.4 Crossed transaction

Spotting the ego states

All of this analysis depends upon being able to diagnose effectively your own and the other person's ego state. How easy is this? Most TA texts will give you a checklist of likely verbal and non-verbal indicators to go with each ego state. For example, the Parent ego state may be recognized by the use of evaluative or moralistic language, accompanied by gestures which imply criticism or support.

But Eric Berne was more cautious, suggesting that a full diagnosis would depend on four different viewpoints – including the other person's behaviour, how this made you feel, the other person's own assessment of their ego state, and analysis of what that person had done in similar situations in the past.

If you want to experiment with these ideas on your own behaviour, then it is worth doing a bit more preparation. Read some more detailed accounts of game analysis; remember to apply a detailed analysis of ego states; and discuss your ideas with others.

Remember that TA was *not* designed to be a manipulative tool to be used on other people.

EXERCISE

Analyse a conversation you have been involved in terms of ego states. Compare your analysis with the other person involved (but remember that this can be quite a revealing exercise).

Neurolinguistic Programming

Neurolinguistic Programming (NLP) was founded in the 1970s by two Americans: Richard Bandler and John Grinder. NLP ideas have since been incorporated into a number of popular management and communication texts, as well as being widely used in training (e.g. S. Knight, 1995, 1999). They claim that you need only three things to communicate well:

■ A clear idea of the outcome you want.
■ Flexible behaviour. You need to find the behaviour which will work in the specific situation.
■ The ability to recognize the responses you are getting from other people. If you can do this, then you will be able to 'home in' on the behaviour which achieves the response you want from the other person.

They also emphasize the importance of non-verbal communication. They advocate specific non-verbal strategies and techniques, such as non-verbal mirroring, but they do *not* claim that each body language signal has a clear and specific meaning. They argue that body language can indicate how a person is responding rather than giving you specific signs or meanings.

Representational systems

One fundamental idea from NLP is that we think using three main representational systems:

- visual, where you see visual images as you think;
- auditory, where you hear sounds inside your head;
- kinaesthetic, where you think in terms of feelings.

For example, if I asked you to tell me about your work, what would go on inside your head as you responded? Would you experience visual images, or sounds, or would you experience some bodily sensations that represent how you feel? NLP claims that we think and *express* ourselves in terms of these systems. It also suggests that we have a favourite system.

Adler (1996) suggests four systems, and offers lists of typical phrases used by someone with preferences for each as follows:

- visual, as in 'I see', 'it appears', 'looking back', etc.;
- auditory, as in 'I hear what you say', 'rings a bell', etc.;
- kinaesthetic, as in 'I feel', 'I'll be in touch', etc.;
- olfactory and gustatory, as in 'fresh as a daisy', 'matter of taste', etc.

Adler goes on to say that you can increase rapport with someone by 'getting to know the thinking preference of the person you are communicating with, and changing your behaviour to literally make more sense to them' (ibid., p. 88). For example, if you are talking to a visual person, then you should use language which corresponds with that representational system. You should say things like 'I see what you mean' or 'that looks fine to me'. By using this technique, '*sometimes almost miraculously*, rapport increases as you share their experience' (Adler and Heather, 1999, p. 62, our italics).

Of course, to use this technique you have to be confident which representation system the other person is using. And that leads to another important idea: that there are reliable ways to recognize somebody's representational system.

Bandler and Grinder (1990) suggest that you can monitor someone's eye movements. You may like to try this out with friends or relatives to see if the generalizations offered by Bandler and Grinder reflect your experience. (See Hartley, 1999, for a fuller discussion, and Adler and Heather, 1999, pp. 92ff. for a recent and typical explanation of NLP thinking.) A reservation concerning this analysis (and with other NLP concepts) is that it has not been supported by systematic research.

EXERCISE

Review your own typical language in terms of the NLP systems. Do you behave consistently as the theory suggests?

Can we believe these popular theories?

Both TA and NLP contain ideas which we think are interesting and useful. But we also have some important concerns:

- Both have suffered by being oversimplified and applied too 'mechanically'.
- Both have been 'oversold'. We believe some of the claims for their success are exaggerated.
- Probably because of the 'overselling', these theories have not attracted the interest of independent researchers. As a result, they both lack independent evidence to show that they really work over a wide range of circumstances.
- Both seem to ignore cultural differences. And this is a general issue for all skills approaches, as we show in Box 11.3.

So one way of looking at any popular analysis of human communication is to ask questions based on these concerns:

- What are the ideas based upon? (Do they come from systematic observation or what?)
- Are the ideas critically examined? (What are the recognized limitations to the ideas?)
- Are they applied in a way which recognizes the specific social context? (Is any account taken of social and cultural differences?)
- Who are the gurus or advocates? (And what is their expertise based on, in terms of experience, training, etc.?)

PUTTING THE SKILLS TOGETHER

Earlier in this chapter we argued that social skills depend upon social understanding. You need to *understand* how and why people are behaving as they do in order to select the appropriate way to behave. We are very suspicious of communication skills training which does not emphasize the need for social understanding and research to accompany the practice of

BOX 11.3 ATTENDING TO CULTURE

So much of the research into interpersonal communication (and so many of the advice texts) is based on US and European examples that it is easy to forget the potential complications of cross-cultural communication. For example:

- Patterns of self-disclosure and relationship development are very different in cultures with strong politeness norms and where the saving of face is critical, like Malaysia.
- NVC has strong cultural variations.
- Assertive behaviour is seen very differently in cultures which do not share the individualistic values of the United States and United Kingdom.

259

techniques. We are not alone in this concern; Deborah Cameron surveyed a range of communication skills courses and training materials and found 'consistent disregard for those bodies of knowledge that derive from the empirical investigation of naturally occurring talk' (2000, p. 51).

One practical way of thinking about this is to approach face-to-face communication as a process with a series of stages, as in Table 11.1. This table emphasizes the planning and preparation which you can undertake before an important face-to-face communication. At first sight this might seem a very deliberate or perhaps even manipulative approach to human relationships. But we are not advocating that you lose all spontaneity and plan *every* encounter in minute detail. We are agreeing with some points made by Peter Honey:

- On many occasions we need consciously to *organize* our behaviour.
- One of the hallmarks of an interactively skilled person is that they frequently declare their objectives openly and explicitly.
- If you have got objectives, your behaviour should be in step with them.

(Honey, 1988, pp. 18ff.)

Honey is very critical of people whose behaviour is 'out of step' with their declared objectives, such as the manager who invites staff to contribute ideas and suggestions and then seems to relish pointing out the defects of every idea but his own. He also comments that planning is not just something we do before an event or activity: 'On-going planning requires us to size up the situation *as we are in it*' (ibid., p. 22). This point highlights a potential criticism of Table 11.1, which implies that we walk into a situation with a single predetermined plan and then simply try to achieve it. Taking the situation described in the table, what would you do if you received a very negative reaction from X when you asked for help/advice? Suppose X's response was 'I'm surprised you don't know that. Aren't you properly qualified for this job?' You need to respond to this not very subtle attack before you can proceed towards your objective. What do you say?

You could respond in a way which allows X to reinforce their negative image of you. For example, if you responded by asserting how well qualified you were, then this could allow X to say, 'Well, you're so well qualified that you obviously don't need my help'. You have just made the relationship worse; X is even more convinced that you are the 'know-it-all' who is just trying to show off your superiority.

So the key to effective interpersonal communication is the flexibility to respond to the other person in order to maintain the original objective. Perhaps asking X for advice is too indirect an approach. Should you adopt a more direct approach and explain how you see the problem to X: 'I feel that we've not managed to sort out how we work together and I'd like to talk about it'? Would this achieve the first step?

We cannot provide a definitive answer to this example because so much depends on the context. What if X feels that all is well and you have misinterpreted his NVC? In this case, a very direct approach might make X feel defensive. And this reflects one of the most important points in this chapter: communicating effectively with other people is *not* just a matter of applying special techniques or behaviours which 'always work'. One fundamental issue is how we perceive the other person and recognize their needs – and this is an important theme of the next chapter.

Table 11.1 *Interpersonal communication as a staged process*

Stage	Content	Points to watch	Example
Decide the general goal	What do you want to achieve overall?		You are a new member of the organization and have been sent to join a new project team. One of the older male members of the team seems to be deliberately unco-operative with you. You want to develop a better relationship with this colleague
Consider the context	What's happened in the past? Who are the participants? What is the setting?	Are there any hidden agendas because of the history? What do your audience need or expect to happen?	What do you know about the history of this group and about X? Suppose you find out from other members that X is generally suspicious of 'new young know-it-alls who want to come in and take over'. So this is the pattern of behaviour which X is expecting of you
Plan	Decide on the objectives. Decide on the structure	Make your objectives realistic and achievable. Make sure your structure leads up to your objective	Your objective is to show X that you value and respect his opinion. You find something which X is very familiar with and you are not: some aspect of the history of the project or some complex company procedure which is new to you. You plan to ask his help by asking him to explain it
Act	Use the relevant skills	What are the most important skills in this situation? e.g. listening, questioning, etc.	You need to choose the right moment so that X feels that the request is genuine and you need to make sure that you listen carefully and don't say anything which X could interpret as criticism
Follow-up	What can make sure that the communication has been effective?	What can you do to reinforce what you have done?	Sometime in the near future you should take the opportunity to thank X for the help and show that you have taken the information seriously

SUMMARY

- The process of interpersonal communication can be complex. Unless you understand some basic features of this process, you can easily behave in ways which the other person does not accept or appreciate.

- You can analyse social interaction as skilled behaviour – it has many of the characteristics of other skills, including the importance of goals and feedback. But it is also important to emphasize that social skills are not just the same as motor skills. There are important differences, including the fact that other people may have different goals, and the importance of personal feelings.

- There are a number of important interpersonal skills, including non-verbal communication (NVC), listening, self-disclosure and assertiveness.

- Many authors stress the advantages of assertiveness without highlighting potential problems. For example, assertive behaviour may be *seen* as aggressive; there are issues of gender roles; and there are important cultural differences to consider.

- There are several 'popular' models of effective communication which are virtually ignored by social science researchers but which are often used in business and management training. We commented briefly on two: Transactional Analysis and Neurolinguistic Programming. Both offer some interesting approaches, but also raise some important concerns. For example, both seem to have suffered by being oversimplified and applied too 'mechanically', and both seem to ignore cultural differences.

- You can approach face-to-face communication as a process with a series of stages, from deciding the goal through planning and on to action. But this must be seen flexibly; effective communication must be based on flexible behaviour which is appropriate to the specific context.

DISCUSSION QUESTIONS

- What social skills are most important in modern business organizations?
- What social skills are most important in your organization?
- What training is available in your organization to help you develop your skills?
- What is the theoretical basis of this training programme?
- Can we confidently recommend assertiveness without worrying about cultural and social context?
- Isn't Honey's approach too mechanical?

FURTHER READING

Cameron, D. (2000) *Good to Talk*. London: Sage. This is an essential read for anyone who is interested in exploring some of the values and critical issues associated with attempts to improve people's communication skills.

Hargie, O. (ed.) (1997) *The Handbook of Communication Skills*, 2nd edn. London: Routledge. Comprehensive collection of articles reviewing research on the main interpersonal skills and their operation in context.

Hargie, O., Saunders, C. and Dickson, D. (1994) *Social Skills in Interpersonal Communication*, 3rd edn. London: Routledge. This has rightly become one of the standard texts on the nature of social skills and a new edition will be available shortly.

Hartley, P. (1999) *Interpersonal Communication*, 2nd edition. London: Routledge. This explores many of the issues we discussed and relates social skills to the model of interpersonal communication used in this chapter.

Chapter 12

Interpersonal skills in action

Communicating face to face

INTRODUCTION

The previous chapter emphasized that effective communication depends on personal aware-ness, interpersonal skills and the context in which people operate. This chapter applies these ideas to common face-to-face situations of two very different types:

■ the more casual, unscheduled or informal interactions and exchanges of information which go on all the time – the conversations and discussions in the office, on the shop floor or service area;
■ the more formal interactions, which are often subject to company rules, regulations and procedures, such as interviews.

In all these situations, we can look at how the participants are working together (or not!) to achieve some understanding which will have an impact on the effectiveness of the orga-nization. As well as highlighting specific skills which we described in Chapter 11, we need to examine the way that participants understand or make sense of the events which unfold, and this is a major theme of the case study which starts the chapter.

OBJECTIVES

This chapter will:

■ show how the principles developed in Chapter 11 can be applied to common face-to-face situations in organizations;
■ analyse a case study which shows how misunderstanding and 'miscommunication' can develop through conversations and discussion in the organization;
■ summarize general principles of selection and appraisal interviews and show how communication influences their outcomes.

CONVERSATIONS IN THE OFFICE – THE CASE OF THE MISSING SERVICE ENGINEER

Jo Brown is General Manager of ABC Computer Services. Jo receives an urgent call from XYZ, an important customer in Durban, who has a 'major fault in his computer system' and demands a service engineer immediately as his whole operation has ground to a halt. Jo tries to contact Edward Smith, the Service Manager, at once but finds he is out visiting PRQ Engineering, another important customer. As Jo considers that the Durban problem is urgent, she goes to the service department and finds service engineer Helen Jones working at her desk. They have the following conversation:

JB: Have you any really urgent work on hand?
HJ: Well, I'm sorting out a few patches for the new system we've sent to PRQ. Mr Smith is expecting me to have them done by tomorrow.
JB: But is it really urgent?
HJ: Well, I don't know . . . I don't suppose so.
JB: Good – you can sort out the Durban problem first.

Jo then decides that Helen should fly to Durban on an afternoon flight so she can start work at XYZ first thing in the morning. Jo suggests that she leave the office immediately to pack and get to the airport. As she is about to leave, Helen says, 'I had better leave a message for Edward Smith.' Jo says, 'Don't worry, I will let Edward know what is happening so he can reschedule your work for the next few days.'

Jo returns to her office and phones XYZ to confirm that Helen Jones will be there first thing in the morning. She then calls Ann Botham, her personal assistant, leaves a number of messages and instructions, and answers some queries. At the end of the call, she says, 'Oh, by the way, let Edward Smith know that Helen Jones will probably be in Durban for a few days working on XYZ's computer problems.'

When Edward Smith returns just after 2 p.m., he finds that Helen Jones is not at her desk, so he leaves a note instructing her to drop everything and go to clear up an urgent problem at PRQ Engineering first thing in the morning. He then leaves the office at 3.30 p.m. to meet another customer and does not return that day.

After working through the other jobs from Jo by around 3.45 p.m., Ann Botham sends an email to Edward Smith saying that Helen Jones will probably be in Durban for a few days on the XYZ job.

Next morning, Edward Smith arrives, notes that Helen Jones is not there, and assumes that she has gone to PRQ Engineering. He has an urgent report to finish, so does not check his email as he usually does first thing. About 9.30 a.m., he receives an irate phone call from PRQ Engineering saying that the promised service engineer has not arrived and threatening to cancel the lucrative service contract. At first no one else in the office knows anything about Helen Jones's whereabouts. As a last resort he checks his email, to find the message from Ann Botham: 'Jo has asked me to let you know that Ms Jones will probably be in Durban at XYZ for a few days.' He is both puzzled and annoyed by the brief message.

About five minutes later, Smith storms into Brown's office and says, 'How the hell do you expect me to run an efficient service department, when you send my staff round the country without letting me know? We will probably lose the PRQ Engineering contract because Helen Jones did not report there this morning as I promised.'

What do you think of communication at ABC?

Before reading on, you might like to consider the following questions:

- What are the most important problems of interpersonal communication illustrated in this case study?
- What are the key factors (both process and meaning) which have created these problems?
- Who was responsible for the problems?
- How could the participants have behaved differently to avoid these problems? (both short-term and long-term).
- Does this case study simply illustrate poor interpersonal communication? Or do you recognize any broader issues?

Our analysis

There are many ways to analyse this incident and we focus on the interpersonal issues. But perhaps there are broader problems in the organization and this conflict is simply a symptom. For example, we have not mentioned the physical surroundings, and researchers have suggested that these can have important influences, as we suggest in Box 12.1.

Moving back to the interpersonal difficulties, we have picked out the following problems. Each one suggests that the participants are not paying much attention to the impact of their communication; they could do with some urgent training in listening, NVC, etc. For each problem, we also suggest an important practical principle which has been ignored.

The request from Jo Brown

Consider the way Jo communicates her own agenda to Helen Jones. If your boss asks you, 'Have you any really urgent work on hand?', this implies that a request is about to follow which *is* really urgent. How is Helen Jones supposed to respond? What does 'really urgent' actually mean? Why did Jo not start on a more neutral note and ask what jobs Helen was undertaking?

And the principle: other people will always try to interpret the *intention* behind what you are saying. This can be a particular problem when status differences are involved.

Jo's reassuring message to Helen

When Helen says she 'had better leave a message for Edward Smith', Jo says, 'Don't worry, I will let Edward know what is happening.' Jo does not do this; she leaves a message for Edward but makes no real attempt to ensure either that Edward has received it, or that the full urgency of the situation is explained.

And the principle: if you give a commitment and a reassuring message, you should make sure that you act on it in the way that you have implied.

BOX 12.1 HOW IMPORTANT ARE THE PHYSICAL SURROUNDINGS IN THE WAYS WE COMMUNICATE?

The idea that our physical surroundings influence how we communicate persuaded many organizations to move to open-plan offices. Sundstrom's review of research studies shows that the outcomes can be more complex. Moving to open plan does give more opportunities for conversations and can lead to perceptions of improved communication. But studies report consistent difficulties in having confidential conversations, and Sundstrom concludes that 'visual accessibility of work spaces is *not consistently associated with communication'* (our emphasis) but does tend to increase 'discretionary, work-related conversations or formal contacts that the initiator considered desirable but not necessary' (Sundstrom, 1986, pp. 266ff.).

As we have discovered many times in this book, communication cannot be determined by a simple change. What have been called 'gathering places' may be more significant than the individual's workspace. These places are where staff typically congregate or meet during their daily routines, by vending machines, photocopiers, in canteens, etc. Organizations should ensure that these places are conveniently situated to encourage communication.

Another aspect of physical space which is relevant to this chapter is the way that staff can manipulate office layouts. For example, Sundstrom cites the case of the executive who arranged his office so that visitors had to sit opposite him, and directly in the light, so it was easier to study their faces.

Jo's message to Edward

Jo does not contact Edward directly but leaves it to Ann Botham. But note the way Jo does this: 'Oh, by the way, let Edward Smith know that Helen Jones will probably be in Durban for a few days working on XYZ's computer problems.' There are several hints in this sentence that the message is not very important: 'by the way' and 'probably'. Ann gives it low priority by leaving it till later.

And the principle: if you delegate a job, then you need to communicate its urgency or priority *explicitly*. Otherwise, the other person will assume the priority from the way you pass it on. In this case, the casual way the message was expressed signalled 'low priority'.

Edward's attempt to contact Helen

When he finds that Helen is not in her office, he leaves a note instructing her to 'drop everything'. If the demand is so urgent, is a note sufficient to explain what needs to happen? Surely not. Edward makes no further attempt to check that the message has been received and understood.

And the principle: always try to receive feedback on messages you send, especially if they are important or urgent.

Edward's confrontation with Jo

How would you respond as Jo to Edward's opening comment: 'How the hell do you expect me to run an efficient service department, when you send my staff round the country without letting me know?' This immediately puts Jo on the defensive, both in the tone and the specific accusation – it is aggressive rather than assertive. Jo will almost certainly respond to the accusation, and the conversation will turn to arguing over who told what to whom, rather than resolving the immediate crisis.

And the principle: the opening to a conversation will establish the tone and the agenda. If you 'say' you want a fight, do not be surprised if you get one.

Resolving the issues

As with so many problems in organizational communication, this crisis could have been avoided if the participants had communicated more carefully. And everyone contributed to the crisis. Even Ann, who simply passed on the message, can be criticized; she did not check whether the message was important or urgent, which she *could* have done.

EXERCISE

How does this case study relate to typical events in your organization? Could it happen where you work? What would/could prevent it happening?

The most significant outcome in our case study is the conflict which has now emerged between Jo and Edward. Of course, we have not explored their history. This may be one symptom of a long-standing personal dispute; Jo does not seem to make much attempt to consult Edward. Or it may be a symptom of confused or sloppy management style. If we assume that there is no personal animosity between them, what could Edward have said? He could have presented the *problem* to Jo: 'We have a crisis as we have both assigned Helen Jones to urgent jobs with different customers. We may lose an important customer if we do not respond promptly.' This form of expression sets out the problem, assumes joint responsibility, does not assign blame, and suggests what needs to happen – it is *assertive* rather than aggressive. Deciding what went wrong, and how it should be resolved long term, is best left till the crisis is over.

One common issue which runs through all these conversations is the way that the participants build up ideas about what an incident means and then translate those into action which may be counterproductive in the long term. One very useful way of analysing this process is described by Linda Ellinor and Glenna Gerard, building on work by Chris Argyris and Peter Senge (Ellinor and Gerard, 1998, pp. 82ff.). They talk about the way we interpret data, make assumptions, draw conclusions and then act on the basis of those conclusions. Other people use a different 'ladder of inference' and arrive at different conclusions from the same event. Table 12.1 shows the steps up the left-hand side and shows how two people (A and B) can arrive at very different conclusions and actions from the same starting point. The logic of Person A is taken from Ellinor and Gerard.

EXERCISE

Analyse an interpersonal misunderstanding which occurred in your worklife. Was this a problem which could be explained in terms of the ladder of inference?

SUPPORTIVE COMMUNICATION

Another way of looking at conversations is to ask whether they are supportive or defensive. Several of the conversations in the case study put the other person 'on the spot', as in Jo's initial request to Helen. This was manipulative and did not encourage Helen to respond openly.

Andrews and Herschel (1996) summarize the way that ideas of supportive communication have developed. They suggest it has five important characteristics (pp. 103–106):

1   It focuses on the problem, not on the person. Contrast what Edward said to Jo in the case study above with our suggestion.
2   It is based on 'congruence', where what we communicate is really based on what we think and feel. In other words, we are not trying to mask what we say – the critical comment delivered with a smile is an example of incongruent behaviour which puts the other person on the defensive.
3   It is descriptive rather than evaluative. Again, compare what Edward said to Jo with what we recommend.

Table 12.1 *The ladder of inference*

	Person A	Person B
Take action	I won't give Sally any key tasks.	I must see Sally for a counselling interview.
Adopt beliefs	Good team players follow the rules and attend meetings on time.	Staff who are on top of their job are able to explain problems to the team.
Draw conclusions	Sally is not a good team player.	Sally is under pressure at the moment.
Make assumptions	Sally does not think this meeting is important.	Sally must be worried about something if she didn't explain.
Add meaning (personal and cultural)	Being late is not acceptable.	People should explain if they cannot attend on time.
Select data (personal and cultural)	Sally came to the meeting late. She didn't say why.	Sally came to the meeting late. She didn't say why.

4   It is 'conjunctive' – in other words, it flows from what has already been discussed and does not interrupt or cut across others.
5   It 'validates' individuals – in other words, it gives the impression that 'whatever the difference in official organisational rank, she or he considers the other individual of equal worth as a person' (pp. 105–106). Box 12.2 gives an example which shows how brief comments can have a very destructive impact.

They also suggest these principles may be especially important in communications between superiors and subordinates, given some of the research which suggests that 'superiors believe they communicate with subordinates more effectively than they actually do' (p. 110).

EXERCISE

How far do staff in your workplace engage in supportive communication? If they don't, why not?

WHEN ORGANIZATIONS PROVIDE THE SCRIPT ...

Many modern organizations train their employees to follow a 'script' in particular situations, for example in sales or telephone conversations with customers, as the following examples illustrate:

- the 'have a nice day' from the restaurant as you leave;
- the 'come again soon' plus 'cheery wave' which restaurant staff were forced to deliver every time;
- the designer clothes shop whose sales staff are forbidden to describe clothes as 'lovely or 'nice' (among the right words are 'exquisite' and 'glamorous');

BOX 12.2 COMMUNICATION CAN DESTROY A RELATIONSHIP IN ONE EASY SENTENCE

The danger of the careless sentence is revealed in the following example, which shows how non-supportive communication can have a powerful and lasting impact: 'The meeting had been quite productive but we had got to a point where we seemed to be a bit stuck and no way forward was emerging. I proposed a possible solution. The senior manager in the meeting immediately responded, "you obviously have not been listening to me. That solution is not appropriate because ... " I felt quite shocked and humiliated by this retort. I had been listening very carefully indeed; we just didn't agree on the way forward. I never trusted that manager again.'

■ the supermarket whose staff must smile and make eye contact with all customers, and are graded on these behaviours as part of performance appraisal (examples from Cameron, 2000, p. 57).

The problem with all such scripts is that they assume the same behaviour means the same thing to all receivers and they assume that everyone can deliver the same script in a completely uniform way. Both these assumptions are suspect. We have argued throughout this book that communication is sensitive to context and is inherently ambiguous. And we have argued that skilled behaviour is flexible. In the long term, organizations who believe that 'good communication' simply equals a 'standard script' may find they have very disgruntled employees.

COMMUNICATION AND INTERVIEWS

One useful definition of an interview comes from Maureen Guirdham (1995, p. 180):

> In an interview, two people meet, face to face, to accomplish a known purpose by talking together. An interview is different from either a negotiation or a problem-solving meeting because it is one-sided – as the words 'interviewer' and 'interviewee' suggest.

This definition ignores the possibility that there might be more than one interviewer in some situations (e.g. a selection panel). But it does highlight the explicit 'known purpose' which is recognized by both sides and the different roles involved. She goes on to discuss the obligations that this places on the interviewers. They are in control and must take responsibility not only to achieve the purpose but also to treat the interviewee fairly and honestly. As we shall see in some later examples, interviewers sometimes ignore this last responsibility and 'play games' which cannot be justified.

The purpose of the interview can also be complex. For example, the purpose of a selection interview is to select the right person for the particular job. But this is not the only goal which the interviewers have to work towards; they must also realize that they are 'representing the organization' to candidates. Candidates will use the interviewers' behaviour and competence as information about 'what the organization is really like' and 'what it might be like to work here'. There is the well-known tale of the organization which decided that the best test for managerial candidates was a series of short, aggressive and stressful interviews. The candidate who performed best in these – staying calm, sticking to his arguments under pressure – was offered the job. He immediately refused it and walked out, commenting that 'if this is how you treat your prospective employees, then I do not want to work for you'.

There are many different types of interview with different purposes, which means that interviewers have to adopt a different approach and use different skills. For example, the typical selection interview will demand good questioning technique; the counselling interview will place more emphasis on reflecting and listening techniques. To illustrate these differences we shall examine two types in more detail: the selection interview and the performance appraisal interview.

Communication in the selection interview

In theory, the selection process is a process of logical steps:

- job description, where the nature and demands of the job are thoroughly reviewed and analysed;
- person specification, where the job demands are translated into the skills and personal characteristics which the person will need to do the job well;
- advertising the vacancy, so that everyone who might meet the specification has the opportunity to apply;
- sorting and short-listing applications, to select candidates who fully satisfy the person specification;
- the selection event itself, which will normally include an interview (see Box 12.3 for some data on how this differs across cultures) but which increasingly includes other tests such as psychometric tests or group tasks.

In practice, this process can be both difficult and time-consuming. For example, the job demands may be changing and there may be some argument as to how the changes should be reflected in the job description and the personal qualities needed. There may also be argument about which of the characteristics in the person specification are the most important. The choice of selection methods may also be controversial. For example, there is debate about the value of psychometric tests. Unfortunately, some organizations do use selection methods which have very dubious validity, such as graphology – the analysis of a person's handwriting.

We do not have the space to explore these issues in this text. Perhaps the most important implication for communication is the possible ambiguity and uncertainty which can creep into the interview room. If the job description and person specification are poorly prepared, then the interviewer might not have a very clear idea of what he or she is looking for. If there is a panel interview then there might be confusion or even clear disagreement between interviewers. The candidate might also have developed a misleading picture of the job depending on how the advertising material was prepared.

EXERCISE

What do you expect to happen if you are a candidate in a selection interview? What behaviour from the interviewer(s) would you consider unacceptable or unexpected? How would you react to this behaviour?

Research on selection interviews has identified many potential problems and pitfalls in the interview process. For example, Mike Smith (1982) suggests five main sources of unreliability:

1   Different interviewers may look for different characteristics in the interviewees. The interviewer who emphasizes technical skills or knowledge may select different

BOX 12.3 SELECTION PRACTICES VARY ACROSS CULTURES

Various studies have shown that there are significant variations between countries in terms of the methods they use to select employees. For example, Hodgkinson and Payne (1998) reviewed how British, Dutch and French organizations selected university graduates. Among the significant differences were the following:

- Traditional interviews were always used by nearly all organizations in Britain and the Netherlands (89 per cent and 85 per cent respectively). Only 45 per cent of French organizations always used them.
- Criterion-referenced interviews were used much more in France than in Britain. Nearly half the British organizations never used them.
- Situational interviews were used much more in France than in Britain. Nearly 63 per cent of British organizations never used them. Sixty-three per cent of French organizations sometimes did.
- Personality tests are used more in Britain than in the Netherlands or in France. Over 40 per cent of British organizations used them all the time.
- References were used much more by British organizations than by the French or Dutch.
- Assessment centres were used very differently. Twenty-six per cent of British organizations used them all the time; none of the French organizations did, although 27 per cent used them sometimes.
- Graphology is used much more in France than in the Netherlands. Eighty-two per cent of French organizations sometimes used it.

Hodgkinson and Payne point out a 'high degree of overall convergence' between these findings and previous studies of selection practices on other employees. What this research does not explain is *why* these differences occur. Hopefully, future research will focus on this question.

candidates from the interviewer who emphasizes personal flexibility or social skills. This highlights the need for a clear person specification.

2   The setting of the interview may influence the interviewee in ways which are un-related to their skills for the job. For example, a candidate recently told us how he had failed his last interview after being 'overwhelmed' by the surroundings. He was expecting a formal panel interview in the committee room with the panel seated behind the long committee table. Instead, he was taken to a corner of the lounge area in the conference block. The seating was low lounge chairs and the panel sat facing him in a circle. He felt very uncomfortable in these unexpected surroundings and came across as nervous and hesitant. One way of minimizing this problem is to give candidates very clear advance information about what the selection event will involve and how it will be organized.

3   The structure of the interview is very important. Common problems are that some interviewers do not structure their interviews carefully so they do not cover all the ground they need to. They will also tend to use a different sequence of questions with different candidates. The same candidate can give a very different impression depending on which sequence of questions they receive.

4   Interviews are interactive. Even interviewers with clear plans and objectives may make unreliable decisions unless they recognize that their behaviour in the interview can influence the way it progresses. For example, Smith (1982, p. 19) quotes a number of interesting research findings, including the following:

■   If the interviewer shows agreement whenever a candidate expresses an opinion, then that candidate will express more personal opinions. Candidates will express fewer personal opinions if they are met by silence and far fewer if they are met by disagreement.

■   Interviewers who self-disclose are more likely to encourage candidates to self-disclose than interviewers who remain impassive.

5   Interviewers may use the information they have gained from candidates in different ways. There are a number of ways we can arrive at a misleading or inaccurate perception of another person. One bias that may be especially important in interviews is the finding that interviewers can place too much emphasis on negative or unusual information.

BOX 12.4 FAIR TREATMENT OR INCOMPETENT PRACTICE?

How would you have responded as a candidate to the following interview situations?

1   'I was straight out of college and this was one of my first interviews, for a copy-writing trainee in an advertising agency. I was shown into the manager's room and sat on the low, comfy chair facing his desk. He looked up and leaned back in his chair, looked me straight in the eye and said, "Hello, Tony". I said "hello" and paused. I was expecting the first question. Nothing happened – he continued to look me straight in the eye. After an awkward pause where I started to panic, I realized he was not going to say something, so I started: "I suppose you'd like to hear something about me." He nodded slightly but still did not say anything. So I started to talk about myself. I wasn't prepared for this and so I didn't feel I was giving a very coherent presentation. After about ten minutes (it seemed a lot longer), I said: "and I'd really like to work for an organization which has exciting development plans. What are your plans?" He leaned back again: "That's a very interesting question – what do you think we should be doing?" After a few more minutes of

desperate improvisation I was told the interview was over. I crawled out of the office, feeling completely dispirited, angry and frustrated. I did not get the job. In retrospect, I'm glad I wasn't offered it.'

2 'I was pleased to be offered an interview for this post in local government as it meant more responsibility, better career prospects, and a useful promotion from my present post. I also wanted to move to that part of the country. I was asked to attend for interview at the local college. When I arrived I was asked to wait as apparently the "interviews are running a few minutes late". Eventually, I was escorted to Lecture Room 6. When I walked in, I was shown to a chair in the position where the lecturer would usually be. I looked up and discovered I was in a banked lecture hall and there must have been about 70 people sitting looking at me. I was asked six questions by different members of the audience – who introduced themselves before their question. None of my answers received any follow-ups or probing questions. If I had known this was going to happen I would have given fuller answers. After my six questions I was thanked and asked to leave. Afterwards, I discovered that these six questions were a standard procedure. The job was controversial because of local politics, so the large audience was because all the interested parties had exercised their formal right to see the candidate.'

3 'I walked into the interview room. The interviewer was standing behind the desk, clutching a stopwatch. He didn't say anything so I sat down in what was obviously the interviewee's chair. He leaned over towards me and said, "Right, you've got ten minutes to sell yourself to me. Go!" He clicked the stopwatch to start the time and sat down with arms folded.'

In all three situations, the candidate expected to receive a conventional interview: a series of relevant questions, some probes and follow-ups, the chance to add their own comments, and the chance to ask questions.

In all three situations, the organization ignored these expectations and presented the candidate with a very different challenge. (Although situation 2 is closest to the expected format, the setting is totally unexpected.) In each case, was the organization behaving legitimately? Does it have a rationale for the specific tactics? How will candidates feel about this 'induction' to the organization? Why weren't candidates told what to expect?

There is no real evidence to suggest that 'shock tactics' help an interviewer arrive at a better opinion of the interviewee's competence and potential. The evidence points the other way. All these three organizations are failing to communicate clear expectations to their candidates. If they make bad selection decisions, they should not be surprised!

Despite continuing concerns about the reliability of interviewer judgements, the interview remains one of the most popular selection methods. Research suggests that its reliability can be improved in several ways, notably by training interviewers to avoid the problems we listed above. If interviewers are sufficiently trained, if they know what characteristics they are looking for, and if they follow a clear (but not over-rigid) interview plan, then they can perform well. They must also have the specific social skills we highlighted in the previous chapter.

The general issues we have identified are summarized in Table 12.2, which applies the model developed in Chapter 11 to the selection interview. This also shows that the specific skills covered in Chapter 11 are all relevant to interview practice. The example of opening and closing will illustrate this.

Opening and closing

The choice of opening can be very important in formal situations such as an interview where the opening can establish either a positive or a negative atmosphere. Which of the following opening techniques would you prefer in a selection interview?

- The interviewer gives you a positive welcome and spends some time in social conversation – breaking the ice – before getting down to business.
- The interviewer starts by describing important features about the company, and the job and then goes straight into critical questions, such as: 'What are the most important attributes you have for this job?'

The first strategy is designed to make you feel relaxed so you can put on the best performance you are capable of. The second is much 'colder' and more official. If it is repeated to every candidate, then you can wonder whether this opening is the best use of interview time – why not have a general briefing of all candidates?

There are also a variety of tactics available to close or conclude the interview. The good interviewer will make sure that the interviewee has a chance to clear up any points they have not understood and will make sure that they know what is going to happen as a result of the interview. We know from our own experience that this does not always happen!

When cultural differences affect a candidate's responses

As we argued in the previous chapter, it is not sufficient just to 'know the techniques' to become a skilled interviewer. The skilled communicator must also be looking for the different meanings which might affect different participants. Many advice books on interview performance are written from a perspective which favours candidates from particular cultural backgrounds (often reflecting middle-class white American values!). Candidates from different cultural backgrounds may not recognize or adapt to the 'hidden rules', as the following examples illustrate (from Hargie, 1997):

- The question 'why have you applied for this position?' may be recognized as an opportunity to show how your skills and background fit you for the position. From a

Table 12.2 The interview as planned communication

Stage	Content	Points to watch	Example
Decide the general goal	What do you want to achieve overall?		You have been asked to carry out the first round of interviews on the candidates for the supervisor position. You have to interview eight candidates, all external, and recommend three for a second interview.
Consider the context	What's happened in the past?	Are there any hidden agendas because of the history?	As all the candidates are external, there should not be any problems because of 'internal politics'.
	Who are the participants?	What does the other person need or expect to happen?	Will the candidates know what this first interview is for? What sort of interview will they expect?
	What is the setting?		What setting will be the best place to interview them to give a professional impression of the organization? (Not a corner of a busy office with phones ringing all the time!)
Plan	Decide on the objectives	Make your objectives realistic and achievable	Your objectives are to: ■ Find which three candidates match the job and person spec. ■ Give them the best chance to show what they can offer. ■ Show them that the organization is a good place in which to work.
	Decide on the structure	Make sure your structure leads up to your objective	You must make sure that you have done your homework: read all the applications; researched the job and person spec. You must have an interview plan which is well structured (and check your questions before the event).
Act	Use the relevant skills	What are the most important skills in this situation? e.g. listening, questioning, etc.	Give the interview a clear, confident introduction. Make sure you listen to each candidate. Make sure you probe the answers to uncover 'the evidence'. Give the candidate the chance to ask questions.
Follow-up			Complete the documentation. Make sure that all candidates are told of the outcome.

different cultural expectation, it may be seen as too obvious to warrant a detailed answer.

■ The question 'Do you have any questions to ask us?' offers an opportunity to impress by asking intelligent questions about prospects and development. It may be ignored by candidates who have the cultural norm of showing respect to the person of high status. From this perspective, asking would be disrespectful.

Organization and structure in the selection interview

Another characteristic which is emphasized in interviewer training is the importance of a clear structure in the interview. Structure can be discussed at two levels: the overall structure of the interview, and the way that questions can be organized in a sensible sequence.

OVERALL STRUCTURE

The simplest way of summarizing the likely structure of a selection interview is to say it will have a beginning, middle and end (Table 12.3).

There are several models of the selection interview which have a more elaborate structure. Problems occur when interviewers 'change the rules' without giving a clear idea of what to expect, as Box 12.4 illustrates.

QUESTION SEQUENCES

In the previous chapter, we introduced the difference between open and closed questions. Open questions invite the candidate to answer in any way they see fit; closed questions ask for a yes/no or specific answer. Hargie *et al.* (1994) suggest that other types of questions are important, including:

■ leading questions, which 'lead the respondent towards an expected response' (Hargie *et al.*, 1994, p. 107) and which could give a misleading impression in a selection interview if the candidate feels obliged to give the 'expected answer';
■ multiple questions, where two or more separate questions are bundled together as one. This confuses candidates – which question should I answer first?

Table 12.3 Stages in the selection interview

Section	What they might contain
Beginning	Candidate is welcomed.
	Interviewer(s) introduce themselves and explain how the interview will be conducted.
	Opening questions are designed to make the candidate feel at ease.
Middle	Interviewer asks main questions and follow-ups.
Ending	Interviewer invites candidate to ask any questions.
	Interviewer explains what will happen next.

Of course, there is no guarantee that a specific type of question will elicit the intended response, as the following examples illustrate:

Q: How long did you spend in the Sales Department? [closed question anticipating short, factual answer]
A: Well, I don't think that I really spent long enough as I felt that I should have been able to . . . [extended answer]

Q: What do you think about expanding the form's international links? [open question anticipating a long answer]
A: Very good idea. [restricted answer]

Interviewers may need to ask a series of open or closed questions to get the response they want from candidates, and this is where *sequences* of questions and the use of probes become important. Probes are designed to 'probe' the previous answer in order to get a more detailed picture. For example, suppose you were interviewing a young graduate and wanted to check their IT competence. You might start with a general question: 'How much IT did you use at college?' Suppose the candidate simply said, 'We used it quite a bit.' This answer could be probed in a number of ways – one sequence could be:

- Which software packages have you used?
- What did you use them for?
- What is the most complex task you've done with IT?

This sequence and further probes should establish both the breadth and depth of the candidate's expertise. Good interviewers will also probe to establish the evidence behind the candidate's answers. For example, does using IT 'quite a bit' mean 'word-processing one essay a month' or 'using the Internet and computerized databases every day'?

Popular sequences of questions include:

- funnel sequence, which starts with open questions and then narrows down, using closed questions and probes;
- inverted funnel, which starts with closed questions and then opens out;
- tunnel sequence where all the questions are at the same level; they are usually closed (Hargie *et al.*, 1994, pp. 102ff.).

EXERCISE

Think back to selection interviews you have undergone. How skilled were your interviewers? What techniques did they use? And how did these techniques affect your performance?

Communication in the appraisal interview

Most modern organizations have an appraisal system (Table 12.4) with the following characteristics:

- A formal meeting takes place between a boss (appraiser) and subordinate (appraisee) which takes place at least once a year and which reviews how the appraisee has performed over the previous period.
- The appraiser gives feedback to the appraisee and the meeting discusses this feedback.
- The meeting is based in some documentation which both parties have to consider before the meeting.
- The outcomes of the meeting are a formal assessment (usually written and kept) of how the appraisee has progressed and what this means for future performance (e.g. future targets agreed) and staff development (e.g. agreed training or development plan).
- These procedures are usually established and monitored by the human resources function within the organization.

Within this broad framework there are important differences in the ways that organizations implement appraisal, including some which will directly affect the communication:

What is the system called and why?

Is it the 'appraisal system' or the 'performance review' or the 'performance development review' or what? The choice of title may well be perceived in particular ways by staff depending on the history and context. When one large organization we know announced its new 'appraisal system' to replace the existing 'staff development system', this aroused widespread suspicion. Many staff saw the change as a management ploy to exert closer control on employees. The human resources department had to work very hard to clarify what the change was designed to achieve.

How does the appraisal link to other systems?

One common research finding is that it is a mistake to link the staff appraisal with the pay or reward system, or with any system of performance-related pay. If it is linked, the appraisees become defensive and manipulative in the way they approach the appraisal. In other words, they approach the appraisal with the goal of scoring points to win a higher award and will try to conceal any weaknesses or problems. The objective of open, honest communication is doomed from the start. Despite this evidence, some organizations persist in linking appraisal to pay and ignore the long-term impact on their organizational culture.

Table 12.4 *Appraisal as planned communication*

Stage	Content	Points to watch	Example
Decide the general goal.	What do you want to achieve overall?		You are a new member of the organization. You have been invited to your first annual appraisal meeting by your manager. You want to convince them that that your first year has been successful and that you want to develop your skills to be considered for regrading.
Consider the context.	What's happened in the past? Who are the participants? What is the setting?	Are there any hidden agendas because of the history? What do your audience need or expect to happen?	Does this organization take appraisal seriously? What is the documentation that you have to fill in beforehand? You need to review this and decide on the best way to fill this in. What is your relationship with the manager? How much are they aware of what you have done since joining? You need to note down the points that you really want to get across.
Plan.	Decide on the objectives. Decide on the structure	Make your objectives realistic and achievable. Make sure your structure leads up to your objective	Your objectives are to: ■ show what contribution you have made so far; ■ find out how you are seen in terms of possible advancement; ■ discover what you have to do to be considered for regrading. In this case, the structure of the interview is decided by the appraiser. But you need to have your script ready in terms of these objectives to make sure these points are covered.
Act.	Use the relevant skills.	What are the most important skills in this situation? e.g. listening, questioning, etc.	You need to explain what you have achieved, without exaggerating, and respecting the contributions of others. You need to respond to any criticism without sounding defensive (and you may need to challenge it assertively if it feels unjustified).
Follow-up.	What can ensure that the communication has been effective?	What can you do to reinforce what you have done?	You need to show that you have acted on what is agreed, e.g. by seeking out development or training opportunities.

What is the documentation like?

The appraisal documentation can be very different in terms of what it focuses on and how it encourages the appraisee to express him- or herself. For example, compare the emphasis in the following very different approaches:

- One example produced by the British arbitration service, ACAS, is based on 'comparison with objectives'. It asks the appraisee to write responses on 'Progress towards achievement of objectives and factors influencing results' and 'Other achievements'.
- The system used by British Petroleum assesses all employees against its 'Essential Behaviours Checklist', which includes 'open thinking', 'building team success' and 'sharing achievement'.

If you are about to be appraised, these different approaches would establish very different expectations of how the process will develop.

How are the appraisees informed about what to expect?

Even if very comprehensive documentation exists, differences can arise. Whether consciously or subconsciously, appraisers will communicate to their appraisees how important the scheme is and what they can expect from it. For example, is the appraisal meeting given priority? Does the appraiser accept any interruptions to the meeting, such as phone calls or messages? How thoroughly does the appraiser prepare?

What happens between appraisal interviews?

If nothing happens between the annual meetings in terms of monitoring and follow-up, the system can easily fall into disrepute.

Do the appraisers have the necessary skills?

If the appraiser does not have the necessary social skills, the system can easily collapse. Is there training to make sure that everyone is adopting a consistent approach?

All these factors will influence the way that the feedback is delivered. Clive Fletcher (1994, pp. 119ff.) summarizes research evidence on the factors which determine the effects of feedback. He identifies six factors:

- *The amount of critical feedback.* He quotes one study which found that appraisees received an average of thirteen criticisms per interview and another where managers were spending on average around one-quarter of the interview criticizing or attacking the appraisee. In these circumstances, it is not surprising if the appraisees adopt a defensive attitude!

- *The balance in the performance review.* The balance between positive and negative feedback is very important.
- *The content of the feedback.* For example, is it clear and unambiguous? Is it relevant to what the person does or does it focus on more personal characteristics?
- *The use of a range of measures.* If there is a wide range of evidence on how well the person is doing and if this evidence is available before the meeting, then this will support the discussion.
- *The way the interview is organized and conducted.* Perhaps the critical factor here is how well and to what extent the appraisee is able to participate in the discussion.
- *The relationship between the appraiser and appraisee.* If there is already a good relationship, this will make the appraisal much easier.

The problems with many appraisal schemes have led to new variations emerging. For example, some organizations have put much more emphasis on self-appraisal as a device for encouraging staff to reflect on their performance and suggest ways they can improve. Another way is to increase the variety of feedback available, as in 360-degree feedback which we describe in Box 12.5.

The skill of feedback?

We have already highlighted the importance of feedback in the appraisal interview, and there are a number of less formal situations where someone might need to receive feedback on their performance. So is there a 'correct' way of delivering feedback so that the person accepts it without becoming antagonistic or defensive?

There are a number of guidelines available. Most of them focus on the issues identified by Harry Levinson, who offers the following advice, especially when giving negative feedback (quoted in Goleman, 1996, pages 153–154):

- *Be specific.* Feedback should highlight specific events or examples rather than just general advice. It should also be specific about what the person did.
- *Offer a solution.* Feedback should suggest ways of resolving any problems. There is little or no point in offering negative feedback where there is no way the person can improve.
- *Deliver the feedback face to face.*
- *Be sensitive.* This is simply a reminder that feedback, even negative feedback, should be delivered in a positive way rather than simply attacking the other person.

BOX 12.5 360-DEGREE FEEDBACK

Peter Ward is one consultant who has used this method in a number of British organizations. He defines the method as 'The systematic collection and feedback of performance data on an individual or group, derived from a number of stakeholders in their performance' (1997, p. 4).

For example, suppose you are a junior manager in a retail company. Data on your performance will be collected from relevant stakeholders such as your staff, your boss, other managers you have to deal with, and your main customers. The data will be collected systematically using questionnaires or interviews, or perhaps both. You will receive a written report which summarizes the results and you will have a chance to reflect on this report before you discuss it with your appraiser. This discussion will cover four areas:

- your strengths – those behaviours where you see yourself as strong and where others also rate you as strong;
- your development areas – those behaviours where you think you need to improve, and so do others;
- discrepancies – those behaviours where you see yourself as strong but where others do not; in other words, where there is a discrepancy between how you see yourself and how others see you;
- hidden strengths – those behaviours where others see you as strong but where you have not rated yourself highly.

As our brief summary implies, this system is both complex and time-consuming. If it is implemented carefully, it can make a significant impact on the culture of a company over time. If it is treated as a 'quick fix', it will probably do more harm than good. As with all such schemes, the quality of communication is critical to its success.

SUMMARY

- The skills and techniques which were explained in Chapter 11 can be applied in common face-to-face situations in organizations, both casual conversations and discussions, and more formal interactions, such as selection and appraisal interviews.
- One important issue is the way that participants understand or 'make sense' of the events which unfold. We can easily jump to misleading or unwarranted assumptions, and base our communication on these. Such false assumptions can very easily lead to confusion and conflict.
- Supportive communication is important, especially in encounters where there is a status difference.

- Organizations which train employees to use standard, inflexible scripts in certain situations are adopting a very limited view of human communication.
- In formal situations such as interviews, the person in control, the interviewer, has special responsibilities to manage the interaction so that communication is open and focused on the specific objectives.
- A range of communication problems can affect the selection interview, and interviewers should be trained to avoid these.
- Similar problems can be found in the appraisal interview, where clarity of objectives and clear communication are critical.
- New methods and models of appraisal are being developed but they all hinge on the skills of delivering feedback.
- Appraisers should understand and use guidelines for achieving effective feedback, as should all staff who have to make comments on others' performance.

DISCUSSION QUESTIONS

- How would you describe the skills and techniques which are used in common face-to-face situations in your organization?
- How important are casual conversations and discussions in the office or on the shop floor? How does the organization encourage or discourage these?
- Our case study showed that staff can easily base their communication on misleading or unwarranted assumptions. What would happen in your organization in similar circumstances?
- Do managers in your organization use supportive communication?
- How are formal situations such as interviews managed and monitored in your organization? Are you aware of typical communication problems? Are interviewers trained to avoid these?
- How does your organization use appraisal interviews? How do the appraisers deliver feedback?

FURTHER READING

Cameron, D. (2000) *Good to Talk*. London: Sage. This offers some very interesting analysis of the formulaic routines which are recommended in some workplaces. See chapter 3, for example.

Duck, S. (1998) *Human Relationships*, 3rd edn. London: Sage. Many of our examples have important implications for the relationships between the participants. This book offers a very clear and comprehensive introduction to the study of human relationships, inside and outside work.

Sypher, B.D. (ed.) (1997) *Case Studies in Organizational Communication 2: Perspectives on Contemporary Work Life*. New York: Guilford. A useful source of case studies which show how communication can work (or not) in real organizations.

Chapter 13

Meetings and presentations

INTRODUCTION

Most people are anxious about standing in front of an audience to deliver a talk. One US survey found that 'giving a speech is the greatest fear people possess; they fear it even more than dying' (Rasberry and Lemoine, 1986, p. 178). A survey by the Aziz Corporation in the United Kingdom found that 76 per cent of people in business believe that public presentations are 'the most daunting task they have to do in the world of commerce' (Aziz, 2000, p. 49).

The problem of ineffective meetings has been described as one of the most important issues facing contemporary organizations. If presentations make us nervous, then meetings seem to make us disappointed and cynical:

- 'Many of us spend too much time in meetings. A lot of organizations have too many meetings and/or ineffective meetings' (Gallagher *et al.*, 1998).
- 'A meeting brings together a group of the unfit, appointed by the unwilling, to do the unnecessary' (quoted in many texts, including Gallagher *et al.*, 1998, and Stanton, 1996).

Both presentations and meetings are often criticized for being poorly organized or badly planned. This chapter concentrates on principles and techniques which can overcome these criticisms. We shall mention some of the group dynamic issues which can also affect meetings, but these will be covered more fully in Chapter 14.

We start by looking at important differences between business meetings and then review various ways to improve their effectiveness. Applying the ideas and principles in this chapter should enable you to run the sorts of meetings which John Tropman (1996) describes as 'excellent', where:

- Decisions are made and agreed.
- The group does not have to revisit or rework 'old' decisions.
- The decisions are good – well worked out and successful.
- Members enjoy the meeting and feel that it has been productive.

We can also improve oral presentations using principles of planning and organization. We explain why they are so important in modern organizations, and look at why giving presentations can cause such anxiety. One important recent development is the use of computer technology. This technology can be used in ways which increase impact and boost the speaker's self-confidence.

OBJECTIVES

This chapter will:

■ analyse the main differences between different types of meetings;

■ identify principles which have been associated with effective meetings, highlight potential pitfalls and problems, and identify important skills for meeting chairs;

■ review different procedures and practical steps which have been proposed to improve meetings;

■ explain why oral presentations are so important in modern organizations;

■ review the main reasons why giving presentations can cause anxiety;

■ summarize the main techniques which speakers can use to improve the chances of success;

■ show how presentation software can be used to make the presentation look more professional and boost the speaker's self-confidence.

TWO CONTRASTING MEETINGS

Consider the following two extracts from business meetings and identify what you think are the most important differences between the meetings.

Meeting A

Speaker 1: OK, well we need to consider John's concerns about the store in Smallville.

Speaker 2: It's just not doing enough business for a store that size. You can see from the figures in Table 3 in the report sent out last week.

Speaker 3: So how can we bump up business?

Speaker 4: The only way is to put up a Slow Down sign and lay a series of small, sharp spikes across the roadway just outside the store.

Speaker 5: Pardon?

Speaker 4: It's obvious. People will slow down, get a puncture and stop. While they're waiting for the breakdown services to arrive, they will have no choice but to go in the store and spend some money.

Speaker 5: You're not serious?

Speaker 4: Of course not. But can you see my point? [pause: some other members of the meeting groan at the very tortured pun]. We do need to get more people in that store. Look at the figures in table 4, which compares different stores across the region. You can see from column 5 that the customers who go in to Smallville spend more on average than customers who visit some of our other stores. We just need to get more people through the door.

Speaker 1: So are we agreed that the best strategy is to work out how to attract more customers to visit the store? OK, so how can we do that?

Meeting B

Speaker 1: We are quorate, so we can now move to the first item on the agenda: the proposal that we close the South Street office in Smallville. You will all have received the paper on this, reference 99/8/2, and I will ask the writer, John Smith, to summarize the main points for us.

Speaker 2: The critical point here is that if we combined the Smallville offices on our main street site then we could offer a much better service to the local community. Apart from some savings due to greater efficiency, we would be more competitive. We could offer a wider range of services by putting the two offices together. We also have no evidence that the existing customers at South Street would be disadvantaged. In fact, we feel that many of them, if not most of them, would find it more convenient to come to Main Street.

Speaker 1: So the proposal is that we merge the two offices on the main street site. Have we any comments or further proposals?

Speaker 3: I have to say that my staff are very concerned about this proposal, in terms of the messages it sends to loyal and hard-working staff. You have glossed over the fact that the South Street office is extremely profitable and has won awards for the quality of its service and management.

Speaker 1: John, can you respond to that?

Speaker 2: We have considered these points. I can assure you are that there will be no redundancies and all of the staff will be accommodated at Main Street.

Speaker 1: Any other comments? [pause]. So if there are no further points then we can move to a vote?

Speaker 4: Point of order, please, chair. According to our terms of reference, I do not believe that we can make this decision without further consultation.

Speaker 1: Yes, we shall need to check that. Rather than hold up this meeting, I shall ask the secretary to check that during the coffee break and we shall return to this item of business at the end of the meeting. Moving on to item 2 on the agenda . . .

So what were the main differences between these two meetings? There are obvious similarities. Both aimed to reach a decision on an important issue. There was an exchange of opinions and the discussion moved towards the final decision.

The differences are more striking. For example:

- More members spoke in meeting A.
- In B, every comment was directed through the chair (speaker 1).
- The style of the conversation was more light-hearted in A (as in the rather feeble joke from speaker 4).

288

- There were several references to formal rules and regulations in B (the debate over the terms of reference, and the check on whether the meeting was quorate).
- The behaviour of the chair was very different (speaker 1 in both cases).
- The procedures were different (e.g. the automatic move to a vote to close the decision in B).

These examples illustrate two of the main dimensions along which meetings can vary:

- the use of formal rules and regulations;
- the degree of structure in the meeting (how clearly it is organized in terms of the items to be discussed and the order in which they are discussed).

These dimensions can be represented as in Figure 13.1, and one can imagine meetings which fall in different sections of the diagram. At position A, we have a meeting which is very tightly structured and which follows formal rules and regulations. An example here would be the annual general meeting of a company or the monthly meeting of a local government committee. At position B, we have a meeting which is tightly structured but which is not subject to very formal rules. An example might be a project or management team meeting.

One obvious implication is that each meeting should be at the appropriate spot on this diagram. For example, suppose you wished to run a meeting to introduce new people to one another and to generate some fresh ideas for new projects. Organizing in style A would be counter-productive, and you would probably use style C. On the other hand, the meeting of a very large official committee might have to follow format A to ensure that the business was seen to be carried out fairly.

EXERCISE

Consider the typical style of meetings in your organization. What are the typical characteristics? Where do they fit on Figure 13.1?

	B	Tight structure	A
Few rules of procedure		Many rules of procedure	
	C	Loose structure	D

Figure 13.1 *Dimensions of meetings*

WHAT MAKES MEETINGS EFFECTIVE?

Every textbook on business communication includes some advice on how to run effective meetings. But much of this advice seems to be based upon the author's personal experience rather than more comprehensive research (for a typical example, see Bell and Smith, 1999, pp. 420–423). Research studies which compare how meetings are conducted in different organizations and in different contexts are relatively thin on the ground, although there are plenty of texts offering advice (e.g. Hodgson and Hodgson, 1992). One notable exception is the work by John Tropman, reporting the conclusions of the Meeting Masters Research Project (Tropman, 1996). This American project aimed to identify individuals who ran excellent meetings and to decide how they did it. The research suggested that 'Meeting Masters' always followed seven main principles, as follows.

The orchestra principle

The orchestra principle emphasizes the high degree of co-operation necessary to complete the task, as you need with the performance of a symphony orchestra. The role of chair is analogous to the role of the conductor: making sure that everyone delivers their best performance, and making sure that everything fits together.

The three characters principle

The three characters principle is based upon the notion that you can do only three things in a meeting:

- announce something;
- decide something;
- discuss something.

Tropman also suggests that each business *item* can do only one of these three things. The meeting should be organized so that members clearly know which item is which. He also suggests that items should be dealt with in that order:

- First you run through all the announcements.
- Then you cover all the items where you need decisions.
- And then you cover the items which need to be discussed but where you do not have to reach a decision.

The role principle

The person in the chair should act as a role model to encourage the other members of the group to contribute openly and positively.

No new business

The meeting should cover only items which have been placed on the agenda and which the members have had some chance to think about. Otherwise, members will not be prepared for the discussion and this will inevitably lead to time being wasted in a fruitless argument.

No more reports

Members are never asked simply to 'give a report from their department', as this can often lead to individuals concentrating on topics which show them up in the best light and failing to identify important issues.

The imperative of proactivity

Meetings should always include some items which deal with future plans or problems, so that issues are discussed before it is too late. Early discussion can enable members to have an impact on future events.

High-quality decisions

Not only are decisions made, but those decisions show 'evidence of quality'. Not only are all the important views discussed and analysed, but the meeting is able to 'construct a decision that advanced the interests of all of the stakeholders' (Tropman, 1996, p. 10).

EXERCISE

Review meetings you have attended in the light of these principles. If they have not been followed, can you explain why?

Tropman suggests rules which can help you apply these principles. Among the most interesting are the rule of six and the rule of two-thirds:

The rule of six

Tropman suggests that:

- About one-sixth of the items on an agenda should be from the past. These have not been completed or perhaps have been deliberately held over from a previous meeting.
- About four-sixths of the items should come from the present. These are important issues that need to be dealt with immediately.
- About one-sixth of the items should relate to the future. These are issues which are likely to be important in the future and which are worth discussing before they become urgent.

291

This way of structuring a meeting also allows Tropman to introduce a sub-rule: the two-meeting rule. This rule suggests that controversial items should be discussed first at one meeting without any decision being taken. They should then be *decided* at the next meeting. This allows members to discuss the item freely and possibly disagree quite strongly, but then leaves some time to reflect upon the issues so that the final decision is not made in the heat of an argument.

The rule of two-thirds

Tropman suggests that all meetings can be divided into three parts, what he calls 'the "get-go", the heavy work, and the decompression'. The middle part of the meeting should contain the important items for decisions, and this is reflected in Tropman's procedure for organizing the agenda, which we talk about later.

The role of the chair

Tropman emphasizes the importance of pre-meeting preparation and the influence of the chair's behaviour. We agree with this emphasis. There is also British research which complements Tropman's analysis of what effective chairs usually do. Rackham and Morgan (1977) showed that effective chairs behaved very differently from the average member of the meetings. For example, they did much more summarizing, and testing of understanding.

Developing the agenda

One of the most important devices for structuring a meeting is the agenda. Tropman proposes seven categories of agenda items, which should be organized as in table 13.1 in a two-hour meeting.

EXERCISE

Do a time analysis of recent meetings you have attended and compare it to Table 13.1. Was the time well managed?

The distribution of time shown in the table gives a bell curve, and so Tropman talks of the 'agenda bell'. Whether meetings follow this exact distribution or not, it is critical that members know the status and priority of each item on the agenda – 'Are we just discussing this or do we have to make a decision?'; 'Do we have to make a decision today?' The agenda should communicate this information to members. Unfortunately, many agendas do not. This may be just a matter of adding a subheading to the title of the item. For example, consider the difference between these two agenda items:

4 Report from J. Smith on the Eureka Project.
5 Report from G. Smith on the Alumni Project:
- review progress to date;
- determine resource allocation for the next financial period;
- decide on the proposal to extend the project to the central site.

Item 4 gives no indication of what should be discussed or decided; item 5 gives very clear information on what needs to be done.

Table 13.1 Tropman's seven categories of agenda items

Category	Item	Type	Time (minutes)
1	Minutes		10
2	Announcements		15
3	Decision	Easy	15
4	Decision	Moderately difficult	15
5	Decision	Hardest item	25–40
6	Discussion		15–30
7	Discussion	Easiest item	10

Source: Adapted from Tropman (1996, pp. 24–27)

Minutes and follow-up

The minutes of a meeting can be very different in style and detail: 'minutes vary from the cursory "bullet" variety to the long "court reporter" variety' (Tropman, 1996, p. 30).

At one end of the scale, we have decisions or action points recorded as a list with no explanation or elaboration of the discussion. This is appropriate for some meetings, say a small project group. At the other end, we have a complete record of what everyone said. A verbatim report of that kind is far too time-consuming, and is unnecessary for most if not all business meetings. A useful compromise is to prepare what Tropman calls 'content minutes' – for each item on the agenda, a minute is written as two separate paragraphs which:

- summarize the main points in the discussion;
- summarize the decision taken or the action agreed, naming whoever has to carry it out, and giving the timescale or deadline.

From this we can suggest that effective minutes must convey all the following information:

Details of the meeting itself	Details of the outcomes
Who was present and who did not attend When and where it took place When and where the next meeting will take place.	What was agreed Who has to take actions as a result, and by when.

There is also the problem of deciding the style and layout of minutes. For example, should the minutes identify who said what? Baguley (1994, p. 94) gives an example of minute structure which includes the following item:

4. Joan Harris reported that software development was on target and still had an anticipated beta version completion date of end of March. There were, however, still problems with Ron Stanning's lack of co-operation over graphics programming availability.

Action agreed: Valerie Williams to set up meeting with Ron Stanning and Joan Harris to resolve problems.
Completion by: 21 Nov 1994.

This example does meet many of the suggestions given above. But there is one important issue: the minutes record that Ron Stanning is being 'unco-operative'. Should this have been recorded? Did the meeting establish this 'fact' or is it simply Joan Harris's opinion? If you were Ron and felt there were good reasons not to supply a graphics programmer, how would you respond to this judgement in the minutes? Should that sentence have read 'Ron Stanning had not supplied a graphics programmer to the project'? Or is a more fundamental change of style required? As minutes remain as a formal record of what has happened, you need to be very careful that they are accurate and that they do not record as 'fact' anything which could be contested later.

EXERCISE

Review the style of minutes which are used in your organization. How would you describe the language style? How was this style developed or agreed? How does this style reflect the culture of the organization?

PROCEDURES AND TECHNIQUES TO IMPROVE MEETINGS

Several techniques have been recommended in order to improve particular aspects of meetings, including:

- brainstorming, which is designed to produce more creative ideas;
- structured problem-solving;
- Nominal Group Technique, also designed to help problem-solving and decision-making;
- Delphi technique, to support a group which cannot physically meet;
- encouraging group innovation;
- clarifying decision-making procedures.

Brainstorming

There are two general principles behind brainstorming: that problem-solving is best done in stages and that each stage should obey certain rules. The first stage is the generating of ideas. *All* the ideas generated during this stage are recorded for later consideration. Brainstorming sessions usually have someone to lead the session who can enforce the rules and act as scribe. This first stage should also have a definite time limit, say ten minutes. During this time, everyone in the group must obey the following rules:

- no evaluation: no one is allowed to criticize or evaluate any of the ideas being expressed;
- no censorship, so all ideas are accepted and recorded;
- participants are encouraged to produce as many ideas as possible in the given time;
- participants are encouraged to hitch-hike, i.e. to build upon the ideas that have been suggested by others in the group.

After the time limit is up, each idea is looked at in turn to see if it is worth pursuing.

But does brainstorming 'work'?

It is difficult to say how useful brainstorming is in practice, which demonstrates some of the problems of undertaking social research (Hartley, 1997). You can find positive and enthusiastic summaries of this technique from practitioners and in some textbooks, but you can also find many researchers who are *very* sceptical of these claims. However, some of the research studies have not been very 'realistic' tests of the method. As we do not have definitive evidence either way, perhaps the best conclusion is to argue that brainstorming is worth considering as a technique but should be used carefully:

> 'I will continue to use brainstorming groups because they can have important social effects – they can act as an "ice-breaker" to help a group develop more of a co-operative spirit. They can also produce good ideas, especially when a group has tried other ways and is getting "stuck" on a particular issue. But they are not a magic solution which will guarantee success.'
>
> (Hartley, 1997, p. 16)

EXERCISE

Is brainstorming used in your organization? If so, when and how? Do participants follow the rules? Is there any evidence that it is useful?

Structured problem-solving

Structured problem-solving is the philosophy on which techniques like brainstorming are based: break down the problem-solving process into discrete stages and then deal with each stage in turn:

- study/discuss/analyse the situation;
- define the problem;
- set your objective;
- generate alternative solutions;
- establish evaluation criteria;
- evaluate alternatives;
- choose among alternatives.

There are many slight variations on this theme. For example, you can argue that deciding the evaluation criteria – on which you judge the possible solutions or decisions – should be done earlier (see Proctor, 1999, for a range of methods).

Nominal group technique

Nominal group technique (NGT) tries to organize the group decision-making to give everyone in the group equal status. The presumed advantage is that everyone will feel able to generate ideas without worrying about how those ideas will be judged by other members who might have higher status. NGT mixes group discussion with independent generation of ideas and independent judgement. Robbins (1996, p. 324) describes it as 'a group decision-making method in which individual members meet face-to-face to pool their judgements in a systematic but independent fashion'.

Usually with an external facilitator to work through the process, the specific steps are as follows:

- The problem is fully explained to the group.
- Individuals work independently to write down ideas and possible solutions.
- Each individual presents one idea to the group in turn until all the ideas are recorded (this could be on a flipchart or whiteboard or using Post-It notes or index cards pinned to the wall).
- Each idea is discussed, clarified and evaluated by the group.
- Individuals privately rank the ideas.
- The group decision is the idea which achieves the highest average ranking.

Delphi

The Delphi technique does not involve a face-to-face meeting. It uses the same steps as NGT and has been used in many different types of organization since its early development in the 1950s (Hargie and Tourish, 2000). The main stages are:

- enlisting the group;
- distributing the statement of the problem to the group members and inviting them to respond;
- compiling the responses;
- sending out the compiled responses for further comment.

These last two phases are then repeated until a consensus is reached. We have used this technique successfully on research projects which demanded that we convene a panel of experts who were unable to physically meet.

Encouraging group innovation

Michael West and colleagues have carried out a number of studies which suggest four factors enourage team innovation:

- vision;
- participative safety;
- climate for excellence;
- support for innovation.

Research suggests that these factors accurately predict whether a team will be able to produce innovative ideas and solutions (West, 1994).

Changing decision-making

A group or committee should consider its present strategy for making decisions – what are its advantages and disadvantages? There are numerous alternatives. Table 13.2 lists many of these and identifies one major advantage and disadvantage of each (from Hartley, 1997).

Table 13.2 Group decision-making methods

Method	Advantage	Disadvantage
Decision by authority without discussion	Speed	Does not use members' expertise.
Decision by authority after discussion	Allows everyone to express opinion	Members may not be committed to the decision.
Decision by expert member	Good decision if really expert	May be difficult to identify the most expert member.
Average members' opinions	Speed	Members may not be committed to the decision.
Majority control	Speed	Minority can be alienated.
Minority control	Can be useful if not everyone can attend	Members may not be committed to the decision.
Consensus	Members will be committed to the decision	Can take a great deal of time, skill and energy.

There are of course additional advantages and disadvantages to each. And we cannot decide on the 'best' unless we know the context and the demands of the situation.

Comparing methods

It is difficult to decide which of these methods to use as there is insufficient research on their everyday applications. The research does suggest a number of general conclusions:

- Groups using systematic procedures probably do make better decisions.
- Members of groups using these procedures seem both more satisfied and more committed.
- Groups which regularly review their own procedures are usually more effective than those that do not. So we should also apply this to committees and working groups in terms of their meetings.

This analysis of meetings has assumed that the members are co-operating and are genuinely interested in problem-solving. We must not forget that many real meetings are constrained or influenced by political factors, as illustrated in Box 13.1.

EXERCISE

Consider specific groups/committees in your organization. How often do they review their own procedures? If not, why not? What sort of improvements could they make?

BOX 13.1 WHEN MACHIAVELLI COMES TO THE MEETING

Political issues and hidden agendas may influence meetings even when the majority of participants are trying to arrive at the most 'rational' decisions. Buchanan and Badham (1999) highlight some of the consequences of 'power games' which can affect events such as meetings: 'Agendas are restricted to "safe" issues; controversial issues are excluded from informal conversations and from formal decision-making processes' (p. 55). Martin (2000) describes bargaining tactics which can be used in meetings to gain an advantage, such as describing a worse situation than actually exists and then backtracking to the position which you wanted in the first place. For example, 'we have to increase prices by 10 per cent' after discussion becomes 'we agree to increase prices by 5 per cent' where 5 per cent was the original hidden objective. The problem with all devious tactics like this is that they can rebound on you if they are discovered. And you may *never* achieve trust if others suspect you of these tactics.

WHY ARE ORAL PRESENTATIONS IMPORTANT?

One reason why oral presentations are important is that they are now very common. Some organizations now use presentations in meetings where previously they might have circulated lengthy written reports. One advantage is that doing so can speed up the decision-making. A disadvantage is that a poor presentation might not do justice to the ideas that are being presented. So organizations want staff who can present convincingly and will not confuse or irritate an audience.

Presentations are also widely used in recruitment, especially for managerial and supervisory positions. Organizations will select staff who can deliver a convincing presentation. This does not mean that they are looking for people who can 'perform' in a theatrical sense, although this sort of skill can come in handy to people who are addressing large audiences. In keeping with the general theme of this book, we are looking for 'effective' speakers. To quote Gordon Wells: 'as in writing, neither rhetoric nor oratory are necessary, just clear competent "plain speaking". With practice anyone can give the impression of being a fluent, confident speaker' (1986, p. 61). The important words here are 'fluent', so that the presentation flows and is clearly organized, and 'confident'. A speaker who is lacking in confidence may well distract an audience from the main topic. One of our most painful memories is the anxious conference speaker who tried to conquer his nerves by preparing far too many overhead slides for his twenty minutes. As the time went on, he went faster and faster in a desperate attempt to fit all the slides in. The audience's attention turned to whether he would finish the race in time. We have met several people who attended that conference; they all remembered the 'battle with the slides' but none remembered what the talk was actually about.

That said, there are certain critical features. You do need to develop your own style, one that suits your personality. For example, some years ago, I (P.H.) met a former student at a conference. I complimented him on the quality of his presentation. He said he developed his technique after a course I had delivered. Before I could take too much credit, he continued:

> 'I realized that I could not deliver a talk in your style which involves quite a lot of "performance" and spoken humour so I worked on developing very clear and engaging slides. This kept the audience's attention on the screen and off me. This helped my confidence. Developing my own style means that I can now deliver presentations very confidently and they come across well.'

And I had to agree.

This anecdote has a very important practical implication. To improve your presentation skills, do you adapt your own style or do you use 'standard' techniques? Guidebooks and training texts offer different approaches, as we illustrate in Box 13.2.

EXERCISE

List the different ways in which oral presentations are used in your organization. What style do presenters typically adopt? Are they usually successful?

WHY ARE PEOPLE SO WORRIED ABOUT GIVING PRESENTATIONS?

The previous paragraphs go some way to answering the question of why people fear presentations so much. One reason is the 'fear of disaster'. We have probably all attended at least one disastrous presentation, and we remember how embarrassing and uncomfortable these experiences were. So we mentally anticipate the possibility that we could be responsible for a similar disaster.

There are two ways to resolve these anxieties:

1   Make yourself feel less nervous both before and during the presentation, accepting that it is perfectly normal to feel nervous to some extent.
2   Behave in ways which are likely to conceal your nerves. In other words, you behave confidently, and this creates confidence in the audience.

There are several techniques which can help you to achieve way 1, including:

■   being really well-prepared;
■   using relaxation exercises such as deep breathing.

Techniques which can help to achieve 2 include:

■   entering the presentation in a very deliberate way;
■   rehearsing not just the presentation itself but also how you will set out your notes, slides, etc.;
■   delivering the talk in a way which does not attract attention to your level of anxiety. For example, if you know that your hand will shake, then do not use cue cards which you have to hold in front of you. Or hold cue cards but use the other hand to keep your arm steady.

EXERCISE

Review how you feel about giving an oral presentation. How do nerves affect you? What could you do to feel and behave more confidently?

BOX 13.2 WHY DON'T THE TRAINERS AGREE?

We noted in Part three that advice on 'effective written communication' is often confused or even contradictory. The same is true for oral presentations. For example, how much rehearsal is appropriate?

- Michael Klepper argues that you should 'Practice. Practice. Practice' until you 'are so bored with the speech you couldn't possibly be afraid of it' (Klepper with Gunther, 1994, p. 120).
- Khalid Aziz recommends 'at least two full rehearsals', while warning of the dangers of over-rehearsal (2000, p. 54).
- Lee Bowman suggests it is 'unwise to do more than one rehearsal' if you are using notes (Bowman with Crofts, 1991, p. 61).

Given all the evidence that communication depends on context, it is unwise to rely on 'golden rules'.

PLANNING THE PRESENTATION

The most popular advice to would-be or developing presenters is to plan what you are doing in terms of key stages or key areas. Two examples can illustrate this:

Rasberry and Lemoine (1986) suggest a four-step process:

- Organize the presentation, which includes deciding when, why, where and to whom the presentation will be delivered. It also involves deciding the way you are going to organize the information you wish to communicate.
- Construct the presentation: make an outline of the presentation and assemble the information.
- Practise the presentation, which includes checking that you can complete it in the time allowed and that you have chosen an appropriate style of delivery.
- Deliver the presentation, which includes relaxing yourself before you perform and making sure that you open and close convincingly.

Gallagher *et al.* (1998) suggest an eight-step approach:

1   Set your objective. They suggest that a simple one-sentence objective is a good way of clarifying your purpose, as in their example: 'As a result of my presentation, my audience will understand and be impressed by the new Customer Services system in Central Branch' (p. 130).
2   Analyse the audience.

3   Analyse the setting (including such things as audio-visual facilities, organization of the event etc.).
4   Write down the 'central theme'. Following the example given in 1, they suggest the theme would be 'the new customer system is effective, and could be applied in other branches of Gold Coin Bank' (p. 133).
5   Write your outline.
6   Develop your visual aids.
7   Prepare your delivery notes.
8   Deliver the presentation.

There is considerable overlap and common ground between these and other common recipes. Table 13.3 uses Tables 12.2 and 12.4 as a starting point from which to analyse other face-to-face situations in order to identify the main stages and the important issues.

Before we try to highlight the most fundamental issues that presenters must deal with, it is worth emphasizing a few notes of caution.

The danger with any series of stages is that it can be interpreted too rigidly. For example, taking the eight-step approach given above, you may have a clear initial objective but decide to amend it on the basis of your audience analysis. As we said earlier in this book when we reviewed strategies for preparing written documents, you need to be flexible, and constantly need to revisit your objectives.

As we suggested in Box 13.2, you do need to find a system for preparation and delivery that suits you rather than follow a recommended recipe from one of the guidebooks. For example, Gallagher *et al.* (1998) suggest that you use a spider diagram to jot down notes when you try to organize your initial ideas (see pp. 152–153) We have also used that idea in this book, but some people find it an unnatural way of organizing notes. Some prefer a more structured or hierarchical method such as the pyramid principle, which we also introduced in Chapter 7. The important thing is to find a method which you can work with – then make sure that it delivers a plan which ensures clear structure in your talk.

The importance of structure

As we say many times in this book, structure is critical. Not only must it be clear to you, but it must be clear to the audience. As Steve Mandel (1987, p. 32) says, 'all effective presentations make the pattern of organisation crystal clear to the audience'.

Which pattern to use?

As with written documents, there are various patterns you can use. Which one is most effective will depend on the audience and context. For example, suppose you have to deliver a presentation which advocates that the company adopts a new procedure for handling customer enquiries. Would the following outline be appropriate?

Give the vision statement (e.g. 'we are leaders in customer care')
State the goal and objective

302

Table 13.3 Planning a presentation

Stage	Content	Points to watch	Example
Decide the general goal.	What do you want to achieve overall?	What amount of research are you expected to do? How far can you offer your personal opinion?	You have been working for the past six months in a sales team, promoting a new product which has only been distributed in your region. You achieved the most sales. You have been asked to deliver a ten-minute presentation to the regional sales management team on the likely prospects if they promote and distribute the product nationally.
Consider the context.	What's happened in the past? Who are the participants? What is the setting?	Are there any hidden agendas because of the history? What do your audience need or expect to happen?	What do you know about the history of the sales management team in terms of their reaction to proposals? Is it usual to ask someone at your level to make a presentation of this type? You need to check whether you might be 'being tested'. You need to find out what criteria have been used to decide on a product's future after test marketing. And you need to know what level of detail the managers expect.
Plan.	Decide on the objectives. Decide on the structure.	Make your objectives realistic and achievable. Make sure your structure leads up to your objective.	Your objectives are to deliver a presentation which: ■ argues that the product should (or should not) be developed more widely on the basis of sensible evidence; ■ shows that you can present effectively to a given brief. Your structure should reflect the criteria which the managers will use to judge the product.
Act.	Use the relevant skills.	What are the most important skills in this situation? e.g. listening, questioning, etc.	Explaining and presenting are obviously critical. You will also need to respond to questions and show evidence of research and preparation. And you must keep to time.
Follow-up.	What can make sure the communication has been effective?	What can you do to reinforce what you have done?	Ask for feedback on the quality of the presentation as soon as possible after the event. This could give useful tips for the next time as well as showing you are willing to learn.

Summarize today's situation
Explain how we got to this position
Summarize available options
Make a recommendation.

This is based on an outline which is offered as one of the templates within Microsoft Powerpoint. It is similar to an outline suggested by Wilder and Fine (1996):

Present situation
Situation problems
Possible solutions
Recommendations
Requirements
Overcoming obstacles
Next steps.

This second outline goes further into the implementation of the recommended solution – overcoming obstacles, and so on. Perhaps the exact outline is not as important as making sure the audience knows where you are heading. There are various ways of achieving this, which highlights the importance of the first few minutes of any talk. Consider the strategies for opening and closing listed in Box 13.3.

CRITICAL ISSUES AND SKILLS IN PRESENTATIONS

Bringing out the common points in the approaches listed above, we suggest that the most critical questions to raise are as follows:

- Do you have clear objectives?
- Do you know your audience? (What are they expecting? What views do they already have on the topic?)
- Do you have a clear structure?
- Is your style of expression right?
- Can you operate effectively in the setting?

Critical skills

Baguley (1994, p. 107) suggests five 'core' skills:

- clarity;
- emphasis;
- using examples;
- organization;
- feedback.

BOX 13.3 STRATEGIES FOR OPENING AND CLOSING PRESENTATIONS

D. Lewis (1996, pp. 133–138) suggests six 'classic openings':

1   Provide a 'startling fact' which relates to your main theme.
2   Tell a 'strong and relevant anecdote'.
3   Give a 'striking example' which illustrates one of your themes.
4   Pay your audience a compliment.
5   Raise a 'challenging question'.
6   Tell a joke.

For all these openings, his advice is that they should clearly relate to the main topic that you are presenting. This can be a particular problem for opening 6. The presenter who starts by telling an irrelevant joke may well be seen by the audience as patronizing or unprofessional.

Lewis (ibid., pp. 139–152) also suggests six 'classic closes':

1   the 'surprise ending', where you make a comment which offers an original twist on your main argument;
2   the summary;
3   a joke;
4   an 'upbeat or uplifting exhortation';
5   a 'call to action';
6   a final compliment to the audience.

Of course, there are alternatives. But do not forget these important principles when you choose your opening and closing:

1   The opening comments establish the tone of what you are going to say and will also establish your credibility. It can be very difficult to rescue a presentation from a poor or indecisive opening.
2   In most business presentations, the opening few minutes should provide clear signposts to the audience so they know where you are going and what you are trying to cover. Otherwise, the audience will place their own interpretation on what you are trying to do.
3   The closing remarks will leave your audience with a particular impression. You need to make sure that this confirms and reinforces the main argument you have offered.

Psychological research suggests that we often remember the opening and closing parts of a presentation and tend to forget the details in the middle.

We have already stressed the importance of organization, so it is worth making comments on the other four skills. As a cautionary tale, we offer an embarrassing example of how not to do it in Box 13.4.

Clarity

As the size and complexity of the audience increases, so your chances decrease of establishing one simple definition of what your audience will understand. You need to be especially careful with technical terms and jargon. Consider the jargon which accompanies many descriptions of computer software or computer systems and see which of the following speakers you would prefer to explain a new package to you. This example illustrates the point that it is possible to explain in a way that most levels of user will follow if you can use everyday analogies.

Speaker A	Speaker B
'I want to explicate and demonstrate the additional functionality.'	'This package can do things we can't do on the present system. I want to explain what the package can do and show you how it does it.'
'We've redesigned the user environment for improved ease of use.'	'We've redesigned how it looks on the screen to make it easier to use.'

Emphasis

Good presenters usually give you a very clear sense of their main points. In other words, they emphasize what they think are the most important parts of what they say. There are various ways of doing this, including the following:

- using NVC to emphasize the verbal message, such as gestures;
- pausing before key points;
- stressing key parts of the sentence;
- using rhetorical devices to emphasize: as in the recent British political party slogan 'We have three priorities: education, education and education'; or by saying 'and if there is one thing I would like you to remember from this talk, it is . . . ';
- signposting that a main point is coming: 'and this highlights one of the most important things I have to say'; 'and so my three main concerns are . . . '

Of course, visual aids can be a major vehicle to convey the emphasis.

One final point which is often overlooked is the value of a brief handout which can summarize main points.

Using examples

Baguley suggests that examples on their own are 'not sufficient' (1994, p. 108). He draws on the work of Brown and Armstrong, who suggest that examples should be used to illustrate general rules in a particular sequence, depending on the audience, as follows:

- If the audience is familiar with the topic but needs to review or be reminded of the rule, then you can use either the rule–example or the example–rule sequence.
- If the audience is not familiar with the topic, then you should use the rule–example–rule sequence. In other words, you tell them the rule, give them an example, and then remind them of the rule.

Another important point about examples is that they must clearly highlight the rule and not be open to very different interpretations or contain too much irrelevant detail.

ELECTRONIC PRESENTATIONS

There are two main ways of using presentation software:

- You can prepare and save the presentation on the computer. At the event, you open the file on the computer, which is hooked up to a projector. You can move from point to point and slide to slide by clicking the computer mouse. Of course, you need to be sure that the computer at the event will cope with whatever software you have used. As the technology has advanced, many lecture, board and conference rooms have been equipped to handle this. The quality and convenience of projection have also improved – for example, in the past few years the weight of portable projectors has gone down by 50 per cent, and the size by 80 per cent (from a manufacturer's quote in *OEN*, October 2000). They have also got much brighter, although it is still worth checking that the room will be dark enough for people to see the screen easily.
- You can prepare the presentation on the computer and then print the slides on acetates to use on an overhead projector. This has the advantage that your slides will

BOX 13.4 HOW TO SHOOT YOUR PRESENTATION IN THE FOOT IN JUST THE FIRST FEW MINUTES

I (P.H.) recently attended a seminar where an experienced speaker from industry opened the afternoon session (using a Powerpoint presentation). He included all the following statements in his opening few minutes:

- 'This is the graveyard slot, just after lunch.'
- 'The previous speakers have said much of what I'm going to say.'
- 'Some of you will have seen these slides before.'
- 'You can go to sleep now.'
- 'This is not the most exciting theme of the day.'

No prizes for guessing how much interest and enthusiasm this presentation generated in the audience!

look professional and uniform in style (assuming the design you select is suitable for acetates). You will have to decide whether to use colour or black-and-white slides.

In making your choice, it is worth remembering points made by Wilder and Fine (1996). If you decide to opt for an electronic presentation, then:

- You need to 'learn how to use the "movement" features' (p. 28). The software will offer various ways of moving between slides, and also bullet points within slides. As well as knowing this, you also need to know how to rescue a mistake. If you press the mouse button too often and move on too far, do you know how to move back? If you make this mistake in a lecture hall watched by 200 people, then you have to think fast if you do not know exactly how to move back. (I can confirm that this is a painful personal experience – P.H.)
- You need to do more equipment planning. Wilder and Fine suggest that this depends on the size of the audience, and Table 13.4 highlights some of their main points which we have found most critical.

There are several advantages in using a computer package like Microsoft Powerpoint:

- It is very easy to learn, especially if your demands are fairly simple.
- It is very easy to edit individual slides, or to change the order of slides in the presentation.
- It is very easy to generate a handout for the presentation which summarizes the main points and shows snapshot pictures of the slides you have used.
- It is also useful to type your notes for each slide so that they can be printed out with the slides.

Table 13.4 *Planning electronic presentations*

Size of audience	Likely equipment need	Points to watch
Up to 10	One or two large monitors, or small portable projector connected to the PC or laptop.	Can everyone see the screen(s)? Where do you stand to deliver the talk and operate the PC?
10–50	Portable projector, connected to the PC or laptop.	Check that everyone can see the screen. What if the audience wish to take notes? Can you supply a handout to help?
50-plus	You will almost certainly need a professional projection unit.	You may also need some sound reinforcement, so some rehearsal in the location is very important.

SUMMARY

- There are different types of business meeting in terms of the level of formality (rules and regulations) and the structure. We need to review organization and communication within all these different types of meeting.

- A series of important recommendations has come from the American Meeting Masters Research Project, which identified those individuals who ran excellent meetings. These 'Meeting Masters' followed seven critical principles, paying special attention to the importance of the role of chair and to structuring the meeting.

- The agenda and the minutes are important documents which can support effective meetings. Both need careful attention to style and approach.

- Various techniques have been suggested to improve different aspects of meetings, including brainstorming, structured problem-solving, Nominal Group Technique, the Delphi technique, encouraging group innovation, and clarifying decision-making procedures. The problem is that we have limited evidence on actual business practice to offer solid recommendations as to which is the most effective in a specific situation. The most important conclusion is that meetings should regularly review their own approaches and procedures and find the most appropriate solutions.

- Presentations are increasingly common in organizations, for example as part of their decision-making and review procedures, and in recruitment and selection. You should be prepared confidently to deliver presentations which are 'fluent', – that is, where the presentation flows and is clearly organized.

- Many people feel very anxious about giving presentations. There are two main ways to resolve these anxieties. First, you can make yourself feel less nervous, both before and during the presentation, by using relaxation techniques and being well prepared. Secondly, you can behave in ways which conceal your nerves.

- If you are a would-be or developing presenter, the most popular advice is to plan what you are doing in terms of key stages or key areas. We summarized a few examples of these and emphasized the importance of a clear structure which is communicated to the audience. Other important issues are having clear objectives, the extent to which you know your audience, your style of expression, and whether you can operate effectively in the setting.

- In addition to your organization, there are other critical skills, including clarity, emphasis and using examples. All depend upon the audience and context.

- There are two possible ways of using IT to support your presentation: either to prepare *and* deliver or just to prepare. If you are confident that the necessary hardware is available, there are considerable advantages in using software such as Powerpoint, including the ease of generating handouts and summaries.

DISCUSSION QUESTIONS

- What are the most appropriate ways of conducting business meetings?
- Does your organization's typical meeting style encourage participants to contribute to the meetings?
- How do people feel about the meetings which take place in your organization? How could they be improved?
- Are any special meeting techniques used in your organization? Is there any evidence that they are useful?
- Are meetings in your organization seriously affected by politics and manipulation, as mentioned in Box 13.1?
- How are presentations used in your organization? And how do people develop the skills of good presentation?
- What style of presentation is favoured in your organization?
- What opportunities do you have to use computer technology in your presentations? Are you making optimum use of this technology?

FURTHER READING

Martin, D. (2000) *Manipulating Meetings: How to Get What You Want, When You Want It.* London: Prentice Hall. This book is not based on any systematic research programme but does offer a wide range of case studies and examples to illustrate how participants and chairs can try to manipulate meetings to their advantage.

Tropman, J.E. (1996) *Making Meetings Work: Achieving High Quality Group Decisions.* Thousand Oaks, CA: Sage. This summarizes the results of the Meeting Masters Research Project and explains the principles which emerged from the research.

Aziz, K. (2000) *Presenting to Win: A Guide for Finance and Business Professionals.* Dublin: Oak Tree Press.

Bowman, L. with Crofts, A. (1991) *High Impact Business Presentations: How to Speak Like an Expert and Sound Like a Statesman.* London: Business Books.

Turk, C. (1985) *Effective Speaking: Communicating in Speech.* London: E. & F.N. Spon. This and the two previous books offer interesting comparisons on effective techniques and approaches. Aziz summarises the techniques which his company teaches to business professionals. Bowman argues that many of the 'standard guides' are wrong and offers his company's training system. The main principle is that you do not learn a range of 'new techniques'; you simply need to develop your normal style of conversation. Although obviously dated in some ways (for example, it makes no mention of computer software), Turk's book offers a very useful overview of techniques and issues, and does refer to some research evidence.

Chapter 14

Building effective teams

INTRODUCTION

According to many organizational analysts, the success of an organization can depend on the levels of teamwork it employs: 'Teams have a great deal of potential to contribute to modern organizational life. Positive working teams encourage flexibility, involvement and efficiency and the introduction of teamworking has been known to transform companies entirely' (Hayes, 1997, p. 25). Some writers have gone even further and suggested that teams will be the 'primary building blocks of company performance in the organization of the future' (Katzenbach and Smith, 1998, p. 173). Certainly, many companies worldwide have invested in team training for staff. For example, the majority of 'top trainers' in the UK use the model of team roles explained in this chapter (according to Belbin, 2000). Stewart *et al.* (1999, p. 7) claim that 'nearly every major US company is currently trying or considering some form of empowered work teams somewhere in the organization'.

We need to know the essential characteristics of a successful team, to define the most important processes which contribute to effective teamwork, and to work out what can go wrong when we try to develop teams. This chapter confronts all these questions and emphasizes that the quality of communication, allied to the quality of the team members, makes the real difference.

This chapter also highlights another important issue. Organizations can consider the more fundamental challenge of moving to a team-based structure. This is not simply about

OBJECTIVES

This chapter will:

- define an 'effective team';
- show how important effective teams are to modern organizations, and comment on the moves to 'empowered' work teams;
- analyse important processes which can influence group and team working, including team roles, leadership and problem-solving;
- discuss how we can develop teams in organizations.

adjusting group relationships; it is a much more radical reorganization of the way work is designed and allocated (Stewart, 1999). We identify some of the main issues.

WE NEED A TEAM!

Consider the following extract from a management meeting and decide whether their plan of action is likely to be successful. Jim is the senior manager:

HUGO: We've been contacted by ABC, who are offering us an upgrade on the network software for a special price.

MO: We'd better check this out carefully before we commit ourselves.

JAN: Then we'd better ask a team to investigate it and report back quickly.

MO: You'll need Harry and Fran from my department – they've got the right technical expertise.

HUGO: We can't forget the finance – Michael and Mika should be involved.

SASHA: Don't forget the users – I would involve Helen from head office and Joe to represent the other sites.

PAT: That team will never work together; they are all too concerned with their own issues. Who is going to co-ordinate them?

JIM: They'll be all right. All they need is a clear deadline. It won't take them more than a couple of meetings.

EXERCISE

What chance would you give the proposed group of working effectively as a team? What confidence would you have in their recommendations after a couple of meetings?

WHAT MAKES A TEAM?

Jim, our senior manager in the conversation above, has no time for the question of what makes a team. As far as he is concerned, all you need to do is put together a group of people with the necessary technical expertise, give them a deadline, and you can expect a clear result. But that result may be disastrous. There are numerous examples of working groups composed of intelligent people, who also had the necessary technical skills, which made terrible decisions.

But what are the most important differences between 'teams' and 'groups'? After commenting that these terms are often 'used interchangeably', one widely used Australian introduction to business communication suggests that teams have three 'key identifiers', namely:

– members are operating within a charter
– they see themselves as having specified roles
– they see the team as accountable for achieving specified organizational goals.

(Dwyer, 1997)

Is this definition sufficient? Leading American experts Katzenbach and Smith distinguish different types of team/group and argue that high-performance teams are much more effective than working groups. Working groups are formed when staff meet together to share information and to co-ordinate and make decisions. Such groups are very different from what they call a 'real team': 'a small number of people with complementary skills who are committed to a common purpose, performance goals, and a working approach for which they hold themselves mutually accountable' (Katzenbach and the Real Change Team, 1996, p. 220). The critical differences they see between teams and working groups are the levels of commitment and the strong sense of mutual support and accountability (which are perhaps not emphasized sufficiently in the definition from Dwyer). Think of a working group that you have been involved in. What happened when something went wrong? Did *everyone* feel *equally* accountable and did they *all* pull together to put it right? Or did the group search out and perhaps 'punish' the member who had made the mistake? According to Katzenbach and Smith, a real team will always do the former: they will always take collective decisions and they will always hold themselves mutually responsible.

They suggest six basic elements of a team. High-performance teams score highly on *all* these elements:

- size (is it large enough to do the job but small enough for easy communication?);
- skills (does the team have all the necessary skills?);
- purpose (is this 'truly meaningful' – do all members understand it and see it as important?);
- goals (are they clear, realistic, specific, shared and measurable?);
- working approach (is this also clear, shared, fair and well understood?);
- mutual accountability (is everyone clear on their individual and joint responsibilities? Do they feel mutually responsible?).

Katzenbach and Smith accept that working groups can be effective and make sensible decisions. But they also argue that 'real teams' will be much more effective. They also define other varieties of group/team, as follows.

The pseudo-team

A working group may call itself a team when actually there is no real shared responsibility; the members act as individuals and are really interested only in the progress of their own department or area. This is the pseudo-team. Its members' failure to share and co-ordinate may make them perform worse than a working group which has fewer pretensions.

The potential team

The potential team is the group which is trying to move to full teamwork but which is probably still not clear on its goals and priorities and which is still struggling with the problem of individual responsibilities and loyalties. Whether it makes the transition will depend on the quality of the leadership or management and the commitment of the members. Box 14.1 gives an example of how *not* to manage this transition.

313

BOX 14.1 HOW NOT TO MOVE TO TEAMS

The workers in the British factory of a large US corporation were called to a mass meeting on Friday afternoon. They received a presentation which talked about the advantages of 'self-managing teams' whereby the work team was responsible for setting targets and monitoring quality and was left to get on with the job, without continual supervision from management. They were then told that the factory was moving to this system the following Monday morning, and that all the existing supervisors had been reallocated to other work within the company. The presentation finished, the workers were thanked for their attention, and everyone went home for the weekend.

What do you think happened on the Monday morning? An immediate upturn in productivity and morale? Or confusion, chaos and anxiety? And why were an intelligent management group surprised when it was the latter?

The other major issue in this discussion about the nature of teams is the amount of control and power which the team has over its operations and progress. Many organizations are not just training workers to work together more co-operatively but also giving the teams more responsibility. These 'empowered' or 'self-managing' teams will have discretion over how the work is completed and the assignment of tasks; they are also likely to be rewarded as a group (Hackman, 1990; Stewart *et al.*, 1999).

GROUP AND TEAM PROCESSES

Turning groups into teams is not easy. It takes time and it depends on an understanding of fundamental group dynamics, issues such as:

- group development;
- team roles;
- leadership;
- problem-solving and decision-making;
- intergroup relationships (relationships *between* groups).

Looking at a few of these will highlight major issues.

Group development

Many business texts paint a very definite picture of how groups change over time, as in:

> [W]hen a group of people form a team, they go through a set of behaviours that help to form the team into a viable working unit. . . . After a team has formed, normed and stormed then, and only then, can it move on to the most successful stage of team behaviour.

> (Nickson and Siddons, 1996, pp. 100–101)

This account – four stages in a definite sequence – is based on the work of Tuckman (1965), who surveyed all the studies of small-group development he could find and suggested that this was the common pattern. Groups start with a period of uncertainty. They then move into a phase of conflict where members argue about the task and on a more personal basis. Roles and relationships then get established, but it takes some time before the group is really ready to get on with the job in hand.

But is this the 'natural' or typical sequence for *all* small groups? Tuckman himself was not so certain, pointing out some limitations in the studies he surveyed. Nonetheless, his account has become the dominant model, as summarized in Table 14.1 in terms of the content – how members approach the task – and the process – how members relate to one another.

In 1977 Tuckman decided that this model could still account for all the studies he could identify, provided that he added a final fifth stage: adjourning. In this final stage, group members know that the group is about to part or split up. They make efforts to complete the task and say their farewells to the other members.

We have certainly experienced these phases in *some* project groups and teams we have been involved in. But is this life cycle inevitable? In fact, several stage theories offer variations on the themes set out by Tuckman, and many of these suggest that stages can occur in various different sequences (Hartley, 1997, ch. 4). For example, Susan Wheelan (1994) proposes five stages which usually occur in the order summarized in Box 14.2. But she also points out exceptions: groups can get 'stuck', or 'regress' to a previous stage. For example, some groups remain dependent for long periods of time and cannot function without the leader present. Another example is the group which gets stuck in a conflict phase and self-destructs.

The important principle here is that members of groups should try to work out what stage of development they are in and act sensitively to 'move the group along' (see Box 14.2 for an example). The problem is that real work groups are not likely to follow the

Table 14.1 *Tuckman's four-stage model of group development*

Stage	Content	Process
Forming	Members try to identify the task and how they should tackle it. The group decide what information they need and how they are going to get it. Members try to work out the 'ground rules'.	Members try to work out what interpersonal behaviours are acceptable. Members will be very dependent on the leader and the reactions of other members.
Storming	Disagreement and argument over the task occur.	Members are hostile to the leader and to other members.
Norming	The group agrees on the task and how it should be done.	Group members start to accept each other and group norms develop.
Performing	The group concentrate on completing the task.	Group members take on roles which enable them to complete the task.

'textbook' sequence of stages in such an orderly and predictable way. There are several good reasons why we can expect more complex and more fluid development:

- membership may change, forcing the group to re-form in some way;
- the task facing the group may change;
- deadlines may change.

Understanding leadership

An enormous range of books claim to unravel the mysteries of leadership: from social science research, through the literature from management and business studies, and on to the various leading personalities who want to tell us how to 'do it right'. You can also find interesting mixtures of fact and fiction, as we illustrate in Box 14.3. Although very diverse (see Shriberg *et al.*, 1997, for a range of examples), many texts agree on a few fundamental points:

- Leaders have special qualities which we can identify;
- Leaders have an important effect on their organizations;
- We need leaders, and only one leader in each situation.

However, all these views can be (and have been) disputed, at least in some contexts. Many researchers do not believe that we really understand enough about leadership and feel that we have ignored cultural factors.

Dominant views on leadership have changed over the years and some views have slipped out of favour. For example, the search for personality traits and characteristics to underpin leadership was very popular in the early twentieth century. But researchers found that different traits were important in different situations. Studies failed to show strong relationships between the leader's character and team performance. More recently, this line of research has been revived, and some modern theorists emphasize the importance of the personality of the leader, and how this is perceived by followers.

One recent example of this interest is the study of so-called charismatic leaders, who are 'regarded by [their] followers with a mixture of reverence, unflinching dedication and awe' (Bryman, 1992, p. 41). Rather than see this form of leadership as just emerging from the leader's personality, this style of leadership is often conceptualized as a particular form of relationship between leader and followers.

A recent return to the traditional notion of the leader as a 'dominant personality' is the work of Edwin Locke. He suggests that 'the prime movers, the creators of great wealth in a free (and even semi-free) economy, possess special qualities' (1997, p. 76). He categorizes these qualities into three groups:

- cognitive qualities, including being honest, independent and self-confident;
- motivation, including 'egoistic passion for the work' and 'commitment to action';
- attitude towards employees, which includes respecting their ability and rewarding them on merit.

BOX 14.2 GROUPS CAN DEVELOP DIFFERENTLY

Susan Wheelan (1994) proposes five stages of group development, usually in the order shown in Table 14.2.

Table 14.2 Wheelan's model of group development

Stage	What happens
Dependency and inclusion	Members are very reliant on the leader.
	Communication is very tentative and polite.
	Members are anxious and fearful.
	Members shy away from the task.
Counterdependency and flight	Conflict either between leader and member(s) or between members.
	Members continue to shy away from the task.
	Individuals try to work out their roles.
Trust and structure	Conflict is successfully resolved.
	Norms and rules can now be decided.
	More open communication.
	Fewer power struggles.
	Members feel more secure.
Work	The group works effectively.
Termination	The group disbands, having completed the task.

Wheelan also offers practical advice to members and leaders. Table 14.3 summarizes critical advice for leaders *and* members of work groups at each stage. It is not just the leader who is responsible for helping the group develop.

Table 14.3 Working through Wheelan's stages of group development

Stage	What leaders need to do	What members need to do
Dependency and inclusion	Enable open discussion of values, goals, tasks and leadership.	Request information about goals. Raise their personal concerns.
Counterdependency and flight	Make sure that the conflicting issues are dealt with constructively.	Work to resolve conflicts constructively.
Trust and structure	Organize in ways that make the group productive.	Organize in ways that make the group productive.
Work	Periodically assess how the group is going to ensure that the group can adjust to any changes.	Periodically assess how the group is going to ensure that the group can adjust to any changes.

BOX 14.3 DIVERSE VIEWS OF LEADERSHIP, FROM PARABLE TO STARSHIP

A recent addition to our bookshelves is Wess Roberts's *Make It So* (Roberts and Ross, 1995). This is a series of leadership lessons supposedly written by Captain Jean-Luc Picard – well known to film and TV audiences across the world as captain of the *Starship Enterprise*. Picard summarizes some of his adventures and highlights the characteristics of the competent leader, including communication, initiative, focus and urgency. But can we transplant the qualities required by a group of intrepid space travellers confronting the unknown on a regular weekly basis to the office or factory? You can ask the same question about Roberts's previous best-seller, *The Leadership Secrets of Attila the Hun*.

To further illustrate this diversity, sample an article in the 1992 *Harvard Business Review*. This contained five parables based upon lessons from the temples of the Kyung Nan province in Korea. These were intended to show:

> the essential qualities of leadership and the acts that define a leader: the ability to hear what is left unspoken, humility, commitment, the value of looking at reality from many vantage points, the ability to create an organization that draws out the unique strengths of every member.

The difficulty with many of these studies is that they focus on the 'movers and shapers' of corporations and other large organizations. Do the same considerations apply when we think of more modest attempts to lead?

The search for leadership functions and style

Looking at what leaders do has taken a number of directions, one of which was to try to define the functions of leadership. For example, a series of US studies suggested that effective leaders should score highly on both the following dimensions:

- initiating structure, i.e. organizing to complete the task;
- consideration, i.e. developing good relations with the members.

In the UK, the work of John Adair has been used for leadership training in a wide variety of organizations. He suggests that leaders fulfil three functions:

- achieving the task;
- building the team, and maintaining good working relationships throughout the team;
- developing the individuals in the team, dealing with the members' needs as individuals (Adair, 1986).

If we know what leaders do, then perhaps we can also define an ideal leader style. Many texts still quote the classic study from the 1930s by Lewin, Lippitt and White in a way which suggests that democratic leadership was unequivocally the 'best'. This is not a very full picture of the results. The democratic groups did report the highest morale and satisfaction, kept working even when the leader was absent, and produced the highest-quality models. The autocratic groups produced the most models but only when the leader was present. When the autocratic leader was absent, their groups quickly turned to misbehaviour as their preferred activity. Later studies produced mixed results, especially when they compared groups from different cultural backgrounds.

Despite mixed research findings, the notion of an ideal style of leadership which blends concern for the task and support for the members is still popular.

Contingency approaches

Given that research on style and functions did not always deliver consistent results, some researchers turned to more complex models, suggesting that effective leadership depends on (is contingent upon) a number of factors. This view can be illustrated by looking at the work of Fred Fiedler, who developed probably the most famous and still the most controversial of these models.

Fiedler's contingency theory

In the 1960s, Fiedler started from the idea that there were two types of leader – task and socio-emotional – and that these were taken on by different types of people. He developed a measure of these leadership styles, and tried to investigate which style was effective in which situation. He concluded that the effective style depended on the amount of control which the leader was able to exert over the group. This control varied from situation to situation as it depended upon three factors:

■ the relations between the leader and the members – how much they liked each other;
■ how structured the task was;
■ the position power of the leader – the amount of authority which the leader can use legitimately in the situation.

His results suggested that

■ Task leadership is most effective where situational control is extremely high or extremely low.
■ Socio-emotional leadership is most effective where situational control is intermediate.

Although Fiedler cites an impressive range of studies which support his conclusons, there have been important criticisms of his approach. In particular, critics have questioned whether leadership style is as fixed as he maintains. Other contingency theories have been developed which incorporate the level of maturity of the group members and the cultural context (see in Smith and Peterson, 1988). Unfortunately, the message from this and other research summaries is that any simple model of leadership behaviour is almost certainly mistaken.

319

Leadership and management

Another important issue is the difference between leadership and management, which are often discriminated in the way summarized in Table 14.4. The general distinction is between the notions of 'direction' and 'vision', associated with leadership, and notions of 'competence' and 'efficient operations', associated with management. This is often summarized in the catchphrase 'Leaders are people who do the right things and managers are people who do things right.'

Another way of dealing with this distinction is to say that leadership is simply *one* of the many roles which managers may play. One influential example of this approach is the work of Henry Mintzberg (1973). He suggests that managers can occupy ten roles: three interpersonal roles, including that of leader; three informational roles, including those of monitor and disseminator of information, and four decisional roles, including those of negotiator and entrepreneur. This concern with the roles associated with leadership is just one of the important recent trends in leadership research to which we now turn.

Recent developments in leadership research

We are still searching for a definitive account of leadership. The most important themes which have emerged from recent research include:

- Vision, communication and networking – emphasizing the leader's need to communicate a clear vision for the group or organization, as in Box 14.4.
- Culture and values – emphasizing the leader's role in building and maintaining an appropriate culture for the group to work in and for the leader to be concerned with values and goals.
- Leadership as 'situated action' – trying to provide a more sophisticated analysis of the situations that leaders find themselves in than is found in earlier contingency theories.
- Leadership as skilled behaviour, making a more detailed analysis of the skills and behaviour which 'good' leaders use.
- Cultural differences, recognizing that there may be some common qualities required of leaders in many cultures but that these will be expressed differently.
- Power and authority structures, looking at the different forms of power which leaders may use and how followers see their power and authority (Hartley, 1997, pp. 103–107).

Table 14.4 Comparing leadership and management

The leader	The manager
Creates and communicates the vision	Controls
Develops power base	Is appointed
Initiates and leads change	Maintains status quo
Sets objectives	Concentrates on results

BOX 14.4 THE LEADER AS COMMUNICATOR

Two recent views emphasize different aspects but both emphasize the importance of communication.

Shackleton (1995) argues that leaders need to 'empower' their teams or individual followers. To do this they must:

- show respect for and belief in the other members;
- act confidently;
- train all the members to make the most of their skills;
- set clear boundaries in terms of responsibilities;
- provide as much relevant information as possible;
- establish a realistic rate of progress.

Georgiades and Macdonell (1998, p. 21) suggest that leaders must carry out four 'explicit imperatives':

- scrutinize the external environment;
- develop a vision and communicate its strategic implications;
- develop the organization's culture so that it can deliver this vision and its strategy;
- specify what management has to do to 'drive the desired culture'.

The search for group roles

Until recently, the typical description of roles in small groups borrowed the three-way distinction originally set out by Benne and Sheats (1948):

- group task roles, such as initiating ideas, requesting or giving information;
- group maintenance roles, such as supporting or encouraging others, or resolving tension;
- individual roles, such as blocker or recognition-seeker.

But this is purely descriptive – it does not tell you which combination of roles is most effective. An important example of work which tries to answer this question comes from Meredith Belbin (1981).

Belbin's team roles

Over a period of around ten years, Belbin and colleagues observed several hundred teams of managers on management games and exercises and found that:

- The behaviours of team members were organized in a limited number of team roles.
- These team roles were independent of the members' technical expertise or formal status.

- Managers tended consistently to adopt one or two of these team roles.
- These preferred team roles were linked to personality characteristics.
- The effectiveness of the team depended upon the combination of team roles adopted by the team members.

EXERCISE

Evaluate Belbin's theory on yourself by completing the questionnaire at the back of his first major book (Belbin, 1981). Check your profile and read on.

Belbin identifies eight team roles, as described below (Belbin, 1993). Their main contribution to the group is summarized in Table 14.5. Belbin's recipe for success is described in Box 14.5.

The titles in brackets are the original labels used in Belbin's earlier book (1981).

Some implications of Belbin's work

There are at least three very important implications of Belbin's approach:

- All the roles are needed and valuable, whereas some other approaches suggest that some roles are destructive or negative.
- Groups *can* develop strategies to adjust any perceived imbalance.
- The third implication is best expressed as a question: using Belbin's role descriptions, who is the leader? Is it the chair or the shaper? Belbin says it depends on the situation.

Table 14.5 Team roles, as identified by Belbin

Role	Main contribution to the group
Chair	Organizes and co-ordinates. Keeps team focused on main objectives. Keeps other members involved.
Team leader (shaper)	Initiates and leads from the front. Challenges complacency or ineffectiveness. Pushes and drives towards the goal.
Innovator (plant)	Provides new and creative ideas.
Monitor–evaluator	Provides dispassionate criticism.
Team worker	Promotes good team spirit.
Completer	Checks things are completed. Monitors progress against deadlines.
Implementer (company worker)	Practical and hard-working. Focuses on the practical nitty-gritty.
Resource investigator	Makes contacts outside the group.

BOX 14.5 BELBIN'S RECIPE FOR SUCCESS

Once you know which roles are strongly represented in the group, you can check whether your group has all the recommended ingredients:

The right person in the chair
Make sure that the person who is carrying out the functions of chairing the group meetings has the appropriate personality and skills.

One strong plant in the group
Do you have at least one person who is both creative and clever in terms of the job at hand?

Fair spread in mental abilities
What is needed is a spread of abilities, including the clever plant and competent chair.

Wide team-role coverage
As many of the roles should be there as possible.

Good match between attributes and responsibilities
Members need to be given roles and jobs which fit their abilities and personal characteristics.

Adjustment to imbalance
If the group can recognize any gaps in its make-up, can it adopt strategies to make good these problems?

We still do not have enough research evidence to assume that Belbin offers the definitive account of group roles. There are both critical and supportive studies, especially concerning his self-report questionnaire. Belbin now uses Interplace, a computer-based system which integrates self-reports and observations. This system is available only on a commercial basis.

Problem-solving and decision-making

There have been many studies which show that groups can fail to solve problems or can make ineffective decisions if they ignore some of the following:

■ Determining the type of task. For example, can the task be divided into subtasks (divisible) or not (unitary)? Does the group need to produce as much as possible (maximizing) or is it trying to achieve some predetermined standard (optimizing)?
■ Problem-solving barriers, biases and traps. For example, we may perceive selectively. We may have subconscious biases. We are very sensitive to contextual influences. We sometimes use inappropriate heuristics (a heuristic is a general rule of thumb). We

use misleading frames of reference. We can fall into problem traps, such as overconfidence, which is usually inversely related to accuracy. The more confident people are, the more likely it is that they are wrong!

Communication and decision-making

On the positive side, we can suggest that the quality of communication is critical on both simple and complex tasks. What is still not clear is some of the relationships between communication, interaction and other components of the decision-making process.

We can say that group goals are important – for example, groups working towards specific, difficult goals perform better than groups without specific goals. Research in this area suggests the following practical strategies:

- setting goals which cover all aspects of the performance;
- providing regular feedback on progress;
- encouraging communication between members;
- encouraging and supporting planning activities;
- helping group members manage failure.

Another problem is that groups may fail to recognize that they are not considering all the alternative information or courses of action which they need in order to arrive at a balanced decision. For example, work by James Stoner in 1961 suggested that groups would tend to move towards more risky decisions than those initially expressed by the individuals involved. He called this the risky shift. Later work by Serge Moscovici and colleagues concluded that the actual group process was what they called group polarization: the group response will be more extreme than the average of the individuals but in the same direction as the individual tendencies. So, if the individual average is on the cautious side, then the group decision will be more cautious than the average of the individual opinions. If the individual average is on the risky side, then the group decision will be more risky than the average of the individual opinions.

But will this group make effective decisions?

How much trust would you place in decisions from a group whose members had the following characteristics:

- They are very cohesive.
- They seem to be insulated from information from outside sources.
- As decision-makers, they rarely make systematic searches through alternative decision possibilities.
- They feel under pressure to make quick decisions.
- They are dominated by a directive leader.

This describes a group which suffers from 'groupthink'. This concept comes from the work of Janis, who looked at historical accounts of poor group decisions. He decided that the particular group processes listed above lead to 'concurrence-seeking tendencies', which then lead to faulty decisions. You need a cohesive group with all these processes at work to fall victim to groupthink, but the good news is that groups can work out strategies to avoid these problems. For example, Janis cited the Kennedy administration as victims of group-think, after the Bay of Pigs crisis. A year later, they successfully managed an even more serious crisis – they had put in place strategies to avoid groupthink. For example, they appointed one member of the group to play 'devil's advocate' at each meeting, making sure this role was rotated round the group so it did not become one person's responsibility. This made sure that every decision was scrutinized with a critical eye.

How widespread is 'groupthink'?

Other investigators have queried some of Janis's conclusions, questioning whether his histor-ical analysis is so clear-cut, and arguing that he might have underestimated political forces. Other researchers have questioned the role of cohesiveness. Some studies suggest the oppo-site relationship – low cohesiveness associated with groupthink – or no strong relationship between the two. The style of the leader has come out as very important in many studies.

EXERCISE

Find an example of a group which seems to have been very 'blinkered' in its decision-making. How would you explain this? Were any characteristics of groupthink present in the situation?

More recent research looking at the detailed impact of group communication and inter-action processes on decision-making has identified five critical functions:

- Has the problem been thoroughly discussed?
- Have the criteria for a successful solution been thoroughly examined?
- Have *all* realistic alternative solutions been proposed?
- Have the positive aspects of each proposal been fully assessed?
- Have the negative aspects of each proposal been fully assessed? (Hirokawa and Poole, 1996).

Problem-solving groups which can honestly claim to achieve all these functions in open communication have the best chances of success.

EXERCISE

Reflect upon a problem-solving group which you have participated in. Did the group achieve the five critical functions listed above? If not, why not?

Intergroup relationships

QUESTION: When is 'a' group not 'one' group?
ANSWER: When it's an intergroup!

In other words, when we communicate with another person we may choose to communicate with them on the basis of the social categories which we occupy, as in the following examples:

- I am lecturer, you are student.
- I am manager, you are trade union representative.
- I am engineer, you are from sales and marketing.

In each case we may be more aware of our 'group responsibilities' than of our more individual characteristics, and this can have a very powerful influence on our behaviour. The easiest way to illustrate this is briefly to describe a classic study from social psychology and explore its implications for organizational behaviour.

The Sherifs (Muzafer and Carolyn) wanted to understand the process of conflict development and discrimination, and wanted to use a 'natural' situation. They chose an American summer camp and did a series of naturalistic experiments in which they manipulated events in the camp without the boys knowing about it. For example, they let boys make friends and then split them into two different groups to see if that would affect subsequent competition; they developed solidarity in groups before they introduced competitive situations; they set up 'frustrations' which affected both groups in camp to see how they would react.

The Sherifs were surprised how easy it was to create discrimination as opposed to 'healthy competition', and noticed how the groups changed to focus on this conflict: both groups developed biased perceptions ('we're OK but they are rubbish!'); groups became more cohesive; leadership became task-centred and authoritarian. They were also surprised how difficult it was to resolve the conflict and to restore open communication between the groups: only a *series* of what they called 'superordinate goals' made any real difference. Superordinate goals are goals where both groups need to co-operate on something which is equally important to both of them.

The Sherifs suggested that this conflict and the breakdown in communication was a product of the conflict of interests: the groups attempted to build their self-esteem by winning the conflict. Later research suggested that intergroup conflict could be much more deep-rooted in the way we build our sense of self-identity by comparing ourselves with other groups (see Hartley, 1997, ch. 9).

We cannot resolve the theoretical issues here, but we can highlight important implications for organizational life. An organizational team which contains members from different areas or functions within that organization may fail because members may have negative stereotypes of the other members and may use the team to foster their own group interests. In other words, the team becomes an arena for intergroup conflict. For example, Putnam and Stohl (1996) describe several studies which show how cross-functional teams can manage and control intergroup differences or can fail to do so. One team was characterized by 'win–lose' negotiation, strong allegiance to the home department, and continuing 'power plays'. The members took every opportunity to highlight departmental differences, including a series of sarcastic wisecracks about ordering and paying for lunch. This continuous conflict 'stifled decision making and led to delays in product introduction' (Putnam and Stohl, 1996, p. 160). It is difficult to see how the techniques for improving meetings we suggested in the previous chapter would make much difference to this situation until the more deep-rooted conflict had been confronted.

In contrast, groups which were sensitive to these problems managed much better – for example, where the different department representatives worked very hard to create 'win–win' negotiations (in other words, trying to create superordinate goals which everyone could commit to). And this highlights the importance of negotiation and communication processes, and recognizing that there are likely to be different views of reality, as illustrated in Box 14.6.

EXERCISE

Identify one example of intergroup communication from your organization. What are the different group perceptions? How do these influence the communication?

BOX 14.6 MULTIPLE VIEWS OF REALITY

One consequence of intergroup difficulties is that there are multiple perceptions of reality. We expect that different groups will have views of reality which reflect their experience and interests, but sometimes these differences can have very serious consequences. An example is the accident which befell the NASA space shuttle *Challenger*, which exploded just after take-off after a component failed. Subsequent investigations showed that the potential for this disaster had been recognized and investigated by NASA engineers. So why was the launch given the go-ahead? Could one problem have been the different perceptions held by different groups in the organization? Yiannis Gabriel contrasts the claims by management that communication was 'open and free' and resolved any technical issues with other testimony that engineers 'agonized over flaws in their equipment' but 'did not feel that they could voice their concerns' (1999, pp. 2–5). For further comment on *Challenger*, see Hartley, 1997; for a personal account of the commission which investigated the accident, see Feynman (1988).

SO HOW CAN WE DEVELOP MORE EFFECTIVE TEAMS AND WORKING GROUPS?

One approach to developing effective teams is simply to identify all the process problems which might be impeding the group progress and try to resolve each one in turn. Robbins and Finley (1997) list fourteen major problems, including confused goals, bad leadership, lack of team trust, and unresolved roles. For each problem they identify the main symptom to observe and a possible solution. For example, consider the problem of unresolved roles. The main symptom is that 'team members are uncertain what their job is', and the solution is to 'inform team members what is expected of them' (1997, p. 14).

Robbins and Finley also suggest that teams must be moved 'through stages towards success' (p. 187). They use Tuckman's four-stage model and again suggest that '*all successful teams* go through all four of these stages' (p. 187, our emphasis) Their strategy for team development depends upon recognizing which stage the group has reached and knowing how to move it on to the next stage.

A similar list of problems comes from Joiner Associates (Scholter, 1988), a leading team of US management consultants. They include clarity in team goals, clearly defined roles, clear communication, beneficial team behaviours (what we described earlier as positive task and social behaviours), well-defined decision procedures, balanced participation, established ground rules, and awareness of the group approach. They also add an improvement plan – including a flow chart of the project in hand which defines necessary resources and assistance – and use of the scientific approach, which is the insistence that opinions are supported by data and that the group avoids jumping to conclusions and unwarranted assumptions.

Many of these notions are very similar to Katzenbach and Smith's high-performing teams which we discussed earlier. Another example based on observation of a real 'world-class' team in action is from Hilarie Owen (1996). Once again the team is characterized by expectations and striving for outstanding performance. Strategies and skills required to create such teams include open communication, negotiating the success criteria, planning both the goals and the process, and effective leadership.

The context in which the team operates is important. McIntyre (1998) argues that management teams face distinctive challenges. For example, they are composed of individuals who will be leaders in their own departments, but who have to work collectively to make critical decisions.

Different ways of mending teamwork

West (1994) suggests five main types of team-building interventions. These have different aims and scope and will satisfy different needs and different situations:

Team start-up

A newly formed team may need work on clarifying the team objectives, deciding the members' roles and co-ordination, and other forming issues.

Regular formal reviews

These may involve 'away-days' where the team takes a day out of the usual routine and environment to reflect on how things are going and being done.

Addressing known task-related problems

This also involves some time out, but perhaps not so much as an away-day, to focus on a very specific problem.

Identifying problems

This is where the focus of the team review is on identifying task-related problems, where a team feels that it is not functioning as effectively as it could but is not sure why. The team may make use of discussion or of questionnaire analysis, or use an external facilitator.

Social process interventions

Here the focus is very much on the social climate and member relationships.

RETURNING TO SELF-MANAGED TEAMS

Richard Hackman (1990) argues that their success depends on three factors:

- The group task is 'well designed' so that members are motivated by a task which is 'meaningful' and receive clear feedback.
- The group is 'well composed' so that members have the necessary range of skills.
- The group's authority and accountability is clearly specified.

Ulich and Weber (1996) emphasize that teams must tackle 'whole tasks', where they can set goals, plan what needs to be done, decide how the work should be done, and receive clear feedback on their performance.

These recommendations complement the points we made at the beginning of the chapter when we looked at the differences between groups and teams. The important implication is that organizations cannot just expect these groups to happen overnight: 'the spread of "self-managing teams" will be a slow process . . . it involves very complex organizational interventions, which must be consistent both with the values of an organization and its technology' (Ulich and Weber, 1996, p. 273).

Research studies reinforce these issues. Kaye and Gilpin (1998) show how moves to teams were influenced by cultural variables in Australian organizations. Stewart *et al.* (1999) provide a number of examples of team interventions in organizations. They highlight some major organizational benefits: for example, Texas Instruments Malaysia (TIM) moved to an organizational design based on self-managing work teams in the 1990s and reported major

329

savings, quality improvements, low absenteeism, etc. They also highlight some of the major lessons which can be drawn from this and other cases:

- Team practices must be compatible with overall company philosophy and values, and with a revised organizational structure.
- Team practices must be supported by senior management.
- Team members will need new social and technical skills to become self-managed.
- Effective implementation is a long and careful process. It took TIM twelve years.

But not everyone is convinced

Not everyone is convinced that the way forward for large organizations is to move to team-based structures. For example, Elliot Jaques (1994) argues that organizations must employ *individuals* who are accountable for the work of their subordinates, and that groups cannot take on this accountability. He argues that improving leadership is the best way forward.

Kanter (1994) suggests that the practical difficulties of implementing team-based structures may not be worth the effort. A recent survey of studies in team-building suggested that many interventions do not have much impact. Some researchers question the nature of any impact. A very detailed case study from Barker (1999) suggests that the move to self-organizing groups may replace external control with an even more demanding regime of control based on peer pressure.

EXERCISE

What is your organization's attitude and policy towards teamwork? How has this view developed and what are its consequences?

SUMMARY

- How do effective teams differ from working groups? Research suggests that the critical differences are the level of commitment and the strong sense of mutual support and accountability.
- In order to create effective teams, we must understand the most important processes which can influence group and team working, including group development, team roles, leadership, problem-solving and intergroup behaviour.
- There are several models of group development but none is inevitable if the members make an open attempt to review their processes.
- The role of leader may be critical, and modern views of leadership place particular emphasis on aspects of communication. This includes the leader's need to

communicate a clear vision for the group and the leader's role in building and maintaining an appropriate culture for the group to work in.

- Belbin suggests that we all have preferred team roles, linked to personality characteristics. The effectiveness of the team depends upon the combination of team roles adopted by the team members. The outcome is not predetermined and the effective group adjusts to any imbalance in roles.
- Recent research has investigated the detailed impact of group communication and interaction processes on decision-making and identified several critical functions, all linked to communication, including thorough discussion of the problem and thorough examination of criteria for success.
- Teams which are sensitive to intergroup issues tend to be more effective, as they can communicate and negotiate in ways which can minimize these problems.
- We can develop teams through improved communication, either by conscious reflection on their major processes and adopting strategies for effective working or by using specific team-building interventions.
- It is important to choose the right team-building intervention to suit the situation; different types have different aims and scope and will satisfy different needs.
- Many organizations now use self-managed teams. They are not a 'quick fix' and involve very complex organizational interventions.

DISCUSSION QUESTIONS

- How do effective teams really differ from working groups? Will the differences be the same in all contexts? What types of group seem to operate in your context?
- Which model of group development is most relevant in your context?
- What is the role of leader in modern organizations? How important is it to communicate a clear vision for the group or organization and what is the leader's role in building and maintaining an appropriate culture for the group to work in?
- Belbin's model of team roles suggests that we all have preferred team roles linked to our personality characteristics. How useful is this model for creating groups and/or diagnosing group problems?
- Which group communication and interaction processes affect decision-making in your context?
- Which team-building interventions are most appropriate in particular organizations? And which are most appropriate in your context? What effect do/would they have?
- Does your organization use self-managed teams? How successful are they? If your organization does not currently use self-managed teams, what could be their application and impact? What would be their likely consequences?

FURTHER READING

Brown, R. (2000) *Group Processes,* 2nd edition. Oxford: Blackwell.

Hartley, P. (1997) *Group Communication.* London: Routledge.

Napier, R.W. and Gershenfeld, M.K. (1999) *Groups: Theory and Experience,* 6th edition. Boston, MA: Houghton Mifflin. Three contrasting reviews (two from the United Kingdom and one from the United States) of major group research which also discuss practical implications.

Frey, L.R., Gouran, D.S. and Poole, M.S. (1999) *The Handbook of Group Communication Theory and Research.* Thousand Oaks, CA: Sage. Comprehensive review of recent research.

Jaques, D. (2000) *Learning in Groups: A Handbook for Improving Group Working,* 3rd edition. London: Kogan Page. The latest version of this text offers another perspective on group dynamics – it aims to help lecturers, managers or trainers help people learn in groups.

Shackleton, V. (1995) *Business Leadership.* London: Routledge. Comprehensive survey of major leadership theories and research.

Stewart, G.L., Manz, C.C. and Sims, H.P. (1999) *Team Work and Group Dynamics.* New York: John Wiley. Interesting combination of research summaries and organizational case studies which highlights the complexities of the move to teams.

Turner, M.E. (ed.) (2001) *Groups at Work.* Mahwah, NJ: Lawrence Erlbaum. Interesting collection of articles summarizing recent research on groups in organizations.

West, M. (1994) *Effective Teamwork.* Leicester: BPS Books. Very readable introduction to team-building processes and interventions.

Part five

Communication and change

Although we have regularly referred to examples of organizational change throughout this book, we need to give special attention to the interplay of communication and organizational change because of the way modern organizations are changing.

So the purpose of Chapter 15 is to look at how communication relates to the pressures and processes of organizational change. Chapter 16 then offers seven overall principles which summarize our approach to communication. The aims of this chapter are to re-emphasize our main themes, to give a few further examples to emphasize their importance, and to stimulate you to further investigation. There is an awful lot we still need to discover about organizational communication and we hope that this introductory text has enthused you to find out more.

Chapter 15

Understanding organizational change

INTRODUCTION

The purpose of this chapter is to discuss how communication relates to organizational change. Various factors can push an organization into some form of change, including political, social, economic, environmental and technological pressures. Management need to be proactive in order to anticipate and adapt to the increasing rate of change.

Modern organizations experience different influences on and different types of change. This shows the importance of recognizing the stage or process which an organization is experiencing and monitoring the environment. Examples of specific strategies for implementing change show how effective communication is essential – in both the acceptance and the implementation of organizational change. Management therefore need to adopt a strategic and planned approach to communication, otherwise even the most imaginative and creative change strategy is likely to misfire.

OBJECTIVES

This chapter will:

■ identify different types of change which modern organizations experience;

■ show how communication is involved in different ways in change processes and strategies;

■ show how communication is an essential feature in both the acceptance and the implementation of organizational change.

WHAT ARE THE DIFFERENT TYPES OF CHANGE IN MODERN ORGANIZATIONS?

We have already looked at some aspects of change in Part two of this book. To provide an overview, some definitions of the organizational environment suggest different types and 'triggers' of change.

The organizational environment

There are several ways of categorizing factors which make up the organization's environment. One of the best-selling European texts on business strategy uses the mnemonic PEST to identify four factors:

- political/legal (including government legislation and ideology, employment law, taxation policy, trade regulations, etc.);
- economic (including business cycles, inflation, interest rates, etc.);
- socio-cultural (including social mobility, lifestyle changes, attitudes to work and leisure, education levels, consumerism, etc.);
- technological (including new discoveries, speed of technology transfer, rates of obsolescence, etc.) (Johnson and Scholes, 1997, pp. 93ff.).

Of course, these factors can combine in particular ways to trigger certain changes. Box 15.1 shows how a complex mix of factors can influence even a small local business.

Barbara Senior summarizes this and other similar approaches by suggesting that organizations operate in at least three types of environment:

- *Temporal*: the historical development over time. This can be seen in two ways: in terms of the general cycle of development which affects all organizations in particular industries or sectors; and in terms of the specific life cycle of the particular organization. We shall review the concept of the organizational life cycle later in this chapter.
- *External*: this is the sum total of the factors identified above in PEST.
- *Internal*: this is what Senior (1997, p. 19) calls 'the first-line responses to changes in the external and temporal environments'. Examples could include the appointment of

BOX 15.1 ENVIRONMENTAL CHANGE AND THE JAPANESE CONVENIENCE STORE

Economic pressures have been a serious threat to many small stores and shops, especially where they have been in direct competition with new super- and hypermarkets. Many Japanese convenience stores (known as *konbini*) responded to these pressures by exploiting several aspects of Japanese culture at the time: the low penetration of the Internet in Japanese homes, the relatively low use of e-commerce, and the fact that *konbini* were so common. They installed online terminals which allowed customers to order items that were not on the shelves, for collection a few days later. This also enabled these stores to offer items which they could not stock normally because of their space limitations. So innovation was triggered by a range of economic, socio-cultural and technological factors.

Will this innovation be successful in the long term? If the *konbini* have shown their customers how easy and useful e-commerce is, will they start using it from home?

new management following a period of poor economic performance, or the installation of new computer software prompted by changes in legal or fiscal requirements.

Triggers and sense-making

This analysis of the organization's environment suggests that change can be 'triggered' in a number of ways. But the occurrence of change depends on the organization noticing or anticipating relevant change and responding appropriately. The history of commerce is full of examples of organizations which failed to appreciate key changes in their environment. For example, the British motorcycle industry refused to believe that new, cheaper machines from Japan would affect its sales, reasoning that customers would pay more for 'traditional quality'. By the time managers recognized the threat, the British industry was in terminal decline.

Many organizations have placed increasing emphasis on 'sense-making', meaning that they try to ensure that their managers and staff are continually scanning the environment and their competitors' behaviour to look for signs of impending change. Management may use particular strategies to ensure this is done. Pettigrew and Whipp (1993) give several examples of these, including:

■ setting up special groups or task forces with members drawn from across the organization;
■ setting up a 'drama' or 'quasi-crisis' to emphasize the consequences of ignoring signals. They use the example of the Jaguar company's 'black museum' of poor product quality which management hoped would 'break open the complacency of its staff' (p. 16).

Such strategies will succeed only if the results of such monitoring are quickly and accurately communicated to the decision-makers within the organization. If these decision-makers do not accept the need for change, then the organization may be in trouble. And this highlights the need for senior management to create an organizational culture which allows information of this sort to surface at high levels.

One issue which might prevent this 'surfacing' is the possible isolation of senior managers. Chaudry-Lawton and Lawton (1992) report that senior executives can suffer from 'feedback starvation', where 'subordinates may constantly try to provide their leader with a flow of support and good news' (p. 7). If this happens, then executives will not receive the full picture of the organization's performance. Four factors seem to be important in creating this kind of atmosphere:

■ Executives' behaviour. If they create an image of being very dominant and single-minded, then many subordinates may not want to 'speak out of turn'.
■ Isolation. Executives may be physically isolated and not have much contact with staff who know what is happening 'on the ground'.
■ 'Exaggerated impact'. Because executives may be seen as having a lot of power (perhaps more than they actually have or want to have), then their every comment

may be carefully scrutinized. Staff may react to a throwaway remark as a direct command or new policy instruction.

■ Autonomy. If executives have freedom to choose their own staff and advisers, they may well (and perhaps unwittingly) surround themselves with staff who share very similar views and who do not look for information contrary to those views.

Careful managements can avoid all these problems. They also need to be open to new suggestions, as Box 15.2 illustrates.

EXERCISE

Select an organization you are familiar with. How does that organization monitor its environment? How are the results of such monitoring communicated? How do they influence decision-making? Is this process effective?

Type and rate of change

We also have to consider the rate and the scale of the change involved. One useful and typical model here comes from Dunphy and Stace (1993), who tested their categories and descriptions with staff in a number of Australian service organizations. They suggest four different types of change, as follows.

Scale Type 1: Fine-tuning

Fine tuning implies that the organization adjusts how it operates at department or division level to improve customer service or to increase employee morale. The adjustments could involve changes in training or staff development.

BOX 15.2 WHO DO YOU CONSULT ABOUT CHANGE?

Many of the on-screen features we take for granted in our modern PC can be traced back to developments by Xerox: the use of icons to represent the desktop; using a mouse to move objects around, etc. So why did not Xerox become the early market leader? Why was it left to Apple, which came along several years later? One factor was the way that Xerox demonstrated the prototype computer with these features (the Alto). The Alto was presented to the male Xerox executives and their wives. Many of the wives had secretarial or administrative experience and were immediately impressed with the machine and its ease of use. But the men did not understand the benefits as they 'had no background, really, to grasp the significance of it' (one of the Alto inventors quoted in Shapiro, 1996, p. 127). You may not be surprised to realize who Xerox listened to!

Scale Type 2: Incremental adjustment

At the next scale up, changes to the business strategy or processes are incremental over time, again to improve customer service or staff commitment. Staff see this as gradual adjustment within the organization rather than radical change. An example might be the expansion of sales or some change of emphasis within existing product lines.

Scale Type 3: Modular transformation

Modular transformation is a radical change that focuses upon only part of the organization. Examples might include outsourcing one aspect of the company's activities, or radically restructuring one division.

Scale Type 4: Corporate transformation

Corporate transformation means radical change right across the organization with major changes to the organization's structures and procedures. It usually means a major overhaul of the organization's values and priorities.

The drawback with this model is that it assumes that everyone in the organization shares the same definition or understanding of the change involved. What senior management see as incremental adjustment might be perceived as a much more fundamental shift by the employees directly involved.

Once again this raises issues of communication. In what terms is the change communicated to staff: how is it described? For example, consider the case of the organization which wished to put all its salaried staff on a new, 'more flexible' contract. Senior management extolled the virtues of the 'new, professional contract' in a series of meetings and in the company newsletter. They saw this as an incremental step towards creating a more flexible organization. Staff saw the new contract as a fundamental shift in their relationship with senior management and reacted very strongly to the implication that their previous contract was somehow 'not professional'.

There is also the question of the pace of change. Where the centre of the organization is very powerful, the organization can change almost literally overnight.

The organizational life cycle

In Chapter 15, we reviewed models which suggest that working groups and teams often progress through a series of stages. A similar approach suggests that organizations have a typical pattern as they grow and develop over time. For example, on the basis of several previous models, Senior suggests four main stages:

■ *Entrepreneurial*: the new organization starts from a small number of people with good ideas. If it becomes successful and grows, it will confront a crisis of leadership – it must decide its future strategy.

339

- *Collective*: the organization has grown, so the appropriate division of labour is critical. Departments or other subdivisions need to be effectively managed and co-ordinated.
- *Formalization*: the organization is now big enough to need more formal systems and procedures. But these could easily become over-bureaucratic and there may be a crisis of 'red tape'.
- *Elaboration*: the company has now reached a plateau and its performance may even be declining. Can it change to remain competitive? (Senior, 1997, p. 40).

A further complication is that organizations can be affected at different times by 'waves' of change. Change does not just happen and go away – it continually reappears in various forms. A period of relative calm involving some incremental change may be followed by one of dramatic and turbulent change in both the internal and the external environment. Box 15.3 gives an example of this: the British railway industry.

EXERCISE

Identify an organization which you know which has recently experienced change. What sort of change was this? Was it defined in the same way by staff at different levels? How would you explain any differences in perception?

STRATEGIES FOR CHANGE

We can also see the importance of communication within the change process if we review various strategies for change. There are a range of alternatives, including:

- education and communication;
- participation;
- intervention/manipulation;
- management direction;
- coercion.

These vary in terms of the amount of control exercised by senior management and the opportunities for involvement for those who will be directly affected by the changes. Each strategy has potential benefits and problems. For example, using participation can be very time-consuming but increases the chances of acceptance. A very directive strategy may be quick but may be resented and obstructed by the staff who have to implement the change.

Four examples illustrate the main issues:

- stage models of the change process;
- Business Process Re-engineering (BPR);
- the dynamics of culture change;
- the 'learning organization'.

340

BOX 15.3 ALL CHANGE ON BRITISH RAILWAY LINES

One example of repeated and sometimes rapid organizational change is that undergone by the British railway system over the past twenty years:

1984: The national system owned by the state (British Rail) was restructured into four sectors (three based on different forms of passenger service and one based on freight and parcels). The government demanded a corporate business plan for the first time.

1992: Reorganization transferred responsibilities held by regions (based on geography) to a business management structure. This new structure was based on different types of rail service (e.g. express passenger).

1993: Government acted to privatize the system. This split the network into no fewer than seventy companies: one (Railtrack) responsible for the infrastructure (track and maintenance, etc.); twenty-six train operators; three rolling stock leasing companies; and various maintenance and freight businesses.

A system of multiple operators makes communication complex. Important issues were highlighted after a serious accident in October 2000 where an express train derailment was blamed on a broken rail. Railtrack immediately set speed limits on similar lines, ran extra safety checks, and even shut some lines for a time – the disruption to the timetables caused 'commuter chaos'. This was followed by government intervention to produce further investment in safety, and intense media debate over what was called a 'nightmarish contrivance' and 'absurd structure' (quotation and statistics from *The Week*, 28 October 2000).

Compare the complexity of this structure with the rail systems in other countries

Stage models of the change process

One of the most common models of the change process suggests three main stages:

- unfreezing;
- changing;
- refreezing.

This three-step model was first proposed by Kurt Lewin (1951) after a series of experiments looking at attitude change. He concluded that people must see a reason to move from their existing attitudes or beliefs. In other words, their existing attitudes must be 'unfrozen' to make way for new ones. After new attitudes have been adopted, there is a period when these new attitudes are tested out to see if they 'work'. The new attitudes will become embedded only if this refreezing process is successful.

A practical example of how this process can be neglected is the effectiveness of management training courses. Suppose such a course is designed to make supervisors more democratic in their leadership style. And suppose the course 'works' if we measure supervisors' attitudes immediately after the course. But what if we send these supervisors back to an autocratic environment where nothing else has changed? Research into situations like this suggests that after a few months, supervisors' attitudes will be more autocratic than they had been before the course! The refreezing stage has been ignored.

Johnson and Scholes (1997) offer a framework for managing strategic change which is an expansion of this three-step model:

Unfreezing: organizational anticipation

Organizational anticipation may be down to management to persuade staff of the need to change, perhaps by highlighting external problems or threats.

Organizational flux

Organizational flux is where 'competing views surface about the causes of, and remedies for, the problems' (p. 453).

Information building

During the information-building stage, managers try to find information which supports their position. A proactive management will try to manage this process rather than leave it to political in-fighting. Johnson and Scholes suggest strategy workshops for management and the use of project groups to make sure that information and options are fully considered.

Experimentation

Some new ideas are tried out.

Refreezing

Once new ideas have been adopted, organizations can use various methods to make sure that the new practices are thoroughly embedded and that staff are supported during this transition.

Dynamics of culture change

As Chapter 4 makes clear, many managers have become concerned about the nature of their organizational culture, and have seen culture change as a major way of resolving problems and increasing competitiveness. Williams *et al.* (1993) suggest six main ways that organizations set about changing their culture.

Changing the people in the organization

Change can be painful, as many large programmes lead to redundancies or early retirement. Are the management open about this in their communication with the workforce? Williams *et al.* quote the very explicit policy adopted by Xerox (p. 84): 'We are very patient with those that have to make the change but, in the end, if they do not adapt, they have to leave.' Of course, this raises many other issues in which communication has an important role. If people fail to adapt, is it because they cannot operate in the new way or because of flaws in the change management? Perhaps they simply do not understand what is required of them. Or is it because they have not received sufficient training to support the new methods?

Another, less painful way of changing the people is to focus on the selection and recruitment process. Improving this process can ensure that new recruits are fully aware of and accept the company ethos before they join. But how can this ethos be communicated effectively? Williams *et al.* use the transcript of the video shown to new recruits at Toshiba as a major example. The following sentences give the flavour of the company culture (p. 83): 'We don't want surprises. We want a clockwork factory. We don't want to get into a situation where we have to use our juggling expertise to get out of trouble.' Again we can highlight potential problems in communication. Will applicants really understand the full implications of the culture before joining? Will they be fully attentive to the company messages at recruitment or induction, or will they be more dismissive of the 'company PR'?

Changing people's positions in the organization

How quickly and how far people move round the organization can have important consequences.

Changing beliefs, attitudes and values

The organizations studied by Williams *et al.* tended to direct their change efforts at specific aspects rather than launch very general programmes of culture change. For example, some focused on customer service, others focused on management style. One common practice was to use a wide range of formal methods to put the message across, sometimes extending beyond the company walls into initiatives which involved the local community.

Changing behaviour

Many conventional psychological models of attitude and behaviour change suggest that you have to change someone's attitudes or beliefs before they will change their behaviour. But there is also evidence to support the view that you can change behaviour directly and that attitude change may then 'follow on'. One example is action taken by many police forces to stamp out racism or other discriminatory behaviour. The focus in training and performance review is on making sure that the police officers *behave* in a non-racist way. If this behaviour is continually reinforced and rewarded, then it will become the norm. Genuine long-term attitude change may then be the long-term result.

Changing systems or structures

The systems often changed are reward, appraisal, budgeting and quality control.

Changing the company image

Trying to increase employees' commitment to the organization is a common goal and often involves internal and external advertising, usually associated with some new logo or slogan. As with all promotional efforts, this must be tied to 'real' activities which the employees can recognize, or the effort may create a more cynical reaction.

The importance of symbolic gestures and clear communication cannot be overemphasized in relation to all these different strategies. But if communication is critical to successful culture change, it is also worth emphasizing that communication must address the right issues. As an example of rapid cultural change in a large organization, Shapiro (1996) cites General Electric in the early 1980s. Described around 1980 as 'thoughtful and slow-moving' (Deal and Kennedy, 1982), this same organization was described by an employee only a few years later as follows: 'At GE, you perform or you die' (Shapiro, 1996, p. 52). This transformation was attributed to the man who became chairman in 1981, Jack Welch. According to Shapiro, Welch had acted directly upon what she calls '"the internal game", the set of implicit, unwritten rules about how to survive and excel within the organization' (Shapiro, 1996, p. 53).

We have already commented many times in this book that messages can be interpreted at various levels, and that what is 'unsaid' can have very powerful meaning. The 'hidden' rules which senior managers had recognized at GE in the 1970s was that good performance meant a level of growth on a par with the overall economy and that managers had to meet this performance level no matter what. Having worked as a senior manager himself under these conditions, Welch changed the rules immediately he took office. The new objective for every business within GE was to be number 1 or 2 within their sector, with a substantial increase in business every quarter. Business units which did not meet these criteria were sold off, and over 100 left in the first four years of his tenure, along with nearly 20 per cent of the staff.

But was this change successful? It did achieve economic gains in the short term, although you might find it difficult to persuade all the 80,000 or so people who left the company. It is difficult to identify the characteristics of long-term health within a company or organization.

A review of organizational change theory and research in the 1990s suggests that an effective change message incorporates five components (Armenakis and Bedeian, 1999):

- This organization needs to change.
- We can change successfully.
- Change is in our best interest.
- The people affected support the change.
- This change is right for this organization.

They also suggest a number of possible influence strategies, ranging from persuasive communication and participation through to symbolic activities and changes to organization structure. Quirke (1995) advises management that different employees will want different things from communication about change. Some will need awareness, others need to become committed. A well-planned change strategy will cater for such differences (Clampitt and Berk, 1996).

Business process re-engineering (BPR)

We mentioned this briefly in Chapter 6. It has been described in various ways, as the following quotation illustrates:

- 'the most ambitious management theory of our time';
- 'the most radical change in business thinking since the industrial revolution';
- 'a clear-cut, no-nonsense guide to rebuilding your business and beating the competition';
- 'the first great management fad of the 1990s, contributing to millions of people losing their jobs and millions more working in entirely new ways'.

All these quotations are taken from a critical review of the growth of BPR by Micklethwait and Wooldridge (1996, pp. 29ff.). The first three echo claims by the founders of BPR, Michael Hammer and James Champy, whose 1993 text *Reengineering the Corporation* profoundly influenced organizations in the United States, Europe and Asia.

BPR tries to redesign work processes without any commitment to existing structures. The key objective is to achieve more efficiency for the customer, and there is usually heavy emphasis on the use of IT to ensure effective flows of information. But can such a radical reassessment always lead to desired outcomes?

Hammer and Champy quote several case studies where BPR seems to have had the desired dramatic effect. For example, the American fast food chain Taco Bell decided to focus on reducing the 75 per cent of its costs which were *not* spent on the food itself. The company's management decided to concentrate on selling the food as opposed to making it, and this enabled them to reverse the internal design of Taco Bell restaurants, cutting the kitchen space by over half and doubling the number of seats for customers. Along with other changes to menus and pricing, this allowed them to make substantial increases to both revenue and profits, even at a time when other fast food chains were declining.

Other examples tell a different story, with even Hammer and Champy admitting that up to 70 per cent of re-engineering projects will fail. And the critics of BPR have high-lighted the fact that many of these failures seem to have occurred because the 're-engineers' have neglected to consider the people in the system and the real impact of the new processes on human interaction and communication (Knights and Wilmott, 2000).

Learning organizations as the answer?

Another solution to problems of increasing and ongoing change which was strongly advo-cated in the 1990s was the notion of the 'learning organization'. This concept was enthusiastically supported by academics and business commentators: 'the most successful corporation of the 1990s will be something called a learning organization, a consummately adaptive enterprise' (quotation from *Fortune* magazine, reproduced in Senge, 1994).

A learning organization is an organization which actively embraces change as an ongoing and inescapable process. The problems are how to harness the positive aspects of change and how to ensure that all employees commit themselves to continuous learning and self-improvement. A positive approach to these problems can develop the learning organization.

This approach challenges traditional models of organizational structure. For example, the traditional separation of research and development (R&D) into a specific department or section is abandoned on the grounds that everyone is responsible for contributing to development. As a result, the R&D function is merged into the production facilities.

Another important aspect of this form of organization is the role and communication of the leader. Senge argues that learning organizations must abandon the traditional view of leaders 'as special people who set the direction, make the key decisions, and energise the troops' (1994, p. 5). Instead, leaders must focus on the 'creative tension' created by the gap between where the organization is at the moment and where it wants to be in the future. And this highlights the need for a coherent vision of where the organization wants to be.

Senge then goes on to highlight how leaders can influence people to view reality at three different levels:

- 'events': this is the analysis of current facts, or what he calls 'who did what to whom';
- 'patterns of behaviour': this is the attempt to identify trends and look for underlying patterns;
- 'systemic structure': this is the 'most powerful' explanation as it looks for what *causes* the patterns of behaviour.

Whereas many organizations seem content to use the first two of these levels, Senge characterizes the learning organization as concerned with all three. An important role for the leader is to enable all staff to contribute to the debate and inquiry which will answer the questions raised at this third level.

AND FINALLY?

The examples reviewed in this chapter highlight the complexity of organizational change. They also show how change and communication are intertwined. And they suggest that management need to adopt a strategic and planned approach to communication in order to support organizational change.

SUMMARY

- Modern organizations experience different types of change, influenced by factors in the environment. Organizations operate in at least three types of environment: temporal (the historical development over time); external (the PEST factors); and the internal environment.

- As a result, many organizations have placed increasing emphasis on 'sense-making', which means trying to ensure that their managers and staff are continually scanning the environment and their competitors' behaviour to look for signs of impending change.

- Even if staff are scanning the environment, this does not mean that issues are fully communicated to management. One problem here which might affect senior managers is 'feedback starvation'.

- We must also consider the rate and the scale of the change involved. This can range from small adjustments at department or division level ('fine-tuning') up to 'corporate transformation', which involves radical change right across the organization.

- Four examples illustrate the main issues in major organizational change: stage models of the change process; business process re-engineering (BPR); dynamics of culture change; and the 'learning organization'. In all these examples, effective communication is an essential feature in both the acceptance and the implementation of organizational change.

- Our main conclusion is that management must adopt a strategic and planned approach to communication in order to support organizational change.

DISCUSSION QUESTIONS

- What factors 'push' your organization into some form of change?
- How proactive are your management in anticipating and adapting to the increasing rate of change?
- What are the different types of change affecting your organization?
- What strategies for implementing change have you experienced? Which was most effective and why? What forms of communication were involve

FURTHER READING

Knights, D. and Wilmott, D. (eds) (2000) *The Reengineering Revolution: Critical Studies of Corporate Change*. London: Sage. These studies of the applications and implications of BPR analyse this important trend and highlight important general issues about the nature of change in a variety of organizations.

Quirke, B. (1995) *Communicating Change*. London: McGraw-Hill. An interesting example of advice to company management from an experienced consultant.

Senior, B. (1997) *Organizational Change*. London: Pitman. A very readable introduction to major theories and change practices.

Stacey, R.D. (2000) *Strategic Management and Organizational Dynamics: The Challenge of Complexity*, 3rd edition. Harlow: Prentice Hall. This offers a more radical approach to strategy than some other texts, emphasizing 'unpredictability and the limitations of control'. It incorporates psychodynamic approaches and management narratives, as well as some very interesting case studies.

Chapter 16

Making communication work

Summary principles

INTRODUCTION

This final chapter does not follow the format of previous chapters. To provide an overall conclusion, we offer seven principles which summarize the perspectives outlined in this book. We explain each principle with some new examples and point to key issues discussed earlier in the book.

All these principles apply to everyday examples of communication in organizations, and so we suggest that you read this final chapter with the following questions in mind:

■ Do the organizations which you know *believe* any/some/all of these principles?
■ Do the organizations which you know *act* according to any/some/all of these principles?
■ If your answer to either of these two questions is 'no', then what are the practical consequences?
■ If you accept that these principles are valid, then how would you implement them fully in the organizations which fill your life?

PRINCIPLE 16.1
You can improve your chances of 'success' in communication if you have clear purpose(s) and select appropriate strategies.

Effective communication depends on selecting the best strategy to achieve some communicative purpose. There is no one 'best way' which will work all the time.

In Part one we reviewed the various factors that affect communication. We emphasized that effective communication requires us to:

■ consider the purpose of our communication;
■ evaluate alternative means of achieving this purpose, taking into account those factors that will affect the communication;
■ select the one which has the greatest chance of success.

In Part one we noted that humans are always interpreting the meaning of events on the basis of the information available. Whatever our message, it will have *some* effect on our audience, and we should at least be clear in our own minds what outcome we wish to achieve. If we are unclear, then our audience will be more so.

This may sound all very elementary, and yet we repeatedly find that people in organizations are vague about their purpose, as we showed in Chapter 7 about formal reports.

PRINCIPLE 16.2
Communication always means more than 'the message'.

To communicate effectively, you need to anticipate how 'messages' will be interpreted in context. You need to consider the meaning which will be 'taken' from your behaviour.

We have highlighted examples where people in organizations took an 'over-simple' approach to communication. They concentrated on the superficial or literal meaning of what was said or written and failed to examine how it would be *interpreted*. In other words, they focused on the surface of 'the message' and omitted to consider how the other people involved would translate this into *meaning*.

For example, ambiguity is an inherent feature of both language and non-verbal communication. As a result, we can use humour to play on double meanings. And perhaps we can have some sympathy for the chief executive who suggested the following motto to celebrate his company's longstanding success: 'Our innovation makes us first – our quality makes us last.' This last anecdote is reported as an 'alleged true story' by Scott Adams in one of his Dilbert books (Adams, 1997, p. 120), which repeatedly figure in the best-selling lists of management books. These very cynical (and very funny) accounts of business life emphasize that management often ignore the implications of communication.

And this also suggests some very simple approaches we can use to support this principle:

- recognizing that ambiguity is an inevitable feature of human communication;
- looking for feedback and checking understanding;
- accepting that others' interpretations are legitimate;
- realizing that discussion is essential to arrive at clear, shared meaning.

Do these approaches characterize everyday interactions in your organization?

PRINCIPLE 16.3
Communication is always based in a specific social and cultural context.

We need to recognize the constraints that influence communication because of the social and historical context in which it occurs, and respond accordingly.

We have criticized attempts to provide guidelines or techniques for communication which ignore the context. For example, many management texts endorse the values of assertiveness without referring to the research which shows that assertive behaviour may be seen as aggressive or inappropriate in certain cultural settings or by certain individuals.

We must analyse both the cultural and the historical context. For example, Chaudry-Lawton and Lawton (1992) describe the experience of a British consultant working on an intensive management training programme in a Middle Eastern country. There were several important levels of cultural awareness which this consultant had to recognize. He had to understand that the historical principles of Islam would influence the managers' approach and expectations. Those principles created a much more fluid approach to agreements and relationships than he expected in comparable Western organizations. In terms of daily interactions, he had to recognize the 'important rituals' of 'lengthy greetings and the tea drinking at every meeting' (p. 42). To ignore or dismiss these rituals would have created deep insult and threatened the relationship on which any effective consultancy is based.

This principle is very important in a situation of change. Management who wish to introduce new processes or procedures should be sensitive to the meaning of the existing patterns of behaviour.

PRINCIPLE 16.4
Communication and action must 'match'.

We can communicate loud and strong but we will not be believed if our actions do not match what we say.

For example, there is the research which shows that verbal and non-verbal communication must express the same meaning if you are to be believed. If your body language contradicts what you say, then the other person will have to choose which channel to believe. Early research suggested that the non-verbal channel would always be believed. We now know that matters are more complicated, but we do know that people are very sensitive to this sort of ambiguity. In other words, if your speech and body language do not agree, then this will almost certainly be noticed and interpreted by your audience.

Linked to this idea is the oft-quoted statement that 'you cannot *not* communicate'. In other words, failing to act can be seen as meaningful. For example, how do staff feel about the chief executive who always stresses the importance of communication in public meetings and in media interviews but who never contributes anything to the staff newsletter?

And this suggests how to follow this principle: act in the way that you say that you do. Of course, there may be some issues of interpretation and these should be sorted out as soon as possible. The management team who announce that they have an 'open door' policy to all employees would be wise to clarify what they mean with some examples or through discussion. It is very easy to set up expectations with a snappy slogan which makes claims that are obviously over-optimistic when you consider the likely interpretation by the audience. A similar fate could await the management who promise 'one computer per desk'. Such a policy could be interpreted as one computer per staff member, or as one computer per office, and so on.

PRINCIPLE 16.5
Communication can always be improved.

Although we accept that some people are inherently more skilled in their communication, we can all improve our skills with the right coaching or preparation.

At first sight, this principle may seem almost obvious. But it is often denied in practice. In other words, if you believe that communication can be improved, then you will devote time to at least some of the following activities:

- reviewing the impact of your own behaviour on others;
- requesting feedback from others;
- developing strategies or plans to improve your communication;
- trying new techniques and reviewing their effectiveness.

This philosophy of review and improvement is often neglected in the pressure of daily business. In the same way that most time management texts argue that you should make some space in the daily routine to plan long-term objectives, we recommend some attention to communication.

PRINCIPLE 16.6
Communication is a fundamental management responsibility.

If management do not accept responsibility for the quantity and quality of communication in the organization, then who will?

This principle can be translated into practice in various ways. For example, we can ask how far the behaviour of managers at all levels throughout the organization reflects concern for and commitment to communication. Werner David (1995) proposes five fundamental steps:

1   making a senior manager formally responsible for 'linking every employee into the communication network' (p. 4);
2   systematic training in communication;
3   building the organization's communication network in a way which uses all the available media and which is especially sensitive to information that indicates the need for change;
4   continually monitoring the network to make sure it works effectively;
5   costing communication so that its effectiveness can be measured.

As with all general strategies, there are possible pitfalls. For example, the notion of making one senior manager 'responsible' could lead to other managers 'leaving it to him or her' rather than taking equal responsibility. Costing is difficult to organize and monitor. Although we have reservations about some aspects of David's approach, we wholeheartedly agree with the overall concept – that management should have an explicit strategy which is regularly reviewed.

PRINCIPLE 16.7
New media can enhance communication.

Most modern organizations now have a much wider choice of communication media than at any time in history. These media can make a profound and positive impact if they are carefully introduced and maintained.

We have discussed various aspects of new media throughout the book, including:

- the potential impact of ICT on organizational structure and functions;
- use of email as a rapid and effective channel for bypassing the possible rigidities of the organizational hierarchy;
- use of intranet and Internet technologies to distribute information both within and outside the organization;
- application of videoconferencing to enable meetings which might otherwise be too expensive to sustain.

All these examples depend upon management strategy – upon management who are able to justify the investment to provide the facilities and then the commitment to sustain the appropriate use of this technology. We do not have to look far to find examples of computer failures and the 'ghastly consequences of some of these failures', including the pessimistic suggestion that 'for both corporate and individual users, software failure is still not only a likelihood but a certainty' (Tenner, 1996, p. 189).

But we can learn from the mistakes of the past and devise effective ways of using ICT to augment human aptitudes. And the same is true of communication in general. Reflecting on some of the problems and pitfalls of human communication in organizations can show us how to avoid them, provided we are prepared to take the responsibility. So we end by emphasizing Principle 5. And if management ignore communication, then we should remind them very quickly of its importance!

Bibliography

Adair, J. (1986) *Effective Leadership: A Modern Guide to Developing Leadership Skills*. London: Pan Books.

Adams, S. (1997) *The Dilbert Principle: A Cubicle's-Eye View of Bosses, Meetings, Management Fads and Other Workplace Afflictions*. New York: HarperBusiness.

Adler, H. (1996) *NLP for Managers: How to Achieve Excellence at Work*. London: Piatkus.

Adler, H. and Heather, B. (1999) *NLP in 21 Days: A Complete Introduction and Training Programme*. London: Piatkus.

Ahmad, C. and Hartley, P. (1999) 'Weapons of the weak: stories from Malaysia.' Paper given at 17th Standing Conference on Organizational Symbolism, Napier University.

Akar, D. and Louhiala-Salminen, L. (1999) 'Towards a new genre: a comparative study of business faxes.' In Bargiella-Chiappini, F. and Nickerson, C. (eds) *Writing Business: Genres, Media and Discourses*. Harlow: Longman.

Albrow, M. (1997) *Do Organizations Have Feelings?* London: Routledge.

Anderson, J.W. (1997) 'A comparison of Arab and American conceptions of "Effective" Persuasion.' In Samovar, L.A. and Porter, R.E. (eds) *Intercultural Communication: A reader*, 8th edn. Belmont, CA: Wadsworth.

Andrews, P.H. and Herschel, R.T. (1996) *Organizational Communication: Empowerment in a Technological Society*. Boston, MA: Houghton Mifflin.

Angell, D. and Heslop, B. (1994) *The Elements of E-mail Style*. Reading, MA: Addison Wesley.

Argyle, M. (1988) *Bodily Communication*, 2nd edition. London: Methuen.

Argyle, M. (1994) *The Psychology of Interpersonal Behaviour*, 5th edition. Harmondsworth: Penguin.

Armenakis, A.A. and Bedeian, A.G. (1999) 'Organizational change: a review of theory and research in the 1990s.' *Journal of Management* 25(3): 293–315.

Arnold, J., Cooper, C.L. and Robertson, I.T. (1998) *Work Psychology: Understanding Human Behaviour in the Workplace*, 3rd edition. London: Pitman.

Aronson, E. (1999) *The Social Animal*, 8th edition. New York: Worth.

Axtell, R.E. (1998) *Gestures: The Do's and Taboos of Body Language Around the World*, revised and expanded edition. New York: John Wiley.

Ayto, J. (1999) *20th Century Words*. Oxford: Oxford University Press.

Aziz, K. (2000) *Presenting to Win: A Guide for Finance and Business Professionals*. Dublin: Oak Tree Press.

Back, K. and Back, K. (1999) *Assertiveness at Work: A Practical Guide to Handling Awkward Situations*. London: McGraw-Hill.

Baguley, P. (1994) *Effective Communication for Modern Business*. London: McGraw-Hill.

Barker, A. (1999) *Writing at Work: How to Create Successful Business Documents*. London: Industrial Society.

Barker, J.R. (1999) *The Discipline of Teamwork: Participation and Coercive Control*. Thousand Oaks, CA: Sage.

Barkham, P. (1999) 'Can surfing get you the sack?' *Guardian Online*, 16 December: 2–3.

Baron, N.S. (1999) *Alphabet to Email: How Written English Evolved and Where It's Heading*. London: Routledge.

Barthe, K., Juaneda, C., Leseigneur, D., Loquet, J.-C., Morin, C., Escanda, J. and Vayrette, A. (1999) 'GIFAS rationalized French: a controlled language for aerospace documentation in French.' *Technical Communication* 46(2): 220–237.

Belbin, R.M. (1981) *Management Teams: Why They Succeed or Fail*. Oxford: Heinemann.

Belbin, R.M. (1993) *Team Roles at Work*. Oxford: Heinemann.

Belbin, R.M. (2000) *Beyond the Team*. Oxford : Heinemann.

Bell, A.H. and Smith, D.M. (1999) *Management Communication*. New York: John Wiley.

Benne, K.D. and Shets, P. (1948) 'Functional roles of group members', *Journal of Social Issues* 4: 41–49.

Bernstein, D. (1984) *Company Image and Reality: A Critique of Corporate Communications*. Eastbourne: Holt, Rinehart and Winston.

Bethune, G. with Huler, S. (1998) *From Worst to First: Behind the Scenes of Continental's Remarkable Comeback*. New York: John Wiley.

Bhatia, V.K. (1993) *Analysing Genre: Language Use in Professional Settings*. Harlow: Longman.

Birchall, D. and Lyons, L. (1995) *Creating Tomorrow's Organization: Unlocking the Benefits of Future Work*. London: Pitman.

Bloch, B. and Starks, D. (1999) 'The many faces of English: intra-language variation and its implications for international business.' *Corporate Communications* 4(2): 80–88.

Boddy, D. and Gunson, N. (1996) *Organizations in the Network Age*. London: Routledge.

Bolton, R. (1986) *People Skills: How to Assert Yourself, Listen to Others, and Resolve Conflicts*. Sydney: Prentice Hall.

Boon, M. (1996) *The African Way: The Power of Interactive Leadership*. Sandton: Zebra.

Bovee, C.L. and Thill, J.V. (1995) *Business Communication Today*, 4th edition. New York: McGraw-Hill.

Bowman, L. with Crofts, A. (1991) *High Impact Business Presentations: How to Speak Like an Expert and Sound Like a Statesman*. London: Business Books.

Brown, R. (2000) *Group Processes*, 2nd edition. Oxford: Blackwell.

Browning, L.D. (1992) 'List and stories as organizational communication.' *Communication Theory* 2: 281–302.

355

Brusaw, C.T., Alred, G.J. and Oliu, W.E. (1997) *Handbook of Technical Writing*, 5th edition. New York: St Martin's Press.

Bryman, A. (1992) *Charisma and Leadership in Organizations*. London: Sage.

Bryson, B. (1990) *Mother Tongue: The English Language*. London: Penguin.

Buchanan, D. and Badham, R. (1999) *Power, Politics and Organisational Change: Winning the Turf Game*. London: Sage.

Buchanan, D. and Huczynski, A. (eds) (1997) *Organisational Behaviour: An Introductory Text*, 3rd edition. Hemel Hempstead: Prentice Hall.

Burgoon, J.K., Buller, D.B. and Woodall, W.G. (1996) *Nonverbal Communication: The Unspoken Dialogue*, 2nd edition. New York: McGraw-Hill.

Buzan, T. with Buzan, B. (1995) *The Mind Map Book*, revised edition. London: BBC Books.

Cairncross, F. (1997) *The Death of Distance: How the Communications Revolution will Change Our Lives*. London: Orion.

Cameron, D. (1995) *Verbal Hygiene*. London: Routledge.

Cameron, D. (2000) *Good to Talk*. London: Sage.

Cannon, T. (1996) *Welcome to the Revolution: Managing Paradox in the 21st century*. London: Pitman.

Carbaugh, D. (1997) 'Finnish and American linguistic patterns: a cultural comparison.' In Samovar, L.A. and Porter, R.E. (eds) *Intercultural Communication: A Reader*, 8th edition. Belmont, CA: Wadsworth.

Castells, M. (1996) *The Rise of the Network Society*. Oxford: Blackwell.

Chambers, H. (1998) *Designers' Handbook of Letterheads and Business Cards*. New York: RC Publications.

Chapanis, A. (1965) 'Words, words, words.' *Human Factors* 7(1): 1–17.

Chapanis, A. (1988) '"Words, words, words" revised.' *International Review of Ergonomics* 2: 1–30.

Chaudry-Lawton, R. and Lawton, R. (1992) *Ignition: Sparking Organizational Change*. London: BCA.

Chesher, M. and Kaura, R. (1998) *Electronic Commerce and Business Communications*. London: Springer-Verlag.

Chu, S. (1999) 'Using chopsticks and a fork together: challenges and strategies of developing a Chinese/English bilingual Web site.' *Technical Communication* 46(2): 206–219.

Clampitt, P.G. (2001) *Communicating for Managerial Effectiveness*, 2nd edition. Thousand Oaks, CA: Sage.

Clampitt, P.G. and Berk, L.R. (1996) 'Strategically communicating organizational change.' *Journal of Communication Management* 1(1): 15–28.

Clark, T. (1998) 'Encouraging critical thinking in business memos.' *Business Communication* 61(3): 71–74.

Clyne, M. (1994) *Inter-cultural Communication at Work: Cultural Values in Discourse*. Cambridge: Cambridge University Press.

Collett, P. (1998) 'What do managers in different countries actually do?' *International Work Psychology Conference Proceedings*. Sheffield: Institute of Work Psychology.

356

Collier, M. J. (1997) 'Cultural identity and intercultural communication.' In Samovar, L.A. and Porter, R.E. (eds) *Intercultural Communication: A Reader*, 8th edition, Belmont, CA: Wadsworth.

Collins, D. (1998) *Organizational Change: Sociological Perspectives*. London: Routledge.

Collins, J. and Porras, J. (1994) *Built to Last: Successful Habits of Visionary Companies*. New York: HarperBusiness.

Collinson, D., Kirkup, G., Kyd, R. and Slocombe, L. (1992) *Plain English*, 2nd edition. Buckingham: Open University Press.

Cooke, C. (1998) 'Not so much "what" you say, but "how" you say it.' *Journal of Communication Management* 3(2): 180–196.

Corman, S.R., Banks, S.P., Bantz, C.R. and Mayer, M.E. (eds) (1990) *Foundations of Organisational Communication: A Reader*. New York: Longman.

Craig, R.T. (1999) 'Communication theory as a field.' *Communication Theory* 9(2): 119–161.

Crawford, J.R. (ed.) (1992) *Language Loyalties: A Sourcebook on the Official English Controversy*. Chicago: University of Chicago Press.

Cronin, M.J. (1994) *Doing Business on the Internet: How the Electronic Highway Is Transforming American Companies*. New York: Van Nostrand Reinhold.

Cupach, W.R. and Spitzberg, B.H. (eds) (1994) *The Dark Side of Interpersonal Communication*. Hillsdale, NJ: Lawrence Erlbaum Associates.

Cutts, M. (1995) *The Plain English Guide: How to Write Clearly and Communicate Better*. London: QPD.

Cutts, M. and Maher, C. (1986) *The Plain English Story*. Stockport: Plain English Campaign.

Czerniawska, F. (1997) *Corporate Speak*. London: Palgrave.

Dale, M. (1999) *The People Dimension: Managing Your People Performance*. Dublin: Blackhall.

Daniels, T.D. and Spiker, B.K. (1994) *Perspectives on Organisational Communication*, 3rd edition. Madison, WI: W.C.B. Brown and Benchmark.

Danziger, K. (1976) *Interpersonal Communication*. Oxford: Pergamon.

David, W. (1995) *Managing Company-Wide Communication*. London: Chapman and Hall.

Davis, S. and Meyer, C. (1998) *Blur: The Speed of Change in the Connected Economy*. London: Capstone.

De Kare-Silver, M. (1998) *E-shock: The Electronic Shopping Revolution: Strategies for Retailers and Manufacturers*. Basingstoke: Macmillan.

Deal, T. and Kennedy, A. (1982) *Corporate Cultures: The Rites and Rituals of Corporate Life*. Reading, MA: Addison-Wesley.

Deal, T. and Kennedy, A. (1999) *The New Corporate Cultures: Revitalising the Workplace after Downsizing, Mergers and Reengineering*. London: Orion.

Deetz, S. (1995) *Transforming Communication, Transforming Business: Building Responsive and Responsible Workplaces*. Cresskill, NJ: Hampton Press.

Delbridge, R. (1998) *Life on the Line in Contemporary Manufacturing*. Oxford: Oxford University Press.

Dertouzos, M. (1997) *What Will Be: How the New World of Information Will Change our Lives*. London: Piatkus.

357

DiSanza, J. R. and Bullis, C. (1999) '"Everybody identifies with Smokey the Bear": employee responses to newsletter identification inducements at the U.S. Forest Service'. *Management Communication Quarterly* 12(3): 347–399.

Dixon, N.M. (1998) *Dialogue at Work: Making Talk Developmental for People and Organizations*. London: Lemos and Crane.

Duck, S. (1998) *Human Relationships*, 3rd edition. London: Sage.

Dunphy, D. and Stace, D. (1993) 'The strategic management of corporate change.' *Human Relations* 45(8): 917–18.

Dwyer, J. (1997) *The Business Communication Handbook*, 4th edition. Sydney: Prentice Hall.

Economist (1996) The Economist Style Guide. London: Profile Books.

Ehrenberg, A.S.C. (1977) 'Rudiments of numeracy.' *Journal of the Royal Statistical Society A* 140: 227–297.

Ekman, P. (1992) 'An argument for basic emotions.' *Cognition and Emotion* 6: 169–200.

Ellinor, L. and Gerard, G. (1998) *Dialogue: Rediscover the Transforming Power of Conversation*. New York: John Wiley.

Ellis, A. and Beattie, G. (1986) *The Psychology of Language and Communication*. London: Weidenfeld and Nicolson.

Fairbrother, L. (1993) *Your Message and the Media: The Complete and Practical Guide to Public Relations*. London: Nicholas Brealey.

Feynman, J.P. (1988) *What Do You Care What Other People Think*, London: Allen and Unwin.

Finan, A. (1998) *Corporate Christ: The World-Changing Secrets of a Management and Marketing Genius*. Chalford, Gloucestershire: Management Books.

Fineman, S. and Gabriel, Y. (1996) *Experiencing Organisations*. London: Sage.

Finn, T. A. (1999) 'A case of telecommunications (mis)management.' *Management Communication Quarterly* 12(4): 575–579.

Fleming, J. (1998) *Web Navigation: Designing the User Experience*. Sebastopol, CA: O'Reilly.

Fletcher, C. (1994) 'The effects of performance review in appraisal: evidence and implications.' In Mabey, C. and Iles, P. (eds) *Managing Learning*. Routledge: London.

Flowers, S. (1996) *Software Failure: Management Failure: Amazing Stories and Cautionary Tales*. Chichester: John Wiley.

Frey, L.R., Gouran, D.S. and Poole, M.S. (1999) *The Handbook of Group Communication Theory and Research*. Thousand Oaks, CA: Sage.

Friday, R.A. (1997) 'Contrasts in discussion behaviours of German and American managers.' In Samovar, L.A. and Porter, R.E. (eds) *Intercultural Communication: A Reader*, 8th edition. Belmont, CA: Wadsworth.

Gabriel, Y. (1998) 'The use of stories.' In Symon, G. and Cassell, C. (eds) *Qualitative Methods and Analysis in Organisational Research: A Practical Guide*. London: Sage.

Gabriel, Y. (1999) *Organizations in Depth: The Psychoanalysis of Organizations*. London: Sage.

Gallagher, K., McLelland, B. and Swales, C. (1998) *Business Skills: An Active Learning Approach*. Oxford: Blackwell.

Gallois, C. and Callan, V. (1997) *Communication and Culture: A Guide for Practice*. Chichester: John Wiley.

358

Gates, B. with Hemingway, C. (1999) *Business @ the Speed of Thought: Using a Digital Nervous System*. London: Penguin.

Gates, B. with Myhrvold, N. and Rinearson, P. (1996) *The Road Ahead*, revised edition. London: Penguin.

Georgiades, N. and Macdonell, R. (1998) *Leadership in Competitive Advantage*. Chichester: Wiley.

Goffee, R. and Jones, G. (2000) *The Character of a Corporation: How Your Company Culture Can Make or Break Your Business*. London: HarperCollins.

Goldman, A. (1994) 'Communication in Japanese multinational organisations.' In Wiseman, R.L. and Shuter, R. (eds) *Communicating in Multinational Organisations*. Thousand Oaks, CA: Sage.

Goleman, D. (1996) *Emotional Intelligence*. London: Bloomsbury.

Goleman, D. (1998) *Working with Emotional Intelligence*. London: Bloomsbury.

Gordon, J.R. (1996) *Organizational Behavior*, 5th edition. Englewood Cliffs, NJ: Prentice Hall.

Gowers, E. (1987) *The Complete Plain Words*, 3rd edition. Harmondsworth: Penguin.

Gralla, P. (1998) *How the Internet Works*, 4th edition. Indianapolis: QUE.

Gray, J. (1993) *Men Are from Mars, Women Are from Venus: A Practical Guide for Improving Communication and Getting What You Want in Your Relationships*. London: Thorsons.

Gudykunst, W.B. (1991) *Bridging Differences: Effective Intergroup Communication*. Newbury Park, CA: Sage.

Gudykunst, W.B., Ting-Toomey, S. and Nishida, T. (1996) *Communication in Personal Relationships across Cultures*. Thousand Oaks, CA: Sage.

Guirdham, M. (1995) *Interpersonal Skills at Work*, 2nd edition. Hemel Hempstead: Prentice Hall.

Hackley, C. (1998) 'Mission statements as corporate communications: the consequences of social constructionism.' *Corporate Communications* 3(3): 92–98.

Hackman, J.R. (1990) *Groups That Work (and Those That Don't): Creating Conditions for Effective Teamwork*. San Francisco: Jossey-Bass.

Hales, C.P. (1986) 'What do managers do? a critical review of the evidence.' *Journal of Management Studies* 23: 88–115.

Hall, E.T. (1959) *The Silent Language*. New York: Doubleday.

Hall, E.T. (1976) *Beyond Culture*. New York: Anchor.

Hall, W. (1995) *Managing Cultures: Making Strategic Relationships Work*. Chichester: John Wiley.

Hammer, M. and Champy, J. (1993) *Reengineering the Corporation: A Manifesto for Business Revolution*. London: Nicholas Brealey.

Hampden-Turner, C. and Trompenaars, F. (2000) *Building Cross Cultural Competence: How to Create Wealth from Conflicting Values*. Chichester: John Wiley.

Hansen, C.D. and Kahnweiler, W.M. (1993) 'Story-telling: an instrument for understanding the dynamics of corporate relationships.' *Human Relations* 44(8): 857–875.

Hargie, O.D.W. (1997) *The Handbook of Communication Skills*, 2nd edition. London: Routledge.

Hargie, O.D.W. and Tourish, D. (eds) (2000) *Handbook of Communication Audits for Organisations.* London: Routledge.

Hargie, O., Saunders, C. and Dickson, D. (1994) *Social Skills in Interpersonal Communication,* 3rd edition. London: Routledge.

Hargie, O.D.W., Dickson, D. and Tourish, D. (1999) *Communication in Management.* Aldershot: Gower.

Harris, L.H. (1996) *Information Graphics: A Comprehensive Illustrated Reference.* Atlanta: Management Graphics.

Harris, M. (1998) 'Rethinking the virtual organization.' In Jackson, P.J. and Van Der Wielen, J.M. (eds) *Teleworking: International Perspectives.* London: Routledge.

Hartley, J. (1994) *Designing Instructional Text,* 3rd edition. London: Kogan Page.

Hartley, J. (1998) 'Return to sender – why written communications fail.' *The Psychologist* 11(10): 477–480.

Hartley, J. (1999) 'Readers as text designers. Personalising the layout the text.' *Innovations in Education and Training International* 36(4): 346–350.

Hartley, P. (1984) 'Principles for effective documents.' Paper given at Scottish Communication Association annual conference.

Hartley, P. (1990) 'The technology of communication.' In Williams, N. and Hartley, P. (eds) *Technology in Human Communication.* London: Pinter.

Hartley, P. (1997) *Group Communication.* London: Routledge.

Hartley, P. (1999) *Interpersonal Communication,* 2nd edition. London: Routledge.

Hayes, J. (1991) *Interpersonal Skills: Goal-Directed Behaviour at Work.* London: Routledge.

Hayes, N. (1997) *Successful Team Management.* London: International Thomson Business Press.

Heckscher, C. and Donnellon, A. (1994) *The Post-bureaucratic Organization: New Perspectives on Organizational Change.* London: Sage.

Heller, R. and Hindle, T. (1998) *Essential Manager's Manual.* London: Dorling Kindersley.

Henning, K. (1998) *The Digital Enterprise: How Digitisation is Redefining Business.* London: Century.

Hirokawa, R.Y. and Poole, M.S. (eds) (1996) *Communication and Group Decision Making.* Thousand Oaks, CA: Sage.

Hirshberg, J. (1998) *The Creative Priority: Driving Innovative Business in the Real World.* Harmondsworth: Penguin.

Hodgkinson, G. and Payne, R.L. (1998) 'Graduate selection in three European countries.' *Journal of Occupational and Organizational Psychology* 71(4): 359–365.

Hodgson, P. and Hodgson, J. (1992) *Effective Meetings.* London: Century.

Hofstede, G. (1994) *Cultures and Organisations: Software of the Mind.* London: HarperCollins.

Honey, P. (1988) *Face to Face: A Practical Guide to Interactive Skills,* 2nd edition. Aldershot: Gower.

Honold, P. (1999) 'Learning how to use a cellular phone: comparison between German and Chinese users.' *Technical Communication,* 46(2): 196–205.

360

Horton, W. (1997) *Secrets of User-Seductive Documents: Wooing and Winning the Reluctant Reader.* Arlington, VA: Society for Technical Communication.

Hosking, D.-M., and Morley, I.E. (1991) *A Social Psychology of Organizing: People, Processes and Contexts.* Hemel Hempstead: Harvester Wheatsheaf.

Howard, G. (1993) *The Good English Guide: English Usage in the 1990s.* London: Macmillan.

Howse, C. (1999) 'Why I'm not wedded to these words.' *Daily Telegraph,* 2 August: 14.

Hussey, M. (1999) 'Marilyn's new platform'. *Daily Express,* 7 May: 23.

Jackson, P. (1997) 'Brusque responses'. *PC Magazine,* August: 101.

Jackson, P.J. and Van Der Wielen, J.M. (eds) (1998) *Teleworking: International Perspectives.* London: Routledge.

Jacobson, R. (ed.) (1999) *Information Design.* Cambridge, MA: MIT Press.

James, J. (1995) *Body Talk: The Skills of Positive Image.* London: Industrial Society.

Janal, D.S. (1999) *Business Speak: Using Speech Technology to Streamline Your Business.* New York: John Wiley.

Jandt, E. (1998) *Intercultural Communication: An Introduction,* 2nd edition. Thousand Oaks, CA: Sage.

Janis, I. (1982) *Groupthink.* Boston, MA: Houghton Mifflin.

Jaques, D. (2000) *Learning in Groups: A Handbook for Improving Group Working,* 3rd edition. London: Kogan Page.

Jaques, E. (1994) 'Managerial leadership: the key to good organization.' In Mabey, C. and Iles, P. (eds) *Managing Learning.* London: Routledge.

Jarboe, S. (1996) 'Procedures for enhancing group decision making.' In Hirokawa, R.Y. and Poole, M.S. (eds) *Communication and Group Decision Making.* Thousand Oaks: Sage.

Jay, R. (1995) *How to Write Proposals and Reports That Get Results.* London: Pitman.

Jenkins, S. and Hinds, J. (1987) 'Business letter writing: English, French and Japanese.' *TESOL Quarterly,* 121(2): 327–354.

Johnson, D. W. and Johnson, F. P. (1997) *Joining Together: Group Theory and Group Skills,* 6th edition. Needham Heights, MA: Allyn and Bacon.

Johnson, G. and Scholes, K. (1997) *Exploring Corporate Strategy,* 4th edition. Hemel Hempstead: Prentice Hall.

Joseph, A. (1998) *Put It in Writing: Learn How to Write Clearly, Quickly and Persuasively.* New York: McGraw-Hill.

Kanter, R.M. (1994) 'Dilemmas of teamwork.' In Mabey, C. and Iles, P. (eds) *Managing Learning.* London: Routledge.

Katz, S. (1998) 'Part 1: Learning to write in organizations: what newcomers learn about writing on the job.' *IEEE Transactions on Professional Communication,* 41(2): 107–115.

Katzenbach, J. and the Real Change Team (1996) *Real Change Leaders: How You Can Create Growth and High Performance at Your Company.* London: BCA.

Katzenbach, J.R. and Smith, D.K. (1998) *The Wisdom of Teams: Creating the High-Performance Organisation.* London: McGraw-Hill.

Kaye, M. and Gilpin, A. (1998) 'Successful Organisational teams: theory and practice from an adult communication management perspective.' *Journal of Communication Management* 2(4): 305–319.

Kennedy, G. (1998) *The New Negotiating Edge: The Behavioral Approach for Results and Relationships*. London: Nicholas Brealey.

Kim, Y.K. and Paulk, S. (1994) 'Intercultural Challenges and personal adjustments: a qualitative analysis of the experiences of American and Japanese co-workers.' In Wiseman, R.L. and Shuter, R. (eds) *Communicating in Multinational Organisations*. Thousand Oaks, CA: Sage.

Kimble, J. (1994/5) 'Answering the critics of plain language.' *The Scribes Journal of Legal Writing* 5: 51–85.

Kirkman, J. (1991) *Full Marks: Advice on Punctuation for Scientific and Technical Writing*. London: ISTC.

Kirkman, J. (1992) *Good Style: Writing for Science and Technology*. London: E. & F.N. Spon.

Klepper, M.M. with Gunther, R. (1994) *I'd Rather Die Than Give a Speech*. New York: Irwin.

Kline, D. (1996) 'The embedded Internet.' *Wired*, November: 54–57.

Knapp, M.L. and Hall, J.A. (1997) *Nonverbal Communication in Human Interaction*, 4th edition. Fort Worth. TX: Harcourt Brace.

Knapp, M.L. and Miller, G.R. (1994) *Handbook of Interpersonal Communication*, 2nd edition. Thousand Oaks, CA: Sage.

Knight, K. (1999) 'Which is Britain's sexiest accent?' *Daily Express*, 4 March: 40–41.

Knight, S. (1995) *NLP at Work*. London: Nicholas Brealey.

Knight, S. (1999) *NLP Solutions: How to Model What Works in Business*. London: Nicholas Brealey.

Knights, D. and Wilmott, D. (eds) (2000) *The Reengineering Revolution: Critical Studies of Corporate Change*. London: Sage.

Knowles, E. with Elliott, J. (eds) (1998) *The Oxford Dictionary of New Words*, 2nd edition. Oxford: Oxford University Press.

Koch, R. (1999) *Moses on Leadership: Or Why Everyone Is a Leader*. Oxford: Capstone.

Kohl, J.R. (1999) 'Improving translatability and readability with syntactic cues.' *Technical Communication* 46(2): 149–166.

Koopman, A. D., Nasser, M. E. and Nel, J. (1987) *The Corporate Crusaders*. London: Lexicon Publishing

Kotter, J. and Heskett, J. (1992) *Corporate Culture and Performance*. New York: Free Press.

Kreps, G.L. (1990) *Organizational Communication*, 2nd edition. New York: Longman.

Lane, G. (2000) 'Email Policies and the Law.' *IT Week*, 28 August: 49.

Lauchman, R. (1998) *Write for Results*. New York: Amacom New Media.

Laudon, K.C. and Laudon, J.P. (1994) *Management Information Systems: Organization and Technology*. New York: Macmillan.

Levinson, P. (1997) *The Soft Edge: A Natural History and Future of the Information Revolution*. London: Routledge.

Lewin, K. (1951) *Field Theory in Social Science*. New York: Harper.

Lewis, D. (1996) *How to Get Your Message Across: A Practical Guide to Power Communication*. London: Souvenir Press.

Lewis, R. D. (1996) *When Cultures Collide: Managing Successfully across Cultures*. London: Nicholas Brealey.

Lichty, T. (1989) *Design Principles for Desktop Publishers*. Glenview, IL: Scott, Foresman.

Linehan, M. and Egan, K. (1983) *Asserting Yourself*. London: Century.

Littlejohn, S.W. (1983) *Theories of Human Communication*, 2nd edition. Belmont, CA: Wadsworth.

Locke, E.A. (1997) 'Prime movers: the traits of great business leaders.' In Cooper, C.L. and Jackson, S.E. (eds) *Creating Tomorrow's Organizations: A Handbook for Future Research in Organizational Behaviour*. Chichester: John Wiley.

Lynch, P.J. and Horton, S. (1999) *Web Style Guide: Basic Design Principles for Creating Web Sites*. New Haven, CT: Yale University Press.

McArthur, T. (1998) *The English Languages*. Cambridge: Cambridge University Press.

McBride, P. (1993) *Excel at Interviews: Tactics for Job and College Applicants*. Cambridge: Hobsons.

McCormack, M.H. (1997) *Mark H. McCormack on Communicating*. London: Arrow.

McDaniel, E.R. (1997) 'Nonverbal communication: a reflection of cultural themes.' In Samovar, L.A. and Porter, R.E. (eds) *Intercultural Communication: A Reader*, 8th edition. Belmont, CA: Wadsworth.

McDaniel, E.R. and Samovar, L.A. (1997) 'Cultural influences on communication in multinational organizations: the Maquiladora.' In Samovar, L.A. and Porter, R.E. (eds) *Intercultural Communication: A Reader*, 8th edition. Belmont, CA: Wadsworth.

McDermott, L.C., Brawley, N. and Waite, W.W. (1998) *World-Class Teams: Working Across Borders*. New York: John Wiley.

McIntyre, M.G. (1998) *The Management Team Handbook: Five Key Strategies for Maximising Group Performance*. San Francisco: Jossey-Bass.

MacKenzie, D. and Wajcman, J. (eds) (1999) *The Social Shaping of Technology*, 2nd edition. Buckingham: Open University Press.

McLean, R. (1980) *The Thames and Hudson Manual of Typography*. London: Thames and Hudson.

Mandel, S. (1987) *Effective Presentation Skills*. London: Kogan Page.

Marquis, K.H. and Cannell, C.F. (1971) *Effect of Some Experimental Interviewing Techniques of Reporting in the Health Interview Study*. Washington, DC: US Department of Health, Education and Welfare.

Martin, D. (1998) *One Stop Communication*. Hemel Hempstead: ICSA Publishing.

Martin, D. (2000) *Manipulating Meetings: How to Get What You Want, When You Want It*. London: Prentice Hall.

Mattelart, A. and Mattelart, M. (1998) *Theories of Commuication: A Short Introduction*. London: Sage.

Mayer, J.C. (1995) '"Tell me a story": eliciting organizational values from narratives.' *Communication Quarterly* 34(2): 210–224.

Meyer, E.K. (1997) *Designing Infographics*. Indianapolis, IN: Hayden.

Micklethwait, J. and Wooldridge, A. (1996) *The Witch Doctors: What the Management Gurus are Saying, Why It Matters and How to Make Sense of It*. London: Heinemann.

Milroy, J. and Milroy, L. (1999) *Authority in Language*, 3rd edition. London: Routledge.

Milsted, D. (1999) *The Cassell Dictionary of Regrettable Quotations*. London: Cassell.

Minto, B. (1991) *The Pyramid Principle: Logic in Writing and Thinking*. London: Pitman.

Mintzberg, H. (1973) *The Nature of Managerial Work*. New York: Harper and Row.

Misiura, S. (1996) *Business Communication*. Oxford: Butterworth-Heinemann.

Mohan, T., McGregor, H., Saunders, S. and Archee, R. (1997) *Communicating: Theory and Practice*, 4th edition. Sydney: Harcourt Brace.

Montgomery, M. (1995) *An Introduction to Language and Society*, 2nd edition. London: Routledge.

Morgan, G. (1986) *Images of Organization*. London: Sage.

Morgan, G. (1997) *Images of Organization*, new edition. London: Sage.

Morris, D. (1994) *Bodytalk: A World Guide to Gestures*. London: Jonathan Cape.

Morrison, T., Conaway, W.A. and Borden, G.A. (1994) *Kiss, Bow or Shake Hands: How to Do Business in Sixty Countries*. Holbrook, MA: Bob Adams.

Mort, S. (1992) *Professional Report Writing*. Aldershot: Gower.

Mulholland, J. (1999) 'E-mail: uses, issues and problems in an institutional setting.' In Bargiella-Chiappini, F. and Nickerson, C. (eds) *Writing Business: Genres, Media and Discourses*. London: Longman.

Murray, D.E. (1995) *Knowledge Machines: Language and Information in a Technological Society*. London: Longman.

Naughton, J. (1999) *A Brief History of the Future: The Origins of the Internet*. London: Weidenfeld and Nicolson.

Negroponte, N. (1995) *Being Digital*. London: Hodder and Stoughton.

Nickson, D. and Siddons, S. (1996) *Business Communications*. Oxford: Butterworth-Heinemann.

Nielsen, J. (2000) *Designing Web Usability*. Indianapolis, IN: New Riders.

Norretranders, T. (1998) *The User Illusion: Cutting Consciousness down to size*. Harmondsworth: Penguin.

Nuttall, R (1999) 'Will Bank of Scotland suffer same fate as the Ford Edsel?,' *Daily Express*, 17 June: 58.

Oakes, P.J., Haslam, S.A. and Reynolds, K.J. (1999) 'Social categorization and social context: is stereotype change a matter of information or meaning?' In Abrams, D. and Hogg, M.A. (eds) *Social Identity and Social Cognition*. Oxford: Blackwell.

Oliver, S (1997) *Corporate Communication: Principles, Techniques and Strategies*. London: Kogan Page.

Orwell, G. (1946) 'Politics and the English language.' Reprinted in *The Collected Essays, Journalism and Letters of George Orwell*, vol. 4: *In Front of Your Nose, 1945–50*, ed. Orwell, S. and Angus, I. (1968). Harmondsworth: Penguin.

Owen, H. (1996) *Creating Top Flight Teams*. London: BCA.

Pacanowsky, M.E. and O'Donnell-Trujillo, N. (1990) 'Communication and Organizational Cultures.' In Corman, S.R., Banks, S.P., Bantz, C.R. and Mayer, M.E. (eds) *Foundations of Organisational Communication: A Reader*. New York: Longman.

Papows, J. (1999) *Enterprise.com: Market Leadership in the Digital Age*. London: Nicholas Brealey.

Penman, R. (1993) 'Unspeakable acts and other deeds: a critique of plain legal language.' *Information Design Journal* 7(2): 121–131.

Peters, T.J. and Waterman, R.H. (1982) *In Search of Excellence: Lessons from America's Best-Run Companies*. New York: Harper and Row.

Pettigrew, A. and Whipp, R. (1993) *Managing Change for Competitive Success*. Oxford: Blackwell.

Pheysey, D.C. (1993) *Organizational Cultures: Types and Transformations*. London: Routledge.

Pickles, H. (1998) 'Play your cards right.' *Livewire*, August/September, published by GNER.

Pinker, S. (1994) *The Language Instinct: The New Science of Language and Mind*. London: Allen Lane.

Plain English Campaign (1993) *The Plain English Story*, 3rd revised edition. Stockport: Plain English Campaign.

Plain English Campaign (1994) *Utter Drivel: A Decade of Jargon and Gobbledygook*. London: Robson.

Plous, S. (1993) *The Psychology of Judgment and Decision Making*. New York: McGraw-Hill.

Proctor, T. (1999) *Creative Problem Solving for Managers*. London: Routledge.

Putnam, L.L. and Cheney, G. (1990) 'Organisational communication: historical development and future directions'. In Corman, S.R., Banks, S.P., Bantz, C.R. and Mayer, M.E. (eds) *Foundations of Organisational Communication: A Reader*. New York: Longman.

Putnam, L.L. and Stohl, C. (1996) 'Bona fide groups: an alternative perspective for communication and small group decision making.' In Hirokawa, R.Y. and Poole, M.S. (eds) *Communication and Group Decision Making*. Thousand Oaks, CA: Sage.

Quirke, B. (1995) *Communicating Change*. London: McGraw-Hill.

Qvortrup, L. (1998) 'From Teleworking to Networking: definitions and trends.' In Jackson, P.J. and Van Der Wielen, J.M. (eds) *Teleworking: International Perspectives*. London: Routledge.

Rackham, N. (1988) *SPIN Selling*. New York: McGraw-Hill.

Rackham, N. and Morgan, T. (1977) *Behaviour Analysis and Training*. London: McGraw-Hill.

Ramey, J.G. (1999) 'Effective technical letters.' *Intercom*, February: 28–29.

Rasberry, R.W. and Lemoine, L.F. (1986) *Effective Managerial Communication*. Boston, MA: Kent.

Ray, D. and Bronstein, H. (1995) *Teaming Up: Making the Transition to a Self-Directed, Team-Based Organization*. New York: McGraw-Hill.

Reid, M. and Hammersley, R. (2000) *Communicating Successfully in Groups: A Practical Guide for the Workplace*. London: Routledge.

Reid, T.R. (1985) *Microchip*. London: William Collins.

Ritzer, G. (1996) *The McDonaldization of Society*, revised edition. Thousand Oaks, CA: Pine Forge Press.

Robbins, H. and Finley, M. (1997) *Why Teams Don't Work: What Went Wrong and How to Make It Right*. London: Orion.

Robbins, S.P. (1996) *Organisational Behaviour: Concepts, Controversies, Applications*, 7th edition. Englewood Cliffs, NJ: Prentice Hall.

Robbins, S.P. (1998) *Organisational Behaviour: Concepts, Controversies, Applications*, 8th edition. Englewood Cliffs, NJ: Prentice Hall.

Roberts, W. and Ross, B. (1995) *'Make It So': Leadership Lessons from 'Star Trek, the Next Generation'*. New York: Pocket Books.

Rogers, P.S., Taylor, J.R., and Finn, T.A. (1999) 'A case of telecommunications (mis)management case analyses.' *Management Communication Quarterly* 12(4): 580–599.

Rosenfeld, L. and Morville, P. (1998) *Information Architecture for the World Wide Web*. Sebastopol, CA: O'Reilly.

Salas, E., Rozell, D., Mullen, B., and Driskell, J.E. (1999) 'The effect of team building on performance: an integration.' *Small Group Research*, 30(3): 309–329.

Samovar, L.A. and Porter, R.E. (1997) *Communication Between Cultures*, 2nd edition. Belmont, CA: Wadsworth.

Samovar, L.A. and Porter, R.E. (eds) (1997) *Intercultural Communication*, 8th edition. Belmont, CA: Wadsworth.

Sarangi, S. and Slembrouck, S. (1996) *Language, Bureaucracy and Social Control*. Longman: London.

Scheibel, D. (1990) 'The emergence of organisational cultures.' In Corman, S.R., Banks, S.P., Bantz, C.R. and Mayer, M.E. (eds) *Foundations of Organisational Communication: A Reader*. New York: Longman.

Schein, E. (1991) 'What is culture?' In Frost, P., Moore, L., Louis, M., Lundberg, C. and Martin, J. (eds) *Reframing Organisational Culture*. London: Sage.

Schiffrin, D. (1994) *Approaches to Discourse*. Cambridge, MA: Blackwell.

Scholes, E. (ed.) (1997) *Gower Handbook of Internal Communication*. Aldershot: Gower.

Scholter, P.R. (1988) *The Team Handbook*. Madison, WI: Joiner.

Schriver, K.A. (1997) *Dynamics in Document Design: Creating Text for Readers*. New York: John Wiley.

Scott, C.R., Connaughton, S.L., Diez-Saenz, H., Maguire, K., Ramirez, R., Richardson, B., Shaw, S.P. and Morgan, D. (1999) 'The impacts of communication and multiple identifications on intent to leave: a multi-methodological exploration.' *Management Communication Quarterly* 12(3): 400–435.

Senge, P.M. (1994) 'The leader's new work: building learning organisations.' In Mabey, C. and Iles, P. (eds) *Managing Learning*. Routledge: London.

Senior, B. (1997) *Organisational Change*. London: Pitman.

Shackleton, V. (1995) *Business Leadership*. London: Routledge.

Shapiro, E.C. (1996) *Fad Surfing in the Boardroom: Reclaiming the Courage to Manage in the Age of Instant Answers.* Oxford: Capstone.

Sharples, M. (1999) *How We Write: Writing as Creative Design.* London: Routledge.

Shimko, B.W. (1990) 'New breed workers need new yardsticks.' *Business Horizons,* November/December: 34–36.

Shriberg, A., Lloyd, C., Shriberg, D.L. and Williamson, M.L. (1997) *Practicing Leadership: Principles and Applications.* New York: John Wiley.

Shuy, R.W. (1998) *The Language of Confession, Interrogation and Deception.* Thousand Oaks, CA: Sage.

Siegel, D. (1996) *Creating Killer Web Sites: The Art of Third-Generation Site Design.* Indianapolis, IN: Hayden.

Sklar, J. (2000) *Principles of Web Design.* Cambridge, MA: Thomson Learning.

Sless, D. (1999) 'The mass production of unique letters.' In Bargiela-Chiappini, F. and Nickerson, C. (eds) *Writing Business: Genres, Media and Discourses.* Harlow: Longman.

Smith, M. (1982) *Selection Interviewing: A Four-Step Approach.* In Breakwell, G.M., Foot, H. and Gilmour, R. (eds) *Social Psychology: A Practical Manual.* London: Macmillan.

Smith, P.B. and Peterson, M.F. (1988) *Leadership, Organizations and Culture.* London: Sage.

Smith, R.C. and Eisenberg, E.M. (1987) 'Conflict at Disneyland: a root-metaphor analysis.' *Communication Monographs* 54: 367–380.

Sparks, S.D. (1999) *The Manager's Guide to Business Writing.* New York: McGraw-Hill.

Spiekermann, E. and Ginger, E.M. (1993) *Stop Stealing Sheep and Find Out How Type Works.* Mountain View, CA: Adobe Press.

Stacey, R.D. (2000) *Strategic Management and Organisational Dynamics: The Challenge of Complexity,* 3rd edition. Harlow: Prentice Hall.

Standage, T. (1999) *The Victorian Internet: The Remarkable Story of the Telegraph and the Nineteenth Century's Online Pioneers.* London: Weidenfeld and Nicolson.

Stanton, N. (1996) *Mastering Communication,* 3rd edition. Basingstoke: Macmillan.

Steenstra, D. (1999) 'Design: from black box into business culture.' In *Proceedings of the Third European Academy of Design Conference: Design Cultures, Sheffield Hallam University.*

Stewart, G.L., Manz, C.C. and Sims, H.P. (1999) *Team Work and Group Dynamics.* New York: John Wiley.

Stewart, R. (1988) *Managers and Their Jobs: A Study of the Similarities and Differences in the Ways Managers Spend Their Time.* London: Macmillan.

Stewart, R. (1991) *Managing Today and Tomorrow.* London: Macmillan.

Stewart, R. (ed.) (1999) *Gower Handbook of Teamworking.* Aldershot: Gower.

Stoner, J.A.F. (1961) *A Comparison of Individual and Group Decisions Involving Risk.* Cambridge, MA: MIT Press.

Suchan, J. (1998) 'The Effect of high-impact writing on decision making within a public sector bureaucracy.' *Journal of Business Communication* 35(3): 299–327.

Sundstrom, E. (1986) *Work Places: The Psychology of the Physical Environment in Offices and Factories.* Cambridge: Cambridge University Press.

367

Sutton, J. and Bartram, A. (1968) *An Atlas of Typeforms*. London: Lund Humphries.

Sypher, B.D. (ed.) (1997) *Case Studies In Organisational Communication 2: Perspectives on Contemporary Work Life*. New York: Guilford.

Tannen, D. (1994) *Talking from 9 To 5: How women's and men's Conversational Styles Affect Who Gets Heard, Who Gets Credit, and What Gets Done at Work*. New York: William Morrow, Ballantine.

Tannenbaum, R.S. (1998) *Theoretical Foundations of Multimedia*. New York: Freeman.

Tapscott, D. (1996) *The Digital Economy: Promise and Peril in the Age of Networked Intelligence*. New York: McGraw-Hill.

Tapscott, D., Lowy, A. and Ticoll, D. (1998) *Blueprint to the Digital Economy: Creating Wealth in the Era of E-Business*. New York: McGraw-Hill.

Taylor, J.T. (1995) *Rethinking the Theory of Organizational Communication: How to Read an Organization*. Norwood, NJ: Ablex.

Taylor, S. (1998) *Gartside's Model Business Letters and Other Business Documents*, 5th edition. London: Pitman.

Taylor, S. (1999) *Communication for Business: A Practical Approach*. Harlow: Longman.

Tenner, E. (1996) *Why Things Bite: New Technology and the Revenge Effect*. London: Fourth Estate.

Thatcher, B. L. (1999) 'Cultural and rhetorical adaptations for South American audiences.' *Technical Communication* 46(2): 177–195.

Thompson, P. and Warhurst, C. (eds) (1998) *Workplaces of the Future*. London: Macmillan.

Thorp, J. and DMR's Center for Strategic Leadership (1998) *The Information Paradox: Realizing the Business Benefits of Information Technology*. Toronto: McGraw-Hill.

Tibballs, G. (1999) *Business Blunders*. London: Robinson.

Timmerman, T.A. (2000) 'Racial diversity, age diversity, interdependence, and team performance.' *Small Group Research* 31(5): 592–606.

Tingley, J.C. (1996) *Say What You Mean, Get What You Want: A Business Person's Guide to Direct Communication*. New York: AMACOM.

Ting-Toomey, S. (1999) *Communicating across Cultures*. New York: Guilford.

Titlestad, P. J. H. (1998) 'South Africa's language ghosts.' *English Today* 54, 14(2): 33–39.

Tourish, D. (1997) 'Transforming internal corporate communications: the power of symbolic gestures and barriers to change.' *Corporate Communications: An International journal* 2(3): 109–116.

Trask, R.L (1997) *The Penguin Guide to Punctuation*. London: Penguin.

Trompenaars, F. (1994) *Riding the Waves of Culture: Understanding Cultural Diversity in Business*. London: Nicholas Brealey.

Tropman, J. E. (1996) *Making Meetings Work: Achieving High Quality Group Decisions*. Thousand Oaks, CA: Sage.

Tuckman, B. W. (1965) 'Developmental sequences in small groups.' *Psychological Bulletin* 63: 384–399.

Tufte, E.R. (1983) *The Visual Display of Quantitative Information*. Cheshire, CT: Graphics Press.

Tufte, E.R. (1990) *Envisioning Information*. Cheshire, CT: Graphics Press.

368

Tunstall, J. (1996) *Newspaper Power: The New National Press in Britain.* Oxford: Oxford University Press.

Turk, C. (1985) *Effective Speaking: Communicating in Speech.* London: E. & F.N. Spon.

Turk, C. and Kirkman, J. (1989) *Effective Writing: Improving Scientific, Technical and Business Communication*, 2nd edition. London: E. & F.N. Spon.

Ulich, E. and Weber, W.G. (1996) 'Dimensions, criteria and evaluation of work group autonomy.' In West, M.A. (ed.) *Handbook of Work Group Psychology.* Chichester: John Wiley.

Vandevelde, H. (1999) *Harnessing Technology for Career Success: From Online CV to Digital Interview.* Richmond: Trotman.

Varey, R. J. (1997) 'A picture of communications management in the UK.' *Corporate Communications: An International Journal* 2(2): 59–69.

Vernon, T. (1980) *Gobbledegook.* London: National Consumer Council.

Vilanilam, J.V. (2000) *More Effective Communication: A Manual for Professionals.* New Delhi: Response Books (Sage).

Waller, D.S. and Polonsky, M.J. (1998) 'Multiple senders and receivers: a business communication model.' *Corporate Communications: An International Journal* 3(3): 83–91.

Ward, P. (1997) *360-degree Feedback.* London: Institute of Personnel and Development.

Waters, C. (1996) *Web Concept and Design: A Comprehensive Guide for Creating Effective Websites.* Indianapolis, IN: New Riders.

Webster, F. (1995) *Theories of the Information Society.* London: Routledge.

Wells, G. (1986) *How to Communicate*, 2nd edition. New York: McGraw-Hill.

West, M. (1994) *Effective Teamwork.* Leicester: BPS Books.

Wheelan, S.A. (1994) *Group Processes: A Developmental Perspective.* Boston: Allyn and Bacon.

Whelan, J. (2000) *E-mail @ Work.* Harlow: Pearson.

Whitehead, M. (1999) 'All Talk.' *Interviewer*, 15 April: 12.

Wieners, B. and Pescovitz, D. (1996) *Reality Check.* San Francisco: Hardwired.

Wilcox, D.L. and Nolte, L.W. (1997) *Public Relations Writing and Media Techniques*, 3rd edition. New York: Longman.

Wilder, C. and Fine, D. (1996) *Point, Click and Wow: A Quick Guide to Brilliant Laptop Presentations.* San Diego, CA: Pfeiffer.

Willcocks, G. and Morris, S. (1996) *Putting Assertiveness to Work: A Programme for Management Excellence.* London: Pitman.

Williams, A., Dobson, P. and Walters, M. (1993) *Changing Culture: New Organisational Approaches*, 2nd edition. London: Institute of Personnel and Development.

Williams, N. and Hartley, P. (eds) (1990) *Technology in Human Communication.* London: Pinter.

Williams, N., Pittard, V. and Hartley, P. (2000) 'Talking to write: towards a framework for voice recognition in writing.' Paper given to European Association for Research on Learning and Instruction, Special Interest Group, University of Verona.

Williams, R. (1992) *The PC Is Not a Typewriter.* Berkeley, CA: Peachpit Press.

Wilson, K. and Gallois, C. (1993) *Assertion and Its Social Context.* Oxford: Pergamon.

Wind, J.Y. and Main, J. (1998) *Driving Change: How the Best Companies Are Preparing for the 21st Century.* London: Kogan Page.

Winder, D. (1999) 'Cyberliability.' *PC Pro,* May: 18–22.

Winston, B. (1998) *Media Technology and Society: A History: From the Telegraph to the Internet.* London: Routledge.

Wiseman, R.L. and Shuter, R. (1994) *Communicating in Multinational Organisations.* Thousand Oaks, CA: Sage.

Wright, P. and Reid, F. (1974) 'Written information: some alternatives to prose for expressing the outcome of complex contingencies.' *Journal of Applied Psychology* 57: 160–166.

Wright, P.L. and Taylor, D.S. (1994) *Improving Leadership Performance: Interpersonal Skills for Effective Leadership,* 2nd edition. Hemel Hempstead:Prentice Hall.

Young, A. (1997) 'Finding the mind's construction in the face.' *The Psychologist,* October: 447–452.

Zuboff, S. (1988) *In the Age of the Smart Machine.* New York: Basic Books.

Index

abbreviations 36
ABCs of organizational culture 77
abortion 53
abstract terminology 176, 228
abstracts of reports 224
accent 34, 60, 132
accountability 80, 330
accuracy in writing 165–6
achievement culture 76–7
action planning 15–16, 27
active listening 251
active verbs 171, 179
Adair, John 318
Adams, Scott 350
Adler, H. 258
administrative system of an organization 117
'adult' ego state 255–6
advertising 107, 344
Advisory, Conciliation and Arbitration Service
    (ACAS) 282
advisory functions 124
agendas 291–3, 309; see also hidden agendas
aggressive behaviour 252–4
algorithms 95, 110
alignment of text 189
Alto computer 338
Amazon (company) 234
ambiguity as a feature of human communication
    350
American style of communication 54, 63, 251
Anderson, J.W. 54
Andrews, P.H. 115, 121, 269
announcements for railway passengers 35
appearance, personal 149
appendices to reports 225–6
appraisal interviews 280–5

'architect' strategy for writing 144
Argyle, Michael 244–5
Argyris, Chris 268
Arial type 191
Aristotle 148–50
Aronson, E. 49
'arrow' approach to management 13–14
Asian Americans 50
assertiveness 251–4, 259, 351; in company
    behaviour 77–8; problems with 254, 262
attitudes and attitude change 53–4, 341–3
audiences 149, 202–4, 237; primary,
    secondary and tertiary 220
Australia 40, 49, 61, 172, 329, 338
autocratic leaders 319
automation 96
away-days 329
Aziz, Khalid 301

Back, Ken and Kate 252–4
back-channelling 61
Badham, R. 4, 298
Baguley, P. 294, 304, 306
Bainbridge, Beryl 34
Bandler, Richard 257–8
banks and banking 81, 97, 132
bar charts 203
Barker, A. 141, 151, 171, 222
Barker, J.R. 330
Basic English 177
Bay of Pigs 325
Beattie, G. 30
Belbin, Meredith 311, 321–3, 331
beliefs 53–4
Bell, A.H. 290
benefits from improved communication xi

Benne, K.D. 321
Berne, Eric 255–7
Berners-Lee, Tim 102
Bernstein, David xi
'bet your company' culture 79
biased perceptions 48, 326
binding of documents 194
'black', use of word 176
Bloch, B. 58–9
body contact 248
body language 39, 257, 351
Boeing (company) 154
Bolton, R. 250
Boon, Mike 76
borrowing of words from other languages 36
Bovee, C.L. xi
Bowman, Lee 301
brainstorming 294–5
'breakout boxes' 196
brevity in writing 166–7
'bricklayer' strategy for writing 144
British Airways 130
British Broadcasting Corporation (BBC) 133
British Petroleum 282
'broken record' technique 253
Brown, R. 306
Browning, L.D. 85
Brusaw, C.T. 140
Bryman, A. 316
Bryson, B. 36, 57
Buchanan, D. 4, 298
bullet points 169
Bullis, C. xii
bureaucratic structures 81, 126–7
Burgoon, J.K. 39
Bush, Vannevar 102
business cards 37–8
business process re-engineering 120–1, 345
Buzan, Tony 154

cable technology 103
Cairncross, F. 107
Cameron, Deborah 181, 260, 270–1
Cannell, C.F. 251
Cannon, T. 127, 133
captions on graphs 204
Carbaugh, D. 63
Caribbean culture 56
Carter, Jimmy 172
Castells, M. 132
Caterpillar Corporation 177

CD-ROMs 94–5
centralized organizational structures 119
chairs: of committees 122; of meetings 290, 292; of teams 322–3
Challenger disaster 327
Chambers, H. 38
Champy, J. 121, 345
change *see* organizational change
change messages 344
channels of communication 18
charismatic leaders 316
charts 200–2
Chaudry-Lawton, R. 337, 351
chess 95
Chicago Manual of Style 181
Christianity 53
chunking 150–1, 160, 212, 219, 235
Churchill, Winston 164
circuit approach to management 13, 19
circular letters 216–17
Clampitt, Philip 13–14, 19, 73
clarity in writing 167–8
Clark, Thomas 212, 222
classification systems 145–6
clichés 177
closed questions 249, 278–9
closing: of interpersonal interactions 250; of oral presentations 305; of selection interviews 276
Clyne, Michael 31, 51, 61–2
codes 6, 9, 17–18, 29–32, 57; practical guidance on 43–5; use in interpersonal communication 242; verbal and non-verbal 37–41
coherence in written communication 158
collectivist culture 55, 76, 131
Collett, Peter xi
Collier, M.J. 51
Collinson, D. 179
colloquial words 176
colour in documents 194
combinations of signals 247
commas, use of 179–80
'commingling' of digital data 95, 110
committee structures and processes 122, 124, 231
communication: culture-laden nature of 52; definition of 5, 11–12, 14; essential components of 19; high-context and low-context 55; history of 90–1; management responsibility for 64–5, 352; matched with

action 351; new media for 353; philosophy of improvement in 352; primary systems of 30; verbal and non-verbal compared 246–7, 351
communication triangle 15
community system of an organization 116
compact discs (CDs) 92; see also CD-ROMs
company policy and practice as regards communication 45, 64, 183, 210, 330
compass model of organizational culture 77–8
complaints 219
complementary transactions 256
computer control 96
computer-mediated-communication (C-m-C) 230
computer-speak 44
computer system failures 108–9, 353
computer technology 67; see also information and communication technology
concrete words 176
congruence in communication 269
conjunctive communication 270
content criteria for business text 165–9
contingency theories of leadership 319–20
control, managerial 80, 87
conversational style of writing 230, 232
conversations in the office (case study) 265–9
Cooke, Chris 43–5
Co-operative Bank 132
corporate culture see organizational culture
corporate-speak 44
corporate transformation 339, 347
creative activity 72
credibility 149–50, 186, 305
Cronin, Mary 107
cross-cultural communication see intercultural communication
cultural context 5, 10, 15, 40, 350–1
'cultural web' of an organization 78
. culture: and assertiveness 254; changes in 342–4; concepts of 51–2; definition of 51; differences in 51–8, 170–1; dimensions of 54–6; and employee selection practices 273; and interpersonal communication 259; and language 61; and leadership 320, 331; in the workplace 57–8, 63; see also organizational culture
curriculum vitae 234–7
customer profiling 96, 99
customer system of an organization 117
customs 53

Cutts, Martin 165, 171–4
Czerniawska, Fiona 44

dance and its similarities to communication 14
Daniels, T.D. 5, 73
Danziger, Kurt 31–2
David, Werner 352–3
Deal, T. 78, 81–2, 344
decentralized organizations 119
decimal numbering for hierarchical headings 192
decision-making processes 297, 324–5
Deetz, Stanley 114
de-layering 120, 127
Delbridge, Rick 75
delegation 267
Delphi technique 294, 296–7
democratic leadership 319
Department of Trade and Industry 130
Dertouzos, M. 91, 93, 96
desktop publishing 104, 185
dialect 34, 60
Digital (company) 154
digital radio 95
digital telecommunications 105
digitization 94–5
DiSanza, J.R. xii
discriminatory behaviour 48, 343
Disneyland and Disney Corporation 24–5, 44, 85
display typeface 190
distance zones (from intimate to public) 42–3
distributed work arrangements 119
divisional form of organization 119
documents for business communication 209–37; design of 143, 186; format, layout and style of 186, 210–11; introductions to 152; legal requirements for 211; structuring of 155–9, 192, 210; visual aids in 210
Donnellon, A. 127
downsizing 120, 127
Dreamweaver software 104
Duck, Steve 4
Dunphy, D. 338
Dwyer, J. 312

e-commerce 101, 107, 109–10, 336
e-procurement 132
'East-style' companies 78
The Economist Style Guide 171, 180
Egan, K. 253

ego states 255–7
Ehrenberg, A.S.C. 200–1
Eisenberg, E.M. 24–5, 85
elbow brushing 248
electric motors 100
electronic data interchange 129
Ellinor, Linda 268–9
Ellis, A. 30
email 209, 214–15, 228–32, 353; monitoring and recording of 232; and organizational culture 231; style in 230–1
embedded technology 100
emoticons 229
emotional intelligence 241
emotions, expression of 40, 149–50, 229
emotive words 176
emphasis on important information 168–9
empowerment 133, 314, 321
enabling role of managers 12
Encarta Encyclopedia 94
Encarta World English Dictionary 32
English language 57–8; gendered personal pronouns in 60; as the language of business 58–61; phonological aspects of 61; 'standard' 34
English-speaking cultures 56
entitative approach to study of organizations 113
environment, organizational 336, 347
espoused values 71, 75
ethical considerations xi–xii
ethnocentrism 52, 62–3
European Union 165
examples used in presentations 306–7
expert systems 97
external communication 2, 164
extinct words 35
extranets 105
eye movement and eye contact 38–41, 247, 251, 258, 271

face-to-face communication 3, 21–2, 27, 241, 264–85
facial expressions 38
fast food restaurants 42,–80–1
fax messages 232
feedback 18, 21–2, 27, 244–5, 248, 267, 282–5
'feedback starvation' 337, 347
feelings, personal 23
fibre optic cable 105

Fiedler, Fred 319
figures of speech 171
File Transfer Protocol (FTP) 101
Finan, A. 146
Fine, D. 304, 308
Fineman, Stephen 83–4
fine-tuning of the way an organization operates 338, 347
Finland 63
Finley, M. 328
Finn, T.A. 12
first day in a new job (case study) 15–17, 20–2, 25–7
'flaming' 229–31
flat organizational structures 127
Fleming, Jennifer 142
Flesch formula 180–1
Fletcher, Clive 282
flexible thinking 14–15, 260, 262
flexible working and contracts 131, 339
Flowers, Stephen 109
fluent speaking 299, 309
folded documents 194
fonts 188–90
formal language 43–5, 176
forming–storming–norming–performing sequence of group development 314–15
forms 212, 221
France 32, 40, 273
Friday, R.A. 63
function statements for reports 222–3
functional structure of an organization 120–2
future search conferences 115
Future Work Forum 129
fuzzy logic 97

Gabriel, Yiannis 83–4, 327
Gallagher, K. 301
Garamond type 191
Gates, B. 91
General Electric 344
General Motors 72
generic terms 176
Georgiades, N. 321
Gerard, Glenna 268–9
Germany and German-speaking culture 56, 61, 63
gestures 39
Gilpin, A. 329
Ginger, E.M. 186
gobbledygook 165

'Golden Bull' awards 165
Goldman, Alan 54
Goleman, D. 239, 241
Gowers, Sir Ernest 171, 173
grammar, rules of 36, 59, 169
grammar checkers, computerized 177–8,
    180–1
grapevine, the 125–6, 216
graphic codes 37
graphic design 186–7
graphics: choice of 203–4; deception and
    distortion in 205–7, 210; uses of 196–7
graphology 272–3
Grinder, John 257–8
group development, stages in 314–17, 328,
    330
group relationships and processes 48, 55, 314,
    326; see also intergroup relationships
groupthink 324–5
Gudykunst, W.B. 51
Guirdham, Maureen 271

Hackman, Richard 329
Hall, Edward 42, 55
Hall, Judith 40
Hall, Wendy 77–8
Hammer, M. 121, 345
handouts 306, 308–9
Handy, Charles 75
Hannah Anderson (company) 86
Hargie, Owen 19, 215, 230, 245, 276–8
Harris, M. 128, 133
Harrison, Roger 75–8, 82
Hartley, James 182
Hartley, P. 190, 243
Hayes, J. 250
Hayes, N. 311
headings 169, 192–3
Heather, B. 258
Heckscher, C. 127
Heller, R. 141
Henning, K. 128
Herschel, R.T. 115, 121, 269
heuristics 323
Hewlett Packard 82–3
hidden agendas 298
hierarchical organizations 64–5
Hindle, T. 141
Hinds, J. 219
Hirshberg, Jerry 72–3
Hodgkinson, G. 273

Hofstede, G. 54–6, 76
holding companies 119
home offices 131
Honey, Peter 260
Horton, William 164
Hosking, D.-M. 113
house style 211, 228
Howard, G. 179
Howse, Christopher 32
Hypercard 102
hypertext and hyperlinks 102, 234
Hypertext Mark-up Language (HTML) 102,
    104, 233
Hypertext Transfer Protocol (http) 100
Hyundai Corporation 83, 86

ideals 53
image of a company 344
incremental adjustments to organizations 339
India 59
individualist culture 55
induction of new staff 27
industrial relations 64–5
informal organization, the 125–7
informating 99
information age, the 91, 127; five pillars of
    93
information and communications technology
    (ICT) 90–110, 129, 353; development in
    business organizations 106; and new ways of
    working 103–7; problems with application
    of 108–9; trends in use of 106
information overload 215, 229
Information Society Initiative 130
'information superhighway' 100
initiative, encouragement of 87
intention behind what is said 266
intercultural communication 47–65, 176; need
    for specialist help with 65; overcoming
    barriers to 62–3
intergroup relationships 48, 326–7, 331
International Labour Process conference 133
Internet, the 94, 100–1, 130–1, 229, 353; use
    for making purchases 107–8; see also Web
    sites; World Wide Web
interpersonal communication 241–62; popular
    theories of 255–9, 262; as a staged process
    260–2
Interplace system 323
interpretation of meaning 23–8, 350
interruptions 59

interviews 250–1; *see also* appraisal interviews; selection interviews
intranets 105, 233–4, 353
Islam 351
Italy 49–50
italic font 188

Jackson, P. 131, 231
Jaguar Cars 337
James, Judi 39
Jandt, E. 49–50, 56
Janis, I. 324–5
Japan and Japanese culture 40, 50, 54–6, 59, 63, 65, 75, 131, 133, 336
Jaques, Elliot 330
jargon 31, 44, 140, 143, 164, 171, 176, 306
Jay, Ros 147
Jenkins, S. 219
Jesus Christ 146
job applications 235–7; *see also* recruitment; selection interviews
Johnson, G. 73, 78, 342
Joiner Associates 328
jokes 31, 305
Joseph, A. 139, 171, 173–4, 224
Jourard, Sidney 251

Kanter, R.M. 330
Katz, Susan 211
Katzenbach, J.R. 311, 313, 328
Kaye, M. 329
Kennedy, A. 78, 81–2, 344
kinesic communication 30
Kirkman, John 4, 139, 164, 179, 228
Klepper, Michael 301
Knapp, Mark 40
Knight, K. 34
konbini 336
Koopman, Albert 64
Kreps, Gary 126

labelling of graphics 204
'ladder of inference' 268–9
language: functions of 31, 60; spoken and written, differences between 37, 61; variety in 33–4, 57–8
language games 60
languages, switching between 59
Latin American culture 56
Lauchman, R. 173–4

Laudon, K.C. and J.P. 126
Lawton, R. 337, 351
leadership 316–22, 330–1, 346; advice on 317; as distinct from management 320; functions of 318; seen as communication 321
leading 189
leading questions 278
'learning organization' concept 345–6
Lemoine, L.F. 301–2
letters 214–20
levels of meaning 31
Levinson, Harry 283
Lewin, Kurt 318–19, 341
Lewis, D. 305
'lie factor' for graphics 206
life cycle: of an organization 339–40; of a team 315
line-fitting in graphs 206–7
line graphs 202–3, 205
line spacing 189
line structure of an organization 120
Linehan, M. 253
linking devices in written communication 158–9
listening skills 249–51
lists, use of 193–4
'lists' organizations 85
Locke, Edwin 316
London Underground 35
'look' of a document 186–7, 207, 210
loyalty cards 99

McArthur, Tom 58
McDaniel, E.R. 40, 63
'McDonaldization' thesis 80–1, 133
Macdonell, R. 321
macho culture 79
McIntyre, M.G. 328
McLean, R. 190
Maher, Chrissie 165, 172
Main, J. 82, 164
Malaysia 85, 259, 329–30
managerial style 12–14, 133
Mandel, Steve 302
margins 194
Marquis, K.H. 251
Martin, D. 298
masculinity of culture 56
'mathematical' theory of communication 17
matrix structure: for a memo 212–13, 222; for an organization 119, 123–4

meaning: extent of verbal and non-verbal
    contributions to 39; interpretation of 23–8,
    350; levels of 31; negotiation of 23–4
medium of communication 18
Meeting Masters Research Project 290, 309
meeting rooms 70
meetings 286–98, 309; dimensions of variation
    in 289; excellence in 286, 290–2, 309;
    preparation for 292; reviewing procedures
    for 298, 309; techniques for improvement
    of 294–8, 309; Tropman's rules for 291–2
memos 211–14
message-taking 211
meta-perception 245–6
metaphors for the way organizations behave
    24–5, 73, 82, 85, 114
Mexico 63
Meyer, Eric 196
microchip technology 91–2, 100
Microsoft 94
Milroy, J. and L. 34
mind maps 154, 160
Ministry of International Trade and Industry
    (MITI), Japan 133
Minto, Barbara 151–2
Mintzberg, Henry 320
minutes of meetings 293–4, 309
Misiura, S. xi
mission statements 5, 71, 82
Mobil Oil 54
modular transformation of an organization
    339
Morgan, G. 9, 70, 114, 125
Morgan, T. 292
Morley, I.E. 113
Morris, S. 252
Moscovici, Serge 324
motivation of employees 74
motorcycle industry 337
MP3 standard 94
Mulholland, J. 230
multiculturalism 51
multimedia 94–5, 234
multiple meanings for words 36
Murdoch, Rupert 98
Murray, Denise 229–30, 232

national culture 76
Naughton, J. 229
negotiation of meaning 23–4
Negroponte, N. 91, 94

Nelson, Ted 102
Netherlands, the 273
networked computers 101
networked organizations 106, 128–9, 133
neural networks 97
neurolinguistic programming (NLP) 255,
    257–9, 262
new technology 3, 12; used to support
    structural change 132; see also information
    and communications technology
news bulletins 150–1
newsletters, corporate xi–xii, 86
newspaper industry, British 96, 98–9
newspapers, visuals in 196, 198
Newspeak 172
Nickson, D. 314
Nielsen, Jacob 233
Nineteen Eighty-four 172
ninsengei 54
Nissan Design International 72–3
noise 18, 21–2
Nominal Group Technique 294, 296
non-verbal communication 37–41, 246–8, 257;
    dependence on context 40–1
norms 42, 53–4
North, Vanda 154
'North-style' companies 78
northern European culture 56

Oakes, P.J. 49
objectives: of groups 324; of spoken
    communication 242, 244, 260; of written
    communication 146–7, 159–60, 222
O'Donnell-Trujillo, N. 70
office layout 130, 267
official forms 172–3
Ogden, C.K. 177
'oil painter' strategy for writing 144
'OK' hand signal 40
open-plan offices 267
open questions 249, 278–9
opening 250; of conversations 250, 268; of
    presentations 305; of selection interviews
    276
opinion surveys of employees 2
Oppenheim, Charles 215
orchestra principle for meetings 290
ordering of information 150–1, 160
'organic' structures 128
organization: of behaviour 260; forms of
    115–19

organization charts 113; 'upside down' 86

organizational change 85, 333–46; types of 335–40

organizational culture 63, 67–88, 236, 337; components of 70–1; consequences of 73–4, 88; definitions of 70, 88; determinants of 85–8; of different parts of a company 82; and email 231; expression of 74, 82–5, 88; and language 175; levels of 71–4; models of 74–82; negative aspects of 84; reflected in documents 211; types of 78–9

organizational flux 342

organizational structure 67, 112–34

Orwell, George 171–2

outlining 154–5, 160

Owen, Hilarie 328

Oxford Dictionary of New Words 32

Oxford English Dictionary 35

Pacanowsky, M.E. 70

page grids 194–5

page layout 192, 207

Papows, Jeff 105

paragraph structure 156–8, 160

paralinguistics 30, 61

'parent' ego state 255, 257

passive voice 171, 178–9, 228

patronizing behaviour 44–5

Payne, R.L. 273

PC Magazine 107

Pease, Alan 248

Penman, Robyn 174–5

perceptions of reality 327; *see also* biased perceptions

personal computers, use of 92

personal pronouns, gendered 60

personal space 42

persuasion 148–50; Arab and American conceptions of 54; in a letter 161

Pescovitz, D. 106

PEST factors 336, 347

Peters, T.J. 80

Peterson, M.F. 319

Pettigrew, A. 337

Philippines, the 59

phone rage 108

phonetics 61

physical surroundings in relation to communication 267

Pickles, Helen 38

piled-up nouns 177

Pitney Bowes (company) 215

Plain English Campaign 164–5, 172–3, 183, 219

plain language 4, 163–4, 171–3; agreement on 173–4; application of 175–80; as a company strategy 183, 210; criticisms of 174–5

Plain Words 171

planned communication: appraisals as 281; interviews as 277

planning triangle 143, 145

Plous, Scott 144

point size of a font 188

polarization within groups 324

politeness 59, 61, 259

'political' issues and behaviour 4, 298

post-it notes 15, 211

posture 39, 42, 253

power culture 76–7

power distance 55–6

power games and power play 298, 326–7

Powerpoint software 304, 308–9

predictability (in products and in the behaviour of workers) 80

prepositions, need for 13

presentation in language (Danziger) 32

presentations, oral 286–7, 299–309; anxiety about 300, 309; critical issues and skills for 304–7; electronic 307–8; planning of 301–4

printed stationery 220

probes used in questioning 279

problem-solving by groups 323–5

process approach to communication 22–3, 28

process culture 79, 91

professional codes of practice 87

project managers 123

pronunciation 36

propaganda 44

prosodic communication 30

protocols (in computer technology) 102

punctuation 58, 159, 179–80

purpose of communication 5, 349–50

'push' technology 234

Putnam, L.L. 326

pyramid principle 151–3, 160, 302

questioning 249; sequences of 278–9

Quirke, B. 344–5

Qvortrup, L. 131

Rackham, N. 292
railway industry 340–1
rapport 258
Rasberry, R.W. 301–2
rational argument 149
rational systems 81
Ratner, Gerald 1
RE scores 181
readability 163, 180–2
'reading' a situation 9
recall of information 144–6
receptiveness 250–1
recommendations in reports 226
recruitment: using the Web 107; see also job
    applications
referential terms 176
reflection, skill of 249
register 33–4
regulatory system of an organization 116
reinforcement 248–9
relational processes 113
relationships with other people 6; see also group
    relationships; intergroup relationships
relativism, cultural 52, 62
report assessors 175
reports 220–8; title pages of 223–4; types
    221
representation in language (Danziger) 32
representational systems (visual, auditory and
    kinaesthetic) 258
representative system of an organization 118,
    124–5
representing one's organization to others 210
research and development (R&D) function
    346
research evidence 4–5
responsiveness in company behaviour 77–8
restrictive and non-restrictive clauses 181
revealing of data and visual aids 195, 207, 210
risky shift 324
Ritzer, George 80–1, 133
Robbins, H. 328
Robbins, S.P. 2, 19, 296
Roberts, Wess 318
role culture 75–7
role models for management behaviour 146
roles in groups 321–3, 331
'rule of six' 291
'rule of two-thirds' 292
rules: applying in different communication
    situations 14; strict observance of 127

sales talk 44
Samovar, L.A. 63
sans serif type 190
satellite technology 103
satellite work centres 131
Scheibel, Dean 82
Schein, Edgar 71, 73
Scholes, E. 126
Scholes, K. 73, 78, 342
Scott, C.R. xi
script typeface 190
'scripts' for interpersonal communication
    270–1, 285
Sears & Roebuck (mail order retailer) 100
second-language users 59–61
selection interviews 42, 247–9, 271–9, 285;
    'shock tactics' in 274–5
self-appraisal 283
self-awareness (of non-verbal communication)
    248
self-disclosure 251, 259, 274
self-fulfilling prophecy 49
semicolons 159
Senge, Peter 268, 346
senior management: commitments needed
    from 2, 71, 330; isolation of 337
Senior, Barbara 73, 336
sense-making 337, 347
sentence structure 177
serif type 190
servers 100–1
Shackleton, V. 321
Shapiro, E.C. 344
shared facility centres 131
shared ideas and/or information 5
shared meanings 24, 350
shareholder system of an organization 116
Sharples, Mike 141, 143
Sheats, P. 321
Sherif, Muzafer and Carolyn 326
Shimko, Barbara 42
Siddons, S. 314
signposting of information 150–1, 160
silicon chips 91–2, 100
simplified language 177
situation for communication 6
'sketcher' strategy for writing 144
slang 32
Sless, David 147
slides, use of 299, 307–8
Smith, D.K. 311, 313, 328

Smith, D.M. 290
Smith, Mike 272–4
Smith, P.B. 319
Smith, R.C. 24–5, 85
social context 5, 10, 15, 67, 92, 242–5, 259,
    350–1
social identity 32, 48, 242
social perception 242, 244
social skills 239, 262
Sophist philosophy 148
sound-bites 36
South Africa 51, 58, 60–1, 64, 176, 211
'South-style' companies 78
space between lines 189
Sparks, Suzanne 158
specialist managers 123–4
speech recognition software 108
spider diagrams 152–4, 302
Spiekermann, E. 186
Spiker, B.K. 5, 73
split infinitives 173
SPQR approach to report-writing 226
spreadsheets 200
Stace, D. 338
staff charters 74
stakeholders 114–15
'standard' language 32, 34
standing committees 122
standing features of communication 30
Stanton, N. 141, 242
Star Wars (films) 96
Starks, D. 58–9
Steenstra, D. 130
stereotyping 49–51, 205, 250, 326;
    unconscious 43
Stewart, G.L. 311, 329
Stewart, Rosemary 114
Stohl, C. 326
Stoner, James 324
stories, organizational culture expressed by
    means of 84–5, 88
strategy for change 340–6
strategy for communication 5
structured problem-solving in meetings 294,
    296
structuring: of documents 155–9, 192, 226–7;
    of information 143–5, 150–5, 160; of
    objectives 147
styles (in word-processing software) 187
subcommittees 122
subcultures 51

subheadings 192–3
submissive behaviour 252–3
subsystems of an organization 116–18
Suchan, Jim 175, 211
suggestion, power of 144
Sun Microsystems 86
Sundstrom, E. 267
supermarkets: checkout technology 96, 99;
    supply chains 129
superordinate goals 326–7
supplier system of an organization 116
support culture 76–7
supportive communication 269–70
symbolic gestures 344
symbols in typefaces 190
synopses of reports 224
syntax 36
systems model of communication 19–20
systems view of the company 57

tables of numerical data 199–201
'tabling' a document 13
Taco Bell (company) 345
Tannenbaum, Robert 233
Tapscott, Don 128
Taylor, Frederick 120
Taylor, James 113
teams 311–31; definition of 312–13; as distinct
    from working groups 313, 329; doubts
    about the effectiveness of 330; elements of
    high performance 313, 328; improving the
    effectiveness of 328; innovation by 297;
    mending of 328–9; roles in 321–3, 331;
    self-managing 314, 329–31
technical reports 228
technical slang 176
technology, creation and development of 91–3;
    see also information and communications
    technology
telephone answering systems 108
telephone call centres 99
telephone technology 100
television shopping 109
teleworking 106, 128–31
templates (in word-processing software) 104,
    187
Tenner, E. 353
terms of reference 225
Texas Instruments Malaysia 329–30
Thill, J.V. xi
third person address 44